A WICCAN FORMULARY AND HERBAL

A.J. DREW

NEW PAGE BOOKS
A division of The Career Press, Inc.
Franklin Lakes, NJ

A WICCAN FORMULARY AND HERBAL
EDITED BY LAUREN MANOY
TYPESET BY STACEY A. FARKAS
Cover design by Cheryl Cohan Finbow
Printed in the U.S.A. by Book-mart Press

To order this title, please call toll-free 1-800-CAREER-1 (NJ and Canada: 201-848-0310) to order using VISA or MasterCard, or for further information on books from Career Press.

The Career Press, Inc., 3 Tice Road, PO Box 687,
Franklin Lakes, NJ 07417
www.careerpress.com
www.newpagebooks.com

Library of Congress Cataloging-in-Publication Data

Drew, A.J.
    A wiccan formulary and herbal / by A.J. Drew.
        p. cm.
    Includes bibliographical references and index.
    ISBN 1-56414-782-7 (pbk.)
        1. Witchcraft. 2. Recipes. I. Title.

BF1572.R4D74 2005
133.4'3--dc22

                                                                    2004055155

For Aubreyahna,
who changed this world on May 14th, 2004, at 3:08 p.m. EST.

Acknowledgments

This book would not be possible without the help of more people than I can count. In the years that it took to complete, I went from bachelor to husband and father; I built a machine shop, started a metalworking business, remodeled my store, and sunk more hours into building an online community at *www.PaganNation.com* than I would like to report. During that time, many people have helped with the actual creation of this book. Paula Newman added her soap recipes, Aimee Carpenter gave some other recipes, which were deleted from this manuscript for political reasons (sorry, not my call), and Angela Howell's reviewing and insights.

But many others gave so much help in other areas of my life so that I could spend the time necessary to complete this book. Sharon Kay (Grandma Kay) for the many hours assuring me that I wouldn't break the baby. Ann P (Grandma Ann) for convincing me that the second try, not the third, is the charm.

Many thanks to Rev. Jennifer Kimball Casto of the New Life Methodist Ministry for performing our nuptials and allowing Christians, Pagans, Jews, Buddhists, and Krishnas to come together in your beautiful church the way I imagine Jesus Christ would have done. Many thanks to Raja from the Columbus Krishna Ashram for taking time to cater my wedding. Many thanks to all those from the Columbus Krishna Ashram who helped at the reception the way I imagine Krishna would have done. Many thanks to our friends at Pagan Nation for their moral support and attendance at a wedding that could have only been better should Dar Williams had performed *The Christians and the Pagans* song.

Many thanks to the matriarch of my wife's father's family, Mammaw, for attending our wedding. Maam, if you will accept the praise of this humble Wiccan, you are a true Christian. Many thanks to Aunt Sharon and Aunt Betty for attending and for helping Mammaw to attend. Many thanks to any other members of my wife's father's side of the family who attended despite the non-Christian ranting of Uncle Mike. Many thanks to Aunt Ruth for driving around Columbus for hours trying to find the wedding. I am sorry the streets in Columbus, Ohio, are so confusing. Many thanks to my wife's mother's side of the family, which is too large to list individually, for being good Christians and demonstrating your understanding of the nature of love.

Many thanks to Tim and Dottie for showing me what a loving couple looks like. Thanks to Jim and Marlana for giving us a fair price on the chateau in the

16th century and the opportunity to provide for my new family. Many thanks to Patty and Charlie, Angie and Jerry, and Jamie and Duane for providing the moral support that we desperately needed. Thanks to Rich and Sandra, even though you don't have kids. You really have to try this!

But most of all, many thanks to my brother-in-law Art (Bubba) Carpenter for introducing me to his sister. For without her, this book would not have been possible.

I acknowledge and thank all the people listed here, all the people I missed, and all the people I have not yet met who have heard the same truth, that God (by whatever name) is Love and that we express our love for God in our love for each other.

Gay, Straight, Black, White,
Same Struggle, Same Fight
Christian, Muslim, Pagan, Jew
There is just one world for me and you

So mote it be!

We all come from the mother
and to her we shall return
like a drop of rain
flowing to the ocean.

We all come from the father
And to him we shall return
Like a spark of flame
Rising to the heavens.

Corn and grain. Corn and grain.
All that falls shall rise again.

Hoof and horn. Hoof and horn.
All that dies shall be reborn.

—Author unknown

Contents

Know Thy Self
Allergy and
Food Sensitivities

On my way into work today, I stopped for a cup of coffee. On the glass door leading into the coffeehouse, I saw a sign that warned that food served in the facility may have come in contact with peanuts, peanut dust, or peanut oil. You can bet that if there is a sign, there has been a problem. Despite the thousands of PB and J sandwiches that most of us have consumed, the peanut is a killer. In fact, people have died after eating food prepared in the same kitchen where peanuts have been used in other food. Yes, even peanut dust can kill. As you can see, allergies and food sensitivities are very serious matters.

In fact, many medical complaints have been related to a food allergy/sensitivity, including arthritis, asthma, autism, chronic fatigue, celiac disease, cardiovascular complaints, epilepsy, fibromyalgia, gastrointestinal problems, headaches, hypertension, hypoglycemia, immune deficiencies, irritable bowel syndrome, migraines, muscle aches, seizures, sinusitis, skin rashes, and many others. The most common foods from the Green World to cause problems are wheat and nuts (especially peanuts).

This is why the first of the 13 Wiccan Goals *is* the first. The 13 Wiccan Goals may have been originally written by Scott Cunningham, but like so many things in the Wiccan religion they have changed and grown as they have been shared. So it is next to impossible to determine who the original author was. And yet with all the many different versions, the first is almost always "Know thy self" or "Know yourself."

So how do *you* know what is safe for *you*? The good news is that with common allergies, there are common tests that your doctor can perform. The bad news is that chances are you will have no reason to ask your doctor to perform such tests until you have already determined you have an allergy or sensitivity. The worse news is that there is absolutely no way your doctor will be able to provide proper testing for each of the thousands and thousands of plants and foods you may encounter. And now for even worse news: The most common form of testing might cause you death.

The Skin Prick Test—The skin prick test should only be conducted by a qualified medical professional. In the simplest terms, the procedure involves cleaning an area of your skin, placing a drop of a solution containing the potential allergen, and then pricking the skin beneath the drop with a needle. If a raised red area forms within 15 minutes, the material being tested is considered a personal allergen. If it does not, generally speaking it is not a personal allergen. Keep in mind, not only could the substance be poisonous (another matter entirely), it could promote a negative response in larger quantities.

The Intradermal Test—The intradermal test should only be conducted by a qualified medical professional. This test involves injecting the allergen solution deeper into the skin. Generally speaking, this test is only performed when the skin prick test produces a negative result, but the substance is still suspected of being a personal allergen.

The Skin Patch Test—The skin patch test is exactly as it sounds. A solution of the suspected allergen is placed on a pad and worn against the skin for 48 hours or until a reaction is noticed. Ah, but the downside of this test is that should you not react to the test, you have only determined that the material does not promote an allergic reaction called *contact dermatitis*. In short, the only thing this test will tell you is if you can place the material on your skin.

More bad news. All of the above listed tests can cause anaphylactic shock and death. That's right, you could go to the grocery store, purchase a ready-made tea blend, drink it, and fall over dead. It's the way life works. Everyone has a potential Achilles's heel and never know about it until just the right arrow hits just the right spot. Then it is entirely too late. Ah, but wait—just when you thought it couldn't get worse, your body has a surprise. You can eat the same thing every day of your life, and then one day find that you have become allergic to it. My wife's father absolutely loved shrimp. So much so that he ate it at least once a week. Then, one day, he developed an allergy to all shellfish. He found this out at an all-you-can-eat seafood buffet when his throat swelled shut. His tongue swelled so large it could no longer fit inside his mouth, and he was rushed to the hospital, where large amounts of antihistamines saved his life.

Now for the good news. Despite the variety of materials we are all exposed to on a daily basis, most people will go through their entire life without ever encountering a serious allergic reaction. This is why so many make fun of that sign in that coffeehouse, even though it is no laughing matter to someone who is allergic to peanuts.

And even more good news. Although any exposure to any plant material may promote a reaction, there is a tried-and-true method of decreasing risk when considering the use of plant material. Test the waters before plunging in. First, check the current

FDA guidelines for the plant material in question (they change too quickly to be included here). With the over-the-counter drug diphenhydramine (Benadryl) at the ready, take a small amount of the substance in the form it will be used and apply it to the inner fold of your elbow. If you are planning on using a water extraction, then test with a water extraction. If you are planning on using an alcohol extraction, then test with an alcohol extraction. Wait 24 hours to see if there is a reaction.

If there is no reaction, then chances are good it will be safe for *topical use* until such time as your body changes its mind. Using the material internally is an entirely different matter. If you have no topical reaction and intend to consume the material, then place a tiny amount in your mouth for 30 seconds. Spit it out and wait 24 hours to see if there is a reaction. If there is no reaction, then chances are good it will be safe to gargle with until your body changes its mind. Swallowing the material is an entirely different matter. If you have had no reaction either on your skin or in your mouth, consume a small amount. Wait 24 hours to see if there is a reaction.

If you should have a mild reaction to either of these tests, take the diphenhydramine in accordance with the instructions on the label and discontinue use of the plant material. If you should have anything more than a mild reaction, then take the diphenhydramine—but also seek medical assistance immediately.

Introduction
Magick
Made Sensible

H i, I am A.J. Drew. I am a hardworking man who is married to the second most beautiful woman in the world. Not long ago, she was the most beautiful woman in the world, but then we had a baby girl on May 14, 2004. I am also a magick worker. I use this term to separate it from the term *magician*, which some believe implies sleight of hand. In fact, I am one of the most powerful magick workers this world has ever known. Why? Because when I wrote a book called *Wicca for Couples*, I ended it with an incantation, and that incantation has brought my new family into manifestation: "I have yet to find her [my love], so here I cast my greatest aspiration to the universe with the words of the greatest storyteller the universe has ever known."

O speak again, bright angel, for thou art
As glorious to this night, being o'er my head,
As is a winged messenger of heaven
Unto the white upturned wond'ring eyes
Of mortals that fall back to gaze on him
When he bestrides the lazy puffing clouds
And sails upon the bosom of the air.

—*William Shakespeare*, Romeo and Juliet *2.1*

I say that I am one of this world's most powerful magick workers because upon hearing this incantation, the most important thing that has ever taken place in this universe happened. I fell in love. Shortly thereafter I was wed to that love, and now we are three. I say that I am *one* of the most powerful magick workers in the world because I know of at least one person who is even more powerful. That is my wife, Aimee. You see, I witnessed the crowning of my baby's head, so I can tell you this: There is no greater magick in this world. Aimee, my beautiful love, thou art Goddess! Aubreyahna, my beautiful daughter, thou art Goddess!

Now with all these goddesses in my life, one might think that I would be content. I am not. Oh, I am not in line for more, but I just cannot seem to let things be when I believe them to be horribly wrong. As a result, I have been rather outspoken in many areas. Surprise, surprise—when you take the time to express an opinion, you will find people who will argue with that opinion.

Although I have been active in the Pagan community since my early teens, I am a relatively new author. I think it was around 1988 that my first short story was published. Years later, I can honestly say I have enjoyed the overwhelming majority of reviews that I have read. Ah, but there are those exceptions, some of which I have come to love for their comic value. Now, before you go thinking I am pompous, let me tell you my secret to being a successful author. All I do is write down what many people already know in their hearts to be true. I have said it time and time again: I am published simply because I got lucky. You could do the same, and, frankly, the Pagan community needs more people doing just that.

If you have not read one of the more colorful reviews of my work, let me tell you that those who predicted that I would become one of the most infamous Witches in the world may have been right. Oh, I didn't really think so at the time, but it does seem like those things that I thought were common sense have risen more than a few eyebrows. Before I discuss this latest radical concept, let me provide a few of my earlier concepts that have been described as radical:

My opinion: If Wicca is an Earth-based religion, protecting the Earth (ecology) is important to our religion.

Response to this opinion: My political views have no place in the Wiccan religion.

Another reviewer announced that the Greek and Roman pantheons have no place in the Wiccan religion. Ah. So Pan (Greek) and Diana (Roman) have no place in modern Wicca? As you might imagine, that one gave me a great chuckle.

Then there is my all-time favorite. In *A Wiccan Bible*, I sought to illustrate the migration of cultural ideas in relation to the migration of humanity out of Africa. First there was the onslaught of racists who insisted that white people did not come from Africa. I say "racist" not out of a scientific disagreement with these folk, but because of the content of their letters, which is not fit for print here. Now wait. The response to the idea of demonstrating cultural ideas in relation to the migration of humanity out of Africa is not my favorite bashed concept because I enjoy receiving letters from racists (although their grammar, spelling, and punctuation was amusing). No, no, my reason for loving the bashing of that concept began when a reviewer announced that I was wrong about Isis being an African goddess form. The reviewer went on to state rather firmly that Isis is an Egyptian, not African, goddess. Apparently she was unaware that Egypt is in Africa.

Please do not understand me to say that I like the few bad reviews that I receive to the exclusion of the good reviews. Not at all. In fact, I have absolutely loved the good ones as well. Especially those that are preceded by "I don't agree with everything A.J. Drew says, but...." You see, after that statement there is usually a great review. But why is that same disclaimer found in so many of the good reviews that I have received? I pondered this for a very long time. The answer is that when I write, I have something to say. Of course, people are not going to agree with everything that I have to say unless I say nothing. My conclusion is that when authors do not receive such a compliment, it is because they have said nothing. That is the point of this long-winded introduction to an herbal and formulary. The publisher and editors probably figured there would be no way that I could be controversial in writing a reference book. Surprise!

Magick Made Sensible

I am tired of spellbooks. I am tired of seeing references with the word "money" followed by a list of herbs that will reportedly fill your pockets. I am tired of books that claim they can teach you how to chant your way to being knee-deep in cash. I am tired of watching author after author and publisher after publisher offer snake oil in the form of words to an unsuspecting public that is desperately hoping to end the pain of living without harmony with the Green World.

I am tired of reading about the latest extinction. I am tired of wondering how many cures for cancer, AIDS, and other modern plagues have not been discovered in the Green World because that part of the Green World no longer exists. I am tired of doctors not being allowed to provide medicine due to political concerns. I am tired of wondering what will be left when I leave this world. Will I leave a world to my daughter that is better than the world my parents left to me?

But what I am most tired of is watching the incredible potential of my beautiful religion presented to the public in a way that helps no one, least of all the Green World. If Wicca no longer teaches our basic principles—that we should live in a symbiotic relationship with the Green World—then what does it teach? That is what I hope this book will teach, the very basic idea that humanity and the Green World living symbiotically is not only a good idea, but it is necessary for the survival of each. No, I will not preach. Well, not often. Instead, I will try to demonstrate to my readers how valuable the Green World is. To do that, I will debunk a few ideas. I will tell you that the people who set down the associations between the planets and the Green World were actually pharmacists and scholars. I will tell you that there is a scientific method behind those associations. I will tell you that magick can make sense. Sure, I will be attacked for such down-to-earth views. But at least I'll be in good company.

Socrates was put to death on the charge of blasphemy because he expressed views that the Pagan elders of his time objected to. It was his stated opinion that the Pagan gods of Greece did not exist in the form that was claimed. He was not an atheist. He believed strongly in the existence of a Supreme Being. However, instead of believing one could climb Mt. Olympus and chat with Zeus, Socrates felt the stories of the gods and goddesses were attempts to explain the nature of the Creator by describing that Creator with stories people could understand. I agree. After all, who but a fool would say they understand the whole of our Creator?

In fact, I believe the knowledge of the ancient pharmacists, scholars, and scientists has been hidden in many of these stories. Hidden in plain sight so that the knowledge could be passed down without the teacher meeting the same fate as Socrates. Although many of those records have been lost forever, the few that have survived have been taken up by the modern Pagan community. Unfortunately, like the citizens of Greece and the stories that Socrates commented on, modern folk just did not understand the author's intent. The modern Pagan community has read the works of the ancients, noted that some plants are "ruled by Venus," and decided that if one burns that plant, then the goddess Venus will descend from the sky to grant three wishes.

Although I in no way believe that I am as learned as Socrates, I am fairly sure I will meet with the same or similar charge for what I am about to say. Fortunately for me, the laws of the day are much more forgiving. So why did Socrates teach what he did without regard for his own life? Because he felt it was right. Why am I about to yet again risk the life of my career? Because it is right.

You see, our community has become littered with spellbooks and other references that provide gender, Elemental, and planetary associations for the Green World in a manner so whimsical that rational people are starting to think the Latin classification for the Wiccan religion is *Wingus Nuttus*. Worse yet, so many Wiccans are gobbling up fast food religion (McWicca) that our community really is starting to look like a collection of complete wing nuts. Of course, every spiritual path has its fair share of lunatics, but this is the community in which I will be raising my daughter. Thus, what follows is an attempt to set the record straight when it comes to such seemingly ridiculous notions as spellcraft and the Green World.

Burning those plants that are ruled by Venus will not get you three wishes any more than rubbing that magic lamp. But finding balance and removing the obstacles that inhibit one's balance is the first step in establishing a symbiotic relationship with the Green World, and that symbiotic relationship is one's first step in the path that is the Wiccan religion. In fact, I consider that first step to be equivalent to the first degree.

Chapter 1
Wicca and
the Green World

The problem with talking about Witchcraft in a historic sense is that, historically speaking, there has never been one group, tribe, or organization that one could definitively state practiced Witchcraft. Certainly there were people who were called Witches, but, historically speaking, to call a person a Witch has been more a matter of opinion than practice. The word Witchcraft has been used to describe a diversity of practices. In fact, the largest number of people put to death on a charge of Witchcraft were probably accused not for any solid reason, but because they practiced a religion that competed with the religion of the accusers.

Contrary to what you might expect, I am not going to state that those competing religions were the remnants of pre-Christian Pagan religions. On the contrary, by the time of the wholesale slaughter of men, women, and children on the charge of Witchcraft, the great majority of those persecuted were themselves Christian. If we look to academia for historic fact, we find that the majority of those charges were not brought against members of ancient Pagan religions. Instead, the term "Witch" was most often used to describe Protestants by Catholics, Catholics by Protestants, and by just about every Church State government against Jewish folk. It's an old and nasty story; those who are in power oppress those who are not in power such that those in power remain in power.

Folklore tells a slightly different story. There have always been people who have excelled in one trade or another. In the English language, the word that is often used for one who has excelled at the art of forging metal is the *blacksmith*. The word that is often used for one who has excelled at the art of making or repairing shoes is *cobbler*; a *tailor* or *seamstress* is one who makes clothing. Of course, let's not forget the *butcher*, *baker*, and *candlestick-maker*. But what of the words *Witch* and *Witchcraft*?

The truth of language is that it changes with word usage. When I was young, I remember hearing that "ain't ain't a word because ain't ain't in the dictionary." Today my spellchecker has no problem with the word, and it is listed in *The American Heritage Dictionary of the English Language*. Making things a bit more confusing is the incorrect idea that any word or phrase in one language can be easily translated into another language. This fallacy was pointed out to me while dating a German woman. Jokingly, I called her an airhead, which I translated into German as *luft koph*. She looked at me as if my IQ had suddenly dropped a hundred points. I explained and she corrected me. In German the expression is *hole koph* (hole head). Then she hit me. The point of this story is that words and phrases do not always translate.

Another example can be found in the recent interest in Pow-Wow folk magick. From speaking to a friend who practices Pow-Wow magick, I understand that the tradition is a blending of Native American and Pennsylvania Dutch practices. However, I know from personal experience that the word *Witch* has a whole different meaning among many of the Pennsylvania Dutch, and one of the last people put to death on a charge of Witchcraft in my neck of the woods was a Native American by the name of Leather Lips. Essentially, Leather Lips was put to death for practicing the elder traditions of his tribe. So we have a modern-day Witch (my friend) speaking favorably about a tradition that melds the traditions of two people who were at a time rather opposed to the words *Witch* and *Witchcraft*. This is possible because when my friend uses the word *witch* to describe herself, she is using one definition. When Leather Lips was put to death for practicing the traditions of his fathers, his accusers were using a different definition. When the Pennsylvania Dutch put up hex symbols on their barns to prevent Witches from spoiling their cow's milk, they were using yet another definition of the word. The word's very definition changes with the context of its use.

Finally, consider the word *strega*. In the Italian language, it simply translates to *Witch*. That is, if an Italian were to say that you are a Witch, he would probably use the word *Strega* without any association to Witchcraft that is culturally Italian. However, if someone speaking English were to call someone Strega, they would likely be indicating that the person practices a culturally Italian form of Witchcraft.

There is yet another use of the word *Witch* that is important in explaining the use of the word in relation to plants. It is fairly common to hear the word used to denote excellence. Calling someone a "Kitchen Witch" within the Pagan community has its own unique meaning, but outside of the Pagan community it often denotes an excellence of culinary skills. In this capacity, the words *Wizard* and *Sorcerer* are also common. As an example, I have a business association with a professor at a local university. His students often call him the "Numbers Wizard," and his license plate reads "Wizard" because of that title. In using the term "Wizard," it is often shortened to "whiz" as in "He is a *whiz* at math" or "He is a whiz kid." Down the street from my shop in Columbus, Ohio, is a wonderful place called Cookware Sorcerer, but don't go looking for Harry Potter items on their shelves because the product in which they excel is as their name implies—cookware.

The Classic Witch and Which Witch is Which

In examining which Witch is which, we find that there are some common grounds on which we can base our usage of the word. Yes, the word has been used as a derogation of followers of other religions. But generally speaking, that derogative was used out of fear. Put simply, the various Church States feared their competition, so the rumor mill started. It's an old story. If one fears the success of another and doesn't want to take the time to examine one's own failures, it is easy to announce that another's success was only had at an expense that you were not willing to pay. If the Church is unable to heal a person with prayer, but the little old lady from the woods can do so with herbs, well, then she must be consorting with Satan. She must be a Witch. If a man is unable to remain faithful to his wife, well, then his mistress must be consorting with Satan. She must be a Witch.

This phenomena is alive and well today in our marketplace. If a town has both a Pagan shop and a New Age shop, it is common to find that folk who shop at one will speak derogatorily of the other. The Pagan shop will become "that Witchcraft shop," and said to be successful only because they merchant in the dark arts or something as equally silly. The New Age shop will become "that fluffy bunny shop," and said to be successful only because they merchant in fluff. If a town has more than one Pagan shop, a rumor will inevitably start about the owner of each being a Satanist or a sacrificer of animals, as if those spreading the rumors believe that worshipping Satan or killing one's pets will bring great wealth.

Fear is the common denominator in the use of the word *Witch* as a derogation. There is an old saying that where there's fear, there's power.[1] There is another old saying that people destroy that which they fear. When one combines the two observations, we see the commonality and understand the derogatory use of the word. When a person becomes particularly skilled at an endeavor, that person is feared, labeled a Witch, and an attempt is made to destroy that person's success.

It is here, in the claim that Witches have been horribly misunderstood, that the Wiccan religion was born. During its infancy, it was popular to believe that Wicca was a form of ancient Witchcraft that had hidden from the persecutions and Witch hunters until such time that it could again be practiced openly. Although most of the claims to antiquity have been proven false, the basis for the claims did set the stage for the religion that would grow from those early efforts.

As a result, you might have noticed a few things in the Wiccan community that just don't seem to make sense. If we are a postmodern religion that is in part based on pre-Christian fertility religions, then why do many Wiccans seem trapped in the Burning

Times? Why all the black clothing, if not to escape into the night should our secret meetings be discovered? For that matter, why the secret meetings? To be honest, I simply do not know.

What I do know is that some of those early popular beliefs have defined Wicca in a very positive way. One of those positive influences was the idea that one of the reasons for the Witch hunts was a business conflict between the rising male medical institution and the predominantly female healers of the countryside. Just how wide this clash was is hard to determine; however, there was certainly a clash between midwives and the Church approved medical profession. Per the medieval Church, the Christian Bible instructed that the pain of childbirth was the punishment women received for original sin. As such, anyone attempting to ease that pain was thought to be practicing against the Church's interpretation of the Christian Bible and, thus, against the word of God. In short, midwifery and other forms of natural healing were often said to be Witchcraft. Thus the popular bumper sticker that reads "Witches Heal."

When we combine the classic view of the Witch and her bubbling brew with the more recent view of the Witch as healer, is there any wonder a religion with connections to the word *Witch* would evolve to include a tradition of working with herbs and the Green World?

Wicca Today

Wicca has grown from those early days. When someone describes Wicca today, the term "Earth religion" is often used. From that description, many have gotten the idea that Wiccans worship the Earth. While I do not speak for all Wiccans, I no more *worship* the Earth than I do my mother and father. Do I wish the best for my parents? Yes. Do I seek a symbiotic relationship with my parents? Yes. Do I worship them? No.

The second term you will likely hear used to describe Wicca is "Goddess centered." From that description, many have the idea that Wiccans worship a goddess. Note the period at the end of that sentence. If we were to replace the word *worship* with the word *praise*, the sentence might be accurate. But there is that pesky period. At the risk of sounding persnickety, the story should not end there. Wiccans give praise to our Lord and Lady (God and Goddess), not to just one or the other.

So when one states that Wicca is an Earth or Earth-based religion, one is not using the word *Earth* to denote our Lady (Earth Mother). Instead, they are making reference to the divine union of our Lady (Earth) and our Lord (Sky). At its very core, the format of Wiccan devotion is the praise of Life, the product of the union between our Mother (Earth) and Father (Sky). This is what I mean when I say Wicca is a "Nature-based" religion: Wicca is a religion that views the Creator as manifest in not only our surroundings, but also in ourselves. Wicca is a religion in which creation is viewed as the interaction between the Divine Feminine (Goddess/Earth Mother) and the Divine Masculine (God/Sky Father). In human terms, the Creator is a marriage. In secular, ecological terms we are speaking about the biosphere.

This is one of the reasons Wicca has so many different faces. It is why some Wiccans call to our beloved parents with only the name Lord and Lady, while others use a pantheon of names. Just as the children of humanity have different appearances, so do the children of our Lord and Lady. Just as black women and white men are members of the same humanity, so, too, are Isis (African goddess) and Odin (Northern European god) members of the same divinity. As above, so below.

Moving towards the macrocosm, this does not mean Wicca stops with the stars. As our parents have parents, so do our Mother Earth and Father Sky have parents. Chances are great that those parents have had other children that have gone on to become parents themselves. While we have not yet discovered these other children, Wicca stands ready to embrace them as kin. As above, so below.

Gender, Sex, and the Magickal Child

Gender is the observation that there are more masculine than feminine traits (or vice versa) in any given thing. Sex, on the other hand, is a reference to the reproductive properties of any living thing. Because Wicca views the Creator as the union of the Divine Masculine (God/Lord) and the Divine Feminine (Goddess/Lady), so do we view their creation (the Magickal Child) as the union of masculine and feminine. Thus, all things are both masculine and feminine.

Any type of plant is considered either masculine or feminine (gender) without respect to the sex of the individual plants that make up the type of plant. In extension, the Green World itself is feminine and is thus more readily associated with our Goddess. Yes, there are both masculine and feminine plants, yes there are male deity forms that are strongly associated with the Green World (the first order of life), but as a whole the Green World is considered feminine. This is why we see numerous chants with similar themes to the one that begins this book. The whole of the chant celebrates both Lord and Lady (animals and plants). As you might have guessed from the chant, the whole of the animal world (the second order of life) is strongly associated with our Lord. But that's another book in itself.

Elevation and the Degree System

Over the years in which Wicca has been available to the seeker, the available books have changed to meet what seems like the community focus of the time. There was a time when the Green World was in focus. Later, more attention was paid to familiars, animals, and totems. Today, the gods and goddesses themselves seem more in focus.

Looking back on the trends, one might think that each was a fad. I doubt many readers can deny observing members of the Wiccan community who were participating in our religion simply because it is fashionable to do so. A few of us, myself included, can even remember a time when we were those very faddists. But something else, something infinitely more important not only to our religion, but the survival of our ecosystem, can now be recognized in the trends that seemed at the time to be nothing more than fads. The three stages or degrees of Wiccan elevation have been established in a deeply meaningful and necessary way.

> **The First Degree**—Associated with the Green World or the First Order of Life as discussed in *A Wiccan Bible*.

> **The Second Degree**—Associated with the Animal World or the Second Order of Life as discussed in *A Wiccan Bible*.

> **The Third Degree**—Associated with the Human World or the Third Order of Life as discussed in *A Wiccan Bible*.

Of course, any system has its upside and its downside. Outside of formal education, those who have moved on to the mindset of the second degree tend to look down upon the first degree. Those who have moved on to the mindset of the third degree tend to look down upon both the first and second degree. It is not until one has completed the third degree that one realizes the truth: that the first, second, and third degrees are actually stages in the awakening of the Wiccan soul. That rather than individual steps of elevation, the degree system in Wicca is as the three legs of a stool. Remove any one, and the stool falls.

However, when looking at the three degrees of initiation in this way, we run into a problem. Wicca is not *predominantly* taught by individuals. It is *predominantly* instructed by books and, thus, by authors, publishers, and shopkeepers. As a result, one who is giving study time to Wicca can easily be guided more by which books are on the end-cap display of their local bookstore than by any sense of order. Also on the downside is the fact that one cannot formalize or test the awakening of one's soul. As a result, this way of addressing the three degrees of Wicca does not translate well when conversing with those who have been fortunate enough to find a qualified teacher and are patient enough to complete formal training.

While the focus of authors, publishers, and stores changes with the growth of the author and market demands of the publishers and stores, the focus of an initiate's interest in Wicca *tends* to follow this same pattern.

First Degree—Goddess-/Earth-/Plant-centered—This is the stage in which you will find most Wiccans because there will always be a larger number of people who are first becoming interested in Wicca than those who have been involved for a long time. Here there is a tendency to rebel against all things masculine and perhaps a stronger tendency to rebel against all things Christian. The flash of incense, oils, and other Witch's brews is at the forefront of the Wiccan's reading interests.

Second Degree—God-/Sky-/Animal-centered—Here you will find the rebirth of God in the hearts of Wiccans. The tendency to rebel against all things masculine has faded, but the tendency to rebel against all things Christian remains. As a result, the Horned God becomes the center of focus, despite the fact that the great majority of historically documented Pagan god forms are without horns.

Third Degree—Lord and Lady-/Earth and Sky-/Humanity-centered—Here we see an interest in the pantheons as interactive. Instead of focusing on one god or goddess, the Wiccan looks towards the interaction between our Lord and Lady. The greetings "Thou art God" and "Thou art Goddess" take on personal meaning.

Elder—The mature Wiccan soul—The formalities of religion take a backseat to the meaning behind those formalities. The degree system that previously seemed to be marking points on a path are seen more as three separate legs of a stool, each one just as important as the next in supporting the stool itself.

Initiation

This structure can also be seen as the conception of the Wiccan soul as the Magickal Child. Step one is the introduction of the feminine. Step two is the introduction of the masculine. Step three is the union of the masculine and feminine (the Great Rite), and step four is the birth of the Magickal Child (the Wiccan soul). Thus, one can look at the processes of informal initiation as an unplanned pregnancy and the process of formal initiation as a planned pregnancy.

It might seem as if the process of informal initiation is superior to the process of formal education. That would be so only if the many failures of the informal initiation system were observed. Generally speaking, they are not. In each system there is a process of elevation. In the case of informal elevations, should one not develop, they tend to leave the Wiccan community because the religion no longer fulfills their maturing needs. In the case of formal elevation, should one not develop, one sometimes sticks around even though the training did not touch the heart and awaken the Wiccan soul as it was intended. No matter what the format of elevation, this is why I believe the Wiccan soul is born and not made. For whatever reason, there are people who simply were not born with Wiccan souls and are thus incapable of truly becoming Wiccan despite any amount of formal or informal education. Call me an elitist if you will, but I rather like believing that those who would harm plants, animals, and humans without cause or a bit of remorse are not and will never be Wiccan.

And so, we start with the first degree. We start where most Wiccans start, with plants, herbs, and the allure of magick that attracts most people to Wicca.

Chapter 2
Traditional Tools
of the Trade

*The least of the Magical Instruments is worth infinitely
more than all that you possess, or, if you like, than all
that you stupidly suppose yourself to possess.* [1]

Did I just use the word *trade*? Isn't Wicca a religion? Doesn't the word *trade* denote a profession? Yes, yes, and yes. Wicca is a religion; however, it is a religion of priesthood. In Wicca, every member must act as his own priest or her own priestess. Each Wiccan is thus charged with learning the *trade* of clergy. The keyword in that statement is *learning*. But don't think for a moment that the education of which I speak is static. As Wiccans, our education is forever ongoing.

Although many Wiccan traditions formally mark elevations of degree, Wicca is not something for which a person generally receives a diploma. It is not a goal or a place to be, it is an unending journey. Perhaps we can even call it a work-study program for the soul. Some of the study comes in the form of reading what others have recorded of their journey, and some of the work comes in the form of on-the-job training. That OJT is living with one's eyes open to the many lessons that life will surely distribute to its students.

On Tradition

One of the more important lessons life handed me, I learned when I first joined the military. There, I learned that for every task, there is a right way, a wrong way, and an Army way. As I rose in the ranks, I discovered that the Army way was most often the best (right) way of doing things. It didn't seem that way earlier because I did not have a full understanding of why things were done as they were. No one had taken the time to explain things, I did not have the initiative to figure it out on my own, and I didn't dare ask questions for fear of additional push-ups.

When talking about Wicca, you have probably discovered there is a right way, a wrong way, and a *traditional* way of doing things. Unlike the Army, there is no single field manual to tell all Wiccans what that *traditional* way is. As there is no one tradition of Wicca to which all Wiccans subscribe, what we are often left with is a right way, a wrong way, and a thousand other ways. Each of those thousand other ways is its own *traditional* way. Making things just a bit more confusing, the only answer many people can give for why something is done in a *traditional* way is that it is tradition. This leaves many in the state of trying to balance the *traditional* way against what seems like the most logical (right) way of doing things.

Let me tell you about one such "tradition." As you probably know, most herbs have common or traditional names. These names have typically been given to plants based on the look of the plant. Some books have gone so far as to call these traditional names Wiccan names. While researching this book, I discovered that Scott Cunningham (an author whose books I adore) cited a common name for valerian as "capon's trailer." As a capon is a castrated rooster, I couldn't imagine how valerian's traditional name could have become capon's trailer. As I compiled more and more references for this book, I soon discovered that many modern Pagan sources and virtually every Pagan Website that provided similar information agreed that one of the folk names for valerian was capon's trailer. However, virtually every reference outside of the Pagan community cited a similar, but different, traditional name, "capon's tail." My best guess is that Scott Cunningham's spellchecker or editor decided to make a switch and he simply did not notice. As a result, it seems as if a new *traditional* name for valerian was born despite the fact that there is nothing *traditional* about it.

Now, before anyone decides I have just attacked Scott Cunningham, let's be perfectly clear that mistakes happen. Shortly after *Wicca for Couples* hit the shelves, I noticed someone's spellchecker (either mine or my editor's) changed the name "Stewart" to "Steward" Farrar. Of course, I immediately apologized to his widow, and for the most part, that was that. But some mistakes, such as capon's trailer, do not die so easily. Try doing an Internet search for the terms "capon's trailer" and "Steward Farrar." You will be amazed.

The other problem with traditions is when they are not explained. The problem is that without the explanation, tradition holds little weight and what seems like a more logical (right) way of doing things will win almost every time. The net result is that the tradition is cast aside when it could have continued to serve the community if only the reason behind the tradition had been explained.

Fortunately for tradition, the best way to determine what is a real tradition and what was made up last week is the same process by which one can determine the best way to accomplish a task. If it works, chances are it has worked for some time and has thus become a tradition. If it does not work, then chances are someone made it up recently despite what that glossy paperback claims.

So when you read what I have to say about tools, understand that this is what has worked for me. I have provided the traditional description and the logic behind that description for each major tool. Should you discover that something else works best for you, then use what works. But in selecting your tools and determining what works best, please do not just consider what seems like the pragmatic attributes of that tool. Oftentimes, the way a tool functions and the function of that tool are two entirely different matters.

General Tools for Working With Herbs

Mortar and pestle—Grinding and pulverizing herbs.

Coffee grinder—Powdering herbs quickly.

Electric blender—For large preparations such as floor wash.

Hammer—For breaking up hard, dried roots and the likes.

Boline—For harvesting fresh herbs.

Work knives—For chopping and mincing herbs.

Mixing bowls—Glass or ceramic.

Brewing bowl/pan—Glass, ceramic, or nonmetallic.

Eyedroppers—Glass tube is best.

Scale—Triple-beam or digital for measuring by weight.

Measuring cups—For measuring by volume.

Censer—For burning light incense and herbs.

Thurible—For burning heavy herbs and mixtures.

Various glass bottles—For storing and mixing herbs, oils, tinctures, and other brews.

Bottle tops, corks, and vents — For closing bottles.

Glass drying trays—Self-explanatory.

Metal spoon—For sprinkling incense over coal.

Small glass funnels—For distributing and pouring essential oils and the likes.

Mortar and Pestle

The mortar is a bowl-shaped tool used to hold herbs while they are being ground. The pestle is a plunger-looking tool that is used to crush the herbs against the mortar. This tool was once so common that it was often used as a generic symbol to denote a pharmacy. In fact, when Wicca was in its infancy, the mortar and pestle was generally purchased at a pharmacy. There, one typically had two choices, glass or white ceramic. Today, the selection is large enough to confuse the shopper.

When it comes to working with herbs, one of the best traditions is that no less than two sets of mortar and pestle are used. At a minimum, one set should be kept for medicinal purposes and one for magickal purposes. The upside to this tradition can be found in the initial reason for its creation. Magickal preparations often include items that should never be ingested.

There is, of course, a downside to this tradition. From a philosophical viewpoint, it enforces a separation between magick and medicine. From a practical viewpoint, it just doesn't get the message across. Some of the preparations made with the mortar and pestle contain ingredients that simply should not be ingested. No matter how much you wash your tools, there is always a chance that something that has no place inside the human body will wind up there if you do not use separate tools for edible preparations and nonedible preparations. Below are the most common choices for your mortar and pestle sets. In order of most preferred to least desired, I would list these materials as glass, ceramic, brass, marble, soapstone, and wood.

Wood—You might be able to find a new mortar and pestle set that has a wood pestle, but chances are you won't find one with a wood mortar. However, there is a really good chance of finding one at a thrift or secondhand store. Wood mortars are often beautiful and seemingly functional, but they should be considered decorative only. At the most, use them only for the preparation of nonedibles. Just like the kitchen cutting board, the wood mortar and pestle contains tiny cracks and pores. Should moisture come in contact with the contents of those cracks and pores, it will provide a breeding ground for bacteria. Further, the contents of one preparation will inevitably mix with the ingredients of the next, no matter how well you clean your tools. Sealing the wood won't help because simply using the mortar and pestle will grind away at that sealant.

Brass—My absolute favorite mortar is made from brass. This antique brass mortar was a gift from a very close friend. As such, it has great meaning, and I use it on special occasions the way one might break out the good china and silverware for a holiday meal. Brass is a fine material for the mortar and pestle if grinding mild herbs and also has magickal properties of its own (Masculine, Fire, Sun). Those properties (and a miniscule bit of the metal itself) will always transfer itself into the mix. Generally speaking, brass is an affordable substitute for gold. Lore tells us that it encourages healing, promotes prosperity, and lends itself to protection spells. In the case of protection, it is of particular use in protecting the home. This might explain why it is often used to adorn the entrance to a home (doorknockers and sills) when there are seemingly much better materials for the task. Ah, tradition again.

Soapstone—Recently, soapstone has become one of the most popular materials for mortars and pestles. This is because soapstone is aesthetically pleasing and, due to the ease of overseas manufacturing, it is much more affordable than other materials. The problem with soapstone is that ease of manufacturing. Because it is an easy stone to machine, it also chips, cracks, and breaks easily.

Marble—When purchasing a marble mortar and pestle, look for machine marks. If you do not see circular machine marks on the bottom or around the base, then chances are it is not marble despite what the salesperson claims. The salesperson often does not know the difference. The market is flooded with reconstituted marble. Even if you do see machine marks, there is a good chance it is just a machined piece of reconstituted marble. Fortunately, reconstituted marble makes a fairly good material from which to create a mortar and pestle. From a manufacturing viewpoint, it is superior to marble because, unlike natural marble, the reconstituted material does not have natural cracks and fissures. On the downside, the material used to reconstitute the chips and powder to make the mortar and pestle is approximately equivalent to plastic. While plastic might be advertised as a wonder material, it just doesn't seem ideal in this instance. Sure, humanity is part of nature and, thus, his creations are natural, but plastic just doesn't seem to fit.

Glass—In my opinion, thick glass is one of the finest materials with which to create both mortar and pestle. It is not nearly as porous as other materials, when it cracks you know it, and it is incredibly easy to clean. About the only downside to glass is that finding a glass mortar and pestle is usually a bit of a challenge. Generally speaking, your local metaphysical or herb shops won't stock it. So check out laboratory suppliers and pharmacies.

Ceramic—My second choice, which is almost as good as the first (glass). When properly constructed, ceramic mortars and pestles (preferably stoneware or porcelain) are almost as good as glass. In addition to quality standards, to be properly manufactured, the ceramic mortar and pestle should be unglazed wherever the tool contacts the herbs (the inside of the bowl and head of the pestle). The ceramic itself should be light colored, preferably white. I say that ceramic is *almost as good* because one of the things that makes glass my first choice is that it is easy to clean. When you can see through the tool, you can see if it is really clean or not. White ceramic is almost as good because you will be able to see any remnants that are not white. The other benefit to the ceramic mortar and pestle is that it is readily purchased at just about any herb or cookware shop.

Coffee Grinders versus Mortar and Pestle

Coffee grinders can be had for less than 30 dollars at just about any coffeehouse or cookery supplier. Most will only process an ounce or two at a time, and virtually all will break if used on a material harder than what they were designed to handle (coffee beans). However, they will make short work of turning herbs and resins into a fine powder. For just about all practical purposes, the coffee grinder is superior to the mortar and pestle. But is the most practical always the best choice?

A good friend of mine and I have had the following discussion. She feels using a coffee grinder instead of a mortar and pestle is better because it is less time consuming. "I just don't have time to sit around grinding herbs," she tells me. I know her schedule and she is right. I conceded, but I think that taking the time improves the final product. I do not believe it improves the mixture itself, but the final product is much more than just that which is tangible. The magick is not just the mixture; it is the process by which that mixture has been created. When making preparations for sale in my store, I am fond of the coffee grinder. Because the finished product will not be used by myself, I do not see how the mixture could benefit from a longer process. However, in making preparations for myself, I know the desired effect of that preparation and exactly how it will be used. Thus, using the mortar and pestle provides an opportunity to focus my intent on the final results.

Blades of the Trade

...buy whatever may be necessary without haggling![2]

Most Wiccans will agree on the basics of the ceremonial knife known as the athame. It is discussed in "Liber ab Quattuor" of *A Wiccan Bible*. Although just about every book is quick to tell you that making one's own athame is the best option, few take the advice. Most rely on the standby advice that "if it feels right, it is right" that now plagues the Wiccan community.

The problem with the "if it feels right, it is right" philosophy is that there are many things that feel right that simply are not right. Morphine might feel right when one has an injury, but it won't stop the bleeding. When it comes to the working blades, incorrect selection will often lead to the same problem...bleeding. In the case of the athame, most traditions stipulate that the blade should never be used to cut anything in the material world. As a result, the pragmatic concerns surrounding the selection of athame are few.

But what of the other working blades? Here you should try to save money. Like the expensive knives of professional chefs, the blades used to harvest and prepare herbs should be selected for function rather than appearance or cost. In the case of working knives, the statement "what feels right is right" does not mean what feels right at the store. Instead, it means what feels right after hours of use without a blister, slip, or stray cut. Unfortunately, if you cannot forge your own blades, this can mean some rather expensive experimentation. So please consider using the following guidelines to aid in your selection and trust that when you arrive at the perfect working knives, that knowledge will have been received after hours of practical use.

The Working Blades

Perhaps you have heard the terms "boline," "hand sickle," and "work knife," but you are not sure what is what and which is which. The easiest answer is that the boline is either the same as a hand sickle or it is a white-handled working knife. I say this is the easiest answer because, unless I defer to authority, there is no complete answer. Should I defer to authority, then I have to pick and choose which authority I will defer to. The truth is, these terms have been used so differently by so many people whose opinions I respect that I cannot say one term is better than the next. So I will default to how I was originally instructed.

The Boline/Hand Sickle

Boline—The boline (sometimes called a hand sickle) is a harvesting tool that looks like a small sickle or a crescent-shaped blade, the inside curve of which has been sharpened. It is used specifically for cutting plants as an act of harvesting. It is not used for chopping, whittling, or otherwise reducing plant material. Many traditions state that this tool should be made from gold, brass (a substitute for gold), bronze, or copper. Some claim iron and steel are offensive to Nature spirits. In fact, there is historic precedence for this belief. However, I do not share this opinion. Instead, I feel steel is the best material because it will hold an edge much better than other metals. The sharper a harvesting tool is, the less damage it will cause when it is used properly. Even if one were to ignore the common ethic that there is no reason to cause unnecessary damage to a plant, many forms of gardening involve a perpetual harvest (trimming repeatedly). In such a harvest method, any unnecessary trauma to the plant will reduce harvest.

Finding a boline is sometimes a bit difficult. Because handmade tools tend to be a bit pricey, one can now find some rather scary-looking, boline-like hunting knives coming in from overseas to satisfy the market. Although marketed by many Pagan and metaphysical shops as an affordable alternative to the more traditional tool, I feel they should be avoided. If you are going to take the time and effort to grow and or harvest your own herbs, why not go the extra step to ensure that you are using an appropriate tool? If you cannot find or make a hand sickle, consider using a straight blade that was made with love rather than purchasing a mass-production blade from Pakistan or China.

The Work Knife

Single Edge With or Without Taper

Working Knives — Although the blade design is seemingly unconventional, these are the best two shapes for the working knife. Each is single-edged with a bulbous handle and a large guard. If you have experience as a chef or a woodworker, the shapes probably seem familiar due to their utilitarian nature. As such, if you can not make your own blades and cannot find a local knife-maker, you can probably find appropriate tools at a kitchen supply shop.

Some people, myself included, choose to own two working knives. The one with the angled tip is best for carving. The one with the square cut is best for chopping. If only one knife is to be used for both purposes, the best is the one whose tip tapers towards the handle (top left). Note that the taper is the opposite of what one might expect, and that the edge is found only on the straight of the blade and not on the angled edge. The blade is typically no less than one-eigth inch and no more than one-quarter-inch thick, and the unsharpened portion is generally rounded at the edges.

The working knife might look a bit odd, but remember that it is strictly utilitarian. The bulbous handles are intended to provide a good grip, the guard to prevent fingers from coming in contact with the blade. In the case of the blade whose tip tapers back, the tapered portion is not sharpened because doing so will remove strength from the tip. Both designs have a rounded back because they are often used for chopping. By holding the tool in the dominant hand, the less dominant hand can be placed on the unsharpened back to provide additional force without cutting or blistering the hand on a sharp or square-cut blade. Like the boline, my preference is steel.

I have now mentioned twice that I prefer steel for working blades. It is important to also mention that there are many different types of steel. If you simply purchase the first blade you see, chances are you will find *Pakistan*, *China*, or *Stainless* printed on that blade. The most common is 440 Stainless. If that is the best you can do, it will work. The best steel I have found for working knives is 1095 tool steel. However, there is nothing 'stainless' about this alloy. You will have to take care of the blade if you choose this or another high-carbon steel. This means keeping it clean and storing it only in a clean and waxed (or oiled) condition.

A good way of looking at your choice of steel is to say that stainless steel is to the working knife (and the athame) as the coffee grinder is to the mortar and pestle. It is the most convenient. Remember that the intention behind your creations is just as important as the creations themselves. Generally speaking, hairdressers do not clip coupons with their work scissors and carpenters do not drive nails with ball peen hammers.

Other Items

Electric Blender

Using an electric blender versus a mixing bowl and spoon is just about the same debate as using a mortar and pestal versus an electric coffee grinder. When making large preparations such as floor wash, the blender can serve well in decreasing time consumption. But it will detract greatly from the experience and the opportunity to focus intent on the final results.

Hammer

While it might seem like a crude tool for use with herbs, the minute you find yourself trying to grind up a large piece of dried ginger, orris, or other root, you will understand. To break hard herbs and roots into smaller pieces, wrap the root in cheesecloth and hit it a few times with your trusted hammer. This works especially well on dragon's blood and other resins when purchased in large chunks.

Mixing Bowls

Only glass or glazed ceramic bowls should be used. If choosing glazed ceramic bowls, make sure that the interior of the bowl does not have cracks or crazing. This is especially true when working with essential oils. Do not use metal bowls, as the metal can adversely interact with many substances. Wood bowls are ill-advised for the same reasons as wood mortars and pestles.

Eyedroppers

Because different liquids have different specific gravity, measuring liquids by volume often gives erroneous results. Unfortunately, the process of measuring small amounts of liquid by weight is difficult under anything short of laboratory conditions. Fortunately, measuring precious oils and other liquids by drops provides a fairly accurate measurement because the specific gravity of the liquid will directly affect the point at which that liquid forms a droplet sufficient enough to leave the dropper. The best eyedroppers to use are glass with a rubber or synthetic bulb. Make sure you do not suck fluids into that bulb or it may melt.

Scale

There are many to choose from. My preference is a good triple-beam, but digital scales are often a bit more accurate. If you cannot afford a good scale, it is just as accurate to use measurements of volume as it is to use a cheap scale. But rather than taking this as an encouragement to measure by volume as opposed to weight, please take this as an encouragement to purchase a good scale.

Measuring Cups

Measurements provided in this book are generally provided in a ratio of one ingredient to the others. That ratio was arrived upon by weight and weight is the best measurement. If you grind material to a powder prior to mixing them, you will be just as accurate using volume (measuring cups) as you would be using weight when that weight is arrived at by using the scales typically found in grocery stores.

Censer and Thurible

The censer is kin to the thurible. Both are typically made of metal, ceramic, or another fireproof material capable of taking high temperatures without shattering. Using an old ashtray is a common mistake, which often results in shards of glass flying every which way. For either, a brass dish will due. Generally speaking, the censer is lighter in weight, more attractive, and is used in ritual; the thurible is heavier in weight, utilitarian, and is generally used in spellcraft or experimentation. Both are filled about halfway with sand or gravel. Atop the gravel is often placed self-igniting charcoal tablets, onto which powdered incense and other mixtures are sprinkled. In some cases, the thurible is also used for burning various other items because it provides a safe container.

Glass Bottles

Depending on what is being created, an assortment of glass bottles will be needed. These can range from tiny one-dram bottles for essential oil combinations to large Mason jars for storing herbs. Most general stores sell a variety of Mason and jelly jars by the dozen or half dozen at a very reasonable price. Thrift stores are often a good source of small decorative bottles, and hardware stores generally offer tiny corks. Avoid using plastic bottles, as some preparations will eat away at the plastic.

Cheesecloth

Cheesecloth is useful to wrap herbs used in a bath mixture. The water is allowed to flow freely through the cloth, but the herbs are held in place such that they do not get stuck in the drain or create unnecessary mess in the tub.

Cotton Bags

Cotton bags in an assortment of colors are often employed to create herbal sachets. Called mojo bags, medicine bags, and gris-gris bags, the practice of carrying magickal and sacred herbs on a person transcends the differences between many religions and magickal traditions.

Charcoal Disks

Charcoal disks are used to burn loose incense. There are two categories of incense used in Wiccan rites. Almost everyone is familiar with stick, cone, and other incense in the self-burning category. The other category is natural or loose incense, which is burned over charcoal disks. The latter is the most common for two reasons. With self-burning incense, you cannot get away from the constant burning of saltpeter. The saltpeter is what keeps the incense lit. When using charcoal disks, the saltpeter in the disks ignites the charcoal, but, after that short moment, the only thing you will smell is the incense that you sprinkle on the disk. The other reason loose or natural incense is most often used is that it is generally easier to prepare than cone incense and is more true to the ingredients than is stick or other "dipped" incenses.

Chapter 3
Homegrown Magick

*It is my Will to inform the World of certain facts within my knowledge.
I therefore take 'magical weapons', pen, ink, and paper; I write
'incantations'—these sentences—in the wish to instruct; I call forth 'spirits,'
such as printers, publishers, booksellers, and so forth, and constrain them to
convey my message to those people. The composition and instruction of
this book is thus an act of MAGICK by which I cause Changes
to take place in conformity with my Will.*[1]

My all-time favorite principle of spellcraft can be expressed thus: Dumb spells work for dumb people. Some think it is a rude way to express the principle, but it is quite to the point. If you are dumb enough to believe that simply burning a green candle has the power to bring you money, then chances are you will be prosperous when you burn green candles—not because the green candle has that power, but because by blindly believing that it does, *you* have the power. Human consciousness has the ability to bring thought into manifestation. The downside to this principle is that most people just do not believe those green candles will make money for anyone except the person selling them. For the most part, that is how spells work.

Wait a minute. Did I just say that the only one who makes money off money spells are the people who make the spells and those gullible enough to think they will work? Yes, I did. But that doesn't mean that spells do not work. It means exactly what I said. Spells work for those who make (craft) them. They also work for those who buy them off the shelf and *blindly believe* they will work.

One of the sweetest people to frequent my shop just came in to ask about an anointing oil that will make him smarter. Alan is a teen with an obvious learning disability. The one thing he wants in this world is to be of normal intelligence—not smarter than the average, just normal. He would gladly pay with every penny in his pocket if someone were to offer him something that would grant that wish. To meet his request, I made up a batch of Aries oil for empowerment. Oh, we had plenty in stock but I thought it would make him feel better if he saw the potion prepared. As I did, we chatted. He asked why my wife wasn't at the store. I told him she was at the doctor's office. He said he would pray for her and I said the anointing oil was in exchange for his prayers. I think both the oil and the prayers will work.

By virtue of your reading this book, chances are you won't benefit from the principle that dumb spells work for dumb people. You see, any discussion on or interest in how magick works will inevitably generate doubt. In short, you will have to rely on *homegrown magick* rather than store-bought magick, and you will have to understand how and why it works to use it effectively.

First, you have to understand that there is nothing *magic* about *magick*. Do not for a moment believe that there is anything sleight of hand or supernatural about magick. No one is trying to trick you. Belief in the supernatural is not only unnecessary, but it is not in keeping with the Wiccan religion. Remember that part about being Nature-based? Wicca is not based in the supernatural. All real things are natural, and nothing unreal exists. So rather than thinking of magick as something supernatural, Wiccans look at magick as a very real part of our natural world.

Like many other aspects of the natural world, we cannot explain exactly why it works, but we have observed time and time again that it does. Effectively, magick is science that has not yet been explained. Conversely, science is magick that has been explained. Like all natural forces, it works whether we fully understand it or not, the same way fire works with or without a full understanding of how it burns.

So what about those green candles that I mentioned earlier and the people who buy them? That is one of the greatest magicks of all, the magick of human consciousness. In fact, all acts of intent are acts of magick even when those acts seem mundane.

If you do not think so, please explain just how it is that human consciousness works. You can't, because it is magick. Your reading this book is an act of magick. My writing this book is magick. When used with intention, it is the magick that causes the arrow of a Zen archer to strike its target before it leaves the bow. When used without intention, it is what causes doubt to destroy even the best of plans.

But magick isn't only mind over matter. It is also matter over mind. It wasn't until just a few years ago that science recognized the scent of lavender as an effective sleeping aid. Prior to that revelation, the term used to describe the effects of lavender was "magick" or "magickal aromatherapy." It wasn't long ago that studies demonstrated the ability of a room's color scheme to affect mood. Prior to that revelation, the term used to describe the effects of color was "magick" or "color magick." Today, the popular term is "color therapy." If it has not already, I wonder when feng shui will become a recognized form of therapy. Time and time again, that which was once magick has become therapy, medicine, or science.

Magick, Spellcraft, and the Green World

This brings us to magick, spellcraft, and the *Green World*. If human consciousness can manifest our world and if external influences can affect human consciousness, then it stands to reason that one can use external influences to affect human consciousness. The study of this relationship between human consciousness and external influences on human consciousness is called *spellcraft*. Let's go back to that green candle.

If that candle contains finely ground patchouli or has been anointed with a blend containing essential oil of the same plant, when it burns, it will release a very powerful scent. That smell appears to stimulate sales no matter where I set up as a merchant and no matter who my potential customers are. The scent does not materialize customers from thin air, but it does seem to increase business when customers are present. My theory is that the patchouli acts as a mild aphrodisiac and lightens the mood of people who are exposed to it. People become a bit looser with their money when they are mildly aroused. Because the relationship between the scent of patchouli and spending habits has not been proven, the scent's apparent ability to increase sales is termed "magick" (as opposed to science). In this case, it is matter (the scent) over mind (the customer's mood).

Now if we want to improve upon *matter over mind*, we can append the simple effects of the scent with a bit of *mind over matter*. While burning the candle, one might visualize the flame working as a magnet to attract customers or see his or her business having a prosperous day. Prior to burning the candle, one might visualize customers working their way to the store, while working anointing oil into the candle. Ultimately, we could work creative visualization into every step of the process, including the making of the candle and the blending of the anointing oil used to anoint that candle. We could also plant and harvest the patchouli used in the creation of the candle.

This does not involve the wiggling of the nose or the waving of a wand. It is the scientific method as applied to things that are not completely understood. It is the alchemists, herbalists, healers, and other learned people practicing their trade without the Church's prohibitions. It is the discovery of natural law and the demonstration of that understanding in a meaningful way. It is what has become known as 'classic' or 'operational' Witchcraft. This is what I call "The Magick of Olde."

When combined with Wicca, it becomes a philosophy that not only instructs that the Green World is sacred, but also demonstrates the very real fact that humanity is dependent on the Green World and mandates its preservation.

Acquiring Supplies

In times of old, there was no mail order or Internet. Supplies were either grown, harvested, or purchased from one who did the growing or harvesting. Today, plants and their concentrates (essential oils) can be had with little difficulty. Although it is impossible to grow or harvest every potential need, you will have better results if you grow what you can, harvest what you can, and only purchase what is unavailable otherwise. Follow this very general rule of thumb:

Grown and harvested by you:	At least 3 times as effective
Harvested, but not grown by you:	At least 2 times as effective
Purchased:	1 time as effective (baseline)

Essential Oils and Absolutes

True essential oils are distilled or expressed from the fragrant part of a plant. A close cousin to essential oils is the *absolute*, which is extracted from the plant material in similar manner to essential oil, but with the assistance of a solvent. Generally speaking, most true essential oils and absolutes are imported from Egypt, India, and the surrounding areas of the Middle East where they have been harvested and extracted for thousands of years.

Sure, a local store could produce their own essential oil if they really put their mind to it, but chances are they would have to mortgage their store, home, car, and just about everything else they might own before producing the first dram. Instead, what most metaphysical and Pagan shops offer is either their own blends or someone else's. The problem with purchasing those blended oils is knowing for sure just what it is that the store has blended. The great majority of so-called "magickal oils" are nothing more than synthetic fragrance and coloring in a cheap (sometimes even petroleum) base oil. Also beware of oils claiming to be the "essence" of a plant. When printed on a bottle of oil, all the word *essence* means is scent, and even that is often a stretch of the imagination.

So where does one go to find true essential oils? Well, due to the misunderstandings surrounding just what constitutes a true essential oil, many Pagan and metaphysical shops have trouble keeping them in stock. Why, the customer asks, does a drop of rose oil cost three dollars in your store when the same money will buy a whole bottle down the street? The result is that if you can find a store fortunate enough to have an educated client base that can keep the store's supply of true essential oil rotated, then give that shop your dedicated business.

Do You Have Strawberry Essential Oil?

If a shop claims to offer strawberry essential oil, it is a good idea to shop elsewhere. The scent of fresh strawberries is entirely water-based. As such, a fragrant essential oil cannot be extracted. While it might be possible to blend other essential oils to arrive at something resembling the scent of fresh strawberries, chances are if it says strawberry on the label, its contents are synthetic. Now, please do not boycott a shop for selling synthetic strawberry oil; the scent can be heavenly, but if they insist that it is essential oil, then they need a bit of an education. The same is true of watermelon oil and (one of my favorites) newly mown hay oil.

Growing Your Own Herbs

I am sure that you remember my friend from Chapter 2 who doesn't have time to grind herbs in a mortar and pestle? As you can imagine, she doesn't do much gardening either. Fortunately for this debate, there is a trump card with which I can win the argument every time. Pick a fresh sprig of sweet basil. If you do not have it growing fresh, check the produce section of your local grocery store. Put it in your mouth and chew on it for a moment. Then rinse your mouth with water and try chewing on some basil you purchased in a bottle.

Fresh basil always tastes better than dried, and recently dried basil always tastes better than basil that was dried last year. When you purchase dried herbs, you have no way of telling just how old they are. When you dry your own herbs, you know exactly when they were dried. If you are still not convinced, compare the flavor of a hothouse tomato to one from a roadside stand or backyard garden.

Of course, taste isn't everything, and some things do improve with age. But if taste dwindles with age, then we can be reasonably sure that many other properties do as well. Properties of a plant will also change with the method of drying and storing. When one adds all of these factors up, growing one's own herbs ensures a higher level of control over the final product.

Gardening With Limits

Of course, we cannot grow everything we might need for either the kitchen or the altar. The word *Pagan* may have once meant "country dweller," but many modern-day Pagans have taken to the city for practical purposes, such as employment. While no one can grow *everything* a person might use in spellcraft, us city Witches are a bit more limited than our country-dwelling counterparts. Some plants just require things that we cannot provide. Sunlight, space, and temperature are often limiting factors.

This does not mean that we have to give up on the idea entirely. The rooftops of New York City, the tiny backyards of condominiums, the balconies of apartments, and even the kitchen windowsills of crafty Pagans burst forth with all order of green life when the will to transform those city spaces is present. And when that will is present, even the indoors will resemble the Green World.

Wild Crafting Your Herbs

Wild crafting your supplies can be rewarding even when you return without that which you were hunting for. Field manuals and pictorial guides are available at most mainstream bookstores. These manuals are often detailed for your particular area of the world. Pass on anything that you cannot be absolutely sure you have identified correctly. Remember that things in the Green World often look like something they are not. Dangerous plants can be easily confused with safe ones.

When gathering your supplies, do so from areas away from freeways, rivers with EPA warnings, and especially farmland. While you might not think about it, the runoff of pesticides and fertilizers is particularly dangerous to wild crafters. Oftentimes, a farmer will use a pesticide on his crop that will dissipate before that crop is harvested. That same pesticide might be alive, well, and active at the time you decide to harvest.

Another consideration in deciding on a location is who owns the land you are looking at. Remember that whoever owns the land that you are harvesting from also owns whatever it is that you are harvesting. While this isn't always a problem, there are some cash crops that you should be extra careful not to disturb unless you are absolutely sure you have the landowner's permission. Ginseng and a few other cash crops come to mind.

Timing Your Harvest

Whether wild-crafted, garden-grown, or even in your kitchen window, there is a right time and a wrong time to harvest different portions of a plant. Just as the tides ebb and flow in accordance with the moon, so do the chemical constituents of plants. Generally speaking, the tops, greens, and flowers of a plant are best harvested when the moon is waxing (growing) and best when the moon is full. The roots or anything that grows below the ground are best harvested when the moon is waning (becoming smaller) and best when the moon is dark.

This does not mean that one should harvest at night. You can determine the cycle of the moon by looking at a calendar or in your local newspaper. While it does not matter for the plant's sake if you are harvesting the entire plant, if you are trimming or topping a plant (perpetual harvest), then you should do so early in the day. The rising sun will help close the plants wounds.

Another consideration is the planetary hour. By looking at Chapter 8, you will be able to determine the planetary ruler for many of the plants that you will use. With that information, you can reference the charts in Chapter 7 to determine the best time to harvest each plant in accordance with the planetary rulers of the plant. Combine this reference with the lunar cycle for the optimum time to harvest.

Fairly Take and Fairly Give

Many books will tell you that when you harvest plants, you should make an offering of bread at their base. Some state that you should dig a small hole next to the plant into which to make that offering. I have even read that if you harvest a portion of a plant's root that you should fill the hole that you created with red wine, honey, raisins, and an assortment of other food goods.

Here we again see that the old saying "what feels right, is right" is wrong. While it may feel right to provide such an offering to a plant for having taken a bit of its green or a flower or two, the truth is that the plant has survived where it is because it lives in balance with its habitat. Pour red wine into a hole at its roots and you will change the pH balance of the soil, likely killing the plant. Bury honey, raisins, or bread, and you will likely attract insects that the plant hadn't found necessary to overcome prior to your intervention.

You should certainly make an offering, especially when wild crafting, but use your head when making those offerings. Better yet, use your local nursery. Chances are great that no matter what it is that you are harvesting, there is something at your local nursery that the plant will like. Miracle-Gro in stick form comes to mind; maybe carry a spray bottle or a couple gallons of water with fish emulsions, bat guano, or other plant food based on what type of plant you are harvesting.

Offerings to indoor, garden, and windowsill plants is a bit different. If you care for your plants, they will already have their favorite food. So instead of a practical offering, it's a great idea to accent the influence of tended plants with semiprecious gems and stones. Simply place the offering at the base of the plant when planting, tending, or trimming. When harvesting flowers or even when planting indoors, consider following these general guidelines:

Blue lends energy to Capricorn and Sagittarius. It encourages a sense of peace and calm. When harvesting or planting garden blues, an offering of aquamarine, blue tourmaline, or silver is very appropriate.

Green lends energy to Cancer. It encourages a sense of prosperity and growth. When harvesting or planting garden greens, rose quartz, tourmaline (green and pink), and emerald make very appropriate offerings.

Indigo lends energy to Aquarius and Pisces. It encourages an increase in willingness to take on ambitious goals. When harvesting or planting garden indigos, an offering of amethyst, sapphire, and tourmaline is very appropriate.

Orange lends energy to Leo. It encourages a sense of energy and heightened emotions. When harvesting or planting garden oranges, an offering of imperial topaz, garnet, red tourmaline, and rose quartz is very appropriate.

Pink lends energy to the union of fire signs with air signs. It encourages a sense of love and friendship. When harvesting or planting garden pinks, an offering of rose quartz is very appropriate.

Purple lends energy to the union of water signs with earth signs. It encourages a sense of power, passion, and sexual forcefulness. When harvesting or planting garden purples, an offering of amethyst is very appropriate.

Red lends energy to Aries and Scorpio. It encourages a sense of love, lust, and romance. When harvesting or planting garden reds, an offering of smoky quartz, tourmaline (black or red), and garnet is very appropriate.

Violet lends energy to Gemini and Virgo. It encourages a sense of empowerment. When harvesting and planting garden violets, an offering of amethyst, diamond, and gold is very appropriate.

White lends energy to all. It encourages a sense of friendship, new beginnings, harmony, and peace. When harvesting and planting garden whites, an offering of clear quartz crystal is very appropriate.

Yellow lends energy to Taurus and Libra. It encourages a sense of happiness and joy. When harvesting and planting garden yellows, an offering of golden beryl, citrine, or tourmaline (green and pink) is very appropriate.

Drying and Preserving versus Fresh Material

In many situations, there will be no reason to dry plant material. In fact, the process of drying tends to damage many of the properties a plant is grown for. If making spaghetti sauce using basil from a kitchen garden, there is absolutely no reason to dry that basil before use. Do be aware that if you are using fresh material for the first time, you will often have to use a larger amount than if using dried herbs. This is because the water that leaves the plant during the drying process makes up a substantial part of its weight. The difference will vary with different types of plants. A general rule of thumb is three times the amount of fresh herbs will be used. In most situations where plant material will be stored, ground, burned, mixed with candles, or used in most capacities other than cooking, the plant material is dried before use.

Prior to any use, the material should be sorted and cleaned. Remove and discard anything that has gone brown or shows signs of blight or insect damage. Wash with purified water and make sure that all contaminants are removed. Lay the plant material out on unbleached, uncolored cotton towels. Then allow the wash water to air dry from the plant material's surface. If you want the material to be movable, put the towels on a drying rack, board, or cookie sheet.

Flowers can be dried on the stalk or separated. Generally speaking, if they are dried on the stalk, they are inverted and hung in a warm, dry place away from direct sunlight. If dried off the stalk, they are generally treated as one would leaves.

Leaves require moving the drying rack to a place where it will not be disturbed. The location should be away from direct sunlight and not subject to sudden or severe temperature changes. A good temperature range is between 65 and 75 degrees Fahrenheit, but exceeding this won't cause too much harm. Turn the material over every morning and every evening until dry. If mold develops, discard the material.

Roots seem like they take forever to dry. I have found that if you harvest them this year and hang them in a warm, dry place, they will be ready by the time of next year's harvest. For this reason, many folk choose to make tinctures out of roots while they are still wet, then store the tincture for later use. While I am not sure why, I have not found this practice to be very successful.

Seeds can be dried loose or still attached to the plant. If drying loose seeds, place them in a cotton or cheesecloth bag. Hang the bag where it may be gently warmed by the sun or a fireplace. Shake the bag at least twice a day so that the seeds rotate. If the seeds are still attached to the plant material, place the bag over the head of the plant, making sure to enclose all the seeds. Then hang the whole plant as you would the bag of seeds. Rotate in the same way, only as the material becomes dry, you can kneed the seedpods so that the seeds are expelled. Once dry, separate seed from husk and stem, saving whatever portion you desire.

Quick Drying— Any form of drying will rob the plant material of some of its properties. The quicker the drying process, the greater the destruction. But if you are in a bind and need dried herbs quickly, commercial food dehydrators will work. You can also speed the process by preheating an oven to about 250 degrees Fahrenheit, turning the oven off, and placing a cookie sheet with one layer of herbs in the oven. After the oven has cooled, check to see if the herbs are dry. If not, repeat the step, but always turn the oven off prior to adding the plant material.

Storing Plant Material

If storing herbs, ensure that they are completely dry before storing, or they will mold during storage. The best way to store herbs is with a vacuum system and heavy plastic bags. These systems are available at most general and cookware stores. The drawback to vacuum packing is that every time you need a portion of what you have packaged, you have to cut and reseal the package.

The next best way of storing herbs is in jars. Mason and jelly jars are available at almost every grocery store. They are affordable and often come with labels that fit the jars perfectly. On those labels, write the name of the herb, where it came from (garden, field, or store), the date, and any other information you might need. First you must boil these jars in water to sterilize them, especially if storing for a long period of time. Then dry them completely before adding your herbs.

Jarred or vacuum-sealed plant material should be stored in a reasonably cool, dry place without direct sunlight and at least a little circulation. A closet that is frequented once every day or two is ideal. Remember that nothing lasts forever. When it comes to dried herbs, it is a very good idea to keep your supply rotated. If harvesting in the Fall, expect that harvest to last no more than the Spring. When discarding old plant material, consider returning it to your garden or the wild.

Purchasing Herbs

The best place and usually only place to purchase fresh herbs is your local grocery store. If you have a gourmet grocery, you'll have a much wider selection. The important thing to remember is that we are talking about *fresh* herbs when we say the best place is your local grocery store. That same resource is one of the worst for dried herbs due to poor quality, length of storage, and high prices.

Try looking up herbs in your local yellow pages. Failing that, frequent your local health food store and ask for their recommendations. Chances are they will know a few places that might not be listed in the book. If that yields no results, try the same of metaphysical and Pagan shops. While most do not carry herbs, they can usually point you in the right direction. Just remember that, generally, the quality of your purchase will increase as the distance between you and the plant decreases.

Suggested Reading

The scope of this book is too far reaching to address the art of negotiating with the Green World and welcoming that Green World into your backyard and living room. For those purposes, I strongly suggest the following books:

Golden Gate Gardening, Environmentally Friendly Gardening, and *Easy Vegetable Garden Plans*, all by Pam Peirce.

Backyard Fruits and Berries, by Miranda Smith.

Rhodale's Pest & Disease Problem Solver, by Gilkeson, Peirce, and Smith.

Garden Witchery, by Ellen Dugan.

Magical Gardens, by Patricia Monaghan.

Chapter 4
Procedure
and Terminology

Procedure

When it comes to herb craft, several titles are available as books intended for a Pagan audience, but most are little more than recipe books. Few go further than to tell you to boil an herb in water to make a tea or grind it into a powder to make incense. With a pharmacist in my new family, I just had to go a bit further and discuss procedure.

There is a reasonable chance that if you grind enough herbs into incense, you will be able to assist a loved one with their properties. However, the amount you will have to burn is prohibitive, and inhaling smoke is not a very good way to deliver most herbs' benefits. This is especially the case with folk who cannot inhale smoke (lung cancer comes to mind).

Steep some herbs in a tea and you might like the flavor, but tea might do nothing to release some herbs' healing properties. This is because the active ingredients in many herbs are not water soluble. No matter how long you steep a tea, the desired active ingredients remain in the plant material. Instead, extracting the active ingredients may need to be accomplished using refluxing or percolating equipment and grain alcohol. You could simply create a tincture by soaking the herb in alcohol (see "Tincture" on page 56), but the result will not be nearly as strong as it would be by using refluxing and percolating techniques.

This brings us to another question that I am often forced to ask whenever I see a formula or concoction that seems overly complicated. Why not just eat it? In the case of many preparations, there is little reason a person could not just eat the plant to receive its benefits. In fact, boiling and cooking often decreases or even destroys the desired properties of a plant. But then there are the exceptions. Sure, eating simply huge amounts of an herb may have an effect. However, the majority of the medicinal properties will simply pass through the patient's system without providing much relief. To assist the body in absorbing many herbal remedies, the active ingredients need to be extracted from the plant material by some kind of extraction. This can be a water-based extraction (as in teas), an alcohol extraction (mentioned earlier), or an extraction using fat, depending on whether the active ingredients are water, alcohol, or fat soluble.

Procedure, Politics, and the Law

In my career as an author, I have often slipped political views into my books—so much so that I have been the bane of many editors and a few reviewers. What do such views have to do with religion and magick they ask? To them I ask, Should not a religion seek to improve the world in which it is practiced? "Should not a religion that embraces magick use that magick to improve the world in which it is practiced?"

After watching my father wither to his death while doctors were prevented by politically inspired laws from prescribing medical marijuana, which would have eased the wasting away syndrome, I decided to educate myself so I will never again be witness to such an atrocity without having the medical knowledge to ease suffering.

The Christian Bible specifically states that a woman's suffering during childbirth is her punishment for original sin. As a result, the Church State that once ruled most of Europe once hunted and murdered midwives for their attempts to ease the suffering of their patients. These brave women were often put to death on a charge of Witchcraft. Better my body burn than allow a loved one's suffering to continue, for doing that would be allowing my soul to burn.

It is my Will that doctors, pharmacists, and those educated in the prescribing of medicine be allowed to prescribe that medicine to those in need without the hindrance of politically inspired laws. "Witches Heal"—It's not just a cool bumper sticker.

To Extract or Not to Extract

As illustrated before, there are reasons to use an extraction of plant material rather than just the plant material itself. Unfortunately, the "if it feels right, it is right" approach to the spellcraft portion of magick seems to have overwhelmed most Wiccans with the idea that spellcraft has nothing to do with the understood laws of nature (otherwise known as science). While I do very much feel that one's own impressions are highly valuable in the art of spellcraft, many are simply lazy. As a result, "if it feels right, it is right" often gets translated into "if it takes the least amount of effort, it's right." If you like the smell of almonds, arsenic tea might feel right when you do not have knowledge of arsenic's effect on the body.

Remember that medicine and magick both follow the laws of nature. They can both be either beneficial or detrimental. Before putting anything into or on your body, be absolutely sure of what it will do. By the way, this applies to incense as well. I have far too many times seen poisonous herbs included in incense recipes without any regard for who will be inhaling the smoke and what that smoke might contain.

Consider the use of cinnamon in spellcraft. Among its many attributes, cinnamon is said to inspire lust. Small amounts of whole (not powdered) cinnamon are sometimes included in bath recipes. As an essential oil, cinnamon is often used in making candles. However, if you put cinnamon oil in your bath or on your body, you will probably burn. It is entirely too concentrated. Put whole cinnamon into a candle, and you will probably cause your home to burn, as the cinnamon will act like a giant wick, as will almost any plant material in whole form. So why does cinnamon inspire lust when added to the bath? Chances are the bath water extracts small amounts of the plant material and that a minute amount of the substance finds its way to the genitals. The mild irritation acts to cause slight inflammation, blood flows to the genitals, and lustful thoughts travel to the mind. Now, if you were to use essential oil of cinnamon on your genitals, chances are it would not be lustful thoughts that travel to your mind.

Other materials are used in their natural or close-to-natural form because that is how they work best. Dried basil is used in money drawing incense and spells. However, dried basil will do next to nothing for a bee sting. Fresh basil, on the other hand, can be rubbed on a bee sting to lessen swelling and decrease irritation. Thus, we see some very practical reasons to use plant materials in different forms.

When shopping for herbs, there are terms that are often confused. At my store, we are often asked if our herbs are *fresh*. I answer, "No, we only carry dried herbs." My wife answers, "We reorder herbs monthly." As you might have guessed, she is the better salesperson. The term "fresh herbs" indicates that the herb has not been dried, but most people just use the word to mean recently purchased.

Other customers have asked if we sell *bulk herbs*. As we tend to prepackage the popular herbs and sell virtually all of what we offer by the ounce, I tend to say that we do not indeed sell "bulk herbs," a term that means herbs that are not prepackaged. My wife asks the customer what herbs they are looking for. You might again have guessed that she is the better salesperson.

Many herbal extracts are readily available. In the case of true essential oils, it is virtually impossible to create them yourself. Others, such as tinctures, are commonly available, but also easily made. Still others are vitally impossible to find in their natural form. Consider some of the most common ingredients used in the preparation of magickal incenses: frankincense, myrrh, and dragon's blood. Although these are generally purchased in a form ready or near ready to use, they are themselves extractions. In the case of these three, the method of extraction is called *expression* (see page 55) in which the pressure used to extract the material is gravity. Incidentally, this form of extraction is also used for medicinal preparations. Raw opium is an expression of the poppy plant. Its traditional method of collection was to cut a small slice in the pod and later collect the expressed raw opium after it is driven from the pod by the force of gravity. Again we see that medicine and magick are not all that different.

What form of extraction is the best? It depends on what constituents one is trying to extract. As I mentioned earlier, some are water soluble, some are alcohol soluble, some are fat soluble, and some are expressed without the use of liquid or solvent. Unfortunately, I have yet to discover a guide that states which constituents can be removed from each plant by each method of extraction. However, by looking at various documented preparations, one can make educated guesses as to the constituents extracted by each method.

By observing and recording the form of extraction and solvent used in recipes that work, one can expand on even the question of which is best. Sometimes a combination of extracts is best. In some cases, a water extraction is often followed by an alcohol extraction. Many constituents that can be extracted by water are also extractable by alcohol. In some cases, the constituents that are water soluble are not desired. Thus, the water extraction removes the undesired constituents prior to the alcohol extraction, which then removes the desired constituents.

Methods of Extraction

In addition to the different solvents (usually water, alcohol, and oil) used to extract the constituents, the method of extraction will vary with the desired product and the material being used.

Decoction—An extraction made with the help of boiling water. Typically, this word is used when the extraction made is boiled into a concentration. Whenever boiling water is used to extract material from a plant, the result is a decoction. However, unless there is further boiling to concentrate (reduce) the strained material, the product is not generally called a decoction. Instead, it is most often referred to as a *tea,* even though the term "decoction" is still appropriate.

It is important to note that the temperature of boiling water is high enough to destroy many medicinal properties found in some plants. When I use the term *tea*, I am referring to a warm water *infusion* intended for consumption, not a decoction. (Please see "Infusion.")

Expression—An extraction made from fresh plant material in which pressure is used to force the plant's juices from the plant material. Although often confused, this is not what a product such as a juicer produces. Instead, the end result is a liquid, as opposed to a pulverized fruit. It is the difference between squeezing an orange to make orange juice (no pulp) and twisting it on an orange juicer (creating a juice/pulp blend).

Infusion—An extraction made with non-boiling water or other non-boiling solvent. Most often, the solvent is water that is brought to a boil, taken off the heat source until it stops boiling, and then poured into a teacup to let it steep. Because the temperature of boiling water is high enough to destroy the properties of some herbs, waiting until the water stops boiling is very important. Please see "Decoction."

It is important to note that *tincture* is another word for an infusion made with high-proof grain alcohol as the solvent. However, for the purpose of discussion, I will use the word *infusion* to indicate a warm water infusion, *tea* to refer to a warm water infusion intended for consumption, *tincture* to refer to a grain alcohol infusion, and make direct reference to any other solvent. Vinegar and wine infusions are great examples of the latter (wine not being a grain alcohol).

Maceration—I have read many books that insist that this word denotes an alcohol infusion. The more common definition for this word is a solvent-based extraction method using any solvent (water, alcohol, oil, etc.), in which the soaking time is so long that the plant material becomes pulp. For the most part, this word is not used in modern herbalism unless the plant material is to soak in the extraction process for an extended period of time. A better word to describe an alcohol infusion is *tincture*.

Percolation—This word is exactly as it sounds. It is the same method by which percolated coffee is made. However, it is not always water that is used with this method of extraction. When flammable liquids such as alcohol are used without the proper precautions, you might need much more than knowledge of medicinal herbs to mend your wounds.

If you are going to attempt an alcohol extraction by percolation or refluxing, it is best to purchase professional equipment rather than build your own. If you should attempt to build your own, never consider using flame as your heat source. For a water extraction using percolation, simple household items may be used.

You will need a large pot, a screen or filter material in the vertical center of the pot, and a domed lid without a handle in the center. Fill the pot with water to a level below the screen or filter. Place the plant material on the screen or filter and place the lid on top of the pot in an inverted position (crown down). Gently warm the water. If all goes well, the water will turn to steam, rise, contact the lid, condense, follow the crown to the center, and then drop onto your plant material. The length of time will vary with the material and the concentration you desire. To speed the process, you can increase the heat and add ice to the dish made by the inverted lid. Please note that professional equipment produces a much better end product.

Refluxing—A system by which a liquid is raised in temperature until it releases vapors (steam). Those vapors rise to a cooling/condensing point, return to their liquid state, and fall back to the bottom of the container where they will be reheated again. Refluxing is often used in conjunction with percolation, such that the falling liquid passes through plant material to extract its properties. The result is that the liquid increases in concentration with each pass through the plant material.

By replacing the plant material with a collection container to catch falling liquid, refluxing becomes a method of concentrating the plant material that has been removed via percolation. The solvent containing the extracted plant material is heated; it turns to a vapor/steam and rises,

> **Percolating and Refluxing: What's in a name?**
>
> Generally speaking, the term "percolation" is used when the solvent used is water and the equipment is as described. When the solvent is alcohol or similar solvents and laboratory equipment is used, the term is "refluxing."

leaving the extracted plant material behind. Then the steam condenses and falls into the collection container.

Tincture—An alcohol extraction. Essentially, a tincture is an infusion in which the liquid used is alcohol. In some cases, this is the word used to describe an extract made using refluxing or percolation techniques with alcohol as the solvent. For the purpose of discussion, when I refer to a tincture, I am referring to the more primitive method of creating an alcohol infusion.

Common Creations and Preparations

Baths

The easiest way to use plant material in a bath is to enclose the material in a cheesecloth wrap and tie the wrap shut. This will prevent the plant material from sticking to your body, the tub, or clogging your drain. Alternatively, some herb shops sell tea bags for the tub. After the herb is placed in the bag, the ends are ironed to create a positive seal.

Do not draw the water as you would a regular bath. Instead, place the bag of plant material in your tub and then draw hot water only. Allow the herb to steep in the tub until the bath is at the desired temperature. An alternative to this method is to create a very strong hot water infusion and then add the infusion to your bath water.

Candles

Commercial candles are most often scented using synthetic oils because essential oils are thought to be too volatile. As essential oils typically evaporate quickly, much of their scent is destroyed when mixed with hot melted wax. Synthetic oils should not be used for medical or magickal practice as there is no lore on which to build. Instead, only pure essential oils and finely ground herbs are used.

Powdered Herbs—Any more than 1 tablespoon of powdered plant material to 1 pound of wax is inviting trouble. In larger ratios, the plant material may act as a wick and produce excessive flame. Be sure that all plant material is ground to a fine powder prior to mixing into the wax, and make sure it distributes evenly.

Essential Oils—Essential oils are added to wax in a ratio of about 1 1/2 ounces (12 drams) of oil to 1 pound of wax. If you are using one of the oil recipes from this book, you will note that those recipes are provided with a base oil. To use those recipes to create candles, do not include the base oil. In fact, remove the word *drops* and replace it with "parts." Example: If an oil recipe reads 9 drops patchouli oil, 7 drops sandalwood oil, 5 drops orange oil, and 1/2 ounce base oil, translate that into 9 parts patchouli oil, 7 parts sandalwood oil, 5 parts orange oil, and omit the base oil. The resulting mixture can then be added to melted candle wax in the ratio of 1 1/2 ounces to 1 pound of wax.

To preserve the properties of the essential oil, it is best to use very low temperature wax with few hardeners. It is best to add the essential oils right before pouring the candles into their molds, as the longer the heat is applied to the essential oils, the more they will vaporize or degrade.

Incense Powder (not self-igniting)—Incense is most often prepared by simply grinding plant material with a mortar and pestle and then mixing the resulting powders in accordance with recipes and guidelines for desired scent and properties. This is the best form of incense for any purpose other than convenience. The resulting powder mixture is burned atop charcoal disks.

Incense powders are also made by selecting a wood powder, which has its own attributes, to aid your intent, and then mixing that into the essential oils and other extractions. As an example, a simple incense for inspiring a combination of spiritual love as well as a bit of lust can be made by adding a small amount of patchouli essential oil to white or yellow sandalwood powder. The sandalwood powder reinforces the properties of patchouli, drawing that energy.

Incense Powder (self-igniting)—Self-igniting incense powder is made by adding saltpeter to an incense powder. Although several books provide an exact ratio, those references are typically following the guidelines set forth by some of the worst powdered incense manufacturers in the world and will only work if the incense you are creating is little more than sawdust and a few drops of essential oil. Typically, these inferior products are sold in a cardboard can with a metal cap at each end.

As you might have guessed, I am not a fan of self-igniting powders. The real problem I see with them is that during the entire time the incense is burning, the saltpeter detracts from the scent and valued properties of the plant material. When one uses charcoal disks, there is a short time while the charcoal is starting when this smell is present, but after a minute or two the only smoke released is that of the incense burning.

But if you really do not want to be bothered by the use of charcoal disks, the secret to mixing in just the right amount of saltpeter is to experiment with different amounts for each recipe. There is no set ratio that will work, as the ingredients will change. The larger the amount of wood and herb pulp used, the lower the amount of saltpeter needed. The larger the amount of resins and moisture used, the higher the amount of saltpeter needed.

Should you ever encounter jars of "handmade" powdered incense that is all one color, be suspicious. If it smells absolutely great, be more suspicious. Both "self-igniting" and "not self-igniting" powdered incenses found in today's market are typically nothing more than colored sawdust with a few drops of essential or even synthetic oil dribbled into the mix. While some believe this is an effective and simple way of making incense, often the colored sawdust is placed into a jar with a few drops of the oil added to the top. Effectively, this creates a product that smells great when you put it to your nose but not so nice when it burns.

Why? Well, to cut costs, many folk who manufacture sawdust-based incense acquire their sawdust at the local lumberyard. A great amount of wood that is cut in such facilities is plywood, particleboard, or other composition lumber. That lumber is created with large amounts of wood glue. So the result is similar to burning Elmer's Glue.

Incense Sticks—There are two procedures used to create what is typically called stick incense. The first procedure is to create a self-igniting incense powder that is high enough in resin and moisture that a small piece of wood can be rolled in the slurry and then allowed to dry. This method is rather uncommon in Western countries, but remains fairly common in and around India. The reason it is uncommon is twofold. First, it takes much more effort than the dipping procedure, and, secondly, the sticks for creating hand-rolled incense are not normally available. I have had some degree of success using bamboo splinters, which I painstakingly separated from a stalk, but I don't see doing it again any time soon. Sticks used for the purpose of hand-dipping incense are typically available in two types, wood or charcoal-based. For scent value, the charcoal sticks are superior. For cleanliness, the wood sticks are superior. The black charcoal will get everywhere and does not clean up easily, but the wood sticks add harshness to the smell of most incense.

The other procedure for creating stick incense is most often called "hand dipped." In the Western world, this is by far the most commonly manufactured and available incense. As you may have guessed, it is also one of the easiest to make. In its simplest form, one just purchases unscented sticks, blends fragrance oil with a solvent at a ratio of about 3 parts base to 1 part fragrance oil, and then "hand dips" the sticks into the oil. If one is actually dipping the sticks, the blended oil will be in a narrow cylinder. However, most people simply pile the unscented sticks in a tray and then use an eyedropper to evenly distribute the oil mixture. After the sticks are saturated, they are set aside in a well-ventilated area and allowed to dry for at least two days before used or sold. Do not try to speed this process by placing them in an oven; it will produce inferior incense.

Note that I said that in its simplest form, fragrance oil is used with a solvent. Typically, incense makers do not use essential oils due to the cost. For any use other than scent alone, only true essential oils should be used. You can use these oils straight (which produces huge amounts of smoke) or go the less expensive route of using a solvent to cut your essential oils. The blending ratio will differ from the ratio used with fragrance oils, but 3 parts solvent to 1 part essential oil (a 25 percent mix) is a very good place to start experimenting. You will discover that some essential oils and blends may be diluted as much as 90 percent without a noticeable difference, while others lose their scent when the solvent is any more than half of the dipping mix.

So, what is the solvent? Most dippers use dipropylene glycol (DPG). It is affordable, virtually scentless, and produces very little smoke of its own. Others use alcohol. In general, alcohol is a bad idea, as the only alcohol that will not leave a large amount of residue to taint the final product is grain alcohol, which is cost prohibitive. Additionally, alcohol is highly flammable. If your drying process does not completely remove the alcohol before the incense is burned, it will burn entirely too fast. It will also eat through the plastic bags that incense sticks are often stored and sold in.

On the rare occasion that I dip incense for my own use, I do not use a solvent or cutting oil. I prefer the increase in smoke when using only essential oils and do not mind the cost. When creating dipped incense for sale, I tend to use the oils used in accordance with the recipes I have collected and have no set oil for using when making dipped incense sticks. Please see further description under "Oils," immediately following.

Oils—When used for either magickal or medicinal purposes, essential oils are most often diluted. There are exceptions, such as lavender oil, but many essential oils are dangerous and should never contact the skin in their undiluted form. This does not mean that synthetic oils are used. Instead, the oils most typically used in both magickal and medical preparations are either diluted essential oils or (more often) diluted mixtures of essential oils. The essential oils are diluted with *carrier* or *base* oils.

I have found the following natural carrier oils very useful: almond, apricot kernel, avocado, coconut, grapeseed, hazelnut, jojoba, olive, palm, sesame, and sunflower. In selecting base oils, one should consult the reference material provided within this book to determine which is best for a particular purpose. To determine the best use of almond oil, just look up almond and read about its properties. For apricot kernel oil, look up apricot, and so on.

With the exception of jojoba oil, each of these carrier oils will eventually go rancid. To prolong their life when creating a blend, the commonly recommended preservative (in Pagan reference material) is 3 drops of wheat germ oil to each 1/2 ounce of final product. A more effective preservative is rosemary oil extract (not the same as essential oil of rosemary). Only a drop or two is needed in 16 ounces of carrier oil.

The mixing ratio is an important consideration when creating blends. The exact ratio of pure essential oil to carrier oil will vary with preparation, intent, and the person who will be using the oil. I have no problem placing pure patchouli oil on my body. Some people show signs of skin irritation when contacting pure patchouli oil but are fine with a 1 part patchouli, 3 parts base oil mixture. Still others are horribly allergic to even the weakest concentration of patchouli. Generally speaking, I mix approximately 21 drops of pure essential oil to each 1/2 ounce of base oil. This is a relatively strong mixture. It is best that you start with a ratio of 2 ounces of base oil to 21 drops of pure essential oil (a 25 percent dilution of my recipes) until you know how the mixtures will affect your skin.

Poultice—The preparation of a poultice will differ with the application. Generally speaking, a poultice is a sterile cloth that has been soaked in a warm water infusion or that is used to keep a paste-like preparation in place on the skin. It is sometimes called a cataplasm. In modern terms, if you were to spray Bactine on a self-adhesive bandage and apply it to a wound, you have used a poultice.

Salve—A simple salve can be made by gently warming either olive or sesame oil with the herb or herbs of choice. If using hard materials, such as dried root or bark, simmer these items first for at least three hours. If dried flowers, herbs, or seeds are used, simmer for only two hours. If fresh material is used, simmer for one hour.

The trick to using a combination of hard, dried, and fresh material is to add them at the appropriate time. Should you have a recipe that includes hard material, dried material, and fresh material, simply heat the oil and add the hard material, simmer for an hour, then add the dried material and simmer for an additional hour, and then add the fresh material. Allow to simmer for an additional hour.

When the material is finished simmering, strain and add beeswax in a ratio of between 1 and 2 ounces of beeswax per pint of oil. With 1 ounce, you will have a thin salve; with 2 ounces you will have a thick salve. Allow the beeswax to melt into the mixture and add 1 teaspoon tincture of benzoin as a preservative. Mix thoroughly, cool, and refrigerate.

Alternatively, solid vegetable shortening can be warmed as a substitute for oil. If this substitute is used, mix 1 ounce beeswax per 1 cup shortening, and again add 1 teaspoon tincture of benzoin as a preservative.

Soaps—Typical recipes for creating homemade soaps are actually instructions for a process called melt and pour. Essentially, this is done by purchasing a soap base, melting it, adding scent, and pouring it into a mold. The process by which soap is made is more involved than many are willing to attempt, and an error can produce a dangerous product.

To use the oil recipes provided in the formulary section of this book to create soaps, do not include the base oil. Instead, remove the word *drops* and replace it with *parts* such that the ratio of essential oils remains the same to each other, but such that the finished blend contains only pure essential oil. Depending on your skin's sensitivity, the typical concentration is 1/2 ounce of this blend of essential oils to 1 or 2 pounds of soap mix. You will have to experiment to find the best ratio for your skin type. Even with dilution, be aware of skin sensitivity and allergic reactions. Other botanicals are commonly added to soap in a ratio of about 1/4 cup of dried plant material to 2 pounds of soap mix.

Tea—The best way to make most teas is to bring water to a boil, allow the boiling to subside, and then pour it over dried plant material in a non-metallic cup or container. Boiling virtually any tea in a metallic container will produce an inferior product. This is why teapots are so valuable in creating these wonderful infusions. Bring your water to a boil in your favorite glass cookware; remove from heat and pour into a teapot over the plant material within.

When entertaining, my preferred way of making tea is to allow the plant material to mix freely with the water in the teapot. After the tea has steeped, I pour the tea into a cup through a bamboo strainer. I do not believe the brief moment that the tea would spend in contact with a metal strainer would

> **Sun Tea**—This is a general recipe with no set ratios. I start with 1 ounce of dried plant material to 2 quarts of water and then increase or decrease the amount of plant material based on flavor. Place plant material and water in a clear glass container and set in the sun for one full day. If you put a lid on the container, it is a good idea to have a small hole for ventilation. Strain and serve over ice.

cause any damage, but I like my bamboo. It's one of the many ways I remind myself not to be too Eurocentric in my magickal and medicinal practices.

Now for a confession. This is not my preferred way of making tea when I am not entertaining. When a special occasion is at hand, the teapot comes out. On those occasions, I am also inclined to grind the tea in a mortar and pestle as part of the immediate preparation. However, I have discovered a wonderful tool for very fast tea creation. It is called the French press, and it is available at almost any gourmet coffee or cookware shop. Essentially, it is a small, round glass pitcher with a top that features a detachable screen attached to a plunger. To use this simple miracle, one places the plant material in the cylinder, pours hot water on top, and places the lid (plunger up) on top. The longer you let it sit, the stronger it will be. When it is just right, you push down on the plunger, driving the plant material to the bottom. Then pour the mixture into a cup and drink. The amount of time this method takes to steep is approximately the amount of time it takes me to shower. I then pour the tea over ice and bring it to work to keep me from drinking soda pop all day.

Additional ways of making tea without getting herbs stuck in your teeth:

* **Tea bags** can be purchased empty and filled with herbs yourself, but they are just as expensive as if you purchase ready-made tea bags. If you are planning on using one-plant teas (chamomile comes to mind) and you don't mind spending a little extra, most of the common plants whose medicinal properties are well known can be found in ready-made tea bags at your local grocery store.

* **Tea balls** are usually made from metal. While a metal screen might not be all that bad, using a metal tea ball will place the metal in contact with the hot water for an extended period of time. This is not desirable. At a certain temperature, portions of the metal may migrate and degrade the constituents of the tea. I am not sure what the chemical changes are, but the taste difference is like drinking beer from the can versus drinking it from the tap. If you absolutely must use metal, use stainless steel.

Tinctures—Tinctures are alcohol infusions. Ideally, they are made with refluxing or percolating devices; however, due to the explosive nature of alcohol fumes, this should only be done with equipment that has been professionally manufactured. Fortunately, there are ways to create tinctures that can produce a finished product that approaches the quality of tinctures made with refluxing equipment.

There are two main reasons for using tinctures. The first is that alcohol extracts material from plants that are not otherwise easily extracted. The second—and probably one of the best reasons—is that plant material can be made ready to use, yet it will not go rancid in any reasonable amount of time. The alcohol is itself a preservative.

The alcohol used should always be grain alcohol (ethanol) and never wood alcohol (isopropyl). Don't bother checking that rubbing alcohol, it won't do. Rubbing alcohol is isopropyl. Isopropyl alcohol is poisonous, and even if the tincture is not going to be used for consumption, it will have a horrible odor even when the alcohol has evaporated.

The best product for making tinctures is commonly sold as Everclear (190 proof/ 95 percent alcohol). The sale of Everclear is restricted in some areas. If you cannot find it and you are fortune enough to be able to find 140 proof vodka (70% alcohol) or stronger, it will work as well. Bacardi 151 will work in a pinch, but your end result will smell like...well, like Bacardi.

To make a simple tincture, grind your plant material into the smallest possible state. If you are using a hard root, it is easiest to purchase it as a powder. Cover the bottom of a Mason jar with the plant material. Then pour in an amount of alcohol equal to twice the volume of the powdered plant material. Screw the lid on tightly and shake vigorously for just a few seconds. Then unscrew the cap to release the pressure. Allow this to sit with the lid off for at least 15 minutes. This will allow any gas formed by the initial blending of the herbs to be released. Generally this is not necessary, but it is always a good idea to be safe. Then tighten the cap and set aside.

Each day, shake the mixture vigorously for three minutes, relieve the pressure, and then reseal the cap. Best results will be had if you do this three times each day for two weeks or longer. After two weeks, strain and test. Place a drop of the tincture on your wrist and allow the alcohol to evaporate. If it smells of the plant material, you have been successful. If it does not, you may want to either return the plant material to the alcohol and soak longer or leave the lid off for a time and allow some of the alcohol to escape, thus strengthening the ratio of plant material to alcohol.

> Using tinctures for their scent is similar to using perfume. When first applied, there is a strong alcohol scent. But your body heat warms the tincture, making the alcohol evaporate and leaving only the scent of the plant material that the alcohol extracted.

Terminology

Abortifacient—A substance that causes abortions.

Anemia—A deficiency of the oxygen-carrying parts of the blood, often the result of low amounts of iron in the diet. It is measured by the ratio of red blood cells found in the blood.

Alterative—Tends to restore the body to normal health.

Anodyne—Decreases or eliminates pain.

Anthelmintic—Destroys or causes parasitic worms to be expelled. See also "taeniafuge."

Antibiotic—Technically, an antibiotic is a substance produced by bacteria and other organisms that is used to kill or inhibit other microorganisms. A good example of an antibiotic is penicillin. However, what you will encounter in this book are recipes and herbs that are used topically for their "antibiotic properties."

Antiseptic—A preparation or plant material that kills or inhibits the growth of microorganisms. Used to battle infection.

Aphrodisiac—A preparation or plant material that stirs lustful thoughts and/or excites the reproductive organs.

Anticoagulant—Decreases the blood's ability to clot.

Antipyretic—Reduces fever.

Antiperiodic—Prevents the reoccurrence of a disease.

Antiscorbutic—Cures or prevents scurvy.

Antispasmodic—Relieves or prevents spasms, especially those of smooth muscles.

Aperient—Gentle laxative that purges the bowls.

Arthritis—Inflammation, pain, and swelling of a joint not caused by a recent injury.

Astringent—A preparation or plant material that draws together or restricts tissues.

Bronchitis—An inflammation of the bronchial system.

Carminative—Encourages the release of gas from the intestines and stomach.

Cathartic—Purges the digestive system. Most often used to describe a laxative.

Colic—Abdominal pain, usually of the intestines or stomach. Most often used to describe such pain in a young child or baby.

Cystitis—An inflammation of the urinary bladder.

Decoction—An extract made with boiling water. Typically called a decoction if boiled further after the plant material is removed to concentrate the extraction.

Demulcent—Sooths and softens mucus membranes to relieve pain.

Dentifrice—Used to clean the teeth.

Deobstruent—Removes obstructions to the flow of body secretions and fluids.

Diaphoretic—Increases perspiration. Useful in cleansing the skin.

Diuretic—Increases urination. Useful in cleansing the system of toxins.

Emetic—Tends to promote vomiting.

Emmenagogue—Tends to induce or quicken menstruation.

Emollient—A substance that softens the skin.

Enzymes—Complicated strings of protein that cause chemical changes in other substances. When it comes to herbalism, these are most often encountered when using a milk infusion.

Expectorant—Assists in the expulsion of phlegm and mucus from the respiratory system.

Febrifuge—Reduces fever. See also "refrigerant."

Homeopathic—A medical preparation or practice in which a tiny amount of a medicine is used to treat a condition that would be brought on by a large amount of the same medicine.

Hypnotic—An agent that causes sleep or a twilight state.

Infusion—An extract made by soaking plant material with warm or hot water (not boiling).

Intoxicant—A preparation or plant material that causes intoxication.

Laxative—A preparation or plant material that raises the level of moisture in the bowls to fight constipation.

Mydriatic—A substance that causes the pupils to dilate.

Narcotic—Soothing, numbing, and pain relieving. Usually addictive, mood altering, behavior altering, and sedative in nature. Most narcotics also stiffen the stool, often to the point of constipation.

Nervine—Preparation or plant material that calms and settles the nerves.

Pectoral—Useful in relieving disorders of the chest.

Prophylactic—Substance that prevents disease.

Purgative—Promotes evacuation of the bowls.

Refrigerant—Reduces fever and may lower body temperature. See also "febrifuge."

Rubefacient—Causes redness of the skin.

Relaxant—Preparation or plant material that relaxes the mind and counters tension.

Sedative—Preparation or plant material that settles the mind. Most often used to induce sleep or relaxation.

Stimulant—Increases the function of a portion of the body. Note that it is possible for a single plant to be a stimulant for one portion of the body and also work as a sedative or a nervine for another part.

Stomachic—Aids in digestion.

Sudorific—See "diaphoretic."

Styptic—Astringent that specifically decreases bleeding by tightening tissues and restricting blood flow.

Taeniafuge—A substance that expels tapeworms from the body. See also "anthelmintic."

Tonic—A preparation or plant material that strengthens the immune system, the body's function as a whole, or any particular organ. Generally speaking, tonics are preventative measures. They are sometimes used to treat deficiencies of certain vitamins, minerals, or other nutrients.

Topical—Applied to the surface of the skin. Used externally.

Vermifuge—Causes parasitic worms to be expelled.

Vulnerary—Useful in treating wounds.

Chapter 5
Herbal Remedies
and Recipes

In ordering this book, I found it extremely hard to separate "Herbal Remedies" from "Kitchen Witchery" (the next chapter). I decided the distinction would be the difference between remedies and preventatives. This chapter will focus on herbal cures, and the next will focus on everyday cooking that can prevent illness and boost the immune system.

But where should I draw the line between the medical properties of the Green World and the magickal? After all, it was not long ago that medicine and magick were not the separate subjects that they seem to be today. For help, I asked my wife what she thought. Her answer was much what I have now found is the most common. Medical considerations are those things that heal by commonly understood methods. So where would I list the scent of lavender oil as a cure for insomnia? Well, that would be medical, of course. After all, research has demonstrated that lavender oil is just as effective as over-the-counter sleep aids. Okay, I'll buy that, but what about asafetida?

Now my bride's family used folk remedies and preventatives as a part of their life without ever considering their use as magick, but she eventually found her way into the Pagan community where belief in magick abounds. So she knew exactly what I was asking. Asafetida is an old folk remedy and preventative. Reportedly, placing it in a sachet and worn around the neck, asafetida will prevent and turn back most illnesses.

So should it be listed as medical? Well, I have seen it work many times, yet I cannot come up with a medical explanation. As you can see, separating the magickal from the medical is not as easy as it seems on the surface.

Using This Chapter With the Herbal and Formulary

I have read many an herbal. Some organize the presented information by herb. Others organize the presented information by illness or complaint. I have used both types of organization. In this chapter, you will find recipes organized by symptom or complaint. For general reference to single plant cures and a guide for creating your own recipes, please refer to the formulary section of this book. For specific herbs, please see the extensive herbal provided at the end of this book.

Using the Recipes

Many recipes given here are provided as *tea mixture*. To prevent redundancy, the method for using these recipes as tea and the standard measurements for infusions and decoctions are described here rather than in each recipe. Simple home remedies and single ingredient recipes are given in text boxes.

To use as tea, place 1 or 2 teaspoons of the powder in an empty tea bag or other appropriate device. Alternatively, place the mixture in a teacup and strain later. Bring water to a boil and then reduce heat. When the water is no longer boiling, pour into a teacup (over the mixture). Allow to sit until it is cool enough to sip.

For an infusion, unless otherwise specified, the general ratio of plant material to liquid is 1 ounce of dried herb in 1 pint of liquid (usually water). Simmer for 30 minutes and strain.

For a decoction, unless otherwise specified, the general ratio of plant material to liquid (usually water) is 1 ounce dried plant material to 1 quart of water. Boil to reduce to 1 pint by volume and then strain.

Arthritis

Oregano Ointment—Simmer 1 part oregano in 4 parts olive oil (by volume), allow to cool, strain, and apply liberally to sore joints.

Arthritis Tea—Combine 1 part parsley and 1 part ginger root. Grind to a powder and serve as tea. Better if you use equal amounts of fresh ginger root and parsley by weight, simmer for 30 minutes.

Arthritis Rub—Combine 2 parts rosemary leaves, 1 part oregano, and 1 part brandy by volume. Allow to sit for at least a month. Strain and massage affected areas.

> Treat Arthritis With Sea Salts—Swimming in the ocean regularly will relieve the pain of arthritis. Most people don't have a handy ocean, so add a couple cups of sea salts to a warm bath. Add a few drops of lavender oil to make it even better. Epson salts (1 cup per bath) will also work. Try both and see which works better for you.

Burns

Burn Salve—Following the instructions for a "simple salve" in the previous chapter, add 1 ounce Irish moss, 1 ounce marshmallow root, and 10 drops tincture of benzoin.

Poultice—A white vinegar infusion of 1 part Irish moss and 1 part marshmallow makes a fine poultice for mild burns.

Sunburns—A white vinegar infusion of 1 part chamomile and 1 part Irish moss.

> Treat Burns with Red Currant Jelly—Keeping homemade red currant jelly in the fridge is a tasty treat. Rubbing it on fresh burns will decrease pain and lessen blisters.

Breathing Problems

See also "Cough, Flu, Colds, and Fevers" and "Expectorants"

Asthma I—Mix equal amounts of rosemary, coltsfoot, thyme, and lavender. This mixture is placed in a water pipe and smoked.

Asthma II—Grind equal amounts of thyme and anise seed. Simmer in sunflower oil for 30 minutes. Strain, cool, and serve 1 tablespoon at night.

> Treat Asthma With Horseradish—A warm skim milk infusion of horseradish.
>
> Treat Asthma With Coffee—Some forms of asthma respond well to a good strong cup of coffee.

Bronchitis—Relief from bronchitis may be had by making a warm skim-milk infusion of lemon balm. Allow to simmer for at least 15 minutes, cool, strain, and then reheat at serving time. Consume an 8-ounce cup with and between every meal, and mild symptoms of bronchitis will probably be gone in a day.

Smoker's Cough—A warm water infusion of 2 parts anise seed and 1 part clove, simmer for 30 minutes, strain, and sweeten with honey. Serve warm.

Cough, Flu, Colds, and Fevers

See also "Expectorants" and "Breathing Problems"

Cough Syrup I (Cherry and Cinnamon)—In a pot, mix 1 pint cherries, 1 lemon sliced thinly, 1 pint honey, 1 tablespoon cinnamon, and enough water to cover the mixture. Mix and simmer for no less than one hour. Mash with a potato masher and simmer for another hour. Strain or remove the lemon rind and cherry pits, but do not remove the pulp. Remove from heat; allow to cool in the refrigerator overnight. Keep refrigerated.

> **Treat Allergies With Locally Harvested Honey**—If you are prone to pollen allergies and you can find a local bee-keeper, you might be in luck. Many folk report relief from pollen-induced allergies from the daily consumption of lo-cally produced honey. Others have a horrible allergic reac-tion to the honey itself.

Cough Syrup II (Sage and Thyme)—In a pot, mix 1/2 ounce sage, 1/2 ounce thyme, and 1 pint water. Simmer for 30 minutes, strain, and mix in 1 pint honey. Allow to cool and keep refrigerated.

Cough Syrup III (Hyssop and Horehound)—Grind 2 parts hyssop and 1 part hore-hound. Bring 1 pint of water to a boil and remove from heat. When the water stops boiling, add 1/4 ounce (about 7 grams) of the herb mixture and allow to simmer for one half hour. Strain hot and return to heat. Add an amount of honey equal to about one half the amount of remaining fluid. Simmer until the volume decreases by approxi-mately half. Allow to cool. The consistency should be approximately that of maple syrup. If it is too thick, warm gently and add water. If it is too thin, warm gently and add honey.

Cough Syrup IV (Horehound and Lemon)—This is my absolute favorite. In a pot, mix 2 ounces of horehound, 1 sliced lemon, and 1 1/2 pints water. Simmer for 30 minutes, strain, and mix in 1 pint of honey. Cool and keep refrigerated.

Cough Syrup V (Red Clover, Mint, and Lemon)—In a pot, mix 1/2 ounce red clover and 1/2 ounce mint and 1 sliced lemon with 1 pint wa-ter. Simmer for 30 minutes, strain, and mix 1 pint honey. Allow to cool and keep refrigerated.

> **Treat Colds With Vinegar, Honey, and Raisins**—Mix 4 parts vinegar, 1 part honey, 1 part raisins, and 1 part wa-ter. Simmer for 30 minutes, strain, and cool. Serve 1/2 cup several times a day.

Cold and Flu Citrus Remedy I—Mix 3 parts orange juice (an expression), 2 parts warm water infusion of sage, and 1 part lemon juice. Simmer (do not boil) until re-duced by one half. Sweeten with honey and serve warm.

Cold and Flu Citrus Remedy II—Make a warm water infusion of equal amounts of sage, lemon peel, and or-ange peel. Simmer 30 minutes, strain, sweeten, and serve warm.

Tea for Flu (Minty)—Grind 3 parts peppermint, 2 parts feverfew, and 1 part elder flowers into a medium powder. Create a warm water infusion of this mixture, simmer for 30 minutes, strain, and sweeten with honey. Serve hot. Eases pain and acts as an expectorant.

Tea for Flu With Fever—Grind equal amounts of fever-few, peppermint, yarrow, and elder flowers. Bring 1 pint of water to a boil and remove from heat. When the water stops boiling, add 1/2 ounce (about 14 grams) of the above mixture and allow to simmer for 30 minutes. While still warm, mix in honey to taste. Strain and serve warm.

Tea for Cold and Flu Symptoms—Mix 2 parts elder flowers, 2 parts peppermint leaves, and 1 part sage. Simmer (do not boil) for 30 minutes, strain, and sweeten with honey. Serve hot.

> **Treat Congestion With Apple Cider Vinegar**—Mix with equal amounts of water, boil, and inhale the rising steam.
>
> **Treat Congestion with Lemon Juice**—Add lemon juice to virtually any tea or other beverage to aid congestion.

Milk and Spice for the Sick—Mix 1 tablespoon honey, 1 teaspoon powdered ginger, 1 teaspoon powdered cinnamon, and 2 cups milk. Simmer for 30 minutes. Serve hot with a cinnamon stick to stir in more honey.

Rose Hip and Spice for the Sick—Make a warm water infusion of 4 parts rose hips, 2 parts lemon peel, and 1 part cinnamon. Simmer for 30 minutes, strain, and sweeten with honey. Serve warm with a cinnamon stick.

Sinus Relief Tea—Grind to a powder 3 tablespoons fenugreek seeds, 1 tablespoon lemon peel, and 1 tablespoon orange peel. Add 1 pint water and bring to a boil. Add 1/2 of a small sliced onion, reduce heat, and simmer for 30 minutes. Strain and serve unsweetened. Believe it or not, it doesn't taste nearly as bad as it sounds. Drink over the course of a day.

> **Treat Fever With Cayenne**—Cayenne will cause sweating and lower fever. It can be mixed into food, but chances are a sick person won't want to eat much. So put cayenne powder into empty gel caps. If using size 00 gel caps, the dose is 1 or 2 caps every three or four hours.

Cuts and Scrapes

Milk and Elder Wash—For topical use only. Make a warm mild infusion of elder leaves. Allow to simmer for 30 minutes, strain, and return liquid to heat until it decreases in volume by one half. Allow to cool and apply to wounds 3 times a day to speed healing.

> **Treat Cuts and Scrapes With Papaya Juice**—Store bought papaya juice is a good topical cleanser for mild cuts and scrapes.
>
> **Treat Cuts and Scrapes With Confectioner Sugar**—Treat minor cuts and scratches with powdered sugar. Decreases healing time when applied daily.

Poultices to Stop Bleeding—Make a poultice from 1 part lemon balm and 1 part witch hazel. Other plants commonly used for this purpose include oak leaves, honeysuckle leaves and root, papaya slices, and St. John's wort.

Prevent Blood Clots—An infusion of fresh ginger root will decrease the formation of blood clots. Typically, the ratio is 2 teaspoons fresh ginger root to 1 pint water. Simmer for 30 minutes, strain, and serve hot.

Infection Fighting I– A decoction of 2 parts comfrey leaves and 1 part garlic will turn back most minor infections when applied topically.

Infection Fighting II—For topical use only. A white wine vinegar infusion of 1 part comfrey leaves and 1 part oak leaves is helpful in treating abrasion wounds that have become infected.

> **Treat Sprains With Buttermilk**—A poultice of warm buttermilk is excellent for pulled muscles and sprains.
>
> **Treat Swollen Joints With Cider Vinegar**—Mix equal amounts of water and cider vinegar, heat gently, and soak affected areas in the warm mixture. Use a cloth if you cannot fit the affected area in the liquid.

Digestive, Nausea, and Stomach Problems

Stomach Settler—Mix 4 parts lobelia, 2 parts chamomile, 2 parts mint, and 1 part mullein. Grind to a powder and use as a tea mix.

Nausea Fighter I—Mix 1 tablespoon oatmeal with 2 tablespoons chamomile and just a pinch of cinnamon. Simmer for 10 minutes in 1/2 pint water.

Nausea Fighter II—Mix equal amounts of chamomile and fennel seed. Serve as tea.

Digestion Helper I– Mix equal amounts of dill and fennel seeds. Serve as tea and sweeten with honey.

Digestion Helper II—Mix equal amounts of marjoram and hops flowers. Serve as tea and sweeten with honey.

End Stomach Cramps—Mix equal amounts of chamomile and lemon balm. Serve as tea.

Ease Constipation—Mix 1 cup apple juice with 1 cup olive oil in the blender. Drink before bed. Drink this quickly (it will separate fast). Relief will come by morning.

Diarrhea Remedy—Slice 1 apple and remove the skin. Simmer the meat of the fruit in 1 cup milk for 30 minutes. Pulverize the softened apple and then put the mixture in a blender on high. Serve warm and sweeten with honey.

> **Treat Constipation With Cloves and Milk**—A warm whole milk infusion of cloves will relieve constipation quickly. Drink a large glass.

Diuretics

Diuretic Syrup—Grind together 1 ounce fennel seeds, 1 ounce mustard seeds, and 1 ounce fresh horseradish root. Add to 2 pints boiling water, reduce heat, and simmer for 3 hours. Remove from heat and allow to stand overnight in the refrigerator. Strain and serve 2 tablespoons several times a day.

Corn Silk and Apple—Cut 3 apples into thin slices. Bring 2 pints of water to a boil, reduce heat, and add apples and the silk of 3 ears of corn. Simmer for 30 minutes and strain. Serve cool. Do not sweeten. This helps with cystitis (inflammation of the bladder).

Urinary Tract Cleanser—Mix 1 part blackberry leaves, 1 part heartsease, and 1 part lemon peel. Serve as tea.

Ear Problems

Earache Drops—Gently warm 1 cup of olive oil and 1 tablespoon of finely ground witch hazel. Simmer for 30 minutes, strain, and allow to cool to body temperature. Add several drops to the affected ear.

Ringing in the Ears—Crush 5 cloves of garlic and add to 1 cup olive oil. Simmer for 30 minutes and let stand for three days in an airtight container. Strain and apply 3 drops to stop ringing of the ears.

Expectorants

Expectorant Tea—Make a warm water infusion of 2 parts mullein flower, 2 parts mallow (dwarf), and 1 part cloves. Simmer for 30 minutes, strain, and flavor with lemon juice and honey to taste.

Headaches

Headache Tea I—Mix equal amounts of sage, peppermint, and rosemary. Grind to a powder and use as a tea. Sweeten with honey.

Headache Tea II—Mix 2 parts chamomile with 1 part willow bark. Grind to a powder and use as a tea. Sweeten with honey.

Headache Tea III—Mix 1 part skullcap, 1 part sage, and 1 part peppermint. Grind into a powder and use as a tea. Sweeten with honey.

High Blood Pressure

Blood Pressure Lowering Tea—Mix 2 parts chamomile, 1 part peppermint, and 1 part tag alder bark. Grind to a powder and serve as tea.

> **Treat High Blood Pressure With Lemonade**—Make lemonade by mixing lemon juice, water, and honey to taste. Do not use sugar. If you simmer this mixture, it will help the honey to dissolve. Serve warm or over ice.

Insect Bites

Bite Paste—A mixture of 1 part baking soda and 1 part powdered sea salt can be combined with water to make a paste that is effective in relieving the skin irritation of insect and spider bites. Or gently moisten the skin in the area of the bite and sprinkle with powdered sea salt to end the irritation.

> **Treat Insect bites With Toothpaste**—Toothpaste acts as a good topical remedy for the itching of insect bites.

Measles

Calendula and Peppermint Remedy—Relief from measles can be had with an infusion of calendula flowers. Bring 4 cups of water to a boil. Reduce heat to a simmer. Add 1 heaping tablespoon of calendula flower and 1 heaping tablespoon of peppermint leaves. Reduce heat and simmer for 15 minutes. Strain and sweeten with sugar (not honey). Will only work if the patient remains in a warm, dark room (preferably in bed). This infusion is useful in treating any condition where you wish to encourage sweating.

Mouth, Throat, Gums, and Teeth

Mouthwash—Do not drink. Mix 4 parts thyme, 4 parts peppermint, 1 part myrrh, and 1 part baking soda. Grind into a powder and then create a warm water infusion. This mixture will treat canker sores, gum infections, and other mouth problems.

Tooth Pain I—Grind together 2 parts whole cloves and 1 part baking soda. Add enough water to create a paste and place on the painful spot just long enough to get to the dentist.

> **Treat Cold Sores With Buttermilk**—Dab some buttermilk on cold sores to speed healing and dry up the affected area.

Tooth Pain II—Grind together 2 parts vanilla bean and 1 part baking soda. Add enough water to create a paste and place on the painful spot just long enough to get to a dentist.

Natural Toothpaste—Grind to a powder 4 parts baking soda, 2 parts peppermint, and 1 part thyme. Mix with water right before using to create a paste, then use as you would a commercial product.

Sore Throat Syrup I—Grind 2 tablespoons cloves and 2 tablespoons slippery elm into a powder. Add 2 pints water and 1 cup honey. Bring to a boil, reduce heat, and allow to simmer for 30 minutes. Strain, cool, and refrigerate. Take a tablespoon or two at a time as needed.

Sore Throat Syrup II—Mix equal amounts of black currant berries, water, and honey by volume. Simmer for 30 minutes and then crush the berries. Strain and return to heat. Reduce until thick. Serve as needed by the tablespoon.

> **Treat Sore Throats With Beet Juice**—Gargle with beet juice to relieve the pain and scratchiness of a sore throat.
>
> **Treat Sore Throats With Brandy and Spice**—Simmer on very low heat 1 cup brandy or cherry brandy, 1 cup brown sugar, and 1 tablespoon finely ground cloves for 15 minutes. Strain and serve warm. Note that you can eliminate a great deal of the alcohol by simmering longer.

Skin Care

Athlete's Foot I—Make a warm water infusion of 3 parts red clover and 1 part chamomile. Simmer for 30 minutes, strain, and reduce to 1/4 volume. Remove from heat, allow to cool, and add enough cornstarch to make a paste. Apply the paste at night, remove in the morning, and repeat as needed.

Athlete's Foot II—Make a warm apple cider vinegar infusion of red clover. Dissolve a bit of sea salt into the infusion and use as a foot wash before sleep.

Diaper Rash—Combine 1 part chamomile flower with 1 part calendula flowers. Grind this into a powder; simmer in water, and then strain. Once cooled, this can be added to bath water or used as a wash to ease diaper rash.

Healthy Skin Bath—Into a bath sachet, mix 1 cup baking soda with 1 ounce medium-ground chamomile flowers. This will also battle mild infections.

Poison Ivy I—Flush the skin with water immediately and dab dry. Slice open a green tomato and express the juice onto the area that has come into contact with poison ivy. After an hour, wash again and apply a paste of baking soda and water. Repeat as necessary.

Poison Ivy II—Grind together 3 parts willow leaves with 1 part chamomile flowers. Mix this with an equal amount of water by volume. Bring to a boil and then simmer for 30 minutes. Strain, cool, and apply to the skin to relieve itching.

Heat Rash Powder—Grind to a powder 2 parts chamomile flowers, 2 parts calendula flowers, and 1 part cornstarch. Sprinkle on affected area.

Sleep and Sedatives

Insomnia Tea—Mix 2 parts peppermint, 1 part rosemary, and 1 part sage. Grind into a powder and use as a tea.

Valerian and Chamomile—Mix equal parts of valerian root and chamomile. Grind into a powder and use as a tea mixture.

Knockout Drops I—Mix 2 ounces skullcap, 2 ounces valerian root, and 1 ounce chamomile. Cover with water and simmer for an hour while adding water as needed to keep the herbs covered. Strain; reduce and concentrate until a teaspoonful is not translucent. At this point, a few teaspoons mixed into another beverage will act as a strong sedative. However, the longer you simmer and reduce this mixture, the stronger it will get.

> **Treat Insomnia With Milk and Honey**—Gently warm whole milk. Add honey to taste and serve warm. The heat activates enzymes in whole milk that will calm the mind and body. Adding oatmeal and simmering for about 15 minutes will greatly improve the effectiveness.

Knockout Drops II—Follow the instructions provided for "Knockout Drops I," but save the discarded plant material. Dry that pulp to remove any remaining water and then create an alcohol extraction using refluxing/percolating equipment. Mix the alcohol extraction with the water infusion created in "Knockout Drops I." Reduce volume by simmering off the alcohol and continue to increase strength. Warning: Depending on how much you reduce, this preparation can be extremely strong. Just a few drops in a cup of tea or other drink will induce sleep.

Hops and Chamomile—Grind equal amounts of chamomile and hops flowers to a medium powder. Bring 1 pint of water to a boil, reduce heat, and simmer as you add 1/2 ounce (about 14 grams) of this mixture. Steep on low heat for 30 minutes. Strain and serve warm. Do not sweeten.

Mullein and Chamomile—Grind a combination of 2 parts chamomile and 1 part mullein to the consistency of down. Bring 1 pint of water to a boil, reduce heat, and simmer as you add 1/2 ounce (about 14 grams) of this mixture. Sweeten with honey.

Five Herb Sleeping Tea—4 parts chamomile, 4 parts skullcap, 4 parts elder flower, 1 part peppermint, and 1 part pennyroyal. Grind to a powder and serve as tea.

Sleepy Sun Tea—Make sun tea (see Chapter 4) with a mixture of 50 percent mint or chamomile and 50 pecent valerian root. Sweeten with natural sugar or powdered honey and serve over ice. Drink it plain and the taste might grow on you. Then again, it might not. Most people describe valerian root as smelling like dirty socks. Cats love this stuff, so hide your stash well. Be aware that most references state that valerian root should be used only once a day and for no longer than three weeks.

Sleepy Night Tea—Mix equal amounts of bee balm, chamomile, and hops. Grind to a powder and use as a tea mix. Sweeten with honey.

Tonics and Immune System Boosters

Hot Weather Tonic—Make an infusion with 2 parts fresh dandelion flowers and 1 part lemon balm. Simmer in water for 30 minutes. Strain, cool, and serve over ice.

Energy Tonic I—Mix 4 tablespoons finely ground marjoram, 1 tablespoon chicory, and 1 pint water. Bring to a boil for just a moment and simmer for 20 minutes. Sweeten with honey and serve warm. It is more eye-opening than a cup of coffee.

Energy Tonic II—Mix 3 parts borage with 1 part chicory. Grind to a powder and use as a tea. Stimulates the adrenal glands.

Study Tonic—Mix 5 parts rosemary, 2 parts goldenseal, and 1 part skullcap. Grind to a powder and use as a tea. Stimulates the mind.

Virility Tonic for Men—Mix 2 parts ginseng root, 1 part shepherd's purse, 1 part corn husk, and 1 part hops. Grind to a powder and use as a tea. Stimulates the prostate and improves blood flow to the genital area.

> Treat Menstrual Cramps With Raspberry Juice—Drinking raspberry juice will decrease painful menstrual cramps. Raspberry leaf tea will help as well.

Virility Tonic for Women—Do not use if pregnant. Mix 4 parts strawberry leaves, 2 parts raspberry leaves, and 1 part ginger root. Grind to a powder and use as a tea blend. Stimulates the reproductive organs.

General Tonic—Mix 4 parts lemon peel, 2 parts orange peel, 1 part hops, and 1 part clove. Grind to a powder and then use as a tea blend. Strain, sweeten with honey, and serve either warm or over ice.

Chapter 6
Kitchen Witchery

Kitchen Witchery is found somewhere between what is often called "Home Remedies" (Chapter 5) and "Making Magick" (Chapter 7). This is why I chose to discuss kitchen witchery right smack in the middle of the two. The truth is that there is no difference between home remedies, kitchen witchery, and making magick when it comes to the Green World. In respect to that world, the ability of valerian root to put a person to sleep is no different than the ability of patchouli to increase sales. The difference is only found in our perception of the Green World and how we relate to it.

You see, nothing unnatural exists in the real world. Those things that seem to be supernatural are actually parts of the natural world, which we *perceive* as being apart from the natural world. Despite hundreds of years of slander by the Church State, herbal remedies are gaining great acceptance in our culture. Thus, such remedies are *perceived* as being part of the natural world. Making magick still has a long way to go before it is generally accepted as part of our world. Kitchen witchery, well, that's the current frontier. Although not entirely accepted, it is making great strides.

I have said that science is magick that has been explained and that magick is science that has not yet been explained. A good way to look at the differences between herbal remedies, kitchen witchery, and making magick follows an expansion of this definition.

Science (herbal remedies) is nature that has been explained. Kitchen witchery is somewhere between science and magick. Magick is nature that has not been explained.

Intent Is the Key

When we think of herbal remedies, we tend to believe we are talking about a chemical reaction. Add vinegar to baking soda and it will fizz whether we want the mixture to fizz or not. We tend to see an illness and apply a cure. Something is broken, so we try to fix it. But what about those times when something isn't necessarily broken? What about those times when we want to sculpt rather than repair? That is kitchen witchery.

Like the sculptor, the first order of business here is our intent. We need a clear mental image of that which we hope to create. In essence, herbal remedies, kitchen witchery, and making magick all require intent. However, with the medical properties of herbal remedies firmly established, the individual's intent is not as critical for success. Some practitioners believe this trend is due to the principles of collective consciousness. Although I am not entirely sure I believe such matters shape our world, it does fit the principle.

Herbal Remedies—Individual intent is least critical. The collective consciousness principal in respect to herbal remedies is such that the principles and properties of the remedy are established so firmly in the collective that the individual intent is not necessary for those principles and properties to manifest. Basically, water is wet because we all say it is wet, and there is nothing you can do about it.

Kitchen Witchery—Intent is more critical. The collective consciousness principal in respect to kitchen witchery is such that the principles and properties of the witchery are partially established in the collective. Thus, the influence of individual intent is partially necessary for those principles and properties to manifest. Basically, water is wet because we think it is wet, and you agree with us.

Making Magick—Intent is most critical. The collective consciousness principal in respect to making magick is such that the principles and properties of magick are not established in the collective. Thus, the influence of individual intent is tremendously important for those principles and properties to manifest. Basically, water is wet because you will it to be.

Again, I remind you that I am not entirely sure that I buy into the principles of Collective Consciousness Theory. However, I do wholly believe that individual intent is key to manifesting one's desire. In the Wiccan religion, one of the methods to focus intent is ritual.

The Daily Ritual of Food

I have been a guest speaker at Indiana University–Perdue University at Fort Wayne (IPFW) on a couple of occasions. On the first occasion, the Pagan Student Alliance asked that I provide two presentations. The first was to be a secular presentation for general consumption. The second was a presentation specifically for the Pagan Student Alliance. So what does a Pagan author speak about that does not involve religion? Well, he speaks on the art of ritual, of course. When I wrote to the organizer with my idea for the secular presentation, I think he wondered if I understood what the word *secular* meant. I secretly wondered if he understood what the word *ritual* meant. By the end of the presentation, we both knew we had been on the same page all along.

So what does the word *ritual* mean? *The American Heritage Dictionary of the English Language* defines ritual as follows:

2A. The prescribed form of conducting a formal secular ceremony: the ritual of an inauguration.

2B. The body of ceremonies used by a fraternal organization.

5A. A detailed method of procedure faithfully or regularly followed: My household chores have become a morning ritual.

We have a tendency to think the word *ritual* refers to a formal religious ceremony. As a result, we tend to forget about the everyday rituals that propel us forward. How many people are able to earn a degree without the ritual of study? But it is these rituals rather than the more formal ones that are key to our advancement. Yes, the rituals of graduation and commencement are important. Magickally speaking, such formal rituals put those in attendance on the same page. They gather the energy from those in attendance to launch the graduate on his or her way. But they are nowhere near as important as the education and study that led to graduation and commencement.

The preparation of meals is among these many overlooked rituals. With these rites, we find an everyday opportunity to practice kitchen witchery. In practicing kitchen witchery, we have the opportunity to become mindful not only of what we consume, but of the relationship between what we consume and the world in which we live. This is the very core of all ritual: to be mindful.

By knowing the properties attributed to the ingredients with which we sustain our bodies, we become aware of what we are. By knowing the relationship between our food and the Green World, we become mindful of the connection between the Green World and ourselves. Yes, kitchen witchery is similar to herbal remedies by the fact that there is clearly an amount of chemistry involved. However, even if there is absolutely no explained reason for a food's attributes and effects, there is still the act of being mindful. After all, even if one believes that kitchen witchery is nothing but hocus pocus, placebo is one of the most powerful medicines a doctor can provide.

Saying Grace

Like the ritual of graduation and commencement, ensuring that guests understand the event is also important. This is where saying grace comes in. Language is one of the most important of the magickal tools. It affords a quick and more or less easily understood way of putting people on the same page. It aids us in being mindful. Now be honest, do you remember what you had for dinner last night? Do you remember why you had dinner last night?

A Brief Discussion of Kitchen Witchery and Ethics

One of the challenges of being Wiccan is making decisions about moral and ethical matters. Our religion is not like others in this department, as Wicca has no set code of ethics. There are no commandments. Even if one accepts the Wiccan Rede as the Wiccan equivalent to the Commandments, one is faced with the fact that the word *rede* implies the material is a set of guidelines, not laws. So what is a Witch to do?

Your best bet is to cast the idea of *magickal ethics* to the wind. But don't ever tell anyone that you feel that way because they will inevitably misunderstand. Instead, when you encounter someone who spouts *magickal ethics*, simply smile and nod. You see, *ethics* are *ethics*. As magick is a part of the real world, it is covered by the ethics that we use for the rest of the real world. Most folk who will tell you differently are just making excuses for their lack of success.

One of the most prevalent of these excuses is the ridiculous magickal ethic that one should not attempt to influence others using magick. Why do I say this is ridiculous? Well, the written word has been thought to be magick from the very beginning. Should I not use the written word to influence your opinion? The challenge is not in seeing and respecting the line between ethical and unethical, but in determining exactly where the lines are drawn.

If you place Rohypnol (one of the "date rape" drugs) in a date's drink without his or her knowledge and consent, I'd say that is over the line. Pretty simple, right? What if you place a natural substance (let's say marijuana or opium) in the meal prepared for someone without their consent or knowledge? I'd say that, too, is over the line. So where am I going with this? Well, was Grandma over the line when she served her homemade eggnog at the family holiday gathering? Did that eggnog contain nutmeg?

If you have any doubt that whole nutmeg is a drug, just consume about three or four tablespoons. Don't say I told you to do so, because chances are that dose is enough to drop you to the floor and probably cause some rather serious medical problems. In small amounts, nutmeg acts as a mood elevator. In large amounts, it acts as a powerful narcotic. In larger amounts, it will kill you. What are those amounts? Well, that depends on your size, constitution, medical condition, and the concentration of active ingredients in the particular nutmeg that you manage to come across. In short, don't try to use it to get high or you might wind up dead.

So did Granny cross the line when she served eggnog to raise the holiday spirits? If you think not, why not? Is it because she used only a small amount of the drug (nutmeg)? Well, if she only used a small amount of Rohypnol, then would you think that was acceptable?

Wicca does not have set ethics, dogma, or commandments because these things are not set. Ethics are fluid. They change with given circumstances. This is an especially important point when it comes to kitchen witchery. You see, many of the recipes that follow will work well if they are allowed to do so in the background. Bringing them to the foreground by announcing your intent can easily interfere with their effectiveness. In short, there are many circumstances where the person you are cooking for should not know the exact intent of the meal. Now that in and of itself might sound overly manipulative, but note that I said the *exact intent*. Should you serve champagne to a lover during a romantic meal without explaining to that lover that champagne is considered an aphrodisiac? Doing so seems rather innocent to me. Unless, of course, you are dating a complete idiot. Sometimes it is the secrecy and suspense (placebo) that will aid in the desired results. Other times, the simple disbelief that a person might hold could interfere with the effect (reverse placebo effect). Of course, in these matters one should maintain one's personal ethics, but don't forget Grandma and her nutmeg.

As with all things, the key is to use this information mindfully. So, in kitchen witchery one incorporates one's intent in the preparation of a meal and then incorporates the general intent to one's guests within the saying of grace. Effectively, kitchen witchery can be likened to Wiccan ritual thus:

> **Preparing the Meal**—Making preparations for ritual. Cleansing the ritual area.
>
> **Saying Grace**—Issuing the challenge. Ensuring that those who are in attendance are there of their own free will.
>
> **Consuming the Meal**—The body of the ritual. In spellcraft, this is the casting of the spell.

A Few of My Favorite Recipes

Consider this section my apology for a few of the herbal remedies. Trust me, I know that a few of them are as horrifically unpalatable as some of the things a doctor might send you home with. These are not.

Aphrodisiacs

Apricot Dessert Topping (aphrodisiac/very mild intoxicant)—Bring a pot of water to a boil and add fresh apricots. Reduce heat and allow to simmer until soft. Place in blender with brandy in a ratio of 4 parts apricots to 1 part brandy by volume. Blend and add honey to taste. Serve over vanilla pie, pudding, or ice cream.

Betel Nut Candy (aphrodisiac)—Warning: Excess use can be dangerous. One betel nut seems to be fine, but more can produce intoxication and problems with digestion.

In the Middle East, where this recipe originated, sweets are often served as appetizers rather than deserts. The lore behind this sweet is that if it is eaten prior to a good meal, you will need to cook nothing for dessert.

    1 betel nut
    2 tablespoons sesame seeds
    2 cardamom seeds
    Honey

Grind to a fine powder, add just enough honey to bind, and mix thoroughly. Carefully slice open dried dates and use this mixture to fill. Cover and allow to sit overnight. The number of dates to use will depend on how much paste you place in each. The general guideline is that one betel nut, however far you stretch the paste, is the dose for one person.

Cake Decorations (aphrodisiac)—Sometimes the magick is in the topping. In this case, it is in the decorations. Soak blue and yellow water lilies in sweet wine overnight. The next morning, lay them out on a cookie sheet, sprinkle with powdered sugar, and let dry. Once dried, they are used to decorate sweets.

Carrot and Plum Wine (aphrodisiac/intoxicant)—Carrots are said to cure impotency, increase stamina in men, and inspire lust in women. Try mixing 1 part carrot juice with 3 parts plum wine. Consume liberally over a romantic dinner and you will probably understand the attributes. Carrot juice is especially effective in relieving sexual dysfunction (impotency and poor lubrication) brought on by doubt and fear after going a great deal of time without sexual intercourse. Do not expect an instant cure, but if the first experience is gentle and prolonged, the second experience will be firm and moist.

Celery Juice Blend (aphrodisiac for women)—Mix 1 part celery juice, 1 part carrot juice, and 2 parts apple juice for a morning breakfast and then again at lunch. By the time you are home from work, you will be ready for physical love and then a sound night's sleep. This blend seems to work with women only.

Cowslip Wine (aphrodisiac/intoxicant)—The Saxons called it *cuy lippe*. Ancient Greeks called it *paralysio*. Both used it to make a mildly narcotic and lust-inspiring wine with recipes such as this:

Mix 1 gallon of the yellow flower rings of the cowslip, 4 pounds of sugar, the rind of 2 lemons, and 14 pints cold water. Pour into a bottle with a vent cap. On the second day, add 1 cup of fresh yeast. Swirl the fluid around the bottle briskly, but not so much that you trap bubbles, each day for a week. After a full week, strain and mix with the juice of the lemons you used earlier. Seal and store undisturbed and away from sunlight in a cool place. After nine months, strain and bottle. If all went well, it will be good drinking at this point, but if all continues to go well, it will be great drinking in about a year. Note that this recipe is primitive. I have had more than one batch go bad. If successful, the final product will have a clear to yellowish tint, never very cloudy. To increase success, please consider purchasing a book on home winemaking. The many concerns of the art of winemaking are far beyond the scope of this work.

Damiana Liqueur (aphrodisiac/intoxicant)—*WARNING:* Not for habitual use. Prolonged use may cause damage to the liver. Soak 1 ounce of dried damiana leaves and 1/4 ounce saw palmetto berries in 1/2 liter of undiluted vodka for one week. Strain the vodka/damiana mixture and set the liquid aside. On the stove, pour 2 liters of filtered water (spring is best, but tap will do in a pinch) over the still-wet leaves. Warm the water/damiana mix and dissolve 21 tablespoons of honey from local hives. Allow to cool to room temperature and then add the damiana/vodka to this mix (you only separated it so the alcohol wouldn't be boiled off). Keep this in a sealed glass container (Mason jars will do) for one month. Strain before serving. Share this liqueur before an evening of lovemaking to enhance passion, lower inhibitions, and increase your psychic awareness of your partner. This mixture will also provide vivid dreams. Approximately 8 ounces seems the proper dose, but experiment, as overdoing it will cause excess intoxication.

Honey Liqueur (aphrodisiac)—If you should find Linden Flower Honey Liqueur on the shelves of your local bottle shop or liquor store, buy a bottle or two and set it aside for a time you might want this mild aphrodisiac. If you try to purchase it when needed, it never seems available.

Kava Kava Coconut Milk Shake (aphrodisiac/mild intoxicant)—This recipe makes enough for two.

    2 ounces finely powdered kava kava root

    1 can (10 ounces or so) coconut milk

    10 ounces coconut or coffee liqueur

    3 tablespoons coconut oil

    2 tablespoons lecithin

    2 large scoops vanilla ice cream

    Place all items into a blender; blend, and serve.

Peppermint Brandy (aphrodisiac/intoxicant)—A simple aphrodisiac can be made by soaking 1 ounce of peppermint in 2 pints of brandy for one moon. Strain and serve to your lover on the night of the full moon or during the waxing moon.

Wild Lettuce and Plum Wine (aphrodisiac)—Place 1 ounce powdered wild lettuce leaves in 1 pint plum wine. Store in refrigerator for one month. Shake every day and relieve the pressure by uncorking for a moment. Strain and serve chilled.

Pumpkin Seed and Spice (aphrodisiac for men)—Remove pumpkin seeds from the pumpkin and soak overnight in saltwater. This will help separate the seeds from the other plant material. Grind into a powder 1 part dill seed, 1 part parsley, and 1 part rosemary. Place a single layer of seeds on a cookie sheet that has been lightly covered in olive oil. Sprinkle this powder over the still damp pumpkin seeds. It is okay to add a bit of salt, but the saltwater soak should be plenty. Preheat the oven to 300 degrees Fahrenheit and bake for 45 minutes or until golden.

Truffle and Spice (aphrodisiac for men and women)—Chop truffles into bite-size pieces. Combine with garlic and dill to taste. Sauté in butter or margarine. Salt to taste and serve as a side dish or over rice.

Calming and Peace Bringing

Rice Tea—This recipe will calm the mind. It will also settle the stomach and digestive system in children.

   1/4 cup rice
   1 vanilla bean
   1 level teaspoon cinnamon
   Honey to taste

   Bring 1 quart water to a boil, add all ingredients, cover, and allow to simmer slowly for half an hour. Strain and serve hot before bedtime.

Love and Romance

Apple Cider, Spiced and Spiked (love inducing/intoxicant)—Grind 1 tablespoon allspice berries, 1 teaspoon cloves, and 1 teaspoon cinnamon into a powder. Into a pot, place 5 cups apple cider, 2 tablespoons butter, and 2 tablespoons honey. Bring to a boil. Lower the heat, add the powdered herbs, and allow to simmer for 15 minutes. Strain and then add 2 ounces dark rum right before serving. Serves two.

Campfire Sweet Potatoes and Spice—Mix equal amounts of cinnamon, sugar, and ginger root. Grind to a powder. Slice sweet potatoes in half lengthwise. Run water over the potatoes and then roll the potatoes in the spice mixture. The right amount is the amount that will stick. Drizzle a bit of honey over the potato halves, add a bit of butter or margarine, and wrap in aluminum foil. Place into a campfire. Poke occasionally; remove when soft. Salt to taste and share with someone you love. This will increase the bonds of love and enhance physical exchange (what better dessert).

Cherry Sauce (Love inducing/intoxicant)—In a blender, mix 4 parts cherries, 1 part honey, and 1 part dark rum by volume. Add cinnamon powder to taste. Blend on high for a few moments, then set in the refrigerator for one week. Remove; warm gently, strain, and then return to the refrigerator to cool. Serve over vanilla ice cream.

Cotiniat Marmalade (strengthens relationships)—The following recipe is used by women to strengthen the relationship between her and her man. It is a French marmalade made from quince fruit.

> Core and pare 1 pound of quinces (save the core), and chop into the smallest possible pieces with a knife. Bring 1 pint of water to a boil with one tablespoon rose petals. Add 1 pound fruit and 1 pound sugar. Lower heat to a mild simmer and simmer until fruit can be mashed into a pulp. Heat again and then bottle or can as one would any preserve, setting it aside for later use. Serve on toast and spend the day with the one you love to strengthen your relationship.

Balm of Gilead Wine (for new love)—A warm, sweet red wine infusion of balm of Gilead will warm the heart and open doors to new love. Simmer 1 pint of sweet red wine with 1/2 ounce balm of Gilead and 1 level teaspoon of cinnamon for 15 minutes. Cool and refrigerate for one week; strain and serve gently warmed. Sweeten with honey, if desired. This mixture will open the heart to new love and bring on a light-headed, almost giddy, intoxication that will quickly fade upon drinking water.

Cardamom Seed Wine (warmth and love)—A warm, sweet red wine infusion of cardamom seeds will warm the heart and bring on a sense of being loved. Simmer 1 pint of sweet red wine with 1/2 ounce ground cardamom seeds for 15 minutes. Cool and refrigerate for one week; strain and serve gently warmed.

Cardamom Seeds and Coffee (warmth and love)—For an after-dinner treat, mix ground cardamom seeds with coffee grinds in a ratio of 1 part cardamom to 3 parts coffee grinds. Prepare coffee as you always do, but substitute honey for other sweeteners. This brings on a feeling of warmth and love.

Carob Treat (warmth and love)—Combine the following in a saucepan and allow to simmer for 15 minutes. Stir often and serve warm.

2 heaping tablespoons carob powder

1/2 teaspoon cornstarch

16 ounces water

Honey to taste (from local producers)

Vanilla extract to taste

Fried Green Tomato for Love—To bring on love, mix equal amounts of rosemary, basil, and dill and grind to a powder. Slice green tomatoes no thinner than 1/4 inch. Dust both sides of the tomato slices with the spice powder. Fry in olive oil, flipping often, until golden brown on both sides.

Raspberry Spread—Bring 1 part water to a boil, reduce heat to a simmer, and add 1 part honey and 1 part raspberry fruit by volume. Allow to simmer rapidly for 30 minutes. Pulverize the berries and then simmer slowly to reduce. Allow to cool and serve on toast to promote love, happiness, and a sense of well-being.

Mood and Perception Altering

Coconut Ginger Rice (improves divination)—Simmer 2 parts shredded coconut meat (not sweetened) with 1 part thinly sliced fresh ginger root in light vegetable oil. Strain and serve over a bed of rice and shredded lettuce. Flavor with rice vinegar.

Kola Nut and Cocoa Appetizer (mild stimulant)—This easy recipe will increase the appetite, settle the stomach, and act as a mild stimulant. It reportedly increases sexual energy. Mix 1 level tablespoon of kola nut powder with just enough honey to bind. Roll the putty into a ball, and dust lightly with cocoa powder. Allow the ball to sit overnight at room temperature. If you wish to store for later use, place in refrigerator until ready to use. This ball will dissolve in coffee, tea, or even hot cocoa. One ball is usually enough.

Lemon Balm Wine (enhances sense of touch)—Gently warm 1 pint of sweet red wine with 1/2 ounce lemon balm herb. When warm, mix in 4 tablespoons honey. Simmer no more than 15 minutes, then store in refrigerator overnight. Strain and serve chilled. Arabian legend praises lemon balm as the bringer of physical pleasures as well as spiritual delights.

Muira-Puama Cordial (heightens sensory perception/enhances sense of touch)—For use in heightening the pleasures of making love, double the dose.

    1 pint high-proof vodka
    8 tablespoons muira-puama bark powder
    4 tablespoons hibiscus flower powder
    4 tablespoons honey (optional)

Bring vodka to a simmer, remove from heat, and add all ingredients. Stir every minute or so for 15 minutes, then strain, cool, and place in the refrigerator for later use. Consume one martini-size glass an hour prior to massage to relax yet increase sensation.

For storage, transportation, and ease of use, omit the honey from the above recipe. Prepare as described and then allow to evaporate until all that is left is a sticky resin. That resin can be rolled into balls or tubes such that they are no longer stuck to their container. Allow these to dry fully and then crush into a powder. The resulting powder still needs to be refrigerated during long storage, but it will easily dissolve into strong alcoholic beverages, making it ideal for travel.

Psychic and Empathic Enhancement

Campfire Potatoes and Spice—Mix equal amounts of dried damiana, rosemary, dill seed, and chives. Grind to a powder. Slice potatoes in half lengthwise. Run water over the potatoes and then roll the potatoes in the spice mixture. The right amount is the amount that will stick. Slice onions and place them in the middle of the two halves like a sandwich. Add butter or margarine if you like, and wrap in aluminum foil. Place into a campfire. Poke occasionally; remove when soft. Salt to taste. Also lends itself to protection.

Tofu and Spice—Mix equal amounts of dried damiana, rosemary, and rose petals. Grind to a powder and add a pinch of saffron. Cut tofu into bite-size chunks and fry in butter until golden brown. Sprinkle this powder onto the chunks and turn to evenly distribute. Serve over a bed of rice and shredded lettuce.

Magickal Properties of Everyday Food and Spices

Allspice—Promotes spiritual healing and opens the pathways to prosperity.

Almond—Promotes spiritual healing. Mends broken hearts and opens paths to prosperity.

Anise—Promotes a sense of love and well-being.

Apple—Both apple cider and fresh apples brings on a sense of love. Apple juice does not seem to have as much effect.

Apricot—Apricots bring on a sense of love and heighten sexual desire.

Artichoke—Flavored with dill and garlic, artichokes lend themselves to protection from baneful influences.

Asparagus—Increases sexual energy and stamina.

Avocado—Included in meals to enhance a feeling of romantic love in men and women. Acts as an aphrodisiac for men.

Bamboo Shoots—Used in oriental cooking to enhance psychic abilities.

Banana—Brings prosperity and a sense of spiritual love.

Basil—Opens the pathways to prosperity, especially when served to one whose income is directly related to the work that he or she does. Promotes a sense of love and well-being. Fresh basil tends to stimulate sexual desire in women.

Bay—Enhances psychic abilities, speeds healing, and promotes a sense of well-being.

Beans—Generally speaking, beans are added to meals to increase prosperity and fertility. For specific bean properties, see the herbal provided with this book.

Beet—Increases the romantic love shared between two people if they eat portions of the same beet as part of a romantic dinner.

Blackberry—Promotes prosperity, brings muses to artisans, and heightens lust.

Black Pepper—Helps to cleanse the psyche of psychic sludge. Use liberally to fight off the effects of psychic/social vampires.

Blueberry—Lends itself to protection.

Brazil Nut—Promotes brotherly love, friendship, and prosperity.

Broccoli—Eaten to lend spiritual protection.

Brussels Sprouts—Eaten to lend spiritual protection.

Buckwheat Pancakes and Noodles—Japanese lore states that if buckwheat noodles are eaten on New Year's Eve, the following year will be prosperous. The commonly available Western equivalent of buckwheat noodles is buckwheat pancakes for breakfast.

Cabbage—Eaten to increase prosperity and lends itself well to spiritual and psychic protection. It also calms the mind, adds energy to the body, and helps one to feel secure in marriage and family relations.

Caraway Seeds—Promotes both love and lust. In women, it works as a mild aphrodisiac. In men, it is much more pronounced.

Cardamom Seeds—Promotes both love and lust.

Carob—Promotes a sense of love. Magickally speaking, carob is a substitute for chocolate. The real thing is a better choice, but carob will work almost as well.

Carrot—Including carrots in your cooking will increase the sex drive of men who eat it.

Cashew—Opens pathways to prosperity. An excellent snack prior to a job interview or during breaks or lunchtime when working in sales.

Cauliflower—Served alone or flavored with dill, garlic, and/or mustard seed, cauliflower lends itself to spiritual and psychic protection.

Cayenne Peppers—Lend themselves protection.

Celery—Filled with peanut butter, celery sticks calm the mind and add a sense of peace to the meal. Celery will reportedly increase sexual passion and desire in women.

Chestnut—Improves cognitive abilities and enhances an existing feeling of love and romance.

Chicory—Promotes love and good fortune.

Cherry—Brings on a sense of love.

Chives—Include in cooking when attempting to break a bad habit. Useful in relieving a broken heart and encouraging one to move on.

Chocolate—Promotes a sense of love and financial well-being. Acts as a mild aphrodisiac in women.

Cinnamon—Promotes love in both men and women, and lust in men more so than women. Also opens the pathways to prosperity.

Cloves—Elevates the mood and encourages a sense of both love and well-being.

Coconut—Improves psychic and divinatory abilities. Coconut milk provides a quick spiritual pick-me-up.

Coriander—Promotes a sense of both love and lust. For a simple aphrodisiac drink, simmer coriander seeds in your favorite wine, sweeten with honey, strain, and serve warm.

Corn—Served on the cob at picnics and other times when the protection of the home is not available. Corn will reportedly protect the event at which it is served from undesired happenstance. Creamed corn is served to women to heighten reproductive fertility.

Cranberry—Lends itself to protection and warding off psychic/social vampires.

Cumin—Promotes a sense of peace, harmony, and happiness. Powdered and sprinkled in warmed wine, it provides a simple and mild aphrodisiac.

Cucumber—Provides a calming effect, decreases lust in men, and quiets a disgruntled home. Particularly effective if used in salad eaten at a picnic just outside the family home. Cucumber seeds will increase lust in a woman.

Date—Serve dried and candied dates to increase physical strength. Serve dried, unsweetened dates to increase spiritual awareness, reproductive fertility in women, and sexual desire in men.

Dill—Inspires lust and passion. Elevates existing feelings of love.

Eggplant—Provides increased prosperity, as well as spiritual awareness. Lends itself to improving the flow/connection between us and the Green World.

Endive—Add to a meal before physical labor. Will increase physical strength. Also good to stir lust in men and women.

Fig—Men who eat figs will experience an increase in sexual desire and virility. Dried and candied figs offer a quick energy boost.

Garlic—Fresh garlic helps to protect a person from psychic/social vampires. Provides an uplifting sense of well-being.

Ginger—Fresh ginger root works to heighten a romantic evening in ways it is hard to imagine from something one can find at the local grocery store. Dried and powdered ginger does not work nearly as well in this respect. Both will open consciousness to opportunities of prosperity.

Grapes and Raisins—Eating either will cause dreams to be more vivid and memorable. Eating grapes will increase reproductive fertility in women and cognitive functions in both men and women.

Grapefruit—Included in meals or eaten as a snack to remove a feeling of spiritual iciness. (Both the fruit and juice work well.)

Green Peppers—Lend themselves to protection.

Hazelnut—Heightens cognitive abilities and lends itself well to improving reproductive fertility.

Horseradish—Aids in cleansing psychic sludge and providing an uplifting feeling. It is powerful when taken from the bottle, better when purchased fresh and cut, and best when harvested fresh, cut, and used in the same evening.

Kumquat—Increases opportunity for prosperity and income.

Leek—Strengthens the bonds of love between those who share a meal, increases strength, and lends itself well to protection.

Lemon—Included in food and beverages to help attune and celebrate lunar events. Encourages an exchange of love and a feeling of happiness. Magickally elevates mood.

Lentil Soup—Brings peace to a family meal and calm to the mind of those who partake; however, it will also stimulate the body and stave off sleep.

Lettuce—An excellent addition to a meal when one is hoping to remain celibate. Served after dinner, it will bring on sleep.

Lime—Promotes love and furthers the relations between kith and kin.

Macadamia—Opens the pathways to prosperity.

Mango—Consuming the meat (not skin) increases sexual desire in both men and women. Also lends itself to protection.

Maple Butter and Syrup—When served with breakfast, it will heighten a sense of love. When served with dinner, that love will turn romantic and lead to lust. If you have never had maple butter with a romantic meal, you just have not lived. Be careful when purchasing maple syrup. Most of what is offered at the grocery store is not the real thing.

Marjoram—Promotes a sense of peace and calm.

Melon—All edible melons provide assistance in spiritual healing and broken hearts.

Mulberry—Eating the fresh berries will improve divinatory skills and enhance psychic awareness.

Mushroom—Generally speaking, mushrooms increase the ability of those dining to communicate without spoken language. Reportedly, they increase psychic abilities.

Nectarine—Improves the nature and exchange of a loving relationship when shared.

Nutmeg—Elevates the mood and provides relief from depression.

Oatmeal—Brings prosperity. Sweeten with honey and flavor with cinnamon to improve sales and when looking for a new job or promotion. Oatmeal muffins and cookies are excellent choices for Beltane celebrations. Oatmeal muffins (called *bannocks*) are a traditional Scottish food during this holiday.

Olive—Eating olives will bring calm and increase sexual appetite in men. Shared, olives will help increase the bonds between sexual partners. Cooking with olive oil is said to maintain general health and increase sexual appetite in men.

Onion—Onions will increase the ability to defend against psychic/social vampires and other forms of psychic and pseudo-psychic attacks. Red onions increase lust.

Orange—Fresh oranges, as well their juice, will promote a sense of warm love while hindering lust at the same time.

Oregano—Promotes a sense of peace and calm.

Passion Fruit—Promotes romantic love and lust, but does so on more of a spiritual rather than physical level.

Parsley—Promotes love, reproductive fertility, and fidelity in monogamous relationships.

Peach—Promotes understanding between lovers and family members. Promotes a sense of ordered love and calm without diminishing passion. Increases reproductive fertility in women.

Peanut and Peanut Butter—Opens the pathways to prosperity. Excellent lunch prior to a job interview or while on break during the business day if your prosperity depends directly on your performance.

Pear—Promotes prosperity and acts as a mild aphrodisiac.

Peas—Eating peas will reportedly open one's heart to new love. Prepare with onions, dill, and basil, and this side dish will not only help you find Prince (or Princess) Charming, it will also help to prevent the occasional run-n with frogs.

Pecan—Promotes prosperity. Exceptionally useful snack when looking for a job.

Persimmon—Include this fruit in meals to stave off depression, especially depression brought on by lack of sunlight and cabin fever.

Pistachio—Helps to break the influence of a lover that you know is bad for you so that you can find another option. Helps one to distinguish the toads from the princes. Improves cognitive function. Pistachio ice cream is the perfect treat when thinking about ending a bad love affair.

Pies—Pies are a wonderful way to incorporate magick into the kitchen. For specific references to the many fillings, look up the potential filling in the herbal provided with this book

Pineapple—Serve pineapple chunks to decrease lust and increase a sense of love and spiritual well-being.

Plum—Strengthens and encourages all forms of love. Acts as a mild aphrodisiac.

Pomegranate—Increases reproductive fertility in women, calls one's muse, and promotes the opening of prosperous pathways. Also helps communication with loved ones who have moved on to other realms.

Poppy Seeds—Promotes love and reproductive fertility.

Potato—Lends itself to protection and enhances empathy.

Pretzels—My Catholic aunt tells me that pretzels were originally made by the Catholic Church and given to good altar boys. Per my aunt, the shape symbolized arms locked in prayer. Scott Cunningham tells us the original European pretzel was in the shape of a sun wheel (a circle with an equilateral cross inside) and that they were served at Winter Solstice to welcome the return of the sun. I think they are a wonderful way to lift the spirit at any time.

Pumpkin—Seeds will increase a man's appetite for sex. The fruit of the plant brings prosperity.

Radish—Lends itself to protection and raises lust in both men and women.

Raspberries—Promotes love, happiness, and a general sense of well-being.

Rice—Calms the mind and stirs reproductive fertility. Eaten as part of a romantic evening followed by lovemaking will increase chances of conception.

Rhubarb—Strengthens established love. Lends itself to protection. Sharing rhubarb pie with your partner is a good way to increase marital bonds.

Rosemary—Increases cognitive functions and opens the heart to love.

Rye—Strengthens the warm ties of a family.

Saffron—Lifts the heart and promotes lust.

Sage—Promotes physical and spiritual healing. Will also lift the heart and provide a sense of well-being.

Sesame Seeds—Cooking with sesame seed oil will add a bit of an aphrodisiac to any meal. The seeds themselves work well for heightening lust, increasing reproductive fertility, promoting a sense of well-being, and opening the pathways to prosperity.

Spinach—Serve fresh, not cooked or from the can. Will increase general prosperity.

Squash—Improves psychic, empathic, and cognitive abilities. Particularly useful when included in meals during the season of Samhain. Aids in communicating with loved ones who have left this realm.

Strawberry—Promotes a sense of romantic love.

Sugar—In small amounts, promotes a sense of romantic love.

Sunflower—Incorporate sunflower oil and seeds into you meals prior to needing an extra bit of energy and luck.

Sweet Potato—Shared with a lover, sweet potatoes will increase the bonds of love and mildly increase the level of lust.

Tangerine—Consumed to ward off psychic/social vampires and to prevent the feeling of spiritual blah.

Thyme—Promotes love and psychic abilities, as well as heightens empathy. Useful in ridding oneself of psychic sludge.

Tofu—Increases psychic abilities, empathy, and cognitive functions. Also lends itself to protection.

Truffles—Added to meals to improve sexual appetite in both men and women. Also increases empathy.

Vanilla—Promotes lust in both men and women. When purchasing extracts, be absolutely sure you are purchasing real vanilla and not the synthetic kind that has been filling the market recently. Real vanilla is expensive, but it is well worth it.

Walnut—Eating walnuts provides heightened cognitive abilities, as well as a sense of well-being.

Watercress—Eaten fresh in salads and sandwiches to increase reproductive fertility in women.

Watermelon—Promotes the healing of a broken heart, lightens the spirit, and staves off depression.

Wheat (whole) Bread—Increases prosperity and potential income.

Chapter 7
Making Magick

An unexpected thing happened to me at 3:08 p.m. Eastern Standard Time on Friday, May 14, 2004 C.E. I had a conversation with God. And no, I do not mean Goddess. Nope, nothing feminine about that conversation. We were talking one father to another. Okay, it wasn't much of a conversation. I did most of the talking. You see, at that precise moment I became the proud father of Aubreyahna ("Mother of Many Nations").

So what did I tell God? I told him I want no less than 18 years. He said, "okay." I said, "Now wait a minute. I mean 18 years prosperous enough that not only will I see my daughter become a healthy adult, but that I can be reasonably sure her educational needs will be met after I leave this world." He said, "okay." I said, "Now wait a minute. I mean 18 years with my wife by my side so that I have someone to do for my daughter what clumsy Yeti-like fathers can't." He said, "okay."

I said, "Now wait a minute." He asked, "Aren't you done yet?" I said, "I mean I want 18 years with my mother still here on Earth to do the things that grandmothers do best." He said, "Now you are reaching a bit. Will you get your mother to quit smoking?" I said I'd see what I could do. He said he'd see what he could do.

I said, "Now wait a minute." He asked, "You again?" I said, "Yep—me again. I want 18 years with my *wife's* mother here on Earth to do the things that grandmothers do best in numbers." He said, "You're reaching again. Will you get your wife's mother to quit smoking?" I said I would see what I could do. He said he'd see what he could do. Guess what? I believed every word he said. After all, he is God.

Right about now, a few of my readers might think I am just a little bit off my rocker. To these I say, if you can witness the birth of your own child and not talk to God, then you have absolutely no heart whatsoever. Another group of readers might think I was awfully arrogant in the way I addressed God. To those I say that when it comes to the well-being of one's child, if God should get in your way, then push him out of the way.

You see if I were God, I imagine I would find my chosen people the way it was done in the Old Testament, only with a bit of a twist. I would tell all who would be my worshipers to kill their firstborn child. Right before they drove the knife into their child, I would stop them. I would then separate those who were willing to kill their child to prove their loyalty to me into one group. Into another group I would put all of those people who told me to bugger off. Then I would announce who my chosen people were. Yep, the ones that told me to bugger off.

The Creator—A Brief Set of Definitions for the Purpose of Discussion

I see the Creator as the union of Lord and Lady. In essence, our Lord is the Father of the household that is the whole of the world and our Lady is the Mother of that same household. Neither alone is the Creator. Instead, the Creator is the marriage of the two, as well as the sum total of all things that have come from that union (parents and offspring) in the way a marriage becomes a family and that family is the sum total of all things that have come from that marriage.

Because many readers may have read New Age titles that do not focus on the idea that one can have a deep and meaningful relationship with the world in which we live, it might help to further our exchange if you substitute the word *Universe* whenever you see me use the word *Creator* in the context of discussing spellcraft.

Prayer and Magick

The subject of talking to our Lord and Lady is one of those issues that most pagan authors like to avoid. Until recently, the word *prayer* was almost missing from books on Wicca. Instead, the party line was that Christians pray and Wiccans cast spells. Recently, it seems someone has figured out that our Lord and Lady understand words and the emotions attached to those words just as well as the traditional trappings of spellcraft. As a result, prayer is back in vogue. Frankly, I do not see much difference between the spoken word and other forms of communication. In fact, I can't even get a handle on why anyone would think there is a difference between saying a prayer and casting a spell.

But does it work?

Well, the first step in knowing if someone is listening is to know whom it is that you are talking to. I cannot tell you who the Creator *is*. I cannot even tell you who most Wiccans think the Creator is. However, I can tell you what I *know* the nature of our Creator to be.

First, please note that I said I *know* the nature of our Creator. I do not in any way need faith, nor do I express this knowledge as a belief. The Creator is just as real as the chair that I am sitting in. Like that chair, if I did not *know* that it existed, I would not be able to allow it to support my Yeti arse. But even without my knowledge of its existence, the chair (and the Creator) would continue to exist.

Note also that in the previous paragraph I was clear in stating that I cannot tell you "who the Creator *is*" or "who most Wiccans think the Creator is." You see, this is one of the Mysteries of the Wiccan religion. Such knowledge as that which will cause you to *know* the Creator is entirely experiential. One cannot transmit this information to you; hence the term "Mystery" to describe that knowledge. Instead, one can point you in the direction of the experiences that may lead you to the same or similar conclusion. That nudge, those things that promote the experience of the "Mystery," are what Wiccans generally refer to as the "Secrets." Now that Wicca has become widely accessible, those secrets are often transmitted via books such as this. Sure, it makes the term "Secrets" a bit out of date, but hey, baby needs a new pair of shoes. Besides, if you have a good heart and know something to be beneficial, you will be driven to share it with those whom will benefit from it.

As the Creator is one of those Mysteries, one of those things that simply cannot be comprehended in its totality, we provide that Creator with an appearance such that we can relate to a portion of the Creator, which is less than its totality. That appearance is what many traditions call the Secrets. These are often specific names, physical attributes, attunements to other deities, and all orders of connections between the Creator and the Green World. These secrets are the methods by which we connect to the Creator. In and of themselves, the Secrets are not magick. They are the tools by which we communicate (pray), and that communication—not the tools of communication—is magick.

The Most Direct Method of Communication

Do I believe one can use magick to move a book through the air from one point to another? Yes. I wholeheartedly believe magick can be used to accomplish such a goal. Do I believe this is accomplished by asking the Creator to do this for us? Yes. I believe I can ask the Creator to lift a book from my desk and cause that book to travel through the air to the other side of the room and that the Creator will listen to my prayer and do as I bid.

If you could see me, I would demonstrate by lifting a book with my hand and tossing it across the room. In using my hand to grasp the book and the muscles in my arm to fling it, I have communicated my intent to the Creator in the most direct method. My movement is prayer, and the action of that book being moved from one location to the next in accordance with my intent is magick.

Of course, most people would not think that my tossing of a book across the room is magick, because it is a very direct and understood method of communicating my intent. It follows laws of science that are reasonably well understood. Instead, they would think it more on the level of herbal remedies rather than making magick. Remember that science and magick are simply words used to describe the same thing with differing levels of understanding. If we can explain how the communication takes place, we use the word *science*. If we cannot explain how the communication takes place, we use the word *magick*. If some people think the explanation is acceptable and other people do not think it is acceptable, then we argue about it.

Thus, the most direct method is the most preferred. That's right, your handy dandy spellbook might tell you that keeping that rose quartz next to a gash in your leg will help your wound to heal, but a few stitches and some disinfectant will go a long way towards the same goal. Why? Because the most direct method is the language the Creator understands best.

Thou Art God/dess

Hey wait a minute. The Creator did not move that book. You did!

Ah, but if I am god (note the lowercase "g") and god is a portion of the Creator, then the Creator did indeed move that book. While I do wholly understand how incredibly pompous such a statement might sound, this is the exact meaning behind the common Wiccan greeting "Thou art God" and "Thou art Goddess." Every living thing is part of the Divine.

Rather than view the Creator as separate from human existence, sitting somewhere in Heaven and looking down on us, Wicca views the Creator as being alive and well right here on Earth: both internally and externally. Our Lord and Lady live within each and every one of us. Hence, there is no reason for a messenger or mediator to communicate our intent between the Divine and ourselves. We are divine. Don't believe me? Look into a child's eyes and tell me that child is not part of the Divine. Now think about how many people once looked into your eyes and saw the Divine looking back at them. Have things really changed since you were an infant or has your self-perception changed that much since you were that young?

Recipes for Making Magick

What follows are recipes for making magick. Each recipe is intended to communicate an intent that you might have. None are in and of themselves magick. Instead, it is the communication that these recipes facilitate that is magick.

Most of these recipes are followed in conjunction with the preparation instructions found in the procedural section of Chapter 4. Instruction on their use and time of preparation is included in Chapter 8. Where additional instructions are necessary, they have been provided with the recipe itself.

It is important to mention that when the content of this book was removed from *A Wiccan Bible* prior to publication, all recipes were removed as well. With the help of a kind editor, I managed to work a few of them back into the context of that work. Thus, some of what follows appear in both books. Where a recipe appears also in *A Wiccan Bible* (as published), I have added an asterisk. Some of the other recipes from *A Wiccan Bible* are duplicated here. In particular, recipes specific to deity forms remain available in the last chapter of *A Wiccan Bible* and are not repeated here.

Bath Recipes

Astrological Baths

Aquarius Bath
 2 parts boneset
 1 part comfrey

Aries Bath
 2 parts coriander seed
 1 part cubeb berries

Cancer Bath
 2 parts gardenia
 1 part eucalyptus

 Note: Adding sliced cucumbers to this bath will greatly improve it.

Capricorn Bath
 2 parts patchouli
 1 part lobelia
 1 part mullein

Gemini Bath
 2 parts peppermint
 1 part red clover

 Note: Adding sliced celery to this bath will greatly improve it.

Leo Bath
 3 parts juniper berries
 2 parts lovage

Libra Bath
 2 parts passion flower
 1 part oats or oatmeal
 1 part mugwort

Pisces Bath
 2 parts sassafras
 1 part sage
 1 part nutmeg

Sagittarius Bath

> 2 parts star anise
> 1 part sassafras
> 1 part clove

Scorpio Bath

> 1 part cubeb berries
> 1 part coriander seeds
> 1 part coffee beans

Taurus Bath

> 4 parts heather flowers
> 2 parts elderberries
> 1 part ginger root

Virgo Bath

> 4 parts lavender flowers
> 2 parts lemongrass
> 1 part mint

Elemental Baths

Air Bath

> 2 parts sage
> 1 part broom flowers
> 1 part anise seeds

Used to communicate the properties of Air (see Chapter 8). If participating in a group ritual in which you have been selected to welcome the East Quarter and the Element Air, this is an excellent choice for your lustral bath.

Earth Bath

> 2 parts patchouli
> 1 part mugwort
> 1 part vetivert

Used to communicate the properties of Earth (see Formulary in Chapter 8). If participating in a group ritual in which you have been selected to welcome the North Quarter and the Element Earth, this is an excellent choice for your lustral bath.

Fire Bath

> 2 parts clove
> 1 part nutmeg
> 1 part cinnamon (Add if you are brave. Remember that cinnamon can cause skin irritation.)

Used to communicate the properties of Fire (see Chapter 8). If participating in a group ritual in which you have been selected to welcome the South Quarter and the Element Fire, this is an excellent choice for your lustral bath.

Water Bath

> 2 parts bladder wrack
> 1 part calamus root
> 1 part feverfew

Used to communicate the properties of Water (see Chapter 8). If participating in a group ritual in which you have been selected to welcome the West Quarter and the Element Water, this is an excellent choice for your lustral bath.

Planetary Baths

Sun Bath

> 2 parts chamomile
> 1 part acacia

Moon Bath

> 2 parts calamus
> 1 part passion flower
> 1 part lemon peel

Mars Bath

> 2 parts allspice
> 1 part damiana
> 1 part ginger

Mercury Bath
  2 parts red clover
  1 part fennel seed

Jupiter Bath
  2 parts anise seed
  1 part clove
  1 part nutmeg

Venus Bath
  2 parts balm of Gilead
  1 part catnip
  1 part hibiscus

Saturn Bath
  2 parts cypress
  1 part lobelia

Sabbat Baths

General Winter Sabbat Bath
  2 parts pine
  1 part clove
  1 part nutmeg

General Summer Sabbat Bath
  4 parts patchouli
  2 parts calendula
  1 part rose

Samhain Bath
  2 parts allspice
  1 part sage
  1 part mugwort

Winter Solstice Bath
  2 parts juniper berries
  2 parts orange peel
  1 part rosemary

Imbolg Bath
  4 parts red sandalwood
  2 parts wildflowers that have
    already bloomed

Spring Equinox Bath
  2 parts jasmine
  1 part sandalwood

Beltane Bath
  2 parts rose petals
  1 part sandalwood

Summer Solstice Bath
  2 parts carnation
  2 parts lavender
  1 part sandalwood

Lughnasadh Bath
  4 parts blackberry leaves
  1 part heather
  1 part lavender

Fall Equinox Bath
  2 parts cypress
  1 part juniper berries
  1 part oakmoss

Powdered Incense and Tincture Recipes

Combined here are incense and tincture recipes, which should be prepared in accordance with the procedures discussed in Chapter 4. (Note: For recipes for sticks and cones that are made by "dipping," see pages 107-110.) In many cases, the only difference between the incense and tincture recipe is how it is prepared and used. In a few, there is a minor change made to the recipe. Where such a minor change is necessary, it has been noted.

General Ritual Incense and Tincture Blends

General Incense/Tincture Blend I *

2 parts frankincense

2 part sandalwood

1 part myrrh

Enough frankincense or sandalwood oil to bind

An incense of choice for initiations. To use this as a tincture, use 1 part frankincense.

General Incense/Tincture Blend II *

2 parts frankincense

2 parts sandalwood

2 parts copal

1 part myrrh

Enough frankincense oil to bind

Another incense of choice for initiations and general ritual use. To use this as a tincture, use 1 part each frankincense and copal, and double the sandalwood.

Astrological Incense and Tincture Blends

Aquarius Incense/Tincture Blend

2 parts benzoin

1 part lavender flowers

1 part patchouli

Enough Aquarius or cypress oil to bind

If making tincture, halve the benzoin and double both the lavender and patchouli.

Aries Incense/Tincture Blend

2 parts frankincense

1 part dragon's blood

1 part clove

Enough Aries or juniper oil to bind

If making tincture, halve the dragon's blood and frankincense, and double the clove.

Cancer Incense/Tincture Blend

2 parts sandalwood powder

1 part myrrh (sweet if available)

1 part rose petals

If making tincture, halve the myrrh and double the rose petals and sandalwood.

Capricorn Incense/Tincture Blend

4 parts myrrh

2 parts patchouli

1 part cypress

Enough Capricorn or patchouli oil to bind

If making tincture, halve the myrrh and double both the patchouli and cypress.

Gemini Incense/Tincture Blend

4 parts benzoin

2 parts lavender

1 part peppermint

Enough Gemini or lavender oil to bind

If making tincture, halve the benzoin and double both the lavender and peppermint.

Leo Incense/Tincture Blend

2 parts sandalwood

1 part frankincense

1 part orange peel

Enough Leo or cinnamon oil to bind

Libra Incense/Tincture Blend

1 part chamomile

1 part petals

1 part gum arabic

Enough Libra or chamomile oil to bind

If making tincture, omit the gum arabic.

Pisces Incense/Tincture Blend

2 parts sandalwood

1 part camphor (natural)

1 part lemon peel

1 part myrrh

Enough Pisces or cardamom seed oil to bind

Sagittarius Incense/Tincture Blend

1 part juniper berries

1 part dragon's blood

1 part frankincense

1 part orange peel

Enough Sagittarius or sweet grass oil to bind

If making tincture, halve the dragon's blood and frankincense, and double the orange peel and juniper berry.

Scorpio Incense/Tincture Blend

2 parts myrrh

1 part clove

1 part violet

Enough Scorpio or ginger oil to bind

If making tincture, halve the myrrh and double both the clove and violet.

Taurus Incense/Tincture Blend

1 part patchouli

1 part rose petals and buds

1 part gum arabic

Enough Taurus or cardamom seed oil to bind

If making tincture, replace gum arabic with cardamom seeds.

Virgo Incense/Tincture Blend

2 parts lavender

1 part lemon balm

1 part gum arabic

Enough Virgo or lavender oil to bind

If making tincture, omit the gum arabic.

Elemental Incense and Tincture Blends

Air Incense/Tincture Blend*

2 parts lavender flower

1 part benzoin

Enough Air or lavender oil to bind

Used to communicate the properties of Air (see Chapter 8). The smoke of this incense is often burned at the East Quarter altar. Its smoke is used to bless and charge a new censer. A tincture made with this recipe can be used to anoint the wrists of those who call and welcome the East Quarter and the Element Air.

Earth Incense/Tincture Blend*

2 parts patchouli

1 part cypress

1 part gum arabic (optional)

Enough Earth or bergamot oil to bind

To use as a tincture recipe, omit the gum arabic. Used to communicate the properties of Earth (see Chapter 8). The smoke of this incense is often burned at the North Quarter altar. Its smoke is used to bless and charge a new pentacle. A tincture made with this recipe can be used to anoint the wrists of those who call and welcome the North Quarter and the Element Earth.

Fire Incense/Tincture Blend*

2 parts cinnamon

1 part dragon's blood

1 part frankincense

Enough Fire or allspice oil to bind

Used to communicate the properties of Fire (see Chapter 8). The smoke of this incense is often burned at the South Quarter altar. Its smoke is used to bless and charge a new athame. A tincture made with this recipe can be used to anoint the wrists of those who call and welcome the South Quarter and the Element Fire.

Water Incense/Tincture Blend*

2 parts jasmine flowers

1 part lemon peel

1 part camphor (natural)

Enough Water or lemon oil to bind

Used to communicate the properties of Water (see Chapter 8). The smoke of this incense is often burned at the West Quarter altar. Its smoke is used to bless and charge a new chalice. A tincture made with this recipe can be used to anoint the wrists of those who call and welcome the West Quarter and the Element Water.

Planetary Incense and Tincture Blends

Sun Incense/Tincture Blend

2 parts cedar powder

1 part copal

1 part benzoin

1 part frankincense

1 part gum arabic

1 pinch saffron

Enough Sun or frankincense oil to bind

If making a tincture, omit the gum arabic and double the cedar powder.

Moon Incense/Tincture Blend

4 parts sandalwood powder
2 parts myrrh (sweet if available)
1 part camphor (natural)
1 part jasmine flower
Enough Moon or lemon oil to bind

Mars Incense/Tincture Blend

2 parts dragon's blood
1 part allspice berries
Enough Mars, galangal, or ginger
oil to bind

Mercury Incense/Tincture Blend

2 parts lavender flowers
2 parts lemongrass
1 part gum arabic
1 part benzoin
Enough Mercury, bergamot, or
clove oil to bind

Jupiter Incense/Tincture Blend

2 parts cedar powder
1 part juniper berries
Enough Jupiter or pine oil to bind

Venus Incense/Tincture Blend

2 parts red sandalwood
1 part red rose petals and buds
1 part lemon peel
Enough Venus, rose, or lemon oil
to bind

Saturn Incense/Tincture Blend

2 parts myrrh
1 part violet
1 part patchouli
Enough Saturn or patchouli oil to
bind

Sabbat Incense and Tincture Blends

General Winter Sabbat Incense/Tincture Blend*

4 parts sandalwood
4 parts frankincense
2 parts myrrh
2 parts benzoin
1 part clove
Enough Winter Sabbat or
sandalwood oil to bind

General Summer Sabbat Incense/Tincture Blend*

4 parts sandalwood
4 parts frankincense
2 parts lavender
Enough Summer Sabbat or
sandalwood oil to bind

If making a tincture, double the lavender and use only 1 part frankincense.

Samhain Incense/Tincture Blend*

1 part allspice
1 part sage
1 part frankincense
1 part gum arabic
Enough Samhain or frankincense
oil to bind

If making a tincture, omit the gum arabic and double the allspice and sage.

Winter Solstice Incense/Tincture Blend*

4 parts frankincense
1 part juniper berry
1 part cedar
Enough Winter Solstice or
frankincense oil to bind

If making a tincture, quarter the frankincense and double the juniper berry and cedar.

Imbolg Incense/Tincture Blend*

6 parts frankincense

4 parts dragon's blood

2 parts red sandalwood

1 part cinnamon

Enough Imbolg or frankincense oil to bind

If making a tincture, halve the frankincense and dragon's blood, and double the red sandalwood and cinnamon.

Spring Equinox Incense/Tincture Blend*

4 parts frankincense

2 parts benzoin

1 part dragon's blood

1 part rose petals

1 part orange peel

Enough Spring Equinox or frankincense oil to bind

If making a tincture, halve the frankincense, benzoin, and dragon's blood, and double the rose petals and orange peel.

Beltane Incense/Tincture Blend*

4 parts frankincense

2 parts gum arabic

2 parts sandalwood

1 part jasmine

1 part rosemary

Enough Beltane or frankincense oil to bind

If making a tincture, halve the frankincense, omit the gum arabic, and double the sandalwood, jasmine, and rosemary.

Summer Solstice Incense/Tincture Blend*

4 parts sandalwood

1 part benzoin

1 part dragon's blood

Enough Summer Solstice or sandalwood oil to bind

Lughnasadh Incense/Tincture Blend*

4 parts frankincense

2 parts lavender

1 part heather

Enough Lughnasadh or lavender oil to bind

If making a tincture, halve the frankincense and double the lavender and heather.

Fall Equinox Incense/Tincture Blend*

4 parts frankincense

2 parts sandalwood

1 part cypress

1 part juniper berries

Enough Fall Equinox or sandalwood oil to bind

If making a tincture, halve the frankincense and double the sandalwood and cypress.

Oil, Dipped Incense, and Soap Recipes

The recipes in this section will work for oils as provided. They will work for dipping incense as described in Chapter 4 by excluding the base oil (the last one listed) and changing the word *drops* for the word *parts* such that the recipe is in the form of a ratio rather than specific volume. Then create the oil in the volume that you require, and use it in accordance with the procedures given for dipping incense found in Chapter 4 and the procedures for soapmaking, which follow after the recipes.

Astrological Oil Blends

Aquarius (Masculine)
9 drops peppermint
6 drops pine
1/2 ounce masculine base oil

Aquarius (Feminine)
9 drops cypress
9 drops patchouli
1/2 ounce base oil

Aries
9 drops allspice
6 drops cinnamon
6 drops clove
1/2 ounce base oil

Cancer (Masculine)
9 drops palmarosa
6 drops chamomile
1/2 ounce masculine base oil

Cancer (Feminine)
9 drops sandalwood
3 drops lemon
3 drops myrrh
3 drops jasmine
1/2 ounce coconut oil

Note: Coconut oil may have to be gently warmed prior to mixing.

Capricorn
9 drops patchouli
6 drops cypress
6 drops myrrh
1/2 ounce base oil

Gemini
9 drops benzoin
6 drops lemongrass
6 drops peppermint
3 drops lavender
1/2 ounce almond oil

Leo (Masculine)
6 drops frankincense
6 drops bay
6 drops juniper
3 drops cinnamon
1/2 ounce sunflower oil

Leo (Feminine)
15 drops sandalwood
6 drops rosemary
1/2 ounce sunflower oil

Libra (Masculine)
9 drops peppermint
6 drops fennel
3 drops chamomile
3 drops thyme
1/2 ounce apricot kernel oil

Libra (Feminine)

9 drops eucalyptus
6 drops geranium
3 drops rose or spearmint
1/2 ounce apricot kernel oil

Pisces

9 drops cardamom
6 drops clove
3 drops myrrh
3 drops sandalwood
1/2 ounce base oil

Sagittarius

6 drops sage
6 drops orange
6 drops sweetgrass
3 drops clove
1/2 ounce base oil

Scorpio

9 drops clove
6 drops black pepper
6 drops ginger
1/2 ounce olive oil

Taurus

6 drops cardamom
3 drops patchouli
3 drops rose
3 drops thyme
1/2 ounce apricot kernel oil

Virgo

6 drops patchouli
3 drops cypress
3 drops fennel
3 drops lavender
1/2 ounce olive oil

Elemental Oil Blends

Air Oil*

9 drops benzoin
9 drops lavender
3 drops pine
1/2 ounce almond or palm oil

Used to communicate the properties of Air (see Chapter 8). This oil is excellent to anoint the wrists and/or forehead of the person who will call the East Quarter and Element Air in Wiccan rituals. It is used regularly to anoint, cleanse, and charge the censer. It may also be worn by men who were born under an Air sign to attract women born under an Earth sign.

Earth Oil*

12 drops patchouli
9 drops bergamot
1/2 ounce base oil

Used to communicate the properties of Earth (see Chapter 8). This oil is excellent to anoint the wrists and/or forehead of the person who will call the North Quarter and Element Earth in Wiccan rituals. It is used regularly to anoint, cleanse, and charge the pentacle. It may also be worn by women who were born under an Earth sign to attract men who were born under an Air sign.

Fire Oil*

6 drops allspice

3 drops bay

3 drops ginger

1/2 ounce base oil

Used to communicate the properties of Fire (see Chapter 8). This oil is excellent to anoint the wrists and/or forehead of the person who will call the South Quarter and Element Fire in Wiccan rituals. It is used regularly to anoint, cleanse, and charge the athame. It can also be worn by men who were born under a Fire sign to attract women born under a Water sign.

Water Oil*

6 drops camphor

3 drops lemon

3 drops eucalyptus

3 drops cardamom

1/2 ounce base oil

Used to communicate the properties of Water (see Chapter 8). This oil is excellent to anoint the wrists and/or forehead of the person who will call the South Quarter and Element Water in Wiccan rituals. It is used regularly to anoint, cleanse, and charge the chalice. It can also be worn by women who were born under a Water sign to attract men that were born under a Fire sign.

Planetary Oil Blends

Sun Oil

9 drops bergamot

6 drops chamomile

6 drops cinnamon

1/2 ounce sunflower oil

Moon Oil

9 drops camphor

3 drops eucalyptus

3 drops lemon

3 drops myrrh

3 drops sandalwood

1/2 ounce grapeseed oil

Mars Oil

6 drops dragon's blood

6 drops allspice

6 drops basil

3 drops coriander

1/2 ounce base oil

Mercury Oil

9 drops lemongrass

6 drops bergamot

3 drops lavender

3 drops clove

1/2 ounce almond oil

Jupiter Oil

9 drops juniper

6 drops clove

6 drops nutmeg

3 drops pine

3 drops sage

1/2 ounce olive oil

Venus Oil

9 drops bergamot
9 drops rose
3 drops ylang ylang
1/2 ounce base oil

Saturn Oil

9 drops patchouli
6 drops myrrh
6 drops cypress
1/2 ounce base oil

Sabbat Oil Blends

General Winter Sabbat Oil*

10 drops pine
4 drops nutmeg
4 drops frankincense
1/2 ounce base oil

General Summer Sabbat Oil*

4 drops patchouli
4 drops otto of rose or
    rose geranium
10 drops pine
1/2 ounce base oil

Samhain Oil*

8 drops allspice
6 drops sage
6 drops frankincense
1/2 ounce base oil

Winter Solstice Oil*

10 drops pine
4 drops clove
2 drops cinnamon
2 drops juniper
1/2 ounce base oil

If making soap, omit the cinnamon oil.

Imbolg Oil*

8 drops frankincense
6 drops rosemary
2 drops cinnamon
1/2 cup base oil

If making soap, omit the cinnamon oil.

Spring Equinox Oil*

8 drops frankincense
6 drops nutmeg
6 drops rose or 3 drops orange and
    3 drops ginger
1/2 cup base oil

Beltane Oil*

8 drops frankincense
6 drops rosemary
4 drops rose
1/2 cup base oil

Summer Solstice Oil*

8 drops lavender
4 drops lemon
4 drops sandalwood
2 drops orange
1/2 cup base oil

Lughnasadh Oil*

10 drops frankincense
10 drops lavender
1/2 cup base oil

Fall Equinox Oil*

6 drops frankincense
6 drops sandalwood
4 drops cypress
2 drops juniper

Soap Recipes

> *****IMPORTANT:** The following equipment should be glass, heavy plastic, or stainless steel. DO NOT USE ALUMINUM.***

Tools

- Safety goggles
- Chemical resistant rubber gloves
- A good scale that measures to tenths of an ounce and preferably with a tare feature
- 3-quart or larger mixing pot or bowl

- 2-cup or larger measuring cup
- Wire whisk or stick blender/ drink mixer
- Scrapping spatula
- Assorted bowls/measuring cups to hold individual ingredients for weighing

All measurements are by weight/mass not volume

Simple French Milling

Grate 4 ounces base soap and mix with 2–4 tablespoons of water or milk (enough that when melted, the mixture has a mashed potato consistency). Melt in a double boiler. Add scent and botanicals. Mix thoroughly. Pour into mold or roll into balls. Allow to cure.

Basic Castile Soap

This recipe yields 2 pounds, which is the smallest you want to go as a beginner "cold process" soap-maker (which does not mean that the soap is poured cold, just that there was no external heat used).

22 ounces olive oil (found in any grocery store; the cheapest brand they have will be fine)

2.8 ounces sodium hydroxide (Red Devil brand lye can be found in the drain-cleaner section of most grocery stores)

7 ounces distilled water

Basic veggie soap

    1 ounce castor oil (usually found in any pharmacy)

    4 ounces coconut oil (found in some grocery stores, but more likely in health food stores and Asian markets)

    10 ounces olive oil

    7 ounces palm oil (health food stores and Asian markets)

    3 ounces sodium hydroxide

    7 ounces distilled water

Basic Cold Process Instructions

Line a mold with a couple of plastic grocery bags or freezer paper. Any box that will hold the above combined 32 ounces will do. While wearing safety goggles and gloves, measure or weigh out individual ingredients. Add sodium hydroxide to water in a glass measuring cup (**do not add water to sodium hydroxide**). Melt hard oils if necessary and mix with liquid oils in a 3-quart mixing bowl/pot. When the temperature of the oils and lye water are approximately between 90 and 125 degrees Fahrenheit, slowly pour lye water into oils while mixing slowly (if using all liquid oils, just the lye water needs to be in this temperature range).

Whisk oils continuously until mixture reaches the trace stage (it will look like thin pudding and a trail of soap sits on top before sinking back into the rest). When mixing by hand, this can take awhile—anywhere from 10 minutes to more than an hour depending on the types of oils used. To speed things up, I would recommend a stick blender (drink mixer), alternating 10 to 15 second bursts with 1–2 minutes of hand stirring.

When mixture reaches the trace stage, one can mix in any fragrance you like (usually 1/2 ounce per pound of oils) or botanicals (around 1/4 cup for a 2-pound batch). Then pour into the mold, cover with plastic, and insulate by wrapping with towels or blankets for 24 hours.

Unmold and cut into bars of desired size and let cure further for 4 to 6 weeks. Curing time makes sure all the lye has saponified and that the bars have hardened, so they will not melt in the shower the first time they are used.

The above 2-pound batch will yield five to seven bars of soap depending on one's preferred bar size. If one wishes not to have five to seven bars of the same type of soap, then skip adding fragrance and botanicals to have a plain base to use for French milling.

Should you decide that creating your own soaps is too involved or complex, please consider contacting Paula Newman at Ravensfyre's Bath and Body for her latest catalog of creations. She is also willing to create custom blends, which is rare in the soap business.

Ravensfyre's Bath and Body
PO Box 28976
Columbus, Ohio 43228-0976

Chapter 8
A Magickal
Formulary

Very shortly after humanity discovered fire, we discovered the beginning of all modern medicine. Some caveman picked up a burning ember, screamed sharply, and tossed it back into the fire. He then observed his hand. There, where his flesh had come into contact with the burning embers, he saw blisters form. Now even though his body had formed the blisters to protect and mend his hand, the burn still hurt. Later, this early relative of ours was retrieving water from the local creek. It was then that he observed the next major breakthrough in science and medicine. When he plunged his burned hand into the water to get a drink, the pain decreased. This was the birth of science and medicine. Later we would observe this scientific law, which states that for every action there is an equal and opposite reaction. When he burned his hand (fire), his body created blisters (water). When he plunged his burned hand (fire) into the creek (water), the pain decreased. A hot injury (fire) was treated with a cold remedy (water). The goal is to find balance.

As humanity grew in knowledge of the Green World, this simple concept of treating hot injuries with cold remedies grew into a set of descriptions for the plants and other items that could be used to reestablish balance. Herbs such as aloe vera were categorized as cold and prescribed for the treatment of hot injuries. In some schools of science and medicine, a connection was made between these two categories and two other categories: masculine and feminine. The category known as *hot* became known as *masculine*, and the category known as *cold* became known as *feminine*.

A World of Gender

This is the basis for virtually every step in Wiccan ritual, not to mention the core of most philosophies that have come from the initiatory path of the religion. While the philosophy of uniting masculine principles with feminine principles is expressed in Wiccan ritual as the symbolic union of male and female, it is extremely important to point out the difference between gender and sex. In reference to the reproductive organs (sex) of an animal or plant, the terms "male" and "female" are used. Of course, there is asexual and hermaphroditic reproduction, but I am addressing the most basic concepts at this point in the discussion. In reference to the basic nature of anything in existence (gender), the terms "masculine" and "feminine" are used. Again, yes, there are things in existence that are generally considered gender neutral, but again we are discussing the most basic concepts at this point.

Unfortunately for the discussion of the Wiccan religion and the philosophy behind it, many people become enraged at the concept of gender identification. Hoping that I will not insult the reader but knowing good and well that there is no way to avoid it, I tell you that it has been my observation that the greatest majority of those who do not like the principles of gender identification are individuals of very low education who speak modern English. You see, virtually every other language in the world relies on gender to identify the basic nature of a thing by incorporating that gender into their language; even the smallest amount of education in other languages and cultures will point this out. In fact, the word *Wicca* was itself a masculine word (*Wicce* being the feminine equivalent), but in modern English the word *Wicca* refers to both men and women. For some reason we have decided that it is bad to use the title of something to help indicate what that thing is. One can no longer use terms like "mailman" and "mailwoman." Today, the politically correct term is "letter carrier," despite the fact that the previous titles were a great deal more descriptive. To be perfectly frank, I think the next assault on the use of gender in our language will be on mothers and fathers. In ten years, I will probably be verbally attacked for referring to myself as a father rather than a parent.

So who decides what is masculine and what is feminine? Generally speaking, the community in which one lives decides. In the Western world, the use of perfumes and body scents is generally considered to be feminine. In the Middle East, one might consider such things masculine. Among humans in the Western world, elegant plumage is generally considered a feminine attribute. In much of the Animal World, elegant plumage is generally considered a masculine attribute. These classifications (*masculine* and *feminine*) are fluid, changing with culture and with cultural developments.

The problem with such a dynamic system is that if the use of the word changes, the system by which things have been cataloged becomes ineffective, until such time that all things that were previously cataloged under the old use of the word are recategorized under the new use of the word. If I use the word *wet* to describe something that is commonly called dry, my use of the word *wet* will not communicate the meaning I intend. If I am not communicating the meaning that I intend, then what was the point? For this reason, standards have been established. Because we are speaking in the most basic of terms, those standards are great, sweeping generalizations; hence, they are the least accurate method of description.

However, despite the negative associations made with words such as *stereotype*, sweeping generalizations are sometimes useful. If you do not believe this is the case, then please ignore such practices as treating a fire (masculine) injury with aloe vera. You see, the aloe vera has the attributes of both feminine and water. But do remember that these are sweeping generalizations. Not every plant associated with water or the female gender is a treatment for a masculine injury.

So we have the first two genders, masculine and feminine. With those genders we have general descriptions for each:

Masculine—strength, power, honor, mirth

Feminine—beauty, compassion, humility, reverence

> *And therefore let there be beauty and strength,*
> *power and compassion, honor and humility,*
> *mirth and reverence within you.*
> —*from* Charge of the Goddess

You will note that in the *Charge of the Goddess,* Our Lady was not cited as saying that in only men shall there be strength, power, honor, and mirth. Nor was Our Lady cited as saying that in only women shall there be beauty, compassion, humility, and reverence. Every man and woman, every boy and girl, is an amalgam of both feminine and masculine principles. Additional associations made with the two basic genders are:

Masculine—hot, positive, light, projective

Feminine—cold, negative, dark, receptive

I should mention that in this context, the word *negative* does not imply evil or bane. In fact, science has given us a wonderful little challenge in this respect. Electricity actually flows from the negative to the positive. In effect, although the term "negative" is listed as feminine, when we are talking about electricity, the negative side of a DC circuit is actually *masculine* and the positive side is actually *feminine*. This serves as a wonderful example of how such terminology changes with time and understanding of the nature of things.

This is key to understanding not only the Wiccan religion, but also the philosophy behind the religion. Although the term "negative" is sometimes tossed around as if it is a synonym for evil, the concept of a manifest evil is not present in the Wiccan religion or its philosophy. Put simply, Wiccans do not believe in the existence of Satan or a Satan-like entity. Ah, but what about such people as Adolph Hitler?

Wicca is a religion of science. Certainly we believe people like Adolph Hitler existed, but our philosophy does not include the existence of a guiding force behind his evil acts. Instead of believing in an all- powerful agent of Good who stands in constant opposition to an all-powerful agent of Evil, we believe in a flow between those things masculine (God) and those things feminine (Goddess), because such belief fits the scientific understanding not only of energy flow, but also the structure of all things in the real world. You see, we believe that one can see the parents (the Creator) in the children (all of creation).

Unfortunately, due to the seemingly overwhelming pressure of the Christian culture in which most Wiccans practice, we do tend to fall into the same trap that so many Christians find themselves. That trap is the belief in such an opposition rather than the natural and scientific understanding of the manifest world, which is the balance of feminine and masculine principles. It is that balance (with a few neutral aspects thrown in) that defines all that is manifest. If you do not believe this, please list an element that is composed entirely of electrons (feminine) or entirely of protons (masculine).

But do not think this means that all things masculine are good and all things feminine are evil (or vice versa). Such thinking is the trap that I spoke about earlier. My parents raised me to believe that God is Love. As I became interested in Wicca, I translated their use of the word God to the word Creator. As I developed as a Wiccan, I realized that my use of the word Creator is a reference to the interaction between our Lord (masculine) and Lady (feminine), neither of which is the Creator without the other. In religious terms, evil is not a force in opposition to the Creator (our Lord and Lady). Instead, Evil is the lack of the Creator (Love), for Love is the force that unites masculine and feminine. It is Love that keeps the electrons and protons united to form atoms.

So what does that have to do with Wiccan spellcraft, the Green World, and this formulary? Everything! You see, in all things magickal we are seeking to create a magickal child—the outcome of our efforts to bring feminine to masculine and masculine to feminine. When an injury is masculine, we use a feminine remedy. The magickal child of that act is the restoration of balance between the masculine and feminine or removal of the obstruction that prevents the interaction between masculine and feminine. Although medicine and magick are often thought of as two entirely different subjects, the same is true of magick. Any deficiency in one's life (be it an injury, sickness, poverty, or even a broken heart) is caused by an imbalance or an impediment of flow. Any magick or medicine that will be effective in addressing such an issue is one that either restores balance or removes the impediment.

Thus, the practice of Wiccan spellcraft is the act of communicating with the Creator about what is not in balance or is causing an obstruction. In essence, spellcraft is the sincere communication between a person and the world in which that person lives in the same way a person might sincerely communicate with his or her spouse or partner about a problem that affects their relationship. The simplest form of that communication is the balance between the masculine and feminine. Thus, the Green World and other materials used in spellcraft are first classified as either masculine or feminine. You see, per Wiccan philosophy, the masculine and feminine are the core building blocks of all things in the real world.

Masculine and Feminine:
The Green World as Two Genders

Masculine Plants (sometimes cited as hot plants)

Acacia, Acanthopanax, Agaric Mushroom, Agrimony, Alder, Allspice, Almond, Amber, American Bittersweet, Anemone, Angelica, Anise, Arabic (Gum), Arbutus, Artichoke, Asafoetida, Ash, Ash (Mountain), Ash (Prickly), Asparagus, Aspen (Big Tooth), Avens, Bamboo, Banyan, Basil, Bay, Benzoin, Bergamot, Bergamot (Orange), Black Bryony, Bloodroot, Bodhi, Borage, Brazil Nut, Broom, Bromeliad, Cacao, Calendula, Caraway, Carnation, Carrot, Cashew, Cattail, Cayenne, Cedar, Cedar (Red), Celandine (Greater), Celery, Centaury, Chamomile (Stinking), Chervil, Chestnut (Horse), Chestnut (Sweet), Chicory, Chives, Chrysanthemum, Cinnamon (Chinese), Cinnamon (Common), Citron, Cloth of Gold, Clove, Clover (Red), Coffee, Cohosh (Black), Cohosh (Blue), Copal, Copal (Black), Coriander, Costmary, Cubeb, Cumin, Curry (Black), Damiana, Dandelion, Deerstongue, Dill, Dock (Yellow), Dragon's Blood, Elecampane, Endive, European White Bryony, Eyebright, Fennel, Fenugreek, Fern, Feverfew, Fig (Common), Five-Finger Grass, Flax, Flax (Mountain), Flax (Perennial), Frankincense, Galangal, Garlic, Gentain, Ginger, Ginseng (American), Goldenseal, Gorse, Grains of Paradise, Gum Mastic, Hawthorn, Hazelnut, Heliotrope, High John the Conqueror, Holly (American), Holly (Common), Honeysuckle, Hops, Horehound (Black), Horehound (White), Horseradish, Hound's-Tongue, Houseleek, Hyssop, Juniper, Kumquat, Lavender, Leek, LemongGrass, Lemon Verbena, Lily of the Valley, Lily (Blue Water), Lime, Lime Tree, Liverwort (American), Liverwort (English), Liquid Amber, Lovage, Lovage (Scotch), Mahogany (Mountain), Mango, Mandrake, Mandrake (American), Marjoram, Masterwort, Meadowsweet, Mint, Mistletoe (American), Mistletoe (European), Morning Glory, Mulberry (Common), Mustard (Black), Mustard (Brown), Mustard (Field), Mustard (Rape), Mustard (White), Nettle (Greater), Nettle (Lesser), Nutmeg, Mace, Oak, Olive, Onion, Orange (Bitter), Orange

(Sweet), Oregano, Peony, Palm (Date), Papyrus, Parsley, Pear (Prickly), Pecan, Pennyroyal, Pepper (Black), Peppermint, Pimpernel (Scarlet), Pine, Pine (Norfolk Island), Pineapple, Pistachio, Pokeweed, Pomegranate, Radish, Rice, Rosemary, Rue, Rue (Goat's), Saffron (Spanish), Sage (Clary), Sage (Common), Sage (Diviner's), Sage (Vervain), Sarsaparilla, Sassafras, Savory (Summer), Savory (Winter), Scabious (Devil's Bit), Sesame, Silverweed, Snapdragon, Sunflower, Sloe, Snake Root (Black), Southernwood, Squash, Star Anise, St. John's Wort, Tangerine, Thistle, Thistle (Blessed), Turmeric, Walnut, Watercress, White Bryony, Wood Betony, Woody Nightshade, Woodruff

Feminine Plants (sometimes cited as cold plants)

Aconite, Adam and Eve Root, Adder's Tongue (American), Ailanthus, Alfalfa, Alismatis Rhizome, Alkanet, Aloe, Amaranth, Apple, Apricot, Aspen (Common), Aspen (American), Aster, Avocado, Balm of Gilead, Bachelor's Buttons, Banana, Barberry (Common), Barberry (Holly-leaved), Barberry (Indian), Barberry (Nepal), Barley, Beech, Beet, Belladonna, Birch, Bistort, Blackberry, Bladderwrack, Bleeding Heart, Blueberries, Blue Flag, Boneset, Broccoli, Brussels Sprouts, Buchu, Buckthorn (Alder), Buckthorn (Californian), Buckwheat, Burdock, Cabbage, Cabbage (Skunk), Calamus, Camellia, Camphor, Caper, Cardamom, Carob, Catnip, Cauliflower, Chamomile (Common), Chamomile (German), Chickweed, Cherry, Cherry (Wild), Cleavers (A), Cleavers (B), Coconut, Coltsfoot, Columbine, Comfrey, Corn, Cotton, Cowslip, Cranberry, Crocus, Cucumber, Cyclamen (Ivy-leaved), Cypress, Daffodil, Daisy (Common), Daisy (Ox-eye), Dittany of Crete, Dodder, Dulse, Eggplant, Elder, Elm (Common), Elm (Slippery), Eucalyptus, Maidenhair (True), Figwort (Knotted), Figwort (Water), Fleabane (Common), Foxglove, Frangipani, Freesia, Fumitory, Gardenia, Geranium, Geranium (Rose), Ginger (White), Goldenrod, Grapefruit, Groundsel (Common), Groundsel (Golden), Groundsel (Hoary), Groundsel (Mountain), Groundsel (Viscid), Guava, Heartsease, Heather, Hellebore (Black), Hemlock, Henbane, Hibiscus, Holly (Sea), Horsetails, Huckleberry, Hyacinth (Wild), Iris, Ivy (Common), Jasmine, Kava Kava, Knotgrass, Lady's Mantle, Lemon, Lemon Balm, Lentil, Lettuce, Lettuce (Wild), Licorice, Lilac, Lily, Lobelia, Loosestrife (Purple), Lotus, Lotus (Sacred), Lucky Hand, Macadamia, Madder, Magnolia, Mallow (Blue), Mallow (Dwarf), Mallow (Marsh), Mallow (Musk), Maple, Marijuana, Millet, Mimosa, Mesquite, Moss (American Club), Moss (Common Club), Moss (Irish), Moss (Corsican), Moss (Cup), Moss (Hair Cap), Moss (Iceland), Moss (Spanish), Moss (Sphagnum), Mugwort, Mullein, Myrrh, Myrtle, Nectarine, Oakmoss, Oats, Oleander, Orris, Palmarosa, Papaya, Passion Flower, Passion Fruit, Patchouli, Pea, Peach, Peanut, Pear, Periwinkle, Persimmon, Plum, Plum (Wild), Poppy (White), Poppy (White), Potato, Plantain (Buck's Horn), Plantain (Common), Plantain (Hoary), Plantain (Ispaghul), Plantain (Psyllium), Plantain (Ribwort), Plantain (Sea), Plantain (Water), Primrose, Pumpkin, Purslane

(Golden), Purslane (Green), Quince, Raspberry, Rhubarb, Rhubarb (Monk's), Rose (White), Rose (Red), Rose (Damascus), Rye, Sage (White), Sandalwood (White), Sandalwood (Red), Scullcap, Solomon's Seal, Soy, Strawberry (Garden), Sorrel (Wood), Spearmint, Spikenard (American), Spikenard (Ploughman's), Spinach, Spurges, Sugarcane, Sweet Potato, Tamarind, Tansy, Tarragon, Thornapple, Thyme, Tomato, Tonka, Truffles, Valerian, Valerian (American), Valerian (Indian), Vanilla, Vetivert, Vervain, Vine, Violet, Watermelon, Wheat, Willow, Wintergreen, Wolf's Bane, Wood Aloes, Yarrow, Yew

Plants and the Elements

Of course, things are rarely black and white. Neither are they just feminine and masculine. There are always shades of grey, and there are always variations in the theme of gender. Some things which are masculine are extremely masculine. Some things that are masculine are not as extreme. Some things that are feminine are extremely feminine. Some things that are feminine are not as extreme. This is where the Four Elements come in. In essence, one could call them the Four Genders as they are an extension of the principles *masculine* and *feminine*.

Fire—Extremely masculine

Air—Masculine

Earth—Feminine

Water—Extremely feminine

A good conceptual way of looking at this is to see the masculine and feminine principles as parents of the Elements.

Fire—Masculine—He takes after his father.

Air—Masculine (predominantly) and a bit Feminine—He takes after both parents.

Earth—Feminine (predominantly) and a bit Masculine—She takes after both parents.

Water—Feminine—She takes after her mother.

The pragmatic concept here is two-fold. The first is that one will not find balance by applying overwhelming force. If an imbalance was of an "Airy" nature, then one would correct that imbalance with Earth. The second is that one will not find balance by applying insufficient force. If an imbalance was of a "Fiery" nature, then one would address that imbalance with Water.

The best analogy I can think of is my experience with blacksmithing over a coal forge. The coal (Earth) is acted upon by the blower (Air) to keep the fire going. However, that fire is kept in check by water that I splash here and there to keep the process in check. Sure, I could decrease the amount of air that is flowing into the forge, but it would not have the immediate response that adding a bit of water here and there does.

Earth, Air, Fire, and Water: The Green World as Four Genders

Earth

Conceptual Lineage—Earth is the conceptual daughter of the concepts of Masculine and Feminine.

> **Associated Ritual Tool**—Pentacle
> **Compliment**—Air
> **Quarter**—North
> **Gender**—Feminine

Earth is the Element of firmament. It is associated with stability, fertility, nurturing, prosperity, success at business, and the rewards associated with hard work. In respect to fertility, prosperity, and success at business, earth rewards efforts in the long term.

Plants associated with the Element Earth are generally used to treat conditions and imbalances associated with Air. Such things as flightiness, instability, fear of commitment, wander lust, indecisiveness, and other similar concerns are prime candidates to be balanced by herbs associated with the element Earth.

Associated Plants—Alfalfa, Barberry (Common), Barberry (Holly-leaved), Barberry (Indian), Barberry (Nepal), Barley, Beech, Beet, Bistort, Buckwheat, Corn, Cotton, Cypress, Eggplant, Fumitory, Honeysuckle, Horsetails, Knotgrass, Loosestrife (Purple), Macadamia, Magnolia, Maple, Millet, Moss (Corsican), Moss (Cup), Moss (Hair Cap), Moss (Iceland), Moss (Spanish), Moss (Sphagnum), Mugwort, Oakmoss, Oats, Oleander, Patchouli, Pea, Peanut, Potato, Plantain (Buck's Horn), Plantain (Common), Plantain (Hoary), Plantain (Ispaghul), Plantain (Psyllium), Plantain (Ribwort), Primrose, Pumpkin, Quince, Rhubarb, Rhubarb (Monk's), Rye, Sage (White), Soy, Sorrel (Wood), Spinach, Tarragon, Vetivert, Vervain, Wheat, Yew

Air

Conceptual Lineage—Air is the conceptual son of the concepts of Masculine and Feminine.

> **Associated Ritual Tool**—Censer
> **Compliment**—Earth
> **Quarter**—Air
> **Gender**—Masculine

Air is the Element of cognitive functions. It is associated with intelligence, thought, visualization, and structured creativity. It is also the Element of flight and is thus associated with both astral and physical travel.

Plants associated with the Element Air are generally used to treat conditions and imbalances associated with Earth. Such things as unwillingness to move forward, the inability to find or accept change, stubbornness, and other similar concerns are prime candidates to be balanced by herbs associated with the Element Air.

Associated Plants—Acacia, Agrimony, Almond, American Bittersweet, Anise, Arabic (Gum), Ash (Mountain), Aspen (Big Tooth), Bamboo, Banyan, Benzoin, Bergamot (Orange), Bodhi, Borage, Brazil Nut, Broom, Bromeliad, Caraway, Carnation, Chervil, Chicory, Citron, Cleavers (B), Clover (Red), Copal, Costmary, Dandelion, Dock (Yellow), Elecampane, Elm (Slippery), Endive, Eyebright, Fenugreek, Fern, Goldenrod, Gum Mastic, Hazelnut, Hops, Horehound (Black), Horehound (White), Houseleek, Kumquat, Lavender, Lemongrass, Lemon Verbena, Lily of the Valley, Lime Tree, Liverwort (American), Marjoram, Meadowsweet, Mint, Mistletoe (American), Mistletoe (European), Morning Glory, Mulberry (Common), Mace, Orange (Bitter), Orange (Sweet), Oregano, Peony, Palm (Date), Papyrus, Parsley, Pecan, Pimpernel (Scarlet), Pine, Pistachio, Rice, Rue (Goat's), Sage (Clary), Sage (Common), Sage (Diviner's), Sage (Vervain), Savory (Summer), Savory (Winter), Southernwood, Star Anise, Tangerine, Thornapple, Turmeric, Woody Nightshade

Fire

Conceptual Lineage—Fire is the conceptual son of the concepts of Masculine and Feminine.

> **Associated Ritual Tool**—Athame
> **Compliment**—Water
> **Gender**—Masculine
> **Quarter**—South

Fire is the Element of rapid change. It is also associated with passion, lust, war, destruction, purification, and rebirth.

Plants associated with the Element Fire are generally used to overwhelm and destroy imbalances associated with Water. Drug and other addictions come to mind, especially those which have come with the flow of lineage (those inherited from our parents). They are also used to break cycles and, in magick, intent on bringing about sudden and forceful change. Such things as complacency, lack of force, the feeling that one cannot effect change, apathy, and similar concerns are prime candidates to be balanced by plants associated with this Element.

Associated Plants—Alder, Allspice, Amaranth, Amber, Anemone, Angelica, Arbutus, Artichoke, Asafoetida, Ash, Ash (Prickly), Asparagus, Avens, Basil, Bay, Bergamot, Black Bryony, Bloodroot, Cacao, Calendula, Carrot, Cashew, Cattail, Cayenne, Cedar, Cedar (Red), Celery, Centaury, Chamomile (Stinking), Chestnut (Horse), Chestnut (Sweet), Chives, Chrysanthemum, Cinnamon (Chinese), Cinnamon (Common), Cloth of Gold, Clove, Coffee, Copal (Black), Coriander, Cubeb, Cumin, Curry (Black), Damiana, Deerstongue, Dill, Dragon's Blood, European White Bryony, Fennel, Fig (Common), Five-Finger Grass, Flax, Flax (Mountain), Flax (Perennial), Frankincense, Galangal, Garlic, Gentain, Ginger, Ginseng (American), Goldenseal, Gorse, Grains of Paradise, Hawthorn, Heliotrope, High John the Conqueror, Holly (American), Holly (Common), Horseradish, Hound's-Tongue, Hyssop, Juniper, Leek, Lily (Blue Water), Lime, Liverwort (English), Liquid Amber, Lovage, Lovage (Scotch), Mahogany (Mountain), Mango, Mandrake, Mandrake (American), Masterwort, Mullein, Mustard (Black), Mustard (Brown), Mustard (Field), Mustard (Rape), Mustard (White), Nettle (Greater), Nettle (Lesser), Nutmeg, Oak, Olive, Onion, Pear (Prickly), Pennyroyal, Pepper (Black), Peppermint, Pine (Norfolk Island), Pineapple, Pokeweed, Pomegranate, Radish, Rosemary, Rue, Saffron (Spanish), Sarsaparilla, Sassafras, Sesame, Silverweed, Snapdragon, Sunflower, Sloe, Snakeroot (Black), Squash, St. John's Wort, Thistle, Thistle (Blessed), Walnut, Watercress, White Bryony, Wood Betony, Woodruff

Water

Conceptual Lineage—Water is the conceptual daughter of the concepts of Masculine and Feminine.

> **Associated Ritual Tool**—Chalice
>
> **Compliment**—Fire
>
> **Gender**—Feminine
>
> **Quarter**—West

Water is the Element of deeply felt emotions. Unlike the associations made with Fire, Water is not passionate in the sense of being greatly active. Instead, it is the Element of calm romantic love rather than lust. It is also the Element of the subconscious, dreams, purification, and prophecy in which visions are received rather than taken. In the practice of divination, it is the Element of scrying.

Water is also an Element of change, but not in the same way that Fire is. Fire causes change by rapid destruction or consumption of something external. Water represents self-change and conformation to one's environment. It is an Element of balance in that Water always finds its own level. However, sometimes self-change tends to destroy with the swiftness of Fire.

Plants associated with the Element Water are generally used to treat conditions and imbalances associated with Fire. Such things as hotheadedness, a tendency to make rapid decisions, allowing one's lust to taint intellectual decisions, and other similar concerns are prime candidates to be balanced by herbs associated with the Element Water.

Associated Plants—Aconite, Adam and Eve Root, Adder's-Tongue (American), Alkanet, Aloe, Apple, Apricot, Aspen (Common), Aspen (American), Aster, Avocado, Balm of Gilead, Bachelor's Buttons, Banana, Belladonna, Birch, Blackberry, Bladderwrack, Bleeding Heart, Blueberries, Blue Flag, Boneset, Broccoli, Brussels Sprouts, Buchu, Buckthorn (Alder), Buckthorn (Californian), Burdock, Cabbage, Cabbage (Skunk), Calamus, Camellia, Camphor, Caper, Cardamom, Carob, Catnip, Cauliflower, Chamomile (Common), Chamomile (German), Chickweed, Cherry, Cherry (Wild), Cleavers (A), Coconut, Coltsfoot, Columbine, Comfrey, Cowslip, Cranberry, Crocus, Cucumber, Cyclamen (Ivy-leaved), Daffodil, Daisy (Common), Daisy (Ox-eye), Dittany of Crete, Dodder, Dulse, Elder, Elm (Common), Eucalyptus, Maidenhair (True), Feverfew, Figwort (Knotted), Figwort (Water), Fleabane (Common), Foxglove, Frangipani, Freesia, Gardenia, Geranium, Geranium (Rose), Ginger (White), Grapefruit, Groundsel (Common), Groundsel (Golden), Groundsel (Hoary), Groundsel (Mountain), Groundsel (Viscid), Guava, Heartsease, Heather, Hellebore (Black), Hemlock, Henbane, Hibiscus, Holly (Sea), Huckleberry, Hyacinth (Wild), Iris, Ivy (Common), Jasmine, Kava Kava, Lady's Mantle, Lemon, Lemon Balm, Lentil, Lettuce, Lettuce (Wild), Licorice, Lilac, Lily, Lobelia, Lotus, Lotus (Sacred), Lucky Hand, Madder, Mallow (Blue), Mallow (Dwarf), Mallow (Marsh), Mallow (Musk), Marijuana, Mimosa, Mesquite, Moss (American Club), Moss (Common Club), Moss (Irish), Myrrh, Myrtle, Nectarine, Orris, Palmarosa, Papaya, Passion Flower, Passion Fruit, Peach, Pear, Periwinkle, Persimmon, Plum, Plum (Wild), Poppy (White), Plantain (Sea), Plantain (Water), Purslane (Golden), Purslane (Green), Raspberry, Rose (White), Rose (Red), Rose (Damascus), Sandalwood (White), Sandalwood (Red), Scullcap, Solomon's Seal, Strawberry (Garden), Spearmint, Spikenard (American), Spikenard (Ploughman's), Spurges, Sugarcane, Sweet Potato, Tamarind, Tansy, Thyme, Tomato, Tonka, Truffles, Valerian, Valerian (American), Valerian (Indian), Vanilla, Vine, Violet, Watermelon, Willow, Wintergreen, Wolf's Bane, Wood Aloes, Yarrow

Planetary Associations

This is a good place to answer a question that I hope you have already asked. Just who came up with all of these associations? Who gets to decide what plant is associated with what planet? Although you have probably heard of intuitive spellcraft or perhaps the "if it feels right, it is right" approach to spellcraft, there is a science behind the traditional associations. So, of course, the answer to the question is that scientists came up with most of the commonly accepted magickal associations and correspondences.

So how did they decide what those associations were? In the case of the planets, they looked into the sky and noticed that certain heavenly bodies moved differently than the stars. Those heavenly bodies were the first planets, of which there were seven. Although, today, the sun and moon are not generally considered planets, and although there have been other planets discovered, the first seven were: Sun, Moon, Mars, Mercury, Jupiter, Venus, and Saturn. Gradually, the planets were assigned attributes.

Now, here is the important part of this story. Those ancient scientists that I spoke about were also doctors and scholars. Their highest aspiration was that humanity understand the Green World. It is to that end that they recorded their observations in ways that future generations would understand. To do that, they related the properties of plants to the planets and not the other way around.

If a plant appeared to inspire love, it was generally associated with the planet Venus. If a plant appeared to be associated with war, it was generally linked to Mars. Ah, but if you look at the ancient records of the Green World, you will see such terms as "ruled by Venus." Does that not mean the planet Venus rules that plant? No, not at all. In fact, it was simply a politically correct way to convey knowledge. To understand this better, consider the execution of Socrates.

He was executed after being found guilty of blasphemy against the gods of Greece. Effectively, he taught his students that the Greek gods did not exist in the way that the myths stated they did. However, he was not an atheist. He believed strongly in the existence of the Creator. He just didn't believe one could climb Mt. Olympus and visit with the Olympian gods and goddesses. Instead, he felt that the stories of the gods were attempts to explain the many facets of the Creator. For this, he was put to death despite the fact that most scholars believed exactly as he did. They just could not express such views openly because they would meet the same fate.

In the modern Pagan community, I am sure I will meet with the same or similar charge for what I am about to say. Fortunately for me, the laws of the day are much more forgiving. So why did Socrates teach what he did without regard for his own life? Because he felt it was right. Why am I about to yet again risk the life of my career? Because it is right.

You see, our community has become littered with spell books and other references that provide gender, Elemental, and planetary associations for the Green World in a manner so whimsical that rational people are starting to think the Latin word for the Wiccan religion is *Wingus Nuttus*. Worse yet, so many Wiccans are gobbling up the fast food of religion (McWicca) that our community really is starting to look like a collection of complete wing nuts. Of course, every spiritual path has its fair share of lunatics, but this is the community in which I will be raising my daughter. Thus, what follows is an attempt to set the record straight when it comes to such seemingly ridiculous notions as spellcraft and the Green World.

The plants do not have their attributes because they are magickally connected to the planets. In the process by which the ancients cataloged plants, the plant was observed, a determination was made as to what that plant's properties were, and then those properties were described as being connected with a planet because the planets had received descriptions earlier. In essence, stating a plant is "ruled by" a planet is a type of magickal shorthand. If one lists a plant as being ruled by Venus, one is stating that the general properties of that plant are the same general properties of the planet Venus, not that Venus actually "rules" the plant.

It is a process similar to medical shorthand. When one wants to note that a plant will bring about an increase in urine output, one simply notes that plant as a diuretic. When one wants to note that a plant will bring about an increase in perspiration, one simply notes that plant as a diaphoretic.

Sun, Moon, Mars, Mercury, Jupiter, Venus, and Saturn: The Green World as Seven Genders

Key: Planet—Day of Week—Gender, Color, Element

Please note that many of these associations will change with particular culture and tradition. This is especially true of the gender associations made with the Sun and Moon. Listed here is what has become most prevalent in today's lore.

Sol/Sun—Sunday—Masculine, Yellow, Air

Conceptual Lineage—Sol/Sun is the conceptual son of the Air and Earth.

Promotes—Authority, Leadership, Healing, Connection with the Masculine aspect of the Creator

The principles of the Sun are often misunderstood. While the Sun lends itself to leadership and authority, such attributes are in the nature of the advice found in the Wiccan Rede, which states that one should "fairly take and fairly give." Thus, while the Sun is associated with the outcome of leadership, this is in the order of equitable trade, a fair price for a fair value, and the establishment of mutually symbiotic relationships.

Associated Base Oils—Sunflower Oil, Sesame Oil, Olive Oil

Associated Plants—Acacia, Amber, Angelica, Arabic (Gum), Ash, Ash (Mountain), Bamboo, Bay, Benzoin, Bergamot, Bromeliad, Calendula, Carnation, Cashew, Cedar, Celandine (Greater), Centaury, Chamomile (Stinking), Chicory, Chrysanthemum,

Cinnamon (Chinese), Cinnamon (Common), Citron, Cloth of Gold, Copal, Copal (Black), Eyebright, Frankincense, Ginseng (American), Golden seal, Gum Mastic, Hazelnut, Heliotrope, Juniper, Kumquat, Lily (Blue Water), Lime, Liquid Amber, Lovage, Lovage (Scotch), Mistletoe (American), Mistletoe (European), Oak, Olive, Orange (Bitter), Orange (Sweet), Peony, Palm (Date), Pineapple, Rice, Rosemary, Saffron (Spanish), Sesame, Sunflower, Squash, St. John's Wort, Tangerine, Walnut

Luna/Moon—Monday—Feminine, Violet, Air

Conceptual Lineage—Luna/Moon is the conceptual daughter of the Air and Earth.

Promotes—Growth, Family Unity, Dreams, Divination, Connection with the Feminine aspect of the Creator

The Moon is associated with the changes found in constant patterns. It is associated with Perfect Love and Perfect Trust, and the eternal passion a spouse might have for his or her partner, as well as the constant devotion of a parent to his or her child.

Transient but returning physical love is also a principle of the Moon. It is the planet of lovers who might not always be fortunate enough to live with one another as well as the planet of those who have lived together for what seems like an eternity and loved every moment of it.

Associated Base Oil—Grapeseed Oil

Associated Plants—Adder's-Tongue (American), Aloe, Bladderwrack, Broccoli, Brussels Sprouts, Buchu, Cabbage, Calamus, Camellia, Camphor, Cauliflower, Chickweed, Coconut, Cotton, Cranberry, Cucumber, Dulse, Eucalyptus, Gardenia, Grapefruit, Jasmine, Lemon, Lemon Balm, Lentil, Lettuce, Lettuce (Wild), Lily, Loosestrife (Purple), Lotus, Lotus (Sacred), Mallow (Blue), Mallow (Dwarf), Mallow (Marsh), Mallow (Musk), Mesquite, Moss (American Club), Moss (Common Club), Moss (Irish), Myrrh, Papaya, Passion Fruit, Poppy (White), Poppy (White), Potato, Pumpkin, Purslane (Golden), Purslane (Green), Rose (White), Sandalwood (White), Soy, Vine, Watermelon, Willow, Wintergreen

Mars—Tuesday—Masculine, Red, Fire

Conceptual Lineage—Mars is the conceptual son of the Fire and Water.

Promotes—War, Competition, Conflict, Lust, Courage, Success at Hunting

Mars promotes high-spiritedness in the effort to effect sudden change. At its core, it is the planet of war. However, war need not be the nasty thing that it is sometimes thought. Mars is the planet of righteousness and the use of force in accordance with that which one knows to be right in a manner detrimental to forces one knows to be wrong. It is also the planet of unity in the face of adversity, especially among men. The message this planet brings is not only "don't tread on me," but also a call to stand up for that which is right.

Associated Base Oil—Olive Oil, Coconut Oil

Associated Plants—Alder, Allspice, Anemone, Arbutus, Artichoke, Asafoetida, Ash (Prickly), Asparagus, Barberry (Common), Barberry (Holly-leaved), Barberry (Indian), Barberry (Nepal), Basil, Black Bryony, Bloodroot, Broom, Cacao, Carrot, Cattail, Cayenne, Cedar (Red), Chives, Coffee, Coriander, Cubeb, Cumin, Curry (Black), Damiana, Deerstongue, Dragon's Blood, European White Bryony, Galangal, Garlic, Gentain, Ginger, Gorse, Grains of Paradise, Hawthorn, High John the Conqueror, Holly (American), Holly (Common), Hops, Horseradish, Hound's-Tongue, Leek, Mahogany (Mountain), Mango, Masterwort, Mustard (Black), Mustard (Brown), Mustard (Field), Mustard (Rape), Mustard (White), Nettle (Greater), Nettle (Lesser), Onion, Pear (Prickly), Pennyroyal, Pepper (Black), Pine, Pine (Norfolk Island), Pokeweed, Radish, Rue, Snapdragon, Sloe, Snakeroot (Black), Thistle, Thistle (Blessed), Watercress, White Bryony, Woodruff

Mercury—Wednesday—Masculine, Yellow, Water

Conceptual Lineage—Mercury is the conceptual son of the Fire and Water.

Promotes—Cognitive Functions, Education, Divination, Intelligence, Communication, Unrest, Travel, Analysis

Mercury is the encouragement to use one's intellect and cognitive functions to question the world in which we live. It is also the encouragement to record and to share those observations in the hope of expanding communal knowledge. To that end, Mercury encourages travel, analysis, and scholarly record-keeping.

Associated Base Oil—Almond Oil

Associated Plants—Agaric Mushroom, Almond, American Bittersweet, Aspen (Big Tooth), Bergamot (Orange), Brazil Nut, Caraway, Celery, Chervil, Clover (Red), Costmary, Dill, Elecampane, Fennel, Fenugreek, Fern, Flax, Flax (Mountain), Flax (Perennial), Horehound (Black), Horehound (White), Lavender, Lemongrass, Lemon Verbena, Lily of the Valley, Mandrake, Mandrake (American), Marjoram, Mint, Moss (Corsican), Moss (Cup), Moss (Hair Cap), Moss (Iceland), Moss (Spanish), Moss (Sphagnum), Mulberry (Common), Mace, Oregano, Papyrus, Parsley, Pecan, Peppermint, Pimpernel (Scarlet), Pistachio, Pomegranate, Rue (Goat's), Sage (Clary), Savory (Summer), Savory (Winter), Southernwood, Turmeric, Woody Nightshade

Jupiter—Thursday—Masculine, Blue, Water

Conceptual Lineage—Jupiter is the conceptual son of the Air and Earth.

Promotes—Organization, Money, Luck, Gambling, Tangible Prosperity, Laws of Man

Jupiter brings tangible prosperity and money via organization. It is the planet of the business owner who conforms to the Laws of Man in an organized manner to accumulate great wealth. Thus, it is the planet of civic leaders, as well as leaders of religious organizations in the capacity of effectively managing funds. Jupiter is also the planet of one who is involved in statistical gambling rather than random (slot machine) gambling.

Associated Base Oil—Olive Oil

Associated Plants—Agrimony, Anise, Avens, Banyan, Bodhi, Borage, Chestnut (Horse), Chestnut (Sweet), Clove, Dandelion, Dock (Yellow), Eggplant, Endive, Fig (Common), Five-Finger Grass, Honeysuckle, Houseleek, Hyssop, Lime Tree, Liverwort (American), Liverwort (English), Macadamia, Maple, Meadowsweet, Millet, Nutmeg, Oakmoss, Peanut, Rose (Red), Sage (Common), Sage (Diviner's), Sage (Vervain), Sarsaparilla, Sassafras, Silverweed, Spinach, Star Anise, Wood Betony

Venus—Friday—Feminine, Green, Fire

Conceptual Lineage—Venus is the conceptual daughter of the Fire and Water.

Promotes—Love, Partnership, Union, Pleasure, Artistic Vision, Creativity, Music

Venus brings good fortune by promoting sound partnerships, love, and creativity. Although it is often whimsically listed as governing prosperity, its message is that love and kindness lend themselves well to prosperity.

Associated Base Oil—Apricot Kernel Oil

Associated Plants—Adam and Eve Root, Alfalfa, Alkanet, Apple, Apricot, Aster, Avocado, Balm of Gilead, Bachelor's Buttons, Banana, Barley, Birch, Blackberry, Bleeding Heart, Blueberries, Blue Flag, Buckwheat, Burdock, Caper, Cardamom, Carob, Catnip, Chamomile (Common), Chamomile (German), Cherry, Cherry (Wild), Cleavers (A), Coltsfoot, Columbine, Corn, Cowslip, Crocus, Cyclamen (Ivy–leaved), Daffodil, Daisy (Common), Daisy (Ox-eye), Dittany of Crete, Elder, Maidenhair (True), Feverfew, Figwort (Knotted), Figwort (Water), Fleabane (Common), Foxglove, Frangipani, Freesia, Geranium, Geranium (Rose), Ginger (White), Goldenrod, Groundsel (Common), Groundsel (Golden), Groundsel (Hoary), Groundsel (Mountain), Groundsel (Viscid), Guava, Heather, Hibiscus, Holly (Sea), Huckleberry, Hyacinth (Wild), Iris, Lady's Mantle, Licorice, Lilac, Lucky Hand, Madder, Magnolia, Mugwort, Myrtle, Nectarine, Oats, Orris, Passion Flower, Pea, Peach, Pear, Periwinkle, Persimmon, Plum, Plum (Wild), Plantain (Buck's Horn), Plantain (Common), Plantain (Hoary), Plantain (Ispaghul), Plantain (Psyllium), Plantain (Ribwort), Plantain (Sea), Plantain (Water), Primrose, Raspberry, Rhubarb, Rhubarb (Monk's), Rose (Damascus), Rye, Sage (White), Sandalwood (Red), Strawberry (Garden), Sorrel (Wood), Spearmint, Spikenard (American), Spikenard (Ploughman's), Sugarcane, Sweet Potato, Tansy, Tarragon, Thyme, Tomato, Tonka, Truffles, Valerian, Valerian (Indian), Vanilla, Vetivert, Vervain, Violet, Wheat, Wood Aloes, Yarrow

Saturn—Saturday—Feminine, Indigo, Earth

Conceptual Lineage—Saturn is the conceptual daughter of the Air and Earth.

Promotes—Endings, Divorce, Funerals, Death, Creation, Creativity

Saturn is the concluding force necessary for new beginnings. In its promotion of divorce, it promotes new marriages. In bringing death, it makes way for new life and reincarnation. It is the planet that speaks to us of the need for endings prior to new beginnings.

Associated Base Oil—N/A

Associated Plants—Aconite, Amaranth, Aspen (Common), Aspen (American), Beech, Beet, Belladonna, Bistort, Boneset, Buckthorn (Alder), Buckthorn (Californian), Cabbage (Skunk), Cleavers (B), Comfrey, Cypress, Dodder, Elm (Common), Elm (Slippery), Fumitory, Heartsease, Hellebore (Black), Hemlock, Henbane, Horsetails, Ivy (Common), Kava Kava, Knotgrass, Lobelia, Marijuana, Mimosa, Morning Glory, Mullein, Oleander, Patchouli, Quince, Scullcap, Solomon's Seal, Spurges, Tamarind, Thornapple, Valerian (American), Wolf's Bane, Yew

Planetary Hours of the Night

The planetary hours of night are not hours as they are commonly thought of. Instead, there are twelve periods of equal length between sundown and sunup. To calculate these "hours," first throw away the idea that an hour has 60 minutes. Instead, use a local reference such as your hometown newspaper to determine the exact time of sunset and sunrise. Calculate the number of minutes between these two times and then divide that number of minutes by twelve. Once you know the number of minutes in each hour, apply that number to the following twelve cycles.

Period	Sun.	Mon.	Tues.	Wed.	Thur.	Fri.	Sat.
A	Jupiter	Venus	Saturn	Sun	Moon	Mars	Mercury
B	Mars	Mercury	Jupiter	Venus	Saturn	Sun	Moon
C	Sun	Moon	Mars	Mercury	Jupiter	Venus	Saturn
D	Venus	Saturn	Sun	Moon	Mars	Mercury	Jupiter
E	Mercury	Jupiter	Venus	Saturn	Sun	Moon	Mars
F	Moon	Mars	Mercury	Jupiter	Venus	Saturn	Sun
G	Saturn	Sun	Moon	Mars	Mercury	Jupiter	Venus
H	Jupiter	Venus	Saturn	Sun	Moon	Mars	Mercury
I	Mars	Mercury	Jupiter	Venus	Saturn	Sun	Moon
J	Sun	Moon	Mars	Mercury	Jupiter	Venus	Saturn
K	Venus	Saturn	Sun	Moon	Mars	Mercury	Jupiter
L	Mercury	Jupiter	Venus	Saturn	Sun	Moon	Mars

Example: If sunset is 5:17 p.m. and sunrise is 7:54 a.m., there will be a total of 877 minutes in the night. Divide 877 by 12, and we see that each hour has 73.0633 minutes. Round to the nearest minute or figure out the seconds depending on how accurate you would like to be.

Period	Sun.	Mon.	Tues.	Wed.	Thur.	Fri.	Sat.
A	Sun	Moon	Mars	Mercury	Jupiter	Venus	Saturn
B	Venus	Saturn	Sun	Moon	Mars	Mercury	Jupiter
C	Mercury	Jupiter	Venus	Saturn	Sun	Moon	Mars
D	Moon	Mars	Mercury	Jupiter	Venus	Saturn	Sun
E	Saturn	Sun	Moon	Mars	Mercury	Jupiter	Venus
F	Jupiter	Venus	Saturn	Sun	Moon	Mars	Mercury
G	Mars	Mercury	Jupiter	Venus	Saturn	Sun	Moon
H	Sun	Moon	Mars	Mercury	Jupiter	Venus	Saturn
I	Venus	Saturn	Sun	Moon	Mars	Mercury	Jupiter
J	Mercury	Jupiter	Venus	Saturn	Sun	Moon	Mars
K	Moon	Mars	Mercury	Jupiter	Venus	Saturn	Sun
L	Saturn	Sun	Moon	Mars	Mercury	Jupiter	Venus

Planetary Hours of the Day

The planetary hours of the day are determined similar to the way the planetary hours of the night are. The exception is that the starting point is sunrise and the ending point is sunset.

Plants, Months, and the Zodiac

In my store, we sell our own line of incense and oils made with the principles that I am about to present. On the label of each product is the Zodiac sign that corresponds to the plant material and/or oils used to create that incense. While one might expect the most common question about this product line to be something in the order of, "How does one determine what scents correspond to the individual signs," that question is only the second most popular. The most popular is, "What is the sign for [insert month]." Generally, I just show the customer a reference with the dates of each Zodiac sign because the full story is entirely too long. Here is the rest of the story.

In astrology, the Zodiac is an imaginary line that resides in the heavens and encircles the Earth. The word *Zodiac* simply means "circle." This line is between 20 and 30 degrees wide (depending on the reference you choose) and is divided into 12 equal parts. That line contains the path of each of the planets recognized by the ancients (including the Sun and Moon). Each of those 12 parts was then assigned one of the 12 astrological signs found therein: Aries, Taurus, Gemini, Cancer, Leo, Virgo, Libra, Scorpio, Sagittarius, Capricorn, Aquarius, and Pisces.

Why 12? Because the great majority of calendars existing prior to the Zodiac were made up of 12 months. Why were so many calendars made up of 12 months? Because the solar year contains 12 full lunar cycles, and the calendars that incorporated both the solar year and the cycles of the moon were a compromise between the two. This is exactly what the Gregorian (modern) calendar is—a compromise.

The Gregorian calendar was instituted by Pope Gregory XIII in 1582. It does not start when the solar year starts (at the Winter Solstice), and it does not have months that are the length of the lunar cycles. Instead, the extra days were worked into some of the months, the actual cycles of the moon were ignored, and the year was started about a week after Winter Solstice. Why a week after the Winter Solstice? Well, my guess is that in the year that it was institutionalized, that is when the first new moon of the year was, and thus it provided an easy transition from the previous Roman calendar.

So what month is Capricorn? Well, depending on how you look at it, it is January, despite the fact that January starts on December 22 on the Gregorian calendar if you were to justify things by the Zodiac calendar or by the Roman calendar should the first new moon fall the day after Winter Solstice. In short, the customer who asked what many would think was a remarkably uneducated question actually hit the nail square on the head.

When it comes to the classification of plants, the Zodiac signs of herbs are established first by the ruling planet of that sign. These are called the *primary associations*. It is these primary associations that most references offer. The second way of establishing the Zodiac sign of a plant is via the Elemental association of the plant—the *secondary association*. Those plants that correspond to both the primary and secondary associations are called *distilled associations*. Note that the reference to distilled associations has nothing to do with suitability of a plant for distillation. Instead the term refers to the alchemical process of refining an association.

Capricorn, Aquarius, Pisces, Aries, Taurus, Gemini, Cancer, Leo, Virgo, Libra, Scorpio, Sagittarius: The Green World as Twelve Genders

Capricorn—First Lunar Cycle—Approx. December 22 till January 19

Names: January (common), Wolf Moon (Celtic 1), Wulf-Monat (Saxon), Gamelion (Greek 2), Januarius (Roman)

Planetary Association—Saturn

Elemental Association—Earth

Encourages practical and efficient exchange with others. This is the Zodiac sign that wants truth, facts, ambition, and pride in one's accomplishments. It is the sign that says, "I know how to play by the rules and I know how to win."

Distilled Plant Associations—Beech, Beet, Bistort, Cypress, Fumitory, Horsetails, Lobelia, Oleander, Patchouli, Quince, Yew

Primary Plant Associations—Aconite, Amaranth, Aspen (Common), Aspen (American), Beech, Beet, Belladonna, Bistort, Boneset, Buckthorn (Alder), Buckthorn (Californian), Cabbage (Skunk), Cleavers (B), Comfrey, Cypress, Dodder, Elm (Common), Elm (Slippery), Fumitory, Heartsease, Hellebore (Black), Hemlock, Henbane, Horsetails, Ivy (Common), Knotgrass, Lobelia, Marijuana, Mimosa, Morning Glory, Mullein, Oleander, Patchouli, Quince, Scullcap, Solomon's Seal, Spurges, Tamarind, Thornapple, Valerian (American), Wolf's Bane, Yew

Secondary Plant Associations—Alfalfa, Barberry (Common), Barberry (Holly-leaved), Barberry (Indian), Barberry (Nepal), Barley, Beech, Beet, Bistort, Buckwheat, Corn, Cotton, Cypress, Eggplant, Fumitory, Honeysuckle, Horsetails, Knotgrass, Loosestrife (Purple), Lucky Hand, Macadamia, Magnolia, Maple, Millet, Moss (Corsican), Moss (Cup), Moss (Hair Cap), Moss (Iceland), Moss (Spanish), Moss (Sphagnum), Mugwort, Oakmoss, Oats, Oleander, Patchouli, Pea, Peanut, Potato, Plantain (Buck's Horn), Plantain (Common), Plantain (Hoary), Plantain (Ispaghul), Plantain (Psyllium), Plantain (Ribwort), Primrose, Pumpkin, Quince, Rhubarb, Rhubarb (Monk's), Rye, Sage (White), Soy, Sorrel (Wood), Spinach, Tarragon, Vetivert, Vervain, Wheat, Yew

Aquarius —Second Lunar Cycle—Approx. January 20 till February 18

Names: February (Common), Storm Moon (Celtic 1), Mire-Monat (Saxon), Anthesterion (Greek 2), Februarius (Roman)

Planetary Association—Saturn (later Uranus)

Elemental Association—Air

Aquarius promotes free-thinking and unorthodox problem resolution. Aquarius speaks of symbiotic relationships, where freedom is ensured but responsibilities are met—the perfect society. Aquarius also promotes idealism, even when the ideals are over the top.

Distilled Plant Associations—Cleavers (B), Elm (Slippery), Morning Glory, Nettle (Greater), Nettle (Lesser), Thornapple

Primary Plant Associations—Aconite, Amaranth, Aspen (Common), Aspen (American), Beech, Beet, Belladonna, Bistort, Boneset, Buckthorn (Alder), Buckthorn (Californian), Cabbage (Skunk), Cleavers (B), Comfrey, Cypress, Dodder, Elm (Common), Elm (Slippery), Fumitory, Heartsease, Hellebore (Black), Hemlock, Henbane, Horsetails, Houseleek, Ivy (Common), Knotgrass, Lobelia, Marijuana, Mimosa, Morning Glory, Mullein, Nettle (Greater), Nettle (Lesser), Oleander, Patchouli, Quince, Sage (Vervain), Scullcap, Solomon's Seal, Spurges, Tamarind, Thornapple, Valerian (American), Wolf's Bane, Yew

Secondary Plant Associations—Acacia, Agaric Mushroom, Almond, American Bittersweet, Anise, Arabic (Gum), Ash (Mountain), Aspen (Big Tooth), Bamboo, Banyan, Benzoin, Bergamot (Orange), Bodhi, Borage, Brazil Nut, Broom, Bromeliad, Caraway, Chervil, Chicory, Citron, Cleavers (B), Clover (Red), Costmary, Dandelion, Dock (Yellow), Elecampane, Elm (Slippery), Endive, Eyebright, Fenugreek, Fern, Goldenrod, Gum Mastic, Hazelnut, Hops, Horehound (Black), Horehound (White), Kumquat, Lavender, Lemongrass, Lemon Verbena, Lily of the Valley, Lime Tree, Marjoram, Meadowsweet, Mint, Mistletoe (American), Mistletoe (European), Morning Glory, Mulberry (Common), Nettle (Greater), Nettle (Lesser), Mace, Orange (Bitter), Orange (Sweet), Oregano, Peony, Palm (Date), Papyrus, Parsley, Pecan, Pimpernel (Scarlet), Pine, Pistachio, Rice, Rue (Goat's), Sage (Clary), Sage (Common), Sage (Diviner's), Savory (Summer), Savory (Winter), Southernwood, Star Anise, Tangerine, Thornapple, Turmeric, Woody Nightshade

Pisces—Third Lunar Cycle—February 19 till March 20

Names: March (Common), Chastle Moon (Celtic 1), Hraed-Monat (Saxon), Elaphebolion (Greek 2), Martius (Roman)

Planetary Association—Jupiter (later Neptune)

Elemental Association—Water

Pisces speaks to us of the whole, of the universe, and of the needs of the whole rather than the needs of the self. Pisces promotes a view of the world from the outside, seeing the interconnectedness of all things. Instead of seeing birth, life, and death, Pisces reminds us that the three are simply parts of a cycle that repeats itself over and over again.

Distilled Plant Association—Nutmeg

Primary Plant Associations—Agrimony, Anise, Avens, Banyan, Bodhi, Borage, Chestnut (Horse), Chestnut (Sweet), Clove, Dandelion, Dock (Yellow), Eggplant, Endive, Fig (Common), Five-Finger Grass, Honeysuckle, Houseleek, Hyssop, Lime Tree, Liverwort (American), Liverwort (English), Macadamia, Maple, Meadowsweet, Millet, Nutmeg, Oakmoss, Peanut, Sage (Common), Sage (Diviner's), Sage (Vervain), Sarsaparilla, Sassafras, Silverweed, Spinach, Star Anise, Violet, Wood Betony

Secondary Plant Associations—Aconite, Adam and Eve Root, Adder's-Tongue (American), Alkanet, Aloe, Apple, Apricot, Aspen (Common), Aspen (American), Aster, Avocado, Balm of Gilead, Bachelor's Buttons, Banana, Belladonna, Birch, Blackberry, Bladderwrack, Bleeding Heart, Blueberries, Blue Flag, Boneset, Broccoli, Brussels Sprouts, Buchu, Buckthorn (Alder), Buckthorn (Californian), Burdock, Cabbage, Cabbage (Skunk), Calamus, Camellia, Camphor, Caper, Cardamom, Carob, Catnip, Cauliflower, Chamomile (Common), Chamomile (German), Chickweed, Cherry, Cherry (Wild), Cleavers (A), Coconut, Coltsfoot, Columbine, Comfrey, Cowslip, Cranberry, Crocus, Cucumber, Cyclamen (Ivy-leaved), Daffodil, Daisy (Common), Daisy (Ox-eye), Dittany of Crete, Dodder, Dulse, Elder, Elm (Common), Eucalyptus, Maidenhair (True), Feverfew, Figwort (Water), Fleabane (Common), Foxglove, Frangipani, Freesia, Gardenia, Geranium, Geranium (Rose), Ginger (White), Grapefruit, Groundsel (Common), Groundsel (Golden), Groundsel (Hoary), Groundsel (Mountain), Groundsel (Viscid), Guava, Heartsease, Heather, Hellebore (Black), Hemlock, Henbane, Hibiscus, Holly (Sea), Huckleberry, Hyacinth (Wild), Iris, Ivy (Common), Jasmine, Lady's Mantle, Lemon, Lemon Balm, Lentil, Lettuce, Lettuce (Wild), Licorice, Lilac, Lily, Lobelia, Lotus, Lotus (Sacred), Lucky Hand, Madder, Mallow (Blue), Mallow (Dwarf), Mallow (Marsh), Mallow (Musk), Marijuana, Mimosa, Mesquite, Moss (American Club), Moss (Common Club), Moss (Irish), Myrrh, Myrtle, Nectarine, Nutmeg, Orris, Palmarosa, Papaya, Passion Flower, Passion Fruit, Peach, Pear, Periwinkle, Persimmon, Plum, Plum (Wild), Poppy (White), Plantain (Sea), Plantain (Water), Purslane (Golden), Purslane (Green), Raspberry, Rose (White), Rose (Red), Rose (Damascus), Sandalwood (White), Sandalwood (Red), Scullcap, Solomon's Seal, Strawberry (Garden), Spearmint, Spikenard (American), Spikenard (Ploughman's), Spurges, Sugarcane, Sweet Potato, Tamarind, Tansy, Thyme, Tomato, Tonka, Truffles, Valerian, Valerian (American), Valerian (Indian), Vanilla, Vine, Watermelon, Willow, Wintergreen, Wolf's Bane, Wood Aloes, Yarrow

Aries—Fourth Lunar Cycle—March 21 till April 19

Names: April (Common), Seed Moon (Celtic 1), Eastre-Monat (Saxon), Mounichion (Greek 2), Aprilis (Roman)

Planetary Association—Mars

Elemental Association—Fire

Aries speaks to us of self-expression, of being the person that one is and letting the rest of the world know who that person is. Aries promotes aggressiveness, assertiveness, enthusiasm, and focus on the immediate future.

Distilled Plant Associations—Alder, Allspice, Anemone, Basil, Black Bryony, Bloodroot, Cacao, Carrot, Cattail, Cayenne, Cedar (Red), Chives, Coffee, Coriander, Cubeb, Cumin, Curry (Black), Damiana, Deerstongue, Dragon's Blood, European White Bryony, Galangal, Garlic, Gentian, Ginger, Gorse, Grains of Paradise, Hawthorn, High John the Conqueror, Holly (American), Holly (Common), Hound's-Tongue, Mahogany (Mountain), Mango, Masterwort, Mustard (Black) Mustard (Brown), Mustard (Field), Mustard (Rape), Mustard (White), Onion, Pear (Prickly), Pennyroyal, Pepper (Black), Pine (Norfolk Island), Pokeweed, Radish, Rue, Snapdragon, Sloe, Snakeroot (Black), Thistle, Thistle (Blessed), Watercress, White Bryony, Woodruff

Primary Plant Associations—Alder, Allspice, Anemone, Arbutus, Artichoke, Asafoetida, Ash (Prickly), Asparagus, Barberry (Common), Barberry (Holly-leaved), Barberry (Indian), Barberry (Nepal), Basil, Black Bryony, Bloodroot, Broom, Cacao, Carrot, Cattail, Cayenne, Cedar (Red), Chives, Coffee, Coriander, Cubeb, Cumin, Curry (Black), Damiana, Deerstongue, Dragon's Blood, European White Bryony, Galangal, Garlic, Gentain, Ginger, Gorse, Grains of Paradise, Hawthorn, High John The Conqueror, Holly (American), Holly (Common), Hops, Horseradish, Hound's-Tongue, Leek, Mahogany (Mountain), Mango, Masterwort, Mustard (Black), Mustard (Brown), Mustard (Field), Mustard (Rape), Mustard (White), Onion, Pear (Prickly), Pennyroyal, Pepper (Black), Pine (Norfolk Island), Pokeweed, Radish, Rue, Snapdragon, Sloe, Snakeroot (Black), Thistle, Thistle (Blessed), Watercress, White Bryony, Woodruff

Secondary Plant Associations—Alder, Allspice, Amaranth, Amber, Anemone, Angelica, Arbutus, Artichoke, Asafoetida, Ash, Ash (Prickly), Asparagus, Avens, Basil, Bay, Bergamot, Black Bryony, Bloodroot, Cacao, Calendula, Carnation, Carrot, Cashew, Cattail, Cayenne, Cedar, Cedar (Red), Celandine (Greater), Celery, Centaury, Chamomile (Stinking), Chestnut (Horse), Chestnut (Sweet), Chives, Chrysanthemum, Cinnamon (Chinese), Cinnamon (Common), Cloth of Gold, Clove, Coffee, Copal, Copal (Black), Coriander, Cubeb, Cumin, Curry (Black), Damiana, Deerstongue, Dill, Dragon's Blood, European White Bryony, Fennel, Fig (Common), Five-Finger Grass, Flax, Flax (Mountain), Flax (Perennial),

Frankincense, Galangal, Garlic, Gentain, Ginger, Ginseng (American), Goldenseal, Gorse, Grains of Paradise, Hawthorn, Heliotrope, High John the Conqueror, Holly (American), Holly (Common), Horseradish, Hound's-Tongue, Hyssop, Juniper, Leek, Lily (Blue Water), Lime, Liverwort (American), Liquid Amber, Lovage, Lovage (Scotch), Mahogany (Mountain), Mango, Mandrake, Mandrake (American), Masterwort, Mullein, Mustard (Black), Mustard (Brown), Mustard (Field), Mustard (Rape), Mustard (White), Nutmeg, Oak, Olive, Onion, Pear (Prickly), Pennyroyal, Pepper (Black), Pine (Norfolk Island), Pineapple, Pokeweed, Pomegranate, Radish, Rosemary, Rue, Saffron (Spanish), Sarsaparilla, Sassafras, Sesame, Silverweed, Snapdragon, Sunflower, Sloe, Snakeroot (Black), Squash, St. John's Wort, Thistle, Thistle (Blessed), Walnut, Watercress, White Bryony, Wood Betony, Woodruff

Taurus—Fifth Lunar Cycle—April 20 till May 20

Names: May (Common), Hare Moon (Celtic 1), Preo-meolc-Monat (Saxon), Thargelion (Greek 2), Maius (Roman)

Planetary Association—Venus

Elemental Association—Earth

Taurus promotes grounding, consistency, and solidification. It promotes permanent love as well as a willingness to accept sexual pleasure.

Distilled Plant Associations—Alfalfa, Buckwheat, Corn, Cyclamen, Magnolia, Mugwort, Oats, Pea, Plantain (Buck's Horn), Plantain (Common), Plantain (Hoary), Plantain (Ispaghul), Plantain (Psyllium), Plantain (Ribwort), Primrose, Rhubarb, Rhubarb (Monk's), Rye, Sage (White), Sorrel (Wood), Tarragon, Vetivert, Vervain, Wheat

Primary Plant Associations—Adam and Eve Root, Alfalfa, Alkanet, Apple, Apricot, Aster, Avocado, Balm of Gilead, Bachelor's Buttons, Banana, Barley, Birch, Blackberry, Bleeding Heart, Blueberries, Blue Flag, Buckwheat, Burdock, Caper, Cardamom, Carob, Catnip, Chamomile (Common), Chamomile (German), Cherry, Cherry (Wild), Cleavers (A), Coltsfoot, Columbine, Corn, Cowslip, Crocus, Cyclamen (Ivy-leaved), Daffodil, Daisy (Common), Daisy (Ox-eye), Dittany of Crete, Elder, Maidenhair (True), Feverfew, Figwort (Water), Fleabane (Common), Foxglove, Frangipani, Freesia, Geranium, Geranium (Rose), Ginger (White), Goldenrod, Groundsel (Common), Groundsel (Golden), Groundsel (Hoary), Groundsel (Mountain), Groundsel (Viscid), Guava, Heather, Hibiscus, Holly (Sea), Huckleberry, Hyacinth (Wild), Iris, Lady's Mantle, Licorice, Lilac, Lucky Hand, Madder, Magnolia, Millet, Mugwort, Myrtle, Nectarine, Oats, Orris, Palmarosa, Passion Flower, Pea, Peach, Pear, Periwinkle, Persimmon, Plum, Plum (Wild), Plantain (Buck's Horn), Plantain (Common), Plantain (Hoary), Plantain (Ispaghul),

Plantain (Psyllium), Plantain (Ribwort), Plantain (Sea), Plantain (Water), Primrose, Raspberry, Rhubarb, Rhubarb (Monk's), Rose (Damascus), Rye, Sage (White), Sandalwood (Red), Strawberry (Garden), Sorrel (Wood), Spearmint, Spikenard (American), Spikenard (Ploughman's), Sugarcane, Sweet Potato, Tansy, Tarragon, Thyme, Tomato, Tonka, Truffles, Valerian, Valerian (Indian), Vanilla, Vetivert, Vervain, Violet, Wheat, Wood Aloes, Yarrow

Secondary Plant Associations—Alfalfa, Barberry (Common), Barberry (Holly-leaved), Barberry (Indian), Barberry (Nepal), Barley, Beech, Beet, Bistort, Buckwheat, Corn, Cotton, Cyclamen, Cypress, Eggplant, Fumitory, Honeysuckle, Horsetails, Knotgrass, Loosestrife (Purple), Macadamia, Magnolia, Maple, Moss (Corsican), Moss (Cup), Moss (Hair Cap), Moss (Iceland), Moss (Spanish), Moss (Sphagnum), Mugwort, Oakmoss, Oats, Oleander, Patchouli, Pea, Peanut, Potato, Plantain (Buck's Horn), Plantain (Common), Plantain (Hoary), Plantain (Ispaghul), Plantain (Psyllium), Plantain (Ribwort), Primrose, Pumpkin, Quince, Rhubarb, Rhubarb (Monk's), Rye, Sage (White), Soy, Sorrel (Wood), Spinach, Tarragon, Vetivert, Vervain, Wheat, Yew

Gemini—Sixth Lunar Cycle—May 21 till June 20

Names: June (Common), Partner Moon (Celtic 1), Saer-Monat (Saxon), Skirophorion (Greek 2), Junius (Roman)

Planetary Association—Mercury

Elemental Association—Air

Gemini promotes curiosity, conceitedness, and the development of skills necessary to satisfy one's curiosity. This is the Zodiac sign of the hacker, always ready to take things apart just to see how they work. Gemini promotes rational and ordered thinking without a great deal of respect for authority.

Distilled Plant Associations—Almond, Aspen (Big Tooth), Bergamot (Orange), Brazil Nut, Caraway, Chervil, Clover (Red), Costmary, Elecampane, Fenugreek, Fern, Horehound (Black), Horehound (White), Lavender, Lemongrass, Lemon Verbena, Lily of the Valley, Marjoram, Mint, Mulberry (Common), Mace, Oregano, Papyrus, Parsley, Pecan, Pimpernel (Scarlet), Pistachio, Rue (Goat's), Sage (Clary), Savory (Summer), Savory (Winter), Southernwood, Turmeric, Woody Nightshade

Primary Plant Associations—Agaric Mushroom, Almond, American Bittersweet, Aspen (Big Tooth), Bergamot (Orange), Brazil Nut, Caraway, Celery, Chervil, Clover (Red), Costmary, Dill, Elecampane, Fenugreek, Fern, Flax, Flax (Mountain), Flax (Perennial), Horehound (Black), Horehound (White), Lavender, Lemongrass, Lemon Verbena, Lily of the Valley, Mandrake, Mandrake (American), Marjoram, Mint, Moss (Corsican), Moss (Cup), Moss (Hair Cap), Moss (Iceland), Moss (Spanish), Moss (Sphagnum), Mulberry (Common), Mace, Oregano, Papyrus,

Parsley, Pecan, Pimpernel (Scarlet), Pistachio, Pomegranate, Rue (Goat's), Sage (Clary), Savory (Summer), Savory (Winter), Southernwood, Turmeric, Woody Nightshade

Secondary Plant Associations—Acacia, Agaric Mushroom, Almond, American Bittersweet, Anise, Arabic (Gum), Ash (Mountain), Aspen (Big Tooth), Bamboo, Banyan, Benzoin, Bergamot (Orange), Bodhi, Borage, Brazil Nut, Broom, Bromeliad, Caraway, Chervil, Chicory, Citron, Cleavers (B), Clover (Red), Costmary, Dandelion, Dock (Yellow), Elecampane, Elm (Slippery), Endive, Eyebright, Fennel, Fenugreek, Fern, Goldenrod, Gum Mastic, Hazelnut, Hops, Horehound (Black), Horehound (White), Houseleek, Kumquat, Lavender, Lemongrass, Lemon Verbena, Lily of the Valley, Lime Tree, Marjoram, Meadowsweet, Mint, Mistletoe (American), Mistletoe (European), Morning Glory, Mulberry (Common), Mace, Orange (Bitter), Orange (Sweet), Oregano, Peony, Palm (Date), Papyrus, Parsley, Pecan, Pimpernel (Scarlet), Pine, Pistachio, Rice, Rue (Goat's), Sage (Clary), Sage (Common), Sage (Diviner's), Sage (Vervain), Savory (Summer), Savory (Winter), Southernwood, Star Anise, Thornapple, Turmeric, Woody Nightshade

Cancer—Seventh Lunar Cycle—June 21 till July 22

Names: July (Common), Mead Moon (Celtic 1), Maed-Monat (Saxon), Hekatombaion (Greek 2), Quinctilis (Roman)

Planetary Association—Moon

Elemental Association—Water

Cancer is the mother sign. It encourages bonds, secure roots, and a desire to nurture those in your life. Cancer promotes emotional bonds, and concern for friends, family, and ancestors.

Distilled Plant Associations—Adder's Tongue (American), Aloe, Bladderwrack, Broccoli, Brussels Sprouts, Buchu, Cabbage, Calamus, Camellia, Camphor, Cauliflower, Chickweed, Coconut, Cranberry, Cucumber, Dulse, Eucalyptus, Gardenia, Grapefruit, Jasmine, Lemon, Lemon Balm, Lentil, Lettuce, Lettuce (Wild), Lily, Lotus, Lotus (Sacred), Mallow (Blue), Mallow (Dwarf), Mallow (Marsh), Mallow (Musk), Mesquite, Moss (American Club), Moss (Common Club), Moss (Irish), Myrrh, Papaya, Passion Flower, Passion Fruit, Poppy (White), Purslane (Golden), Purslane (Green), Rose (White), Sandalwood (White), Vine, Watermelon, Willow, Wintergreen

Primary Plant Associations—Adder's-Tongue (American), Aloe, Bladderwrack, Broccoli, Brussels Sprouts, Buchu, Cabbage, Calamus, Camellia, Camphor, Cauliflower, Chickweed, Coconut, Cotton, Cranberry, Cucumber, Dulse, Eucalyptus,

Gardenia, Grapefruit, Hellebore (Black), Jasmine, Lemon, Lemon Balm, Lentil, Lettuce, Lettuce (Wild), Lily, Loosestrife (Purple), Lotus, Lotus (Sacred), Mallow (Blue), Mallow (Dwarf), Mallow (Marsh), Mallow (Musk), Mesquite, Moss (American Club), Moss (Common Club), Moss (Irish), Myrrh, Papaya, Passion Flower, Passion Fruit, Poppy (White), Potato, Pumpkin, Purslane (Golden), Purslane (Green), Rose (White), Sandalwood (White), Soy, Vine, Violet, Watermelon, Willow, Wintergreen

Secondary Plant Associations—Aconite, Adam and Eve Root, Adder's-Tongue (American), Alkanet, Aloe, Apple, Apricot, Aspen (Common), Aspen (American), Aster, Avocado, Balm of Gilead, Bachelor's Buttons, Banana, Belladonna, Birch, Blackberry, Bladderwrack, Bleeding Heart, Blueberries, Blue Flag, Boneset, Broccoli, Brussels Sprouts, Buchu, Buckthorn (Alder), Buckthorn (Californian), Burdock, Cabbage, Cabbage (Skunk), Calamus, Camellia, Camphor, Caper, Cardamom, Carob, Catnip, Cauliflower, Chamomile (Common), Chamomile (German), Chickweed, Cherry, Cherry (Wild), Cleavers (A), Coconut, Coltsfoot, Columbine, Comfrey, Cowslip, Cranberry, Crocus, Cucumber, Cyclamen (Ivy-leaved), Daffodil, Daisy (Common), Daisy (Ox-eye), Dittany of Crete, Dodder, Dulse, Elder, Elm (Common), Eucalyptus, Maidenhair (True), Feverfew, Figwort (Water), Fleabane (Common), Foxglove, Frangipani, Freesia, Gardenia, Geranium, Geranium (Rose), Ginger (White), Grapefruit, Groundsel (Common), Groundsel (Golden), Groundsel (Hoary), Groundsel (Mountain), Groundsel (Viscid), Guava, Heartsease, Heather, Hemlock, Henbane, Hibiscus, Holly (Sea), Huckleberry, Hyacinth (Wild), Iris, Ivy (Common), Jasmine, Lady's Mantle, Lemon, Lemon Balm, Lentil, Lettuce, Lettuce (Wild), Licorice, Lilac, Lily, Lobelia, Lotus, Lotus (Sacred), Madder, Mallow (Blue), Mallow (Dwarf), Mallow (Marsh), Mallow (Musk), Marijuana, Mimosa, Mesquite, Moss (American Club), Moss (Common Club), Moss (Irish), Myrrh, Myrtle, Nectarine, Orris, Palmarosa, Papaya, Passion Flower, Passion Fruit, Peach, Pear, Periwinkle, Persimmon, Plum, Plum (Wild), Poppy (White), Plantain (Sea), Plantain (Water), Purslane (Golden), Purslane (Green), Raspberry, Rose (White), Rose (Red), Rose (Damascus), Sandalwood (White), Sandalwood (Red), Scullcap, Solomon's Seal, Strawberry (Garden), Spearmint, Spikenard (American), Spikenard (Ploughman's), Spurges, Sugarcane, Sweet Potato, Tamarind, Tansy, Thyme, Tomato, Tonka, Truffles, Valerian, Valerian (American), Valerian (Indian), Vanilla, Vine, Watermelon, Willow, Wintergreen, Wolf's Bane, Wood Aloes, Yarrow

Leo—Eighth Lunar Cycle—July 23 till August 22

Names: August (Common), Wort Moon (Celtic 1), Wyrt-Monat (Saxon), Metageitnion (Greek 2), Sextilis (Roman)

Planetary Association—Sun

Elemental Association—Fire

Leo is the proudest of all the Zodiac signs. It promotes pride, honor, self-worth, integrity, and confidence.

Distilled Plant Associations—Amber, Angelica, Ash, Bay, Bergamot, Calendula, Carnation, Cashew, Celandine (Greater), Centaury, Chamomile (Stinking), Chrysanthemum, Cinnamon (Chinese), Cinnamon (Common), Cloth of Gold, Copal, Copal (Black), Frankincense, Ginseng (American), Goldenseal, Heliotrope, Juniper, Lily (Blue Water), Lime, Liquid Amber, Lovage, Lovage (Scotch), Oak, Olive, Pineapple, Rosemary, Saffron (Spanish), Sunflower, Squash, St. John's Wort, Walnut

Primary Plant Associations—Acacia, Amber, Angelica, Arabic (Gum), Ash, Ash (Mountain), Bamboo, Bay, Benzoin, Bergamot, Bromeliad, Calendula, Carnation, Cashew, Cedar, Celandine (Greater), Centaury, Chamomile (Stinking), Chicory, Chrysanthemum, Cinnamon (Chinese), Cinnamon (Common), Citron, Cloth of Gold, Copal, Copal (Black), Eyebright, Frankincense, Ginseng (American), Goldenseal, Gum Mastic, Hawthorn, Hazelnut, Heliotrope, Juniper, Kumquat, Lily (Blue Water), Lime, Liquid Amber, Lovage, Lovage (Scotch), Mistletoe (American), Mistletoe (European), Oak, Olive, Orange (Bitter), Orange (Sweet), Peony, Palm (Date), Pineapple, Rice, Rosemary, Saffron (Spanish), Sesame, Sunflower, Squash, St. John's Wort, Tangerine, Walnut

Secondary Plant Associations—Alder, Allspice, Amaranth, Amber, Anemone, Angelica, Arbutus, Artichoke, Asafoetida, Ash, Ash (Prickly), Asparagus, Avens, Basil, Bay, Bergamot, Black Bryony, Bloodroot, Cacao, Calendula, Carnation, Carrot, Cashew, Cattail, Cayenne, Cedar, Cedar (Red), Celandine (Greater), Celery, Centaury, Chamomile (Stinking), Chestnut (Horse), Chestnut (Sweet), Chives, Chrysanthemum, Cinnamon (Chinese), Cinnamon (Common), Cloth of Gold, Clove, Coffee, Copal, Copal (Black), Coriander, Cubeb, Cumin, Curry (Black), Damiana, Deerstongue, Dill, Dock (Yellow), Dragon's Blood, European White Bryony, Fennel, Fig (Common), Five-Finger Grass, Flax, Flax (Mountain), Flax (Perennial), Frankincense, Galangal, Garlic, Gentain, Ginger, Ginseng (American), Goldenseal, Gorse, Grains of Paradise, Heliotrope, High John the Conqueror, Holly (American), Holly (Common), Horseradish, Hound's-Tongue, Hyssop, Juniper, Leek, Lily (Blue Water), Lime, Liverwort (American), Liquid Amber, Lovage, Lovage (Scotch), Mahogany (Mountain), Mango, Mandrake, Mandrake (American), Masterwort, Mullein, Mustard (Black), Mustard (Brown), Mustard (Field), Mustard (Rape), Mustard (White), Nettle (Greater), Nettle (Lesser), Nutmeg, Oak, Olive, Onion, Pear (Prickly), Pennyroyal, Pepper (Black), Pine (Norfolk Island), Pineapple, Pokeweed, Pomegranate, Radish, Rosemary, Rue, Saffron (Spanish), Sarsaparilla, Sassafras, Sesame, Silverweed, Snapdragon, Sunflower, Sloe, Snakeroot (Black), Squash, St. John's Wort, Thistle, Thistle (Blessed), Walnut, Watercress, White Bryony, Wood Betony, Woodruff

Virgo—Ninth Lunar Cycle—August 23 till September 22

Names: September (Common), Barley Moon (Celtic 1), Gust-Monat (Saxon), Boedromion (Greek 2), September (Roman)

Planetary Association—Mercury

Elemental Association—Air

Virgo is adaptation for the purpose of self-improvement. Virgo encourages one to meet responsibilities with honor and to complete one's duty.

Distilled Plant Associations—Moss (Corsican), Moss (Cup), Moss (Hair Cap), Moss (Iceland), Moss (Spanish), Moss (Sphagnum)

Primary Plant Associations—Agaric Mushroom, Almond, American Bittersweet, Aspen (Big Tooth), Bergamot (Orange), Brazil Nut, Caraway, Celery, Chervil, Clover (Red), Costmary, Dill, Elecampane, Fennel, Fenugreek, Flax, Flax (Mountain), Flax (Perennial), Horehound (Black), Horehound (White), Lavender, Lemongrass, Lemon Verbena, Lily of the Valley, Mandrake, Mandrake (American), Marjoram, Mint, Moss (Corsican), Moss (Cup), Moss (Hair Cap), Moss (Iceland), Moss (Spanish), Moss (Sphagnum), Mulberry (Common), Mace, Papyrus, Parsley, Pecan, Pimpernel (Scarlet), Pistachio, Pomegranate, Rue (Goat's), Sage (Clary), Savory (Summer), Savory (Winter), Southernwood, Turmeric, Woody Nightshade

Secondary Plant Associations—Alfalfa, Barberry (Common), Barberry (Holly-leaved), Barberry (Indian), Barberry (Nepal), Barley, Beech, Beet, Bistort, Buckwheat, Carob, Catnip, Corn, Cotton, Cypress, Eggplant, Fern, Fumitory, Honeysuckle, Horsetails, Knotgrass, Loosestrife (Purple), Macadamia, Magnolia, Maple, Millet, Moss (Corsican), Moss (Cup), Moss (Hair Cap), Moss (Iceland), Moss (Spanish), Moss (Sphagnum), Mugwort, Oakmoss, Oats, Oleander, Oregano, Patchouli, Pea, Peanut, Potato, Plantain (Buck's Horn), Plantain (Common), Plantain (Hoary), Plantain (Ispaghul), Plantain (Psyllium), Plantain (Ribwort), Primrose, Pumpkin, Quince, Rhubarb, Rhubarb (Monk's), Rye, Sage (White), Soy, Sorrel (Wood), Spinach, Tarragon, Vetivert, Vervain, Wheat, Yew

Libra—Tenth Lunar Cycle—September 23 till October 22

Names: October (Common), Blood Moon (Celtic 1), Wyne-Monat (Saxon), Puanepsion (Greek 2), October (Roman)

Planetary Association—Venus

Elemental Association—Air

Libra promotes one-to-one relationships, balance, peace, and social awareness. This is the sign of the happy marriage, where each member contributes to the whole.

Distilled Plant Associations—Goldenrod

Primary Plant Associations—Adam and Eve Root, Alfalfa, Alkanet, Apple, Apricot, Aster, Avocado, Balm of Gilead, Bachelor's Buttons, Banana, Barley, Birch, Blackberry, Bleeding Heart, Blueberries, Buckwheat, Caper, Cardamom, Carob, Catnip, Chamomile (Common), Chamomile (German), Cherry, Cherry (Wild), Cleavers (A), Coltsfoot, Columbine, Corn, Cowslip, Crocus, Cyclamen (Ivy-leaved), Daffodil, Daisy (Common), Daisy (Ox-eye), Dittany of Crete, Elder, Feverfew, Figwort (Water), Fleabane (Common), Foxglove, Frangipani, Freesia, Geranium, Geranium (Rose), Ginger (White), Goldenrod, Groundsel (Common), Groundsel (Golden), Groundsel (Hoary), Groundsel (Mountain), Groundsel (Viscid), Guava, Heather, Hibiscus, Holly (Sea), Huckleberry, Hyacinth (Wild), Iris, Lady's Mantle, Licorice, Lilac, Lucky Hand, Magnolia, Maidenhair (True), Mugwort, Myrtle, Nectarine, Oats, Orris, Palmarosa, Passion Flower, Pea, Peach, Pear, Periwinkle, Persimmon, Plum, Plum (Wild), Plantain (Buck's Horn), Plantain (Common), Plantain (Hoary), Plantain (Ispaghul), Plantain (Psyllium), Plantain (Ribwort), Plantain (Sea), Plantain (Water), Primrose, Raspberry, Rhubarb, Rhubarb (Monk's), Rye, Sage (White), Sandalwood (Red), Strawberry (Garden), Sorrel (Wood), Spearmint, Spikenard (American), Spikenard (Ploughman's), Sugarcane, Sweet Potato, Tansy, Tarragon, Thyme, Tomato, Tonka, Truffles, Valerian, Valerian (Indian), Vanilla, Vetivert, Vervain, Violet, Wheat, Wood Aloes, Yarrow

Secondary Plant Associations—Acacia, Agaric Mushroom, Almond, American Bittersweet, Anise, Arabic (Gum), Ash (Mountain), Aspen (Big Tooth), Bamboo, Banyan, Benzoin, Bergamot (Orange), Blue Flag, Bodhi, Borage, Brazil Nut, Broom, Bromeliad, Caraway, Chervil, Chicory, Citron, Cleavers (B), Clover (Red), Costmary, Dandelion, Elecampane, Elm (Slippery), Endive, Eyebright, Fenugreek, Fern, Goldenrod, Gum Mastic, Hazelnut, Hops, Horehound (Black), Horehound (White), Houseleek, Kumquat, Lavender, Lemongrass, Lemon Verbena, Lily of the Valley, Lime Tree, Madder, Marjoram, Meadowsweet, Mint, Mistletoe (American), Mistletoe (European), Morning Glory, Mulberry (Common), Mace, Orange (Bitter), Orange (Sweet), Oregano, Peony, Palm (Date), Papyrus, Parsley, Pecan, Pimpernel (Scarlet), Pine, Pistachio, Rice, Rue (Goat's), Sage (Common), Sage (Diviner's), Sage (Vervain), Savory (Summer), Savory (Winter), Southernwood, Star Anise, Tangerine, Thornapple, Turmeric, Woody Nightshade

Scorpio—Eleventh Lunar Cycle—October 23 till November 21

Names: November (Common), Snow Moon (Celtic 1), Blot-Monat (Saxon), Maimakterion (Greek 2), November (Roman)

Planetary Association—Mars (later Pluto)

Elemental Association—Water

Scorpio speaks of encouraging transformation, change, and personal improvement. It says you can break those imagined limitations and boundaries.

Distilled Plant Associations—None that I have found thus far.

Primary Plant Associations—Alder, Allspice, Anemone, Arbutus, Artichoke, Asafoetida, Ash (Prickly), Asparagus, Aspen (American), Barberry (Common), Barberry (Holly-leaved), Barberry (Indian), Barberry (Nepal), Basil, Black Bryony, Bloodroot, Broom, Cacao, Carrot, Cattail, Cayenne, Cedar (Red), Chives, Coffee, Coriander, Cubeb, Cumin, Curry (Black), Damiana, Deerstongue, Dragon's Blood, European White Bryony, Galangal, Garlic, Gentain, Ginger, Gorse, Grains of Paradise, Hawthorn, High John the Conqueror, Holly (American), Holly (Common), Hops, Horseradish, Hound's-Tongue, Leek, Mahogany (Mountain), Mango, Masterwort, Nettle (Greater), Nettle (Lesser), Onion, Pear (Prickly), Pennyroyal, Pepper (Black), Pine, Pine (Norfolk Island), Pokeweed, Radish, Rue, Snapdragon, Snakeroot (Black), Thistle, Thistle (Blessed), Violet, Watercress, White Bryony

Secondary Plant Associations—Aconite, Adam and Eve Root, Adder's-Tongue (American), Alkanet, Aloe, Apple, Apricot, Aspen (Common), Aster, Avocado, Balm of Gilead, Bachelor's Buttons, Banana, Belladonna, Birch, Blackberry, Bladderwrack, Bleeding Heart, Blueberries, Blue Flag, Boneset, Broccoli, Brussels Sprouts, Buchu, Buckthorn (Alder), Buckthorn (Californian), Burdock, Cabbage, Cabbage (Skunk), Calamus, Camellia, Camphor, Caper, Cardamom, Cauliflower, Chamomile (Common), Chamomile (German), Chickweed, Cherry, Cherry (Wild), Cleavers (A), Coconut, Coltsfoot, Columbine, Comfrey, Cowslip, Cranberry, Crocus, Cucumber, Cyclamen (Ivy-leaved), Daffodil, Daisy (Common), Daisy (Ox-eye), Dittany of Crete, Dodder, Dulse, Elder, Elm (Common), Eucalyptus, Maidenhair (True), Feverfew, Figwort (Water), Fleabane (Common), Foxglove, Frangipani, Freesia, Gardenia, Geranium, Geranium (Rose), Ginger (White), Grapefruit, Groundsel (Common), Groundsel (Golden), Groundsel (Hoary), Groundsel (Mountain), Groundsel (Viscid), Guava, Heartsease, Heather, Hellebore (Black), Hemlock, Henbane, Hibiscus, Holly (Sea), Huckleberry, Hyacinth (Wild), Iris, Ivy (Common), Jasmine, Lady's Mantle, Lemon, Lemon Balm, Lentil, Lettuce, Lettuce (Wild), Licorice, Lilac, Lily, Lobelia, Lotus, Lotus (Sacred), Lucky Hand, Madder, Mallow (Blue), Mallow (Dwarf), Mallow (Marsh), Mallow (Musk), Marijuana, Mimosa, Mesquite, Moss (American Club), Moss (Common Club), Moss (Irish), Mustard (Black), Mustard (Brown), Mustard (Field), Mustard (Rape), Mustard (White), Myrrh, Myrtle, Nectarine, Orris, Palmarosa, Papaya, Passion Flower, Passion Fruit, Peach, Pear, Periwinkle, Persimmon, Plum, Plum (Wild), Poppy (White), Plantain (Sea), Plantain (Water), Purslane (Golden), Purslane (Green), Raspberry, Rose (White), Rose (Red), Rose (Damascus), Sandalwood (White), Sandalwood (Red), Scullcap, Solomon's Seal, Strawberry (Garden), Sloe, Spearmint, Spikenard (American), Spikenard (Ploughman's), Spurges, Sugarcane, Sweet Potato,

Tamarind, Tansy, Thyme, Tomato, Tonka, Truffles, Valerian, Valerian (American), Valerian (Indian), Vanilla, Vine, Walnut, Watermelon, Willow, Wintergreen, Wolf's Bane, Wood Aloes, Woodruff, Yarrow

Sagittarius—Twelfth Lunar Cycle—November 22 till December 21

Names: December (Common), Oak Moon (Celtic 1), Yule-Monat (Saxon), Poseidon (Greek 2), December (Roman)

Planetary Association—Jupiter

Elemental Association—Fire

Sagittarius speaks to us of finding and joining our tribe. It talks of the importance of the community and one's involvement in the community. Sagittarius promotes seeing the big picture, the value of wisdom, and moving forward.

Distilled Plant Associations—Avens, Chestnut (Horse), Chestnut (Sweet), Clove, Fig (Common), Five-Finger Grass, Hyssop, Liverwort (American), Sarsaparilla, Sassafras, Wood Betony

Primary Plant Associations—Agrimony, Anise, Avens, Banyan, Bodhi, Borage, Chestnut (Horse), Chestnut (Sweet), Clove, Dandelion, Dock (Yellow), Eggplant, Endive, Fig (Common), Five-Finger Grass, Honeysuckle, Houseleek, Hyssop, Lime Tree, Liverwort (American), Liverwort (English), Macadamia, Maple, Meadowsweet, Millet, Nutmeg, Oakmoss, Peanut, Rose (Red), Sage (Common), Sage (Diviner's), Sage (Vervain), Sarsaparilla, Sassafras, Silverweed, Spinach, Star Anise, Wood Betony

Secondary Plant Associations—Alder, Allspice, Amaranth, Amber, Anemone, Angelica, Arbutus, Artichoke, Asafoetida, Ash, Ash (Prickly), Asparagus, Avens, Basil, Bay, Bergamot, Black Bryony, Bloodroot, Cacao, Calendula, Carnation, Carrot, Cashew, Cattail, Cayenne, Cedar, Cedar (Red), Celandine (Greater), Celery, Centaury, Chamomile (Stinking), Chestnut (Horse), Chestnut (Sweet), Chives, Chrysanthemum, Cinnamon (Chinese), Cinnamon (Common), Cloth of Gold, Clove, Coffee, Copal, Copal (Black), Coriander, Cubeb, Cumin, Curry (Black), Damiana, Deerstongue, Dill, Dragon's Blood, European White Bryony, Fennel, Fig (Common), Five Finger Grass, Flax, Flax (Mountain), Flax (Perennial), Frankincense, Galangal, Garlic, Gentain, Ginger, Ginseng (American), Goldenseal, Gorse, Grains of Paradise, Hawthorn, Heliotrope, High John the Conqueror, Holly (American), Holly (Common), Horseradish, Hound's-Tongue, Hyssop, Juniper, Leek, Lily (Blue Water), Lime, Liverwort (American), Liquid Amber, Lovage, Lovage (Scotch), Mahogany (Mountain), Mango, Mandrake, Mandrake (American), Masterwort, Mullein, Mustard (Black), Mustard (Brown), Mustard (Field), Mustard (Rape), Mustard (White), Nettle (Greater), Nettle (Lesser), Oak, Olive, Onion,

Pear (Prickly), Pennyroyal, Pepper (Black), Pine (Norfolk Island), Pineapple, Pokeweed, Pomegranate, Radish, Rosemary, Rue, Saffron (Spanish), Sarsaparilla, Sassafras, Sesame, Silverweed, Snapdragon, Sunflower, Sloe, Snakeroot (Black), Squash, St. John's Wort, Thistle, Thistle (Blessed), Watercress, White Bryony, Wood Betony, Woodruff

Chapter 9
Plants and Their Lore

This reference has taken me years to compile. It is incomplete and would be incomplete if I spent years more making it ready. There are two reasons for this. The first is the enormity of the subject matter. The second is that the available material continues to grow as any reference is written. With our understanding of DNA, many plants are being categorized differently and given new Latin names. The old system of classifying a plant based on its look is being replaced with a system of classification based on its genetic code. While the new system is far better, the transition has created great confusion.

If one were to purchase an herb in a botanical or other herb supplier, chances are one would be best to ask for that plant by its common name as listed here, but to cross-reference by its traditional Latin name. This is because most herb suppliers use those same botanical references that have been around for as long as hundreds of years. If, however, one were to purchase the living plant at a greenhouse or nursery, that common name might be one of the other several that I have listed. This is because that thing which we call a *common name* is only common in a cultural context. But even if you identify the right common name, there will be a chance the plant's Latin name will have changed by the time you have read this book.

For these and other reasons, you should not use any of the herbs listed here without checking with your doctor or other learned medical practitioner. This material is presented for educational purposes only. Only the most severe warnings have been listed. So please, double-check any information here with a medical professional before using.

Key

ATTENTION! The symbol (☠) preceding an entry denotes a POISONOUS plant.

☠**Common Name**—*Latin Name*—Gender, Planet, Element.

Also known as (list of other names that may refer to the entry).

See also (any other plants that are indicated for cross-reference).

WARNING: Any applicable warnings.

ASTROLOGICAL: *Primary*: (signs associated with the plant); *Secondary*: (other signs associated).

GODS: List of gods associated with the plant.

GODDESSES: List of goddesses associated with the plant.

MEDICAL: Classification (for example, Diuretic, Sedative, or Antibiotic).

PARTS USED: Specific parts used in medical applications.

   Any notes or instructions follow.

MAGICKAL: Details the plant's magickal application.

GENERAL: Lore, notes, and suggestions for use.

NOTE: Any notable information.

Aaron's Rod—*See* Mullein

Abscess Root—*Polemonium reptans*
Also known as American Greek Valerian, Bluebells, False Jacob's Ladder, Sweatroot
MEDICAL: Astringent, Alterative, Diaphoretic, Expectorant. The active ingredients of this root are alcohol soluble. Contrary to instructions provided in the procedure section, whiskey is the alcohol of choice to make a tincture of this root.
PARTS USED: Roots

Absinthe—*See* Wormwood

Acacia—*Acacia Senega* —Masculine, Sun, Air
See also Gum Arabic
Also known as Cap Gum, Egyptian Thorn, Gum Arabic, Kikwata, Mkwatia, Mgunga, and Mokala
ASTROLOGICAL: *Primary*: Leo; *Secondary*: Aquarius, Gemini, Libra
GODS: Adonis, Amun Ra, The Buddha, Apollo, Krishna, Osiris, Ra, Vishnu, Babalu Aye
GODDESSES: Astarte, Diana, Ishtar
MAGICKAL: In the Middle and Far East, the wood of the Acacia plant is used to build temples and sacred sites as it is believed that structures built of its wood offer protection

against far more than the weather. Most readers are not fortunate enough to have access to large amounts of Acacia wood. When ordering herbs, if you ask for whole Acacia, you will usually receive enough twigs to braid small charms. These simple charms are worn for protection. When given as gifts, they promote friendship and kindred love. Acacia flowers can be powdered and mixed with equal amounts of Sandalwood. When burned, this mixture may stimulate areas of the brain responsible for psychic abilities.

GENERAL: Acacia flowers attract bugs rapidly. Always store in an absolutely sealed container, but don't be surprised if insects seem to spawn spontaneously. Chances are that no matter how thoroughly the plant material is cleaned, it will include near-microscopic insect larvae.

Acanthopanax—*Cortex Acanthopanacis Radicis*—Masculine

Also known as Wu jia pi

MEDICAL: A decoction of 5 to 8 grams of the bark taken once a day will strengthen and speed the healing of bones and tendons.

PART USED: Bark

Aceca Nut—*See* Betel Nut

Achi Uea—*See* Yarrow

Achyranthes—*Radix Achyranthis identatae*

Also known as Niu Xi

MEDICAL: Emmenagogue. A decoction of 8 to 10 grams of the root increases menstrual flow and decreases cramps associated with menstruation. Decreases lower back muscle pain. To be used once a day for no more than one week.

PART USED: Root

☠**Aconite**—*Aconitum napellus*—Feminine, Saturn, Water

Also known as Auld Wife's Huid, Blue Rocket, and Friar's Cap

ASTROLOGICAL: *Primary*: Aquarius, Capricorn; *Secondary*: Cancer, Pisces, Scorpio

GODDESSES: Hecate, Medea

MEDICAL: Anodyne, Diaphoretic, Diuretic. The active chemicals in Aconite are alcohol soluble. Thus, it is typically prepared in a tincture. This plant has been used for a range of medical complaints from the stopping of the heart to tonsillitis. However, today it is best avoided due to its tremendously poisonous nature.

MAGICKAL: Aconite has been known and used as a poison for thousands of years. Per Greek lore, Hecate created it from the foam of Cerberus. Aconite is one of the ingredients often found in traditional flying ointments. However, it is entirely too dangerous to use. How dangerous? It has also been extracted and concentrated for use in making poison arrows and darts. Aconite is still used to charge and bless the athame and tools used in protection. However, such practices can be very hazardous.

Acrid Lettuce—*See* Lettuce, Wild

Actaea—*See* Cohosh, Black

☠**Adam and Eve Root**—*Orchis spp.*—Feminine, Venus, Water

Also known as Lover's Root and Come-to-Me Root

ASTROLOGICAL: *Primary:* Libra, Taurus; *Secondary*: Cancer, Pisces, Scorpio

GODDESSES: Ochun, Venus, Vesta

MAGICKAL: Adam and Eve Root is said to promote romantic love and to ensure fidelity between a loving couple. It has sometimes been used as a protection talisman for the marital home or bed. Although the plant is generally considered to have feminine properties, the root comes in two varieties: male and female. Determining which is which is not difficult as they are most often sold in pairs (one male and one female), and one look at the two is enough to understand why. The male root has convex veins and the female has concave veins. Traditionally, a single male and female root are sewn into a pink sachet and given as a gift to each member of a relationship to ensure the love, fidelity, and happiness of the couple. However, if the couple is of the same sex or the partnership includes more than two, there is no reason the combination of roots should not match the combination of genders in the relationship being blessed.

GENERAL: Although originally separate roots, today the name Adam and Eve Root is used to refer to a wide variety of roots that cross with Lucky Hand Root. It seems that in today's marketplace, the difference between Adam and Eve Root and Lucky Hand Root is based only on the look of the root. Due to the tremendous number of citations in which they share Latin names, it is impossible to separate the two.

Adam's Flannel—*See* Mullein

Adder's Eyes—*See* Pimpernel, Scarlet

Adder's Mouth—*See* Adder's Tongue and Chickweed

Adder's-Tongue, American—*Erythronium americanum*—Feminine, Moon, Water
Also known as Adder's-Mouth, Dog Tooth Violet, Serpent's-tongue, and Yellow Snowdrop

Adder's-Tongue

ASTROLOGICAL: *Primary*: Cancer; *Secondary:* Cancer, Pisces, Scorpio

GODS: Adonis, Attis

GODDESS: Ceres

MEDICAL: Emetic. Taken internally, Adder's-Tongue will cause vomiting.

PART USED: Leaves

MAGICKAL: Lore tells us that Adder's-Tongue will draw even the poison of a viper's bite from the body. Adder's-Tongue is most often used in poultices. The herb is soaked in cold water and then applied to bruises and superficial scratches. When the poultice is discarded, it is widely believed that pain and infection will be discarded with it.

GENERAL: Should you find yourself to have indeed been bitten by a viper, please ignore this reference and go straight to the emergency room.

Note: You might also be looking for English Adder's-Tongue (*Ophioglossum vulgatum*) listed in this reference with the other ferns (see Fern).

Adder's Tongue, English—*See* Fern

Adelfa—*See* Oleander

Adonis—*See* Hellebore, False

Aaron's Rod—*See* Goldenrod

African Ginger—See Ginger

African Pepper—See Cayenne and Grains of Paradise

☠**Agaric Mushroom**—*Amanita muscaria*—Masculine, Mercury, Air
Also known as Asumer, Amrita, Bolong Gomba, Bug Agaric, Death Angel, Death Cap, Fly Agaric, Fly Fungus, Magic Mushroom*, Narren Schwamm, Pank, Pongo, Pong, Soma

ASTROLOGICAL: *Primary*: Gemini, Virgo; *Secondary:* Aquarius, Gemini, Libra

GODS: Dionysus, Soma

MEDICAL: The active ingredients in Agaric Mushroom are water soluble.

MAGICKAL: Agaric Mushroom has been used for religious purposes by the ancient Greek, early Hindu, Siberians, pre-Columbian Americans, the Sami, and the Japanese. Most often it was used for the purpose of obtaining visions and to achieve an altered state in which sexual union could be enjoyed and understood with a different mind-set. Sometimes this was achieved with a complicated recipe of sacred herbs, of which the Agaric Mushroom was included. Other times it was achieved simply by boiling the mushroom in water. The most repulsive method was by drinking the urine of other animals (including humans) that had consumed the mushroom. Many authors have put forth the idea that the active ingredients in Agaric Mushrooms were responsible for the behavior of Berserkers found in Viking lore.

Far be it from me to tell anyone not to follow their heart or any legitimate religious path, but perhaps it is best to avoid the use of this herb, because identification is difficult, determining a safe dose is next to impossible, and possession may be illegal. However, if in a place where it is legal, without children, and where everyone who might come into contact with it (or you) consents, placing the dried mushroom under one's bed is said to encourage conception.

*Note: This is not the only mushroom sold under the name "Magic Mushroom."

Aggastache—*Herba Agastachis*

Also known as Huo Xiang

Medical: Stomachache. Will settle the stomach and prevent vomiting. Also assists with headaches, fever, and diarrhea. As a tea, it sooths summer heat. The active ingredients are water soluble. 6 to 10 grams of the herb in a decoction or 15 to 30 grams fresh herb.

Magickal: Weave the twigs together and carry as an amulet against negative energy and undesired influences.

Agrimony—(*Agrimonia eupatoria/Herba Agrimoniae*)—Masculine, Jupiter, Air

Also known as Church Steeples, Cocklebur, Garclive, Philanthropos, Sticklewort, Stickwort, Umakhuthula, Ntola, Xian he cao

Astrological: *Primary*: Pisces, Sagittarius; *Secondary*: Aquarius, Gemini, Libra

Medical: Astringent, Diuretic, Tonic. Resolves diarrhea, relieves headaches, and slows bleeding. 10 to 15 grams of the herb in a decoction.

Parts used: Herb

Magickal: Agrimony has long been held to protect from all forms of attacks, including poison. In a time when such things seemed prudent, Agrimony tea and honey consumed each morning was sometimes used to protect one from attack by poison.

If it be leyd under mann's heed,
He shal sleepyn as he were deed;
He shal never drede ne wakyn
Till fro under his heed it be takyn.
　　　　—From my Book of Shadows, cited as
　　　　　　"An Old English Herbal"

Worn in a sachet around the neck or carried in the pocket, Agrimony helps protect the user. Sewn into a pillow, Agrimony aids sleep. Fill a bowl of Agrimony with white vinegar, let sit for three days, strain, and bottle. This easy mixture can be sprinkled outside the home to turn back baneful magick.

Ague Grass—*See also* Ague Root, but you might also be looking for Boneset (commonly called Agueweed) as the names are often confused.

Ague Root—*Aletris farinosa*

Also known as Ague Grass, Aletris Farinseu (French), Aloe Root, Bettie Grass, Bitter Grass, Black Root, Blazing Star, Colic Root, Crown Corn, Devil's Bit, Mehlige Aletria (German), Stargrass, Star Root, Starwort, True Unicorn Root, Unicorn Root, Aletris

Medical: Cathartic, Emetic, Narcotic (mildly). When dried, the medicinal properties of this plant are vastly decreased. Fresh root is used in the making of a tincture. A typical dose is 10 drops diluted in a glass of water.

Part used: Fresh root

Magickal: Powder the root and then sprinkle in a circular pattern around an area you seek to protect. Warm a mixture of 1 part ground Ague Root, 1 part water, and 2 parts red wine vinegar. Allow to soak for no less than three hours. The resulting mixture can be strained, bottled, and then used for returning and unhexing spells.

Agueweed—*See* Boneset, but you might also be looking for Ague Root (commonly called Ague Grass) as the names are often confused. Could also be a reference to Sassafras.

Ague Tree—*See* Sassafras

Agurk—*See* Cucumber

Ahuacotl—*See* Avocado

Ailanthus—*Cortex Ailanthi*—Feminine
Also known as Chun pi
MEDICAL: Historically used to treat diarrhea with bloody discharge. However, a better suggestion would be to visit your doctor immediately upon finding blood in your stool.

Ail Civitte—*See* Chives

Ailum—*See* Cardamom

Aipo—See Celery

Airelle—*See* Huckleberry

Ajo—*See* Garlic

Alantwurzel—*See* Elecampane

Albahaca—*See* Basil

Albizia—*Cortex Albiziae*
Also known as He Huan Pi
MEDICAL: Sedative. Used to decrease depression, anger, and sleeplessness. Sometimes prescribed to help speed the mending of bones and flesh. Daily use will speed healing of cuts and burns. A typical dose is 10 to 15 grams of the bark as a decoction.
PART USED: Bark

Alcaravea—*See* Caraway

Alder Buckthorn—*See* Buckthorn, Alder

Alehoof—*See* Ivy, Ground

Aletris—*See* Ague Root

Aletris Farinseu—*See* Ague Root

Alexanders—*See* Lovage, Black

Alfalfa—*Medicago saliva*—Feminine, Venus, Earth
Also known as Bubbalo Herb, Lucerne, Purple Medic, Jat, Qadb
ASTROLOGICAL: *Primary*: Libra, Taurus; *Secondary:* Capricorn, Taurus, Virgo
MAGICKAL: Burn Alfalfa in ritual fires and as incense during focused works for prosperity. Scatter the ashes outside your home to keep its residents from wanting for food. Alfalfa can be carried in a green sachet to encourage prosperity, especially when job hunting or when putting forth that extra effort at jobs where one is paid commission. If you own your own business, try sprinkling it on the floors at night and then thoroughly sweeping in the morning. An infusion of Alfalfa can be mixed into your mop water and then used to clean the home of properties that might prevent prosperity.

Alfalfa

Alder—*See List*—Masculine, Mars, Fire

> **Black Alder** – *Prinos verticillatus*
> MEDICAL: Antiseptic, Astringent, Cathartic
> PART USED: Fresh bark
> **Common Alder**—*Alnus glutinosa*
> MEDICAL: Astringent
> PARTS USED: Bark, leaves
> **European Alder**—*Alnus incana*
> Also known as Grey Alder
> **Italian Alder**—*Alnus cordata*
> **Tag Alder**— *Alunus serrulata*

MEDICAL: Alterative, Astringent, Emetic, Tonic
PARTS USED: Bark, Cones
ASTROLOGICAL: *Primary*: Aries, Scorpio; *Secondary:* Aries, Leo, Sagittarius
GODS: Apollo, Bran the Blessed, King Arthur, Lugh, Odin
GODDESS: Arainrhod

CELTIC TREE CALENDAR (Fearn)—March 18th thru April 14th—The fourth month of the year.

GENERAL: The bark and fruit of the Black Alder are used to cleanse the body of toxins. A warm water infusion is used to cleanse the liver. The bark of Tag Alder is used as a diuretic and assists in lowering blood pressure.

MAGICKAL: Alder wood is an excellent choice for talismans intended to protect. It was used by the ancients for both shields and weapons, and speaks to us of the decision of knowing when to attack and when to retreat.

Algaroba—*See* Carob

Al-Henna—*See* Henna

Alisanders—*See* Lovage, Black

Alismatis Rhizome—*Rhizoma Alismatis*—Feminine

Also known as Ze xie

MEDICAL: Diuretic. Used to rid the body of excess fluids. Promotes urination. It is especially useful for relief of the bloating and water retention associated with menstruation. Typical dose is 10 to 15 grams of the herb in a decoction.

PART USED: Herb

Alison—*See* Alyssum

Alkanet—*Alkanna tictoria/Lithosfermum tinctorium*—Feminine, Venus, Water

Also known as Dyer's Bugloss, Ocanet, Dyer's Alkanet

ASTROLOGICAL: *Primary*: Libra, Taurus; *Secondary:* Cancer, Pisces, Scorpio

MEDICAL: Tonic for the blood. Historically, Alkanet root was sometimes prescribed for blood and liver disorders.

PART USED: Root

MAGICKAL: Mix Alkanet with equal amounts of Sandalwood and Frankincense for simple purification incense. Grind into a powder and place in your shoes while job hunting or when attempting to acquire a raise or promotion. If you own your own business, dusting your floors at night with powdered Alkanet and then thoroughly sweeping the next morning will aid in prosperity. An infusion of Alkanet is useful in mop water for the same purpose.

GENERAL: There is some argument over the attributes of Alkanet. Generally speaking, the gender, Elemental, and secondary astrological associations are agreed upon, but the planet and primary astrological associations are argued. The provided associations are the ones that I have found to be most often cited.

Al-Khanna—*See* Henna

All-Heal—*See* Valerian

Alligator Pear—*See* Avocado

Allseed—*See* Knotgrass

Allspice—*Pimenta officinalis / Pimenta dioica*—Masculine, Mars, Fire

Also known as Basheen, Eddo, Kouroubaga, Madere

ASTROLOGICAL: *Primary*: Aries, Scorpio; *Secondary*: Aries, Leo, Sagittarius

GODS: Aeacus, Babalu Aye, Shango, Eleggua, Obatala, Ochosi, Oko, Olocun

GODDESSES: Ochun, Yemaya

MEDICAL: Carminative, Stimulant (mild)

PART USED: Fruit

MAGICKAL: Allspice is a common component of incenses for money and healing. Place a handful of dried Allspice berries in a green sachet for luck at gambling and in all matters of finance.

NOTE: Sometimes listed as Feminine, Jupiter, and Earth

Almond—*Prunus communis*—Masculine, Mercury, Air

Also known as Greek Nuts, Bitter Almond (*Amygdalus communis var. amara*), and Sweet Almond (*Amygdalus communis var. dulcis*)

ASTROLOGICAL: *Primary*: Gemini, Virgo; *Secondary:* Aquarius, Gemini, Libra

GODS: Attis, Babalu Aye, Chandra, Hermes, Jupiter, Liber Pater, Mercury, Obatala, Odin, Oko, Olocun, Ptah, Thoth, Zeus

GODDESSES: Artemis, Diana, Ochun, Yemaya

MAGICKAL: Almonds have a bit of lore that I have difficulty including while keeping a straight face. Their folk name is Greek Nuts, and they were sacred to the self-castrated Greek god Attis. Almond wood has been carved into charms to promote prosperity, wealth, and riches. Climbing an Almond tree prior to beginning a business venture is said to guarantee success. Eating and carrying Almonds pro-

Almond

motes prosperity, speeds emotional healing, and mends broken hearts. A green sachet containing Almonds makes a wonderful gift to kith and kin when moving into a new home or starting a new venture. Almond wood is an excellent choice for the crafting of wands.

Aloe—*Aloe Vera, Aloe Perriy*—Feminine, Moon, Water

Also known as Burn Plant, Medicine Plant, Saqal, Zabila

ASTROLOGICAL: *Primary*: Cancer; *Secondary*: Cancer, Pisces, Scorpio

GODS: Aeacus, Amun-Ra, Chandra, Indra, Minos, Rhadamanthus, Vulcan

GODDESS: Artemis

MEDICAL: Cathartic, Purgative (very mild). Expression of Aloe Vera will ease the pain of burns, cuts, and other skin disorders. Used internally, it acts as a mild laxative. Chop fresh Aloe Vera into chunks, add water, and let stand refrigerated overnight. The resulting tonic will act as a general tonic for the kidneys and a mild laxative. You can experiment with other herbs to add flavor, but avoid anything

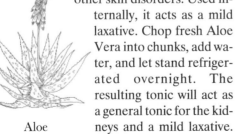

Aloe

that contains caffeine.

PART USED: Leaves

MAGICKAL: Aloe Vera has been hung over the entrance to homes and rooms to welcome good luck and to drive out forces contrary to a content home. An expression of the Aloe Vera is rubbed into the hands to bring prosperity and to improve luck at games of chance.

Aloe Root—*See* Ague Root and Aloe, might be a reference to either.

Aloe, Wood—*See* Wood Aloe

Alpinia Cardamom—*See* Cardamom

Alraun—*See* Mandrake

Alsidium Helminthocorton—*See* Moss, Corsican

Alsine media—*See* Chickweed

Alstonia—*See* Dita Tree

Alum Bloom—*See* Geranium

Alum Root—*See* Geranium

Alycompaine—*See* Elecampane

Alyssum—*Slyssum spp.*

Also known as Alison and Madwort

MAGICKAL: Simmer and allow the scent to fill the home. This will calm and aid in anger management. Alyssum is also carried in a sachet for this same purpose. If you can remember this sachet before you respond to impulses of anger, it will help greatly.

Amantilla—See Valerian

Amaranth—*Amaranthus hypochondriacus*—Feminine, Saturn, Fire

Also known as Flower of Immortality, Huauhtli, Love-Lies-Bleeding, Red Cockscomb, Velvet Flower, Princess Flower, and Floramon

ASTROLOGICAL: *Primary:* Aquarius, Capricorn; *Secondary:* Aries, Leo, Sagittarius

GODS: Amun-Ra, Buddha, Vishnu

GODDESSES: Artemis, Athena, Nut

MAGICKAL: Dried Amaranth flowers scattered as you cast the Circle of a Samhain rite will help you to make contact with past loved ones. Carried in the pocket or in a sachet against the breast will ease a broken heart and sooth the pain of loosing a loved one.

Amaranth

Amber—*Succinum*—Masculine, Sun, Fire

Also known as Hu Po

See also Liquid Amber and St. John's Wort

ASTROLOGICAL: *Primary*: Leo; *Secondary:* Aries, Leo, Sagittarius

MEDICAL: Emmenagogue. 1.5 to 3 grams very finely ground material promotes menstruation and relaxes the mind. May be mixed as a suspension in other fluids, but generally consumed as a powder or placed in capsules.

MAGICKAL: Amber is often worn for protection. In some traditions of Wicca, it is worn as a necklace with alternating Jet beads to represent the union of our Lord (Amber) with our Lady (Jet).

NOTE: The amber that is listed here is a fossil resin from the extinct coniferous tree. It is most often listed as a gemstone in Western references. If your source material is of Western origin, chances are you are looking for Liquid Amber or St. John's Wort. If it is of Eastern origin, it is probably a reference to Amber as a fossil.

Amber Resin—*See* Liquid Amber

American Club Moss—*See* Moss, American Club

American Cranesbill Root—*See* Geranium

American Daisy—*See* Daisy, Common

American Ginseng—*See* Ginseng, American

American Greek Valerian—*See* Abscess Root

American Ground Pine—*See* Moss, American Club

American Hellebore—*See* Hellebore, Green

American Liverwort—*See* Liverwort, American

American Nightshade—*See* Poke Weed

American Sarsaparilla—*See* Sarsaparilla

American Spikenard—*See* Spikenard, American

American Spinach—*See* Pokeweed

American Valerian—*See* Valerian, American

Amerikanische scharlachbeere—*See* Pokeweed

Amomum Cardamomum—*See* Cardamom

Amyroot—*See* Dogbane

Anemone—*Anemone pulsatilla*—Masculine, Mars, Fire

Also known as Meadow Anemone, Pasque Flower, Passe Flower, Wind Flower

ASTROLOGICAL: *Primary:* Aries, Scorpio; *Secondary*: Aries, Leo, Sagittarius

GOD: Adonis

GODDESS: Venus

MAGICKAL: Planted in the four corners of a plot of land, red Anemone will lend its influence toward protecting those who call that land home. Growing Anemone around a ritual Circle will cause that Circle to be twice smiled upon by those forces that watch over the rites that take place within. The fresh flowers can be picked and worn in a green sachet to drive away spring fever and minor colds.

Anemone

Anthropomophon—*See* Mandrake

☠**American Bittersweet**—*Celastrus scandens*—Masculine, Mercury, Air

Also known as Wax Works and False Bittersweet.

ASTROLOGICAL: *Primary:* Gemini, Virgo; *Secondary*: Aquarius, Gemini, Libra

GENERAL: If you are looking for Bittersweet, then you are probably looking for European Bittersweet. This can be a costly mistake as American Bittersweet is a poisonous herb.

American Club Moss—*See* Moss, American Club

American Dittany—*See* Basil

American Everlasting—See Life Everlasting, Perl Flowered

American Ivy—*See* Ivy, American

American Mistletoe—*See* Mistletoe, American

American Saffron—*See* Saffron, Mexican

Amrita—*See* Agaric Mushroom

Anbar—*See* Jasmine

Aneton—*See* Dill

Angelica—*Angelica archangelica/Angelica atropurpurea*—Masculine, Sun, Fire

Also known as Archangel, Bingo Root, Masterwort, Garden Angelica

ASTROLOGICAL: *Primary:* Leo; *Secondary:* Aries, Leo, Sagittarius

GODS: Shango, Eleggua, Obatala, Oggun, Oko, Olocun, Babalu Aye

GODDESSES: Venus, Yemaya

MEDICAL: Carminative, Diaphoretic, Expectorant, Stimulant, Tonic. Angelica root is sometimes included in remedies for bronchial problems and some digestive issues. However,

in large doses it is toxic. Extended use may increase sensitivity to sunlight and may increase chances of skin cancer.

PARTS USED: Root, Leaves, Seeds

MAGICKAL: A warm water infusion of Angelica root can be used in bath or mop water to ward off menacing forces. To strengthen that infusion, use white wine vinegar instead of water. Carried in a green sachet, Angelica root is said to be lucky to the gambler. There is some lore that visions will occur when the leaves of the Angelica plant are smoked, but this practice is ill-advised.

Anise—*Pimpinella anisum*—Masculine, Jupiter, Air

Also known as Anneys, Aniseed, Yanisin, Sweet Cumin

ASTROLOGICAL: *Primary*: Pisces, Sagittarius; *Secondary*: Aquarius, Gemini, Libra

GODS: Babalu Aye, Shango, Eleggua, Ochosi, Oggun, Olocun, Orunla

GODDESSES: Ochun, Oya

MEDICAL: Carminative, Diuretic, Expectorant, Pectoral, Stimulant, Tonic. Anise seeds will sooth gastric problems and increase milk production in nursing women. Grind Anise seed into a powder and mix with your favorite decaffeinated coffee or tea. Serve sweetened with honey. Acts as a stimulant to the lungs, but relaxes the mind. Also acts as an expectorant, tonic, and diuretic. Simmer Anise seeds in sunflower oil for a simple asthma treatment. Alternatively, a few drops of Anise essential oil may be added to a tablespoon of honey. Either can be taken by the tablespoon as needed up to five times a day.

Anise

PART USED: Seeds

MAGICKAL: Sewn into a pillow, Anise seeds ward off unpleasant dreams and nightmares. An infusion of Anise seeds or Anise seeds mixed with bay leaves makes an excellent purification bath, especially for the lustral bath.

Powder Anise seeds and mix with your coffee grounds. A pot brewed with this mixture will greatly enhance your feeling of youthfulness throughout the day, especially if sweetened with local honey. Mix one to one with bay leaf and then use to create an infusion for adding to a purification bath. Will promote a sense of love when used in cooking.

Aniseed—*See* Anise

Anneys—*See* Anise

☠ **Apple**—*Pyrus malus*—Feminine, Venus, Water

Also known as Fruit of the Gods, Fruit of the Underworld, Silver Branch, Silver Bough, Tree of Love

ASTROLOGICAL: *Primary*: Libra, Taurus; *Secondary*: Cancer, Pisces, Scorpio

GODS: Apollo, Shango (blossom), Dionysus, Olocun (blossom), Tegid, Zeus

GODDESSES: Athena, Aphrodite, Astarte, Cerridwen, Diana, Freya, Gaia, Hera, Ochun (blossom), Venus, Pomona, Nemesis, Ishtar, Olwyn, Gwen, Arwen

CELTIC TREE CALENDAR (Quert)—September 2nd thru September 29th—The tenth month of the year.

MEDICAL: Diuretic. Apples are a good diuretic and provide relief from summer heat. Eating apples will assist in sleep and serve as good treatment for diarrhea. One interesting use is to slice and dry the fruit, and make a warm water infusion with the dried fruit. Reportedly, this infusion is good for the treatment of gout.

PARTS USED: Bark, Fruit

MAGICKAL: One of the nine woods said to be best for ritual fires.

Apple

Apples are often used to decorate the Wiccan altar, especially on Samhain. Apples are considered one of the favorite foods of the dead, but consider the personal preferences of ancestors to be more important than this general suggestion. Apples are an almost universal love food. Sharing Apples as part of a romantic dinner will further the pursuits of love. Substituting hard sparkling cider for champagne is said to encourage lovemaking. Apple wood is ideal for use in making love charms, as is the dried fruit. If two amulets are made from the same branch or two slices from the same Apple are dried, the bond of love is strengthened and the romantic portion of the relationship is heightened when the amulets are worn by each member of a loving partnership. To experience purity in the act of love, let the lovers' first night be spent under an Apple tree. Better this be on their wedding night, surrounded by an encampment of family and friends who wish the couple well. If the following morning is met with mist, any child conceived of that night is said to be blessed twice by our Lord and Lady. More so than with Apricots, Apples seem to heighten sexual desire in men. They are especially useful in pursuits of women by men, but gay men have told me that they are completely useless when one man is attempting to woo another into anything other than the bedroom. The scent of the Apple flower is intoxicating. Although they do not fit well into a vase, they can be used to scent a person and home by adding the fresh flowers to a bath. Alternatively, the fresh flowers can be added to a potpourri or simmer pot, but do not use dried flowers, as they simply do not seem to work. If you want to experiment with the many Apple blossom oils on the market, please do, but do not expect good results, as everything I have found is synthetic.

NOTE: Apple seeds are poisonous.

Apple of Peru—*See* Thornapple

Appleringie—*See* Southernwood

Apricot—*Prunus armeniaca*—Feminine, Venus, Water

Also known as Apple's Partner, Umublinkosi, Xing Ren

ASTROLOGICAL: *Primary*: Libra, Taurus; *Secondary*: Cancer, Pisces, Scorpio

GODS: Shango, Oko

GODDESSES: Ochun, Venus

MEDICAL: The oil is used to smooth the skin and as a base for soap and other products.

PARTS USED: Kernels, Oil

MAGICKAL: Apricot pits carried in a pink sachet will attract love. Served with Apples and honey, Apricots will enhance a romantic evening. Add a few slices of Apricot and a bit of honey from local fields to your favorite Apple pie recipe for the perfect dessert when you want your lover to be the perfect dessert. More so than with Apples, Apricots seem to heighten sexual desire in women. They are especially useful in pursuits of women by women, but can be equally effective in helping men to woo women.

Apricot

Apricot Vine—*See* Passion Flower

Aquifolius—*See* Holly, Common

Arabic, Gum—*Acacia sengal*—Masculine, Sun, Air

See also Acacia

Also known as Arabic, Egyptian Gum, Indian Gum

ASTROLOGICAL: *Primary*: Leo; *Secondary*: Aquarius, Gemini, Libra

MAGICKAL: Gum Arabic is one of the most widely used herbs in most Wiccans' collections. Alone, it is burned on charcoal for purification and to aid in connecting with an inner sense of spirituality. However, it is also widely used as a binding agent in many incense blends.

Aralia Quinquefolia—*See* Ginseng, American

Arbutus—*Arbutus unede*—Masculine, Mars, Fire

ASTROLOGICAL: *Primary*: Aries, Scorpio; *Secondary*: Aries, Leo, Sagittarius

GODDESS: Cardea

MEDICAL: Narcotic. In large amounts, the fruit is a narcotic.

PART USED: Fruit

MAGICKAL: Arbutus can be sewn into sachets and placed out of reach in a child's room for protection. If you ever have the fortune to find Arbutus wine, you are indeed in luck. The wine is a strong aphrodisiac, but the fruit itself tastes horrible.

Archangel—A reference calling for Archangel is usually referring to Angelica or White Dead Nettle. *See also* Angelica, Nettle (White Dead), Nettle (Purple Dead), and Nettle, (Yellow Dead).

Arched Fig—*See* Banyan

Armstrong—*See* Knotgrass

Arrow Root—*See* Yarrow

Artemis Herb—*See* Mugwort

Artemisia—*See* Mugwort

Arthritica—*See* Cowslip

Artetyke—*See* Cowslip

Artichoke—*Cynara scolymus*—Masculine, Mars, Fire

ASTROLOGICAL: *Primary*: Aries, Scorpio; *Secondary*: Aries, Leo, Sagittarius

MAGICKAL: Consumed and included in meals for spiritual protection.

Artichoke

Asafoetida—*Ferula assafoetida, Ferula foetida, Ferula rurbicaulis*—Masculine, Mars, Fire

Also known as Assyfetida, Devil's Dung, Food of the Gods, Ungoozeh

ASTROLOGICAL: *Primary*: Aries, Scorpio; *Secondary*: Aries, Leo, Sagittarius

GODS: Babalu Aye, Shango, Eleggua, Ochosi, Oggun

GODDESSES: Athena, Oko, Yemaya

MEDICAL: Calmative. Typical dose is 3 grains.

PARTS USED: An extract of the root

MAGICKAL: When eaten, promotes cognitive functions. I have spoken to several people whose parents insisted they wear sachets of Asafoetida around their necks to ward off childhood illness. Chances are the foul-smelling herb also drove away many childhood friends. Asafoetida is sometimes used in exorcisms and is thrown into the censer when wanting spirits to depart quickly (along with your worldly guests). Warning: This is by far the single worst smelling herb you will ever have the misfortune of smelling. So disgusting is its stench, grown men have been known to vomit upon one sniff. Cunningham says not to feed Asafoetida to a child with colic, but I would shorten that to just, "Do not feed to a child"— or anyone else, for that matter.

Ash—*Fraxinus excelsior, Fraxinus americana*—Masculine, Sun, Fire

Also known as Nion, Asktroed, Jasen Beli, Freixo

ASTROLOGICAL: *Primary*: Leo; *Secondary*: Aries, Leo, Sagittarius

GODS: Brahma, Gwydion, Mars, Nemesis, Neptune, Odin, Poseidon, Saturn, Thor, Uranus

GODDESS: Athena

CELTIC TREE CALENDAR (Nion)—February 18th thru March 17th—The third month of the year.

MEDICAL: Astringent, Antiperiodic. Typical preparation is decoction or infusion of 1 ounce in 1 pint of water.

PARTS USED: Leaves, Bark

MAGICKAL: The strongest association one can find for the Ash is the Norse association with the World Tree, Ygdrasill. For this reason, the Ash has been associated with the working of magick for countless years. Its wood is sacred to Poseidon, and, as such, is often used in charms and spells to ensure the safe passage over water. Sleeping in a bed made of Ash wood or on a pillow with Ash leaves is said to encourage prophetic dreams, as well as visions of the past, which one might have overlooked. When given as a gift to a new couple, a besom (broom) whose staff is made of Ash is not only a great blessing, it is also a good protective talisman when hung on or over the front door. Charms made of Ash are said to keep away snakes. As a love charm, Ash leaves are often carried in the pocket to attract the opposite sex. Planting an Ash tree at each of the corners of a homestead or around ritual areas will protect that area. The Ash is referred to in the British Tree Fairy Triad, as well as the many others that have sprouted up, citing three sacred trees as Oak, Ash, and Thorn

Ash-Colored Ground Liverwort—*See* Liverwort, English

Ash, Mountain—*Sorbus acuparia*—Masculine, Sun, Air

Also known as Delight of the Eyes, Quickbane, Rain Tree, Ran Tree, Roden-Quicken, Roden-Quicken-Royan, Rowan Tree, Roynetree, Sorb Apple, Thor's Helper, Wand Wood, Whitty, Wicken-Tree, Wiggin, Wiggy, Wiky, Wild Ash, Witchbane, Witchen, Witchwood

ASTROLOGICAL: *Primary*: Leo; *Secondary*: Aquarius, Gemini, Libra

GOD: Thor

GODDESSES: Brigantia, Brigit, Virgin Mary

Ash, mountain

CELTIC TREE CALENDAR (Luis)—January 21st thru February 17th—The second month of the year.

MAGICKAL: The Mountain Ash (Rowan) is one of the nine woods cited in the Wiccan Rede as best for ritual fires. Although it is not actually a member of the Ash family, I have listed it under its folk name, Mountain Ash, because that is the name I have been most able to find it referenced in the United States. Many Wiccan traditions instruct that Mountain Ash (Rowan) is the best wood for constructing wands. It is also an ideal wood for athame handles, staffs, and walking sticks. Mountain Ash is protective when grown by the home. Hand-carved talismans of Mountain Ash are both protective and empowering, especially when carved in the shape of a hammer.

Ash, Prickly—*Xanthoxylum americanum*—Masculine, Mars, Fire

Also known as Suterberry, Toothache Tree, Yellow Wood

ASTROLOGICAL: *Primary*: Aries, Scorpio; *Secondary*: Aries, Leo, Sagittarius

MEDICAL: Stimulant

PARTS USED: Bark of root, berries

MAGICKAL: A tincture of Prickly Ash berries works as a love-drawing perfume.

Asian Marsh Pennywort—*See* Gotu Kola

Asktroed—*See* Ash

Asthma Weed—See Lobelia

Asparagus—*Asparagus officinalis*—Masculine, Mars, Fire

ASTROLOGICAL: *Primary*: Aries, Scorpio; *Secondary*: Aries, Leo, Sagittarius

MEDICAL: Diuretic, Cathartic, Laxative

PARTS USED: Herb

MAGICKAL: Increases sexual energy and stamina when consumed.

Asphodel—*See* Daffodil

Aspen, Common—*Poplus tremula*—Feminine, Saturn, Water

See also Aspen, Big Tooth or Aspen, American

ASTROLOGICAL: *Primary*: Aquarius, Capricorn; *Secondary*: Cancer, Pisces, Scorpio

GODS: Brahma, Hades, Jupiter, Pluto, Zeus

GODDESSES: Leuce, Mut, Valkyries

CELTIC TREE CALENDAR (Eadha)—Fall Equinox

Aspen, American—*Populus tremuloides*—Feminine, Saturn, Water

Also known as Aspen, Poplar, Quaking Aspen, Trembling Aspen

ASTROLOGICAL: *Primary*: Aquarius, Capricorn; *Secondary*: Cancer, Pisces, Scorpio

GODS: Brahma, Jupiter, Pluto, Zeus

GODDESSES: Leuce, Oya

CELTIC TREE CALENDAR (Eadha)—Fall Equinox

MAGICKAL: The fresh leaves of Poplar are shredded and then gently warmed with olive oil for several hours. Cool, allow to sit for one week, warm again, and strain while warm. Mix equal amounts of beeswax by volume, warm and stir; then warm until all the beeswax has melted. When this mixture cools, it can be used as a substitute for the more dangerous flying ointments.

Aspen, Big Tooth—*Populus grandidentata*—Masculine, Mercury, Air

Also known as Aspen, European Aspen, Large Tooth Aspen

ASTROLOGICAL: *Primary*: Gemini, Virgo; *Secondary*: Aquarius, Gemini, Libra

MAGICKAL: Plant the Aspen in your front yard to cause potential thieves to move on without striking.

Assaranaccara—*See* Avens

Assear—*See* Comfrey

Ass's Ear—*See* Comfrey

Ass's Foot—*See* Coltsfoot

Assyfetida—*See* Asafoetida

Aster—*Callistephus chinensis*—Feminine, Venus, Water

Also known as China Aster, Michaelmas Daisy, Starwort

ASTROLOGICAL: *Primary*: Libra, Taurus; *Secondary*: Cancer, Pisces, Scorpio

GODDESS: Venus

MAGICKAL: Aster was grown outside Greek temples as a tribute to all of the Greek (and to a lesser degree, the Roman) gods and goddesses, but especially as an honor to the goddess Venus. Plant it in your home or garden to attract love. Give thanks to the plant for its flowers, then carry the flowers to triumph in the game that love sometimes becomes. Statuary of Venus surrounded by fresh Aster flowers goes a long way towards winning a bit of divine guidance or intervention in an often troublesome or conflicted relationship.

Asumer—*See* Agaric Mushroom

Althea—*See* Mallow, Marsh

Athyrium Filix-foemina—*See* Fern

Augentrost—*See* Eyebright

Augentrosgras—*See* Chickweed

Autumn Crocus— *See* Saffron, Spanish

Ava—*See* Kava Kava

Avocado—*Persea americans*—Feminine, Venus, Water

Also known as Ahuacotl, Alligator Pear, Persea, Zaboca

ASTROLOGICAL: *Primary*: Libra, Taurus; *Secondary*: Cancer, Pisces, Scorpio

MAGICKAL: Reportedly, eating Avocado will infuse a man with lust. This, as well as the fruit shape might be why the Aztecs called it Ahuacotl, which means "testicle tree." Then again, it probably has more to do with the look of the plant. Growing an Avocado tree in your bedroom will reportedly infuse the area with a healthy desire for the act of love. Wands and

Avocado

the hilts of athames made of Avocado wood are reportedly especially powerful, which makes me wonder if the associations given might be less than perfect.

Ava Pepper—*See* Kava Kava

Ava Root—*See* Kava Kava

Avens—*Geum urbanum*—Masculine, Jupiter, Fire

Also known as Assaranaccara, Bennet, Blessed Herb, Clove Root, Colewort, Golden Star, Goldy Star, Harefoot, Herb Bennet, Minarta, Pesleporis, Star of the Earth, Way of Bennet, Yellow Avens

ASTROLOGICAL: *Primary:* Pisces, Sagittarius; *Secondary*: Aries, Leo, Sagittarius

MEDICAL: Antiseptic, Astringent, Diaphoretic, Febrifuge, Stomachic, Styptic, Tonic. A wine decoction will aid greatly in digestion.

PARTS USED: Herb, Root

MAGICKAL: Avens are worn by men to attract women. It is also worn as an amulet of protection.

Aubergine—*See* Eggplant

Auld Wife's Huid—*See* Aconite

Aunee—*See* Elecampane

Autumn Gentian—*See* Gentian

Awa Root—*See* Kava Kava

Ayron—*See* Houseleek

Ayegreen—*See* Houseleek

Baaras—*See* Mandrake

Bacove—*See* Banana

Badiana—*See* Star Anise

Bad Man's Plaything—*See* Yarrow

Bairnwort—*See* Daisy, Common

Balanoi—*See* Basil

Balessan—*See* Balm of Gilead

Balm, Lemon—*See* Lemon Balm

Balm of Gilead—*Populus balsamifera*—Feminine, Venus, Water

Also known as Balessan, Balsam Tree, Balsumodendron Gileadensis, Bechan, Poplar Buds, Mecca Balsam

ASTROLOGICAL: *Primary*: Libra, Taurus; *Secondary*: Cancer, Pisces, Scorpio

GODS: Babalu Aye, Shango, Eleggua

GODDESS: Yemaya

MEDICAL: Astringent, Diuretic, Expectorant, Stimulant. An alcohol infusion (sweet red wine is good) of the closed buds is useful in treating coughs and helping the sick to achieve a good night's sleep. In alcohol or warm water, Balm of Gilead will act as an expectorant. May also act as an aphrodisiac. A warm water infusion acts as a mild stimulant, topical astringent, and diuretic.

PARTS USED: Fruit, Buds

MAGICKAL: Balm of Gilead (usually the buds) is carried in a white sachet to mend a broken heart. When that heart is mended, take the same buds out and place them in a pink sachet to attract a new love interest—but NEVER let things turn pink before you are absolutely sure the reason for the white sachet has diminished or you will just be putting those buds into a white sachet again before long.

GENERAL: As pointed out in the introduction, many plants share common names. Balm of Gilead is often confused with Poplar and Aspen.

Balsam Tree—*See* Balm of Gilead

Balsam, White—*Gnaphalium polycephalum / Gnaphalium Obtusifolium*

Also known as Catsfoot, Fragrant Everlasting, Indian Posy, None-So-Pretty, Old Field Balsam, Silver Leaf, Sweet-Scented Life Everlasting

Balsumodendron Gileadensis—*See* Balm of Gilead

Bamboo—*Bambusa vulgaris*—Masculine, Sun, Air

Also known as Common Bamboo, Ohe, Kauayan-Kiling

ASTROLOGICAL: *Primary*: Leo; *Secondary*: Aquarius, Gemini, Libra

MAGICKAL: Bamboo shoots are eaten to enhance psychic abilities. The wood and growing plant are used for protection. Popular in feng shui, Bamboo flutes are often used to call forth positive energy and desirable spirits.

Bamboo

GENERAL: Contrary to popular belief, there are strains of Bamboo that will grow quite well in North America. If grown near your home, it is said that Bamboo will lend to the good fortune of your family. Although many folk consider ground Bamboo to be a cheap fill for powdered incense, Bamboo powder is a traditional incense for sending away both baneful magick and spirits.

Banewort—*See* Belladonna

Banilje—*See* Vanilla

Barguthi—*See* Plantain, Psyllium

Basheen—*See* Allspice

Bachelor's Buttons—*Centaurea cyanus*—Feminine, Venus, Water

Also known as Bluet, Blue Bottle, Bluebow, Blue Cap, Corn Flower, Hurtlesickle, Red Campion

See also Feverfew, which is sometimes called Bachelor's Buttons.

ASTROLOGICAL: *Primary*: Libra, Taurus; *Secondary*: Cancer, Pisces, Scorpio

GODS: Robin Goodfellow, Green Man

MEDICAL: Tonic, Stimulant, Emmenagogue. The active chemicals may be extracted by warm water infusion or decoction.

PART USED: Flowers

MAGICKAL: Just the opposite of what the name might imply at first glance, the Bachelor's Button is not worn by bachelors but is instead worn by maidens to attract the bachelor in the delicate dance of courtship where the lines between pursued and pursuer are often unclear at best.

Baie—*See* Bay

Bastard Cinnamon—*See* Cinnamon, Chinese

Brake Root—*See* Fern

Baino—*See* Lotus

Balangot—*See* Cattail

Baldmoney—*See* Gentian

Banal—*See* Broom

Banana—*Musa sapientum/Musa paradisiaca*—Feminine, Venus, Water

Also known as Maia, Bacove, Fruit Plantain, Sanging

ASTROLOGICAL: *Primary*: Libra, Taurus; *Secondary*: Cancer, Pisces, Scorpio

GOD: Kanaloa

MAGICKAL: Until 1819, the Hawaiian punishment for a woman eating certain kinds of Banana was death. Banana stalks have been used to represent both humans and gods. In the culture that developed naturally on the Hawaiian Islands, the Banana tree is thought to have similar properties as the Apple tree when it comes to marriages and the consummation of marriage. But the Hawaiian lore goes one step further to say that

Banana

the marriage will be more blessed when the ceremony is held under Banana trees. Dried chunks of Banana are a common ingredient for sachets intended to bring wealth and to cure issues of male virility. More than just for amusement, I add that they make a tasty snack. You see, chances are the Banana received its magickal properties when it was observed that their consumption increased health, and who isn't more virile or wealthy when they have good health? Warning: Lore does state that Banana should be torn and chunked (not cut), or it may have the opposite effect on a man's virility. I think this lore probably comes from the sight of seeing a knife taken to an obviously phallic-shaped food. Remember that your subconscious often picks up on messages your conscious mind does not.

Banewort—*See* Heartsease

Banwort—*See* Heartsease

Banyan—*Ficus benghalensis*—Masculine, Jupiter, Air

Also known as Arched Fig, Indian Fig Tree, Indian God Tree, Vada Tree

ASTROLOGICAL: *Primary*: Pisces, Sagittarius; *Secondary*: Aquarius, Gemini, Libra

GODS: Maui, Shu, Vishnu, Kurma

GODDESS: Diana

MAGICKAL: Like the Apple and Banana tree, lore tells us that being wed under the Banyan tree will greatly bless the union. In the Middle East, particularly among Hindus, the Banyan is planted outside of homes and temples for its blessings. Unlike the lore of the Apple and Banana tree, the Banyan is not generally cut or used in any way. Simply gazing at or planting it around the home will bring on blessings, so tempting fate by cutting it might not be a good idea.

Barbe de Capucin—*See* Chicory

Barberry, Common—*Berberis vulgaris/Berberis dumetorum*—Feminine, Mars, Earth

Also known as Berbery, Holy Thorn, Piperidge Bush

ASTROLOGICAL: *Primary*: Aries, Scorpio; *Secondary*: Capricorn, Taurus, Virgo

GENERAL: The folk name Holy Thorn comes from Italy where it is thought that the crown of thorns worn by Jesus prior to crucifixion was partly made of Common Barberry.

Barberry, Holly-leaved—*Berberis aquifolium/ Mahonia aquifolia*—Feminine, Mars, Earth

Also known as California Barberry, Oregon Grape, Oregon Grape Root, Rocky Mountain Grape, Trail Grape, Trailing Grape, Wild Oregon Grape

ASTROLOGICAL: *Primary*: Aries, Scorpio; *Secondary*: Capricorn, Taurus, Virgo

MEDICAL: Alterative, Tonic

PART USED: Root

MAGICKAL: The root of the Holly-leaved Barberry is carried in a green sachet to attract money.

Barberry, Indian—*Berberis asiatica*—Feminine, Mars, Earth

Also known as Darlahad

ASTROLOGICAL: *Primary*: Aries, Scorpio; *Secondary*: Capricorn, Taurus, Virgo

MEDICAL: Antipyretic, Antibacterial. The root and wood of the Indian Barberry is used in India to make an extract called Rusot. This extract is a powerful antimicrobial ointment, due to an abundance of the active ingredient Berberine.

PARTS USED: Root, Wood

Barberry, Nepal—*Berberis aristata*—Feminine, Mars, Earth

Also known as Ophthalmic Barberry, Darlahad

ASTROLOGICAL: *Primary*: Aries, Scorpio; *Secondary*: Capricorn, Taurus, Virgo

MEDICAL: Antibacterial, Antiperiodic, Antipyretic, Diaphoretic. Used similarly to Indian Barberry, due to its content of Berberine.

PART USED: Stems

Bardana—*See* Burdock

Barley—*Hordeum spp. vulgare*—Feminine, Venus, Earth

Also known as Malt

ASTROLOGICAL: *Primary*: Libra, Taurus; *Secondary*: Capricorn, Taurus, Virgo

GOD: Taliesin

GODDESSES: Albina, Anna Perenna

MEDICAL: A warm water infusion of barley taken on a daily basis will help arthritis pain.

PART USED: Seeds

MAGICKAL: Barley has been associated with the richness of the earth for many years.  Carried in sachets, it is believed to be a powerful agent for attracting love and improving health. Scattered outside the home or the magick Circle, it is said to keep out evil spirits. Barley is used in family cooking to increase prosperity of the household and the fertility (especially sexual fertility) of the heads of the household. It is an ideal choice for inclusion in a handfasting/wedding feast and is said to heighten male sexual performance.

Barley

Barweed—*See* Cleavers (B)

Basam—*See* Broom

Bashoush—*See* Rue

Basil—*Ocimum basilicum*—Masculine, Mars, Fire

Also known as Albahaca, American Dittany, Balanoi, Feslien, Njjlika, Our Herb, St. Joseph's Wort, Sweet Basil, Witches Herb

ASTROLOGICAL: *Primary*: Aries, Scorpio; *Secondary*: Aries, Leo, Sagittarius

GODS: Babalu Aye, Shango, Eleggua, Obatala, Ochosi, Oggun, Oko, Vishnu

GODDESSES: Erzulie, Ochun, Yemaya

MEDICAL: Anodyne, Astringent, Diuretic, Nervine

PART USED: Herb. Fresh Basil or an expression of fresh Basil can be rubbed on bee stings to decrease the pain and swelling. A warm water infusion works as a fine astringent. Basil is used in cooking to aid digestion and calm the mind. It is also a diuretic and natural laxative.

MAGICKAL: Basil is one of those herbs that has a long-standing relationship with Witchcraft. So much so that one of its common names is "Witches Herb." This probably comes, as do many modern Wiccan traditions, from Italian folklore and witchery. Basil plants make great housewarming presents, especially if you feel that everyone should have a window garden in the kitchen. If you have the opportunity to give a wedding present when fresh Basil is available, decorating

Basil

the gift box with a fresh sprig is considered a blessing. Hung over a doorway, fresh sprigs of Basil are said to calm the hearts of guests who enter your home. If you and your lover quarrel, agree to set the quarrel aside until after dinner. Then pick fresh Basil together and use it in your dinner sauce. If both of you are still quarrelsome after dinner, at least you won't go hungry, but chances are you will be less interested in fighting and more interested in making up. Lore says that men who simply cannot grow Basil will never be faithful. After showering thoroughly, but prior to making love, a woman can heighten her man's desire by rubbing her body with fresh Basil leaves. Making love after being anointed with fresh Basil is said to help ensure fidelity. Alternatively, fresh Basil may be added to a hot bath, simmered on the stove, or added to humidifiers to promote similar results (but on the body is best). Do not substitute Basil oils or extracts

for this purpose, as the effects seem to be associated with the plant in its natural state and concentration. Because Basil promotes both love and prosperity, it is commonly used in incense recipes designed to improve retail sales by increasing the good mood of your customers. Sprinkled lightly in the shoes it is said to increase the income of someone who works on commission or who is self-employed. Essential oil of Basil is diffused to calm a quarrelsome home and to both restore and maintain a sense of peace and well-being. It is sometimes used to dampen powdered incenses designed to draw wealth and money.

GENERAL: Excess use of Basil scent may cause headaches. According one source, excess inhalation will cause a scorpion to grow in a man's head. On a more serious note, essential oil of Basil should not be taken internally.

Bastard Rhubarb—*See* Rhubarb

Bastard Saffron—*See* Saffron, Mexican

Bat's Wings—*See* Holly

Bay—*Laurus nobilis*—Masculine, Sun, Fire

Also known as Baie, Bay Laurel, Bay Tree, Daphne, Grecian Laurel, Laurel, Laurier d' Apollon, Laurier Sauce, Lorbeer, Noble Laurel, Roman Laurel, Sweet Bay

WARNING: Do not serve or consume the leaf. Remove and discard before serving.

ASTROLOGICAL: *Primary*: Leo; *Secondary*: Aries, Leo, Sagittarius

GODS: Adonis, Asclepius, Apollo, Babalu Aye, The Buddha, Shango, Faunus, Eros, Cupid, Krishna, Obatala, Oggun, Olocun, Ra, Vishnu

GODDESSES: Demeter, Ceres

MEDICAL: Diaphoretic, Emetic (in large doses), Narcotic, Stomachic. Add whole Bay leaf

Bay

to cooking to help with digestion. A warm water infusion of Bay leaf will calm hysteria.

PARTS USED: Fruit, Leaves, Oil

MAGICKAL: The Bay leaf reminds us that ancient Pagan traditions are still embraced by our modern society, even when that society does not recognize the Pagan origin of our modern customs. Millions of people tune in to the broadcasts of our modern Olympics but rarely notice the symbolic use of the Bay leaf. No, we no longer follow the ancient tradition of crowning the Olympic victors with Bay leaf, but the symbolism continues on the medals. Lore tells us that chewing Bay leaves and breathing the steam rising off a simmering pot of Bay leaves aids in all forms of divination. For this reason, the dried leaves are often included in incense recipes and dream pillows. A sprig of Bay is an ideal tool for asperging (sprinkling of water), and a weak infusion of Bay is often used for asperging when one wants an extra element of purification. Planted by the home and used in family recipes, Bay is an excellent guardian against sickness and is widely believed to help with healing the common cold. A mixture of 1 part powdered Bay leaf and 3 parts Sandalwood powder produces incense that can be burned for both healing and cleansing (especially of undesired energy). Bay is said to ward off evil spirits. If a couple wants to stay together, matching charms can be made for both members of a relationship from the same twig or branch of Bay. Once a week, the couple should trade charms and remind each other why they carry the twig. In cooking, Bay enhances psychic abilities, helps battle psychic sludge, speeds healing, and promotes a sense of well-being. The scent of Bay was used by the oracles of ancient Greece. Its essential oil can be diffused to bring on relaxation and preparation for divination.

Bay Laurel—*See* Bay

Bay Tree—*See* Bay

Bear's Bed—*See* Moss, Hair Cup

Bear's Foot—*See* Lady's Mantle

Bear's Weed—*See* Yerba Santa

Beaver Poison—*See* Hemlock

Bechan—*See* Balm of Gilead

Bee Balm—*Monarda didyma*
See also Lemon Balm and Bergamot (Wild), as both of these plants share this common name. Most references to Bee Balm seem to be calling for Lemon Balm. Most references to Bergamot are looking for either Bee Balm or Wild Bergamot.

MEDICAL: Antiseptic, Sedative (mild). A warm water infusion of Bee Balm leaves and stems acts as an antiseptic. Used internally, it makes for a mild sleeping aid.

Bee Nettle—*See* Nettle, White Dead

Bee Pollen

MEDICAL: Tonic. Bee Pollen improves the respiratory system. If you are fortunate enough to find Bee Pollen that has been collected locally, it may help with allergies when you consume 1 teaspoon every morning. Bee Pollen is an excellent tonic for vegetarians and anemics. One tablespoon a day will do.

Beech—*See List*—Feminine, Saturn, Earth

> **Common Beech**—*Fagus sylvatica*
> MEDICAL: Antiseptic, Expectorant, Stimulant
> PARTS USED: Oil of nuts
>
> **American Beech**—*Fagus grandifoila*
> Also known as Bok, Boke, Buche, Buk, Buke, Dreamer's Tree, Faggio, Fagos, Faya, Haya, Hetre
> WARNING: Large amounts of the nut can be dangerous.

ASTROLOGICAL: *Primary*: Aquarius, Capricorn; *Secondary*: Capricorn, Taurus, Virgo

GODS: Cronus, Hermes, Mercury, Odin, Thoth

Celtic Tree Calendar (Phagos)—The whole of the year.

MAGICKAL: Beech is the artist's tree. A branch of Beech on an altar or easel will greatly increase you creativity, as will the Beechnut in small quantities.

Beechwheat—*See* Buckwheat

Beer Flower—*See* Hops

Beet—*Beta vulgaris*—Feminine, Saturn, Earth
Also known as Mangel, Mangold
ASTROLOGICAL: *Primary*: Aquarius, Capricorn; *Secondary*: Capricorn, Taurus, Virgo
MEDICAL: To reduce the pain of a sore and scratchy throat, gargle for one minute with beet juice.
PARTS USED: Leaves, Root
MAGICKAL: If a love spell calls for blood that does not depart the body naturally or accidentally, substitute beet juice. A single beet shared by two people is said to cause those two to fall in love.

Beggar's Buttons—*See* Burdock

Beggar's Blanket—*See* Mullein

Beggar's Stalks—*See* Mullein

Beggarweed—*See* Dodder

Beggary—*See* Fumitory

Beithe—*See* Birch

Belladonna—*Atropa belladonna*—Feminine, Saturn, Water
Also known as Banewort, Black Cherry, Deadly Nightshade, Death's Herb, Devil's Cherries, Divale, Dwale, Dwaleberry, Dwayberry, Fair Lady, Great Morel, Nightly Man's Cherries, Sorcerer's Berry, Witch's Berry
ASTROLOGICAL: *Primary*: Aquarius, Capricorn; *Secondary*: Cancer, Pisces, Scorpio
GODDESSES: Athena, Bellona, Circe, Hecate, Saturn

MEDICAL: Antispasmodic, Diuretic, Mydriatic, Narcotic, Sedative. Due to its content of atropine, Belladonna has been used in medicine for centuries. However, the difference between a dose that will bring on sleep and a dose that will cause death is hard to determine due to the variance in the concentration of active ingredients.
PARTS USED: Leaves, Roots, Tops
MAGICKAL: One of the common ingredients in flying ointments. Belladonna produces delirium. When combined with other herbs and a vehicle by which the chemical properties can be absorbed through the skin, one can see that so-called flying ointments were little more than topical intoxicants. Belladonna is one of the herbs that has caused bad PR for Witchcraft. So fearful was King James of the Witch that he allowed his translation of the Christian Bible to be influenced by his fears. In his translation, he ordered the Latin word for "poisoner" be replaced by the Latin word that many incorrectly translated to "witch." This is a very important point. You see, the Latin word *malefica* does not translate to the word *Witch* unless one believes the lies that a Witch is a vicious, wicked, female criminal. *Malefica* is a feminine word describing a lawbreaker who is vicious and wicked. For modern Pagan authors to continue to promote the lie that *malefica* is the Latin word for Witch is a slap in the face of every Wiccan attempting to

Belladonna

set the record straight. Reportedly, it was Belladonna that was used to poison the troops of Marcus Antonius, changing the path of the Parthian wars. But even that was a forward assault when considering the history of this herb. When Duncan was King of Scotland, invading Danes were poisoned by an infusion of Belladona mixed with liquor. Overcome by slumber brought on by the poison, they were easily slaughtered by the Scots. What makes this a particularly sneaky use of the herb? Not that it was hidden in the liquor, but the fact that the Scots acquired the poison from the Danes during a period of truce. Before even thinking about using this herb for any purpose (including ornamental), think about this: *Atropa Belladonna* in part comes from the Greek *Atropos*. According to Greek lore, Atropos is the one who held the scissors with which the thread of human life was cut. Of course, history is full of people who weren't scared by its Latin name, not to mention the common names, which include such words as death, bane, and deadly. The priests of Bellona reportedly consumed a tea of Belladonna to invoke her aid. As Bellona is a Roman Goddess of war, I imagine this practice was kin to the use of Agaric by Viking Berserkers. Many old herbals offer instructions on using Belladonna to induce sleep; however, one can never be sure of the concentration of the active ingredients, so it is best avoided—as are the old herbals except for purposes of education and entertainment.

Besom—*See* Broom

Ben—*See* Benzoin

Benjamen—*See* Benzoin

Bennet—*See* Avens

Benzoin—*Styrax benzoin*—Masculine, Sun, Air
Also known as Ben, Benjamen, Gum Benzoin, Siam Benzoin, Siamese Benzoin
ASTROLOGICAL: *Primary*: Leo; *Secondary*: Aquarius, Gemini, Libra
GODS: Apep, Anubis, Ares, Hanuman, Hermes, Kephra, Loki, Mars, Odin, Osiris, Parashurama, Thoth, Vishnu
GODDESSES: Nike, Venus
MEDICAL: Antiseptic, Carminative, Diuretic, Expectorant, Stimulant. Although it has been prescribed for use internally (in greatly diluted form), this plant is best reserved for topical use

only. In a tincture, it is used topically to treat minor skin irritations.
PART USED: Resin
MAGICKAL: By itself, Benzoin is burned over charcoal for purification. It is an excellent choice for smudging a Circle. It is also used for prosperity and to increase business. Like Arabic Gum, Benzoin is used as a binding agent in many incense recipes, but its rich smell can sometimes cover the scent of lighter herbs. Essential oil of Benzoin is diffused to bring energy to the physical body and to stimulate the conscious mind. Diffuse and inhale when you need an extra bit of energy to complete a physical task or after work on Friday night when you almost have enough energy to go out with friends, but not quite enough. Inhaling it offers a safe and sane alternative to those little energy drinks, which sometimes tax the body a bit too much.

Berbery—*See* Barberry, Common

Berenjena—*See* Eggplant

Bereza—*See* Birch

Bergamot—*Citrus bergamia*—Masculine, Sun, Fire
See also Bergamot, Orange and Bergamot, Wild
ASTROLOGICAL: *Primary*: Leo; *Secondary*: Aries, Leo, Sagittarius
GOD: Shango
Essential oil of Bergamot is diffused to sooth the nerves. It is one of the most effective oils to use in the home to keep the stresses of work from affecting personal relationships.
GENERAL: The word *Bergamot* is clearly used to describe two clearly separate plants and perhaps a third. Orange Bergamot (*Mentha citrata*) and Wild Bergamot (*Monarda fistulosa*) are most certainly separate plants. However, when the word *Bergamot* is used by itself, the reference is sometimes to *Citrus bergamia* and other times to *Mentha citrata*.

I believe the confusion is simply due to poor labeling of products. Generally speaking, if a reference is simply Bergamot essential oil, then it is *Citrus bergamia* that the recipe is calling for.

Bergamot, Orange—*Mentha citrata*—Masculine, Mercury, Air

Also known as Orange Mint

ASTROLOGICAL: *Primary*: Gemini, Virgo; *Secondary*: Aquarius, Gemini, Libra

GODS: Babalu Aye, Eleggua, Oggun, Oko, Olocun

MAGICKAL: Orange Bergamot is often used in incense and oil recipes to promote the accumulation of wealth. Fresh leaves of Orange/ Mint Bergamot are added to potpourri pots and simmered over the stove to lighten the mood while promoting the sense of self-worth necessary to advance in the workplace.

Bergamot, Wild—*Monarda fistulosa*

Also known as Horsemint, Bee Balm, Monarda

MAGICKAL: Generally speaking, Wild Bergamot is associated with magickal workings to aid in organization and clarity.

Bergamot, Wild

Berke—*See* Birch

☠ **Be-Still**—*Thevetia peruviana*

Also known as Trumpet Flower, Yellow Oleander, Flor Del Peru, Lucky Bean, Lucky Nut

MAGICKAL: Unless you already have a great amount of luck, my advice is to steer clear of the Be-Still. If you already have great amounts of luck, there is no reason to have this creature around. It is absolutely beautiful and absolutely poisonous. If you absolutely must have such things, please grow it only as an ornamental and keep away from children and animals. The seed of the Be-Still is often called Lucky Bean or Lucky Seed. I first heard about the Lucky Bean from a friend who worked for a local pizza parlor. Although we aren't exactly sure how it happened, over the course of about three months, just about everyone who worked in the kitchen was replaced with immigrants from Sri Lanka. One of these kind folks explained that his necklace of "lucky beans" was what was responsible for getting him his new job making pizzas. I tell you this story because one man's good luck can sometimes be another man's bad luck. If you find a recipe that calls for Lucky Bean or Lucky Nut, do not follow it if the last step is ingestion. This plant is poisonous and should only be used as a general good luck amulet. Even then, never use it in a situation where anyone might be tempted to put it in their mouth. There is some question whether these things are even safe against the skin.

Betel Nut—*Areca catechu*

Also known as Aceca Nut, Pinang, Sirir, Supari, Ping lang

MEDICAL: Astringent, Dentifrice, Stimulant, Intoxicant, Taeniafuge. Consumed to treat tapeworms. Betel Nut is most often used in the Middle East as a mild intoxicant and aphrodisiac.

PART USED: Nut

MAGICKAL: Betel Nut is a well-known stimulant in the Middle East and South Pacific Islands. Because it both stimulates and elevates the mood, it is widely considered an aphrodisiac. One nut is the typical dose, but it is often mixed with other ingredients to create a tasty and more effective delicacy. To this day, these very intoxicating treats are available in the open-air markets of India and other countries of the Middle East.

Betony, Wood—*See* Wood Betony

Bettie Grass—*See* Ague Root

Bevilacqua—*See* Gotu Kola

Bharout—*See* Carob

Bicuiba Acu—*See* Nutmeg

Bigardarier Orange—*See* Orange, Bitter

Bindweed—*See* Morning Glory

Bindweed, Jalap—*See* High John the Conqueror

Bingo Root—*See* Angelica

Bipinella—*See* Pimpernel, Scarlet

Birch—*See List*—Feminine, Venus, Water
Also known as Beithe, Bereza, Berke, Beth, Bouleau, Lady-of-the-Woods
> **Black Birch**—*Betula lenta*
> **Downy Birch**—*Betula pubescens*
> **Silver Birch**—*Betula pendula*
> **White Birch**—*Betula alba*

ASTROLOGICAL: *Primary*: Libra, Taurus; *Secondary*: Cancer, Pisces, Scorpio

GODS: Thor, Thoth

GODDESSES: Arianrhod, Blodeuwedd, Frigga, Freya, Eostra

CELTIC TREE CALENDAR (Beth)—December 24th thru January 20th—The first month of the year.

MEDICAL: (*Betula lenta*) Febrifuge. A tea made from the leaves of the Black Birch will relieve headaches, fevers, muscle cramps, and mild arthritis.

MAGICKAL: Birch is one of the nine woods cited in the Wiccan Rede as being best for ritual fires. Planted around the home, Birch is said to win the favors of Thor and protect the home from lightning. Some evidence points to the idea that ritual besoms used Birch twigs for straw. An especially powerful besom can be made by attaching Birch twigs to the end of a shaft of Ash.

GENERAL: It just screams out, "Don't drink me in tea!" In this case, it is not due to a bad taste, but because you have not lived until you have had a tall cold glass of real Birch beer on a hot summer day. My favorite brand is probably the smallest soda company in the world, Boylan's

Original Birch Beer, which was first made in an apothecary in 1890. So why do I mention Birch beer? Is it a hint for the kind folk who bring me gifts every Witches Ball? Well, maybe. But more so because I worry that Wiccans may have fallen into the "Boil and Push" philosophy, thinking the only way to use an herb is to boil it in water or push it into a sachet. There are so many other ways to experience the wonders of plants. Wonderful ways like—well like Birch Beer, which should be consumed over ice on a hot summer day to ensure that your picnic is not plagued by storms. The aroma of simmering Birch leaves clears congestion

Birdlime Mistletoe—*See* Mistletoe, European

Bird's Foot—*See* Fenugreek

Bird's Tongue—*See* Knotgrass

Bird Pepper—*See* Cayenne

Bird's Nest—*See* Carrot

Beth—*See* Birch

Bignonia Caroba—*See* Carob

Bilberry—*See* Blueberries and Huckleberry

Bird's Eye—*See* Heartsease

Bishops' Leaves—*See* Figwort, Water

Bishopwort—*See* Wood Betony

Bisom—*See* Broom

Bistort—*Polygonum bistorta*—Feminine, Saturn, Earth
Also known as Dragonwort, Easter Giant, English Serpentary, Osterick, Passions, Patience Dock, Red Legs, Snakeweed, Sweet Dock

ASTROLOGICAL: *Primary*: Aquarius, Capricorn; *Secondary*: Capricorn, Taurus, Virgo

MEDICAL: Astringent. Helpful in the treatment of diarrhea and dysentery. The root of the Bistort is a very powerful astringent. In a poultice, it is an excellent choice to halt bleeding. A typical dose is 1 teaspoon decocted in 1 cup of water.

PART USED: Root

MAGICKAL: Bistort ground and powdered will encourage fertility when worn in a green sachet. Add an infusion of Bistort to the bath water of a gentleman friend an hour before making love. Ensure that the bath water is as cold as possible. Soak for an hour and then have fun warming him up. Repeat the bath each evening, but repeat the lovemaking only every two weeks. Don't worry, the cold baths will go a long way towards making this possible even in the most physical relationships. Bistort is occasionally used in money and wealth attracting incenses, but there are far better herbs for that. Patchouli comes to mind.

Bitter Almond—*See* Almond

Bitter Ash—*See* Quassia

Bitter Bark—*See* Dita Tree and Buckthorn, Californian

Bitter Grass—*See* Ague Root

Bitter Nightshade—*See* Woody Nightshade

Bitter Orange—*See* Orange, Bitter

Bitter-root—*See* Dogbane and Gentian

Bittersweet—*See* Woody Nightshade and American Bittersweet

Bittersweet, American—*See* American Bittersweet

Bittersweet, European—*See* Woody Nightshade

Bitter Wood—*See* Quassia

Bitterwort—*See* Gentian

Bizzon—*See* Broom

Black Alder—*See* Alder

Black Cherry—*See* Belladonna

Black-berried White Bryony—*See* European White Bryony

Blackberry—*Rubus villosus/Rubus fructicosus*—Feminine, Venus, Water

Also known as Bly, Bramble, Bramble-Kite, Bumble-Kite, Cloudberry, Dewberry, Goutberry, High Blackberry, Thimbleberry

ASTROLOGICAL: *Primary*: Libra, Taurus; *Secondary*: Cancer, Pisces, Scorpio

GOD: Lugh

GODDESS: Brigit

MEDICAL: Astringent, Tonic. A warm water infusion of the leaves will help to rid the kidneys of stones. The fruit of the Blackberry is a good treatment for diarrhea. The root has strong astringent properties.

PARTS USED: Fruit, Leaves, Root

MAGICKAL: Blackberry pies baked and served on Lughnasadh (Lugh's Night) are a great way to celebrate the harvest. No, we don't all have to actually harvest Blackberries. The pies can also be tasty symbols of other harvests that have come from hard work. Because Blackberries are sacred to both Lugh and Brigit, both patrons of arts and crafts, the Blackberry makes a wonderful snack

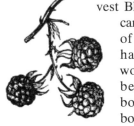

Blackberry

while working on art and craft projects. If you can bear to part with such a lovely thing, bake fresh Blackberry pies and donate them to a local shelter on or around Lugh's night for the Lord and Lady's blessings upon your craft. Eating Blackberries will bring on lust and promote prosperity.

☠**Black Bryony**—*Tamus communis*—Masculine, Mars, Fire

Also known as Blackeye Root, Briony

ASTROLOGICAL: *Primary*: Aries, Scorpio; *Secondary*: Aries, Leo, Sagittarius

MEDICAL: Diuretic, Rubefacient. Historically, a white wine infusion of this plant has been used in medical preparations. However, an overdose does not just cause death, but a very painful death. As you might imagine, it has been just about abandoned for medical use.

PART USED: Root

MAGICKAL: If you have a place in your home or business where you store cash, store also the root of the Black Bryony, but remove neither the cash nor the root for a year and a day. As the year passes, add to this pile any unexpected cash you attribute to this simple spell. On the day after the year, share your fortune with friends and it will be returned several times.

Black Cherry—*See* Cherry, Wild

Black Cohosh—*See* Cohosh, black

Black Currant—*See* Currant, Black

Black Hellebore—*See* Hellebore, Black

Black Horehound—*See* Horehound, Black

Black Jack—*See* Plantain, Ribwort

Black Maidenhair—*See* Fern

Black Nightshade—*See* Henbane

Black Pepper—*See* Pepper, Black

Black Sampson—*See* Echinacea

Black Spleenwort—*See* Fern

Blackeye Root—*See* Black Bryony

Black Dogwood—*See* Buckthorn, Alder

Black Mulberry—*See* Mulberry, Common

Black Mustard—*See* Mustard, Black

Black Plantain—*See* Plantain, Ribwort

Black Pot-Herb—*See* Lovage, Black

Black Root—*See* Ague Root

Black Snakeroot—*See* Cohosh, Black and Snakeroot, Black

Blackthorn—*See* Sloe

Black Whortles—*See* Huckleberry

Blackwort—*See* Comfrey

Bladder Fucus—*See* Bladderwrack

Bladderpod—See Lobelia

Bladderwrack—*Fucus vesiculosus*—Feminine, Moon, Water

Also known as Bladder Fucus, Cutweed, Kelp, Sea Spirit, Seawrack, Seetang, Meeriche, Sea Oak, Black Tang

ASTROLOGICAL: *Primary*: Cancer; *Secondary*: Cancer, Pisces, Scorpio

MEDICAL: Excellent food for vegetarians and as a preventative and treatment for anemia and goiters. Bladderwrack contains a large amount of iron.

PARTS USED: Root, Stem, Leaves

MAGICKAL: Carry in a blue sachet as a talisman against drowning.

Blanket Herb—*See* Mullein

Blanket Leaf—*See* Mullein

Blazing Star—*See* Ague Root

Bleaberry—*See* Huckleberry

Bleeding Heart—*Dicentra spectabilis*—Feminine, Venus, Water

ASTROLOGICAL: *Primary*: Libra, Taurus; *Secondary*: Cancer, Pisces, Scorpio

MAGICKAL: Grow the plant in your home to attract love, but plant a grounding stone (hematite comes to mind) or metal object with it. It is said that if you don't, Bleeding Heart will generate jittery energy, like static electricity for the soul.

Bleeding Heart

Blessed Herb—*See* Avens

Blind Nettle—*See* Nettle, White Dead

Blindweed—*See* Shepherd's Purse

Blood—*See* Dragon's Blood

Bloodroot—*Sanguinari canadensis*—Masculine, Mars, Fire

Also known as King Root, Red Root, Tetterwort

WARNING: Bloodroot should not be worn against the skin.

ASTROLOGICAL: *Primary*: Aries, Scorpio; *Secondary:* Aries, Leo, Sagittarius

MEDICAL: Cathartic, Emetic, Emmenagogue, Expectorant. Tends to lower blood pressure. The taste is so horrid that it may bring on vomiting. Bloodroot is best avoided for internal use.

PARTS USED: Root, Whole Plant

MAGICKAL: Acquire a supply of Bloodroots and drill a hole in each. Those with the darkest insides are the best; select the two with the darkest insides, string a red ribbon through each, and knot loosely so that they will hang loosely on a black cord or chain around your neck. This will bring potential lovers into your life. Once you have three potential suitors, no

Bloodroot

more and no less, untie the red ribbons. Restring both ribbons such that they each go through both roots. Use this to tie the two roots together, and back onto that black cord or necklace it goes. The first potential suitor that notices the change will be your best bet. For protection, the same can be done with only one root; best not to use Bloodroot for protection unless the other attribute (love) is desired. Can be used at doorways and windows to protect the home, but it is best to place it on top so children, pets, and the curious-minded will not touch.

Bloody Butcher—*See* Valerian

Bloody Fingers—*See* Foxglove

Blooming Sally—*See* Loosestrife, Purple

Blowball—*See* Dandelion

Bluebell—*Campanula rotundifolia*

Also known as Harebell and Abscess Root

See also Hyacinth, Wild

MAGICKAL: In your left palm, place freshly picked Bluebell with your palm up. Ask your lover to do the same, and then cover your lover's left palm with your right. Your lover should do the same. Look into each other's eyes, and it will be hard for either to speak anything that is not true and from the heart.

Blue Bells—See Abscess Root

Blueberry Root—See Cohosh, Blue and Blueberry

Blueberry—Feminine, Venus, Water

Potential Latin names and varieties include *Vaccinum frondosum, Vaccinum angustifolium, Vaccinum corymbosum, Vaccinum pallidum*

Also known as Bilberry

See also Huckleberry

ASTROLOGICAL: *Primary*: Libra, Taurus; *Secondary:* Cancer, Pisces, Scorpio

MEDICAL: An infusion of the leaves (*Vaccinum frondosum*) may be useful to lower blood sugar.

PART USED: Leaves

MAGICKAL: Eaten to fortify the mind against psychic attacks. Serve sprinkled with sugar or dipped in honey over stimulating conversation to further exchanges of intellect and mind.

Blue Bottle—*See* Bachelor's Buttons

Bluebow—*See* Bachelor's Buttons

Blue Buttons—*See* Periwinkle

Blue Cap—*See* Bachelor's Buttons

Blue Dots—*See* Periwinkle

Blue Cohosh—*See* Cohosh, Blue

Blue Eyes—*See* Potato

Blue Flag—*Iris versicolor*—Feminine, Venus, Water

Also known as Flag Lily, Fleur-de-Lys, Iris, Liver Lily, Poison Lily, Poison Flag, Snake Lily, Water Flag, Water Iris

ASTROLOGICAL: *Primary*: Libra, Taurus; *Secondary*: Cancer, Pisces, Scorpio

MEDICAL: Diuretic

PART USED: Root

MAGICKAL: The root of the Blue Flag is placed in cash registers and boxes to increase the income of small business owners. I have found it especially useful when conducting business at arts and crafts shows. Less so in a permanent store, but it can't hurt.

Blue Gum Tree—*See* Eucalyptus

Blue Mallow—*See* Mallow, Blue

Blue Magnolia—*See* Magnolia

Blue Mountain Tea—*See* Goldenrod

Blue Pimpernel—*See* Scullcap

Blue Rocket—*See* Aconite

Bluet—*See* Bachelor's Buttons

Blue Violet—*See* Violet

Blue Water Lily—*See* Lily, Water

Blume—*See* Dragon's Blood

Bly—*See* Blackberry

Bodhi—*Ficus religiosa*—Masculine, Jupiter, Air

Also known as Bo-Tree, Peepul Tree, Pipul, Sacred Tree

ASTROLOGICAL: *Primary*: Pisces, Sagittarius; *Secondary*: Aquarius, Gemini, Libra

GODS: The Buddha, Vishnu

MAGICKAL: Vishnu was said to have been born under the Bodhi tree, making this tree particularly sacred to Hindus. It is also said to be a favorite place for the Buddha to meditate, so its leaves are often used in meditation incenses. The Bodhi has been long associated with fertility. Lore tells us that if a couple bathes together in a cold spring each night for seven days and then makes love under the Bodhi, their chances of conception will greatly increase. Children conceived under the Bodhi are said to be granted the grace and patience of Buddha.

Bog Moss—*See* Moss, Sphagnum

Bog Onion—*See* Fern

Boilean—*See* Gotu Kola

Bok—*See* Beech

Boke—*See* Beech

Bolong Gomba—*See* Agaric Mushroom

Boneset—*Eupatorium perfoliatum*—Feminine, Saturn, Water

Also known as Agueweed, Crosswort, Feverwort, Indian Sage, Sweating Plant, Teasel, Thoroughwort, Wood Boneset

ASTROLOGICAL: *Primary*: Aquarius, Capricorn; *Secondary*: Cancer, Pisces, Scorpio

MEDICAL: Expectorant, Febrifuge, Laxative, Stimulant. A strong warm water infusion will aid in relieving flu and flu-like symptoms and help with sinus problems. Works as a great expectorant and mild muscle relaxant. In particular, it will provide relief from the general aches and pains.

PART USED: Herb

MAGICKAL: An infusion of Boneset can be used to ward off undesirable spirits and influences from the home, however there are much better herbs for this purpose. If Boneset is all you have, try making an infusion with white vinegar instead. Mix well with table salt and then sprinkle on your front porch.

NOTE: If your recipe calls for Boneset, it may be calling for *Eupatorium perfoliatum* (listed here) or it may be calling for *Symphytum officinale*, which is listed here as Comfrey because Boneset is sometimes listed as a folk name for Comfrey.

Bonewort—*See* Heartsease

Bonin—*See* Sesame

Bookoo—*See* Buchu

Borage—*Borago officinalis*—Masculine, Jupiter, Air

Also known as Bugloss, Burrage, Herb of Gladness, Star Flower, Borak, Lisan Selvi, Lesan-El-Tour

ASTROLOGICAL: *Primary*: Pisces, Sagittarius; *Secondary*: Aquarius, Gemini, Libra

MEDICAL: Astringent, Demulcent, Diuretic, Emollient, Expectorant, Nervine. A warm water infusion of Borage flowers and leaves will reportedly relieve depression. I believe this is so because it stimulates the adrenal glands, thus providing a natural mood-lifting boost of energy. It also helps to lower fevers, aids in relieving bronchitis symptoms, and acts as a mild diuretic, topical astringent, and expectorant. Relieve sore throats by gargling with a strong warm water infusion.

PARTS USED: Leaves, Flowers

MAGICKAL: Drinking warm Borage tea will encourage astral projection and psychic abilities. If you have a specific destination in mind for an astral voyage, sweeten the tea with honey from the location you wish to visit. This also seems to encourage dreams of that place. By far, the best use for Borage is in spells for courage to face an exchange with others. Dress in your best shirt and tie and wear a fresh Borage flower to overcome the fear of a job interview or while asking the person of your unspoken affection out on the first date. Also very useful for meeting your date's parents.

Borak—*See* Borage

Bo-Tree—*See* Bodhi

Bottle Brush—*See* Horsetails

Bouleau—*See* Birch

Bouncing Bess—*See* Valerian, Red-Spur

Bouncing Bet—*See* Heartsease

Bourse de Pasteur—*See* Shepherd's Purse

Bowl—*See* Myrrh

Boy's Love—*See* Southernwood

Bracken—*See* Fern

Brain Thief—*See* Mandrake

Brake Fern—*See* Fern

Bramble—*See* Blackberry

Bramble of Mount Ida—*See* Raspberry

Bramble-Kite—*See* Blackberry

Branching Everlasting—*See* Gnaphaliums

Brandy Mint—*See* Peppermint

Brank—*See* Buckwheat

Bras—*See* Rice

Braune Weiderich—*See* Loosestrife, Purple

Brazilian Cocoa—*See* Guarana

Brazil Nut—*Bertholletia exellsa*—Masculine, Mercury, Air
ASTROLOGICAL: *Primary*: Virgo, Gemini; *Secondary*: Aquarius, Gemini, Libra
MAGICKAL: Drill a hole in a whole Brazil Nut when looking for brotherly love. May work for romantic love, but there are better herbs for that. When consumed, promotes prosperity and friendship.
NOTE: Sometimes listed as Feminine, Venus, Earth.

Brazil Nut

Bread and Cheese Tree—*See* Hawthorn

Breeam—*See* Broom

Bridewort—*See* Meadowsweet

Brinjal—*See* Eggplant

Bringham Weed—*See* Ma Huang

Briony—*See* either White Bryony, Black Bryony, or European White Bryony

British Oak—*See* Oak

British Tobacco—*See* Coltsfoot

Brittanica—*See* Vervain

Broad-leaved Elm—*See* Elm, Common

Broad-leaved Plantain—*See* Plantain, Common

Broad-leaved White Sage—*See* Sage, Common

Broccoli—*Brassica spp.*—Feminine, Moon, Water
ASTROLOGICAL: *Primary*: Cancer; *Secondary*: Cancer, Pisces, Scorpio
MAGICKAL: Lends itself to spiritual protection.

☙ **Broom**—*Cytisus scoparius*—Masculine, Mars, Air
Also known as Banal, Basam, Besom, Bisom, Bizzon, Breeam, Broom Tops, Brum, Genista Green Broom, Irish Broom, Irish Tops, Link, Scotch Broom, Hog Weed
See also Gorse
ASTROLOGICAL: *Primary*: Aries, Scorpio; *Secondary*: Aquarius, Gemini, Libra
GODS: Bacchus, Mercury, Morpheus, Ochosi,
GODDESS: Blodeuwedd
CELTIC TREE CALENDAR (Ngetal)—October 28th thru November 24th— The twelfth month of the year.
MEDICAL: Cathartic, Diuretic.
PART USED: Tops
MAGICKAL: An infusion of Broom flowers can be used in mop water to drive away ghosts and undesired spirits. Lore tells us that a mild infusion will aid in divination and to see ghosts. The problem with this lore is that Broom is considered a poison, so internal use could indeed cause folks to see a ghost. Of course, I am speaking about yours. As an invitation to the East Quarter, whose Element is Air, try throwing a handful of Broom flowers in a salute. However, be ready, as this practice is said to call for the winds. To calm those winds, burn Broom and bury the ashes to ground the winds. Dried or fresh flowers can be scattered in the ritual area and then swept away by the besom. With them, the Broom flowers will take the Outsiders (those forces unwelcome in your Circle). Fresh Broom flowers are used in potpourri and simmer pots to settle the mind and encourage peace and a sense of purification. The aroma seems to carry off the nasties that come from the outside world and often cling to us as unwanted hitchhikers into our homes.

Broom Tops—*See* Broom

Bromeliad—*Crypanthus spp.*—Masculine, Sun, Air

Also known as Chameleon Star, Earth Star

ASTROLOGICAL: *Primary*: Leo; *Secondary*: Aquarius, Gemini, Libra

MAGICKAL: A beautiful plant with long, broad leaves, perfect for growing indoors. Will lend itself to protection and wealth.

Brown Mint—*See* Spearmint

Brown Mustard—*See* Mustard; Mustard, Black; and Mustard, Brown

Brownwort—*See* Figwort, Water

Bruisewort—*See* Comfrey and Daisy, Common

Brum—See Broom

Brussels Sprouts—*Brassica spp.*—Feminine, Moon, Water

ASTROLOGICAL: *Primary*: Cancer; *Secondary*: Cancer, Pisces, Scorpio

MAGICKAL: Lends itself to spiritual protection.

Bubbalo Herb—*See* Alfalfa

Buche—*See* Beech

Buchu—*Barosma betulina*—Feminine, Moon, Water

Also known as Bookoo, Bucoo, Buku, Oval Bachu, Short Buchu, Sab, Pinkaou

ASTROLOGICAL: *Primary*: Cancer; *Secondary*: Cancer, Pisces, Scorpio

MEDICAL: Stimulant, Tonic. A warm water infusion is made in a ratio of 1 ounce of leaves to 1 pint of water.

PART USED: Leaves

MAGICKAL: Drink tea made from Buchu to enhance divination. Do not sweeten nor add milk. Mix 1 part Buchu to 3 parts Frankincense to produce incense that will encourage dreams of the future. Burn in the bedroom an hour before sleep, but make sure all the coals are out before lying down or your future might be filled with flames.

Buchweizen—*See* Buckwheat

Buckeye—*See* Chestnut, Horse

Buckles—*See* Cowslip

Buckshorne—*See* Plantain, Buck's Horn

Buck's Horn Plantain—*See* Plantain, Buck's Horn

Buckthorn—*See also* Buckthorn, Alder; Buckthorn, Californian; and Buckthorn, Sea

NOTE: If you found a recipe in a magickal reference, you are probably looking for the plant listed here as Buckthorn, Alder *(Rhamnus Frangula)*. Your second best bet is Buckthorn, Californian *(Rhamnus purshianus)*. However, references that list the herb simply as Buckthorn will rarely be referring to Buckthorn, Sea *(Hippophae rhamnoides)*. This is also true of medicinal uses of the herb Buckthorn, as both Alder and Californian contain many of the same active constituents in varying amounts, but the other is an entirely different natural order.

Buckthorn, Alder—*Rhamnus Frangula*—Feminine, Saturn, Water

Also known as Black Dogwood, Frangula Bark, Hart's Thorn

ASTROLOGICAL: *Primary*: Aquarius, Capricorn; *Secondary*: Cancer, Pisces, Scorpio

MEDICAL: Cathartic, Laxative, Tonic. One ounce is decocted in 1 quart of water. Reduce volume by boiling until 1 pint of fluid remains. Strain and administer 1 tablespoon at a time.

PART USED: Bark

MAGICKAL: Alder Buckthorn can be used as a barrier against the magickal workings of others. He suggests that its branches can be placed next to doors and windows to keep those forces from one's home. Scott Cunningham tells of an old legend that states that to summon an elf, one should dance in a circle of Buckthorn until the elf appears, then say to the elf, "Halt and grant my boon!" The elf will then grant you one wish. I have not found this lore to be accurate. However, I have found the Alder Buckthorn to be particularly useful in providing that extra bit of luck that one needs in legal matters. Wear a pendent made of Alder Buckthorn and tell the truth in court, and it is said that an innocent man cannot be found guilty.

Buckthorn, Californian—*Rhamnus purshianus*—Feminine, Saturn, Water

Also known as Bitter Bark, Cascara Sagrada, Cittim Bark, Ecorce Sacree, Sacred Bark, Yellow Bark

ASTROLOGICAL: *Primary*: Aquarius, Capricorn; *Secondary*: Cancer, Pisces, Scorpio

MEDICAL: Laxative (mild), Stomachic

PART USED: Bark

MAGICKAL: An infusion of Californian Buckthorn can be lightly sprinkled on money prior to being spent to cause it to return many times over. Sprinkle on your front yard's grass the night before going to court, and then tell only the absolute truth. Lore says you will win your court case. Tell one lie, no matter how small, and you will more than likely lose worse than if you had not tried to use spellcraft to prove your case.

Buckthorn, Sea—(*Hippophae rhamnoides*)

Also known as Shallow Thorn

Buckwheat—*Fagopyrum esculentum/Polygonum fagopyrum*—Feminine, Venus, Earth

*Note: Planet is sometimes listed as Jupiter

Also known as Beechwheat, Brank, Buchweizen, French Wheat, Heidekorm, Le Blé Noir, Saracen Corn, Sarrasin

ASTROLOGICAL: *Primary*: Libra, Taurus; *Secondary*: Capricorn, Taurus, Virgo

MEDICAL: Astringent. Typically used as a warm water infusion.

PART USED: Fruit

MAGICKAL: Buckwheat has been popular to use in the casting of Circles since the casting of Circles became something you didn't want your neighbors to know about. Being very common in the kitchen, few would question its owner for having it available. It is additionally used to stave off poverty, but does not seem to aid in the acquisition of money or riches. Instead, the rewards of using buckwheat in spells seem to prevent one from going underfed or unclothed. For this purpose, it is included in meals and carried in brown sachets.

Bucoo—*See* Buchu

Bug Agaric—*See* Agaric Mushroom

Bugbane—*See* Cohosh, Black

Bugloss—*See* Borage

Buk—*See* Beech

Buke—*See* Beech

Buku—*See* Buchu

Bullock's Eye—*See* Houseleek

Bullock's Lungwort—*See* Mullein

Bull's Blood—*See* Horehound, White

Bull's Foot—*See* Coltsfoot

Bullweed—*See* Heartsease

Bumble-Kite—*See* Blackberry

Bumweed—*See* Compass Plant

Burdock—*Arctium lappa*—Feminine, Venus, Water

Also known as Bardana, Beggar's Buttons, Burrseed, Clot-Bur, Cockle Buttons, Cocklebur, Fox's Clote, Great Burdock, Happy Major, Hardock, Hurrburr, Lappa, Love Leaves, Personata, Philanthropium, Thorny Burr

ASTROLOGICAL: *Primary*: Libra, Taurus; *Secondary*: Cancer, Pisces, Scorpio

MEDICAL: Alterative, Diaphoretic, Diuretic, Tonic. A warm water infusion of seeds works as a good diuretic and helps with kidney stones. A warm water infusion of the bark is a good tonic but must be simmered for at least 30 minutes.

PARTS USED: Herb, Root, Seeds

MAGICKAL: Worn around the neck, the dried Burdock root is said to protect from all forms of undesired influences.

Burn Plant—*See* Aloe

Burrage—*See* Borage

Burrseed—*See* Burdock

Butterbur—*See* Coltsfoot

Butter Daisy—*See* Daisy, Ox-Eye

Butter Dock—*See* Dock, Round-leaved

Butter Rose—*See* Primrose

Butter Winter—*See* Pipissewa

Buttonhole—*See* Fern

Buttons—*See* Tansy

Button Snakeroot—*See* Snakeroot, Button

Buzzalchippet—*See* Dill

Bryony—*See either* White Bryony, Black Bryony, or European White Bryony

Caaroba—*See* Carob

Cabbage—*Brassica oleracea*—Feminine, Moon, Water

ASTROLOGICAL: *Primary*: Cancer; *Secondary*: Cancer, Pisces, Scorpio

MAGICKAL: When a couple moves into a home, they should plant cabbage before any other plant. Lore says this will ensure a good marriage and a good garden. Cabbage increases prosperity and lends itself well to protection.

Cabbage, Skunk—*Symplocarpus foetidus/Dracontium foetidum*—Feminine, Saturn, Water

Also known as Dracontium, Meadow Cabbage, Polecatweed, Skunkweed, Suntull, Swamp Cabbage

ASTROLOGICAL: *Primary*: Aquarius, Capricorn; *Secondary*: Cancer, Pisces, Scorpio

MAGICKAL: According to Appalachian folklore, 1 part powdered Skunk Cabbage root can be mixed with 4 parts honey and served on toast. One teaspoon was said to win court cases, but any more may make you sick.

Cacao—*Theobroma cacao*—Masculine, Mars, Fire

Also known as Cocoa, Chocolate, and Chocolate Tree

ASTROLOGICAL: *Primary*: Aries, Scorpio; *Secondary:* Aries, Leo, Sagittarius

MEDICAL: Helps to lower blood pressure by dilating blood vessels.

PART USED: Seeds

MAGICKAL: When consumed, promotes a sense of love and acts as a mild aphrodisiac in women.

Cacao

Cactus

GODS: Apep, Ares, Kephra, Typhon

MAGICKAL: Volumes of books could and have been written on our prickly little friends. Best to just briefly touch the surface. All kinds of Cacti are excellent housewarming presents as they are said to protect the home. Large Cacti spines are an excellent substitute for porcupine quills in most spells.

Calamus—*Acorus calamus*—Feminine, Moon, Water

Also known as Cinnamon Sedge, Gladdon, Myrtle Flag, Myrtle Grass, Myrtle Sedge, Sweet Cane, Sweet Flag, Sweetgrass, Sweet Rod, Sweet Rush, Sweet Sedge, Lubigan

WARNING: Potentially dangerous in large volumes.

ASTROLOGICAL: *Primary*: Cancer; *Secondary*: Cancer, Pisces, Scorpio

GODS: Babalu Aye, Eleggua, Obatala, Oko, Olocun, Orunla

GODDESSES: Ochun, Oya, Yemaya

MEDICAL: Carminative, Stimulant, Tonic

PART USED: Root

MAGICKAL: An infusion of Calamus is an excellent choice for home blessings and protection. If you have carpeted floors, just scatter the pleasant-smelling herb on the floor, leave overnight, and vacuum. This practice has been followed for centuries and has just recently been abandoned by the Norwich Cathedral, where the church once scattered Calamus root prior to festivals. Sometimes referenced as a hallucinogen, there is much confusion as to variety and dose. The powdered root is often a part of the recipe for healing incenses, but do not eat or it may have the opposite effect. Of Calamus root, *The Magical and Ritual Use of Herbs*, by Richard Alan Miller, says: "Stimulant when a dried root 2 inches long and the thickness of a pencil is eaten; a hallucinogen when over 10 inches is eaten."

Calamus

GENERAL: To list this botanical, I choose the name Calamus because in current Wiccan lore the word *Calamus* is used to refer to this botanical much more than in other fields of study where it is more often referenced as Sweet Sedge.

Calamus Draco—*See* Dragon's Blood

Calendula—*Calendula officinalis*—Masculine, Sun, Fire

Also known as Marigold

ASTROLOGICAL: *Primary*: Leo; *Secondary*: Aries, Leo, Sagittarius

GODS: Shango, Eleggua, Obatala, Oko, Orunla

MEDICAL: Astringent, Diaphoretic, Stimulant. Expression of fresh plant material will decrease the pain and speed the healing of mild cuts and scratches. A poultice made with either dried or fresh material will provide relief from bruises. A warm water infusion acts as a mild stimulant and astringent. The same infusion will relive chapped skin and slow bleeding when used topically.

PARTS USED: Flower, Herbs, Leaves

MAGICKAL: Dried Calendula flowers are used in incense recipes for divination. A simple incense for burning while reading the tarot can be made by mixing 1 part Calendula, 1 part Gum Arabic, and 1 part Lavender. Grind into a powder and burn over charcoal as you conduct tarot readings. Fresh flowers can be mixed with a salad to promote a sense of well-being and an uplifting feeling. The fresh flowers are brought or grown in the bedroom to promote psychic dreams. They are simmered to promote calm and health.

Calf's Snout—*See* Snapdragon

California Barberry—*See* Barberry, Holly-leaved

Californian Buckthorn—*See* Buckthorn, Californian

Californian Spikenard—*See* Spikenard, Californian

Call-Me-to-You—*See* Heartsease

Calmouc—*See* Lime

Camellia—*Camellia japonica*—Feminine, Moon, Water

ASTROLOGICAL: *Primary*: Cancer; *Secondary*: Cancer, Pisces, Scorpio

MAGICKAL: Camellia, especially fresh flowers, is said to lend itself well to spells for money and wealth.

Camomyle—*See* Chamomile, German and Chamomile, Common

Camphire—*See* Camphor

Camphor—*Cinnamonum camphora*—Feminine, Moon, Water

Also known as Kafoor, Camphire, Chang Nao, Laurel Camphor, Gum Camphor

ASTROLOGICAL: *Primary*: Cancer; *Secondary*: Cancer, Pisces, Scorpio

GODS: Babalu Aye, Chandra, Eleggua, Oko, Olocun, Orunla

GODDESSES: Artemis, Yemaya

MEDICAL: Antiseptic. Inhalation of its fumes aids in clearing the bronchial passageways. Internal use has been abandoned, due to side effects.

PART USED: Gum extract

MAGICKAL: Small amounts of natural Camphor are used in brews and mixtures to aid divination. These mixtures are not consumed. Instead, boil equal amounts (by weight) of natural Camphor and Lavender flowers in a pot of water. Inhale the fumes as you gaze into a scrying mirror or other scrying device. Small amounts mixed with Sandalwood makes a pleasant divination incense. Inhaling Camphor is also said to quiet sexual appetite and is used in celibacy preparations. Obtained from the *Cinnamonum camphora* tree, real Camphor is off-white, sticky, crystalline material. However, historically speaking, the word *Camphor* has been used to describe several different extracts from pungent plant material. In the modern world, we have yet another concern: synthetic camphor. Always check for the Latin name on this one. Yes, natural Camphor costs a great deal more than synthetic, but the synthetic offers none of the magickal benefits. Hint: There are exceptions, but natural Camphor usually is sold as an off-white resinous granular powder, and synthetic Camphor is usually sold as a

Camphor

yellowish material in square blocks that are about an inch across. True essential oil of Camphor does exist, but the great majority of what is on the market is synthetic. If you can find the real thing, buy it on sight if it is not already in your cabinet. Its scent clears the mind of bodily desires, especially lust. It is most useful diffused in a hotel room while traveling away from a monogamous relationship to aid that relationship in remaining monogamous. Although admitting temptation sounds like we are weak, doing so allows us to become strong. Pack this one even if you think you won't give in to occasional temptation. The essential oil is also diffused to speed healing, especially from the common cold. However, it should not be used directly from the bottle because it tends to cause headaches in pure form.

Canadian Fleabane—*See* Fleabane, Canadian

Cancer Root—*See* Pokeweed

Candlewick Plant—*See* Mullein

Canella—*See* Cinnamon, White

Canellae Cortex—*See* Cinnamon, White

Cannabis—*See* Marijuana

Cannabis, Chinese—*See* Marijuana

Cankerwort—*See* Dandelion

Canton Cassia—*See* Cinnamon, Chinese

Capalaga—*See* Cardamom

Caper—*Capparis spinosa*—Feminine, Venus, Water

Also known as Fakouha, Lasafa, Shafallah

ASTROLOGICAL: *Primary*: Libra, Taurus; *Secondary*: Cancer, Pisces, Scorpio

MAGICKAL: If a woman wants to ensure her gentleman's attention and performance in the act of love, she should serve him a dish rich in Capers. Add some garlic, thyme, and some red peppers, and he will certainly come to your bed at attention.

Cap Gum—*See* Acacia

Capon's Tail—*See* Valerian

Capon's Trailer—*See* Valerian

Capri-Foglio—*See* Honeysuckle

Caraway—*Carum Carvi*—Masculine, Mercury, Air

Also known as Alcaravea, Caraway Seed, Kummel

ASTROLOGICAL: *Primary*: Gemini, Virgo; *Secondary*: Aquarius, Gemini, Libra

GODS: Shango, Olocun, Oggun

MEDICAL: Carminative, Stimulant. Caraway seeds act as a mild stimulant.

PARTS USED: Seeds, Oil

MAGICKAL: Scattering Caraway in a footlocker, money box, or other place where valuables are hidden well will ward off thieves. Caraway inspires lust when used as an ingredient in breads and cakes without a lot of sugar. For help in school, chew Caraway seeds while you study. When it comes time for a test, slip a few between your cheek and gum when you enter the classroom, and chew during the test. Eating the seeds will also stimulate a strong sense of both love and lust. They are an excellent choice for inclusion in a romantic dinner. Essential oil of Caraway will improve the physical and conscious act of lovemaking when diffused into a room. Its scent promotes reciprocity and can greatly enhance the act of love should one lover have inhibitions based on social taboo, but don't think it will work on the receiving end of a sexual act alone. Here, the word reciprocity is key. If using this oil to enhance lovemaking, remember that you will only receive that which you first give. Generally speaking, its scent stimulates both mind

Caraway

and body; however, it does not stimulate love itself. That, you and your partner will have to provide for yourselves.

Caraway Seed—*See* Caraway

Cardamom—*Elettaria cardamomum*—Feminine, Venus, Water

Also known as Amomum Cardamomum, Alpinia Cardamom, Matonia Cardamomum, Cardamomum Minus, Cardamomi Semina, Cardamon, Malabar Cardamums, Ebil, Kakelah Seghar, Capalaga, Gujatatti Elachi, Ailum

ASTROLOGICAL: *Primary*: Libra, Taurus; *Secondary*: Cancer, Pisces, Scorpio

GODDESS: Erzulie

MEDICAL: Carminative, Stimulant. Chewing or otherwise consuming uncooked Cardamom seeds will aid in relieving gas and other digestive problems. In the Middle East and Mediterranean, Cardamom is ground and mixed with coffee beans for an after-dinner treat that also serves this medical purpose.

PARTS USED: Oil, Seed

MAGICKAL: To inspire lust, soak ground seeds in a sweet red wine overnight. As you drift off to sleep, imagine yourself in your lover's arms. The next day, strain the seeds from the wine, sweeten with honey from local fields, and serve warm over a romantic dinner. In Germany, smart shopkeepers use similar recipes during the Yule season, giving out hot spiced wine to potential customers. What better way to increase the amount they will spend on a gift for their lovers than to heighten their desires? If your lover does not drink wine, serve a romantic dinner. With dessert, serve coffee brewed with ground Cardamom seeds and sweetened with natural sugar (not honey). The seeds can also be included in sachets and incenses, but these practices are much less effective than the wine potion mentioned above. Essential oil of Cardamom is diffused to increase appetite. Used prior to and in conjunction with the ideas listed above, it is a most excellent scent to promote love—and if the timing is right, tender lovemaking.

Carenfil—*See* Clove

Carnation—*Dianthus carophyllus*—Masculine, Sun, Fire

Also known as Gillies, Gillyflower, Jove's Flower, Nelka, Scaffold Flower, Sops-In-Wine

ASTROLOGICAL: *Primary*: Leo; *Secondary*: Aries, Leo, Sagittarius

GODS: Babalu Aye, Shango, Jupiter, Obatala, Oggun

GODDESS: Yemaya

MAGICKAL: A fresh Carnation is a perfectly functional—as well as covert—talisman of protection. Wear in the buttonhole of an off-white shirt with a nice tie, and it will build the confidence needed to guard against a hostile workplace or an often unpleasant world. Given as gifts to travelers, they are said to ensure a safe journey. They help to speed healing when given to sick friends as living

Carnation

plants, and the dried flowers are used for the same purpose in incense and sachet recipes. Like the Rose, the scent of fresh Carnations has been almost lost due to selective breeding for appearance. Unlike the Rose, a true essential oil of Carnation is rarely (if ever) available. If you should receive red Carnations, it is possible their scent will stir love. However, other colors seem to have no effect, and there are much better fresh flowers for this purpose.

Carob—*Ceratonia siliqua*—Feminine, Venus, Water

Also known as Algaroba, Bharout, Caaroba, Caroba, Carobinha, Bignonia Caroba, Jacaranda Caroba, John's Bread, Locust Pod, Subar Pod

ASTROLOGICAL: *Primary*: Libra, Taurus; *Secondary*: Cancer, Pisces, Virgo

MEDICAL: Laxative. Carob and carob products act as a mild laxative.

PART USED: Fruit

MAGICKAL: Carob is used for both protection and to ensuring health. As it is a magickal substitute for chocolate, it will also stir feelings of love. You can usually find it in powder form at your local grocery store. If not, try a health or natural food store. It can be mixed into just about anything warm.

Carob

Caroba—*See* Carob

Carobinha—*See* Carob

Carpenter's Square—*See* Figwort, Knotted

Carpenter's Weed—*See* Yarrow

Carrageen—*See* Moss, Irish

Carrahan—*See* Moss, Irish

Carrot—*Daucus carota*—Masculine, Mars, Fire

Also know as Bird's Nest, Philtron, Gizri, Queen Ann's Lace

ASTROLOGICAL: *Primary*: Aries, Scorpio; *Secondary*: Aries, Leo, Sagittarius

MEDICAL: Deobstruent, Diuretic, Stimulant. Eating fresh Carrots will improve eyesight and act as a mild diuretic. Cooked Carrots will help with treating diarrhea. The greens may be useful in stabilizing and normalizing blood sugar. Carrots are a natural deobstruent of the pours. Eating them will help with acne.

PART USED: Whole plant

MAGICKAL: Eating Carrots (fresh or cooked) will increase a man's sex drive.

Carthage Apple—*See* Pomegranate

Cascara Sagrada—*See* Buckthorn, Californian

Case-Weed—*See* Shepherd's Purse

Cashew—*Anacardium occidentale*—Masculine, Sun, Fire

Also known as Mbiba, Kasui, Mkanju

ASTROLOGICAL: *Primary*: Leo; *Secondary*: Aries, Leo, Sagittarius

MEDICAL: The expression of fresh Cashew nuts is said to remove warts when applied topically.

PART USED: Nut

MAGICKAL: Cashews can be worn in a green sachet as a money-drawing talisman as well as a tasty snack.

Cassia Aromaticum—*See* Cinnamon, Chinese

Cassia Bark—*See* Cinnamon, Chinese

Casse-Lunnette—*See* Eyebright

Cassilata—*See* Henbane

Cassilago—*See* Henbane

Castor—*Ricinus communes*

Also known as Castor Oil Bush, Palma Christi, Palms Christi Root, Mamona, Makula Kula, Mbono, Mdogo, Racznick

MEDICAL: Laxative. Castor oil is one of the most powerful natural laxatives. A typical dose is 1 or 2 tablespoons. My wife and I argued over the use of Castor oil to induce labor. My stance was that it was a bad idea. Her stance was that it was a good idea. I lost the arguement. It did not work, but in the large amounts she took, it did cause great volumes of intestinal discomfort, pain, and false labor.

PART USED: Oil

MAGICKAL: Drill a tiny hole in dried Castor beans and string on a necklace cord. Wear for protection.

Castor Oil Bush—*See* Castor

Catchweed—*See* Cleavers (B)

Catnip—*Nepeta cataria*—Feminine, Venus, Water

Also known as Cat, Catmint, Catnep, Catrup, Cat's Wort, Field Balm, Nepeta, Nip

ASTROLOGICAL: *Primary*: Libra, Taurus; *Secondary*: Cancer, Pisces, Virgo

GODDESSES: Bast, Ochun

MEDICAL: Antispasmodic, Diaphoretic, Carminative, Emmenagogue (mildly), Febrifuge, Nervine, Refrigerant, Stimulant (mildly), Tonic. Relief from mild fever, insomnia, and flatulence can be had from this wonderful plant. A strong warm water infusion of Catnip makes a wonderful sleeping aid. Consume 1 cup an hour right before going to bed. If you don't like the taste, try using a blend of Chamomile and Catnip, but do not sweeten. If you still cannot stand the taste, add small amounts of honey. Will also combat colic.

PART USED: Herb

MAGICKAL: When we were young, many of us became "blood brothers" by cutting our palms with a friend and then holding hands. In a day when we are more aware and concerned about disease, Catnip is a good substitute. To remain forever friends, place fresh Catnip in your hand and shake the hand of your best friend while telling him or her what you are up to with the herb. Dried Catnip is mixed with Rose petals and placed in a pink sachet to attract love. A tincture

Catnip

of dried Catnip and Roses can be made for the same purpose. Use the mixture as perfume. Growing Catnip in your garden and outside the house will cause baneful spirits to depart and pleasant spirits to be attracted. But be careful, because if the field is large enough, the pleasant spirits will ride in on the backs of—you guessed it—cats! They love the stuff. If grown without a barrier, it will spread at a rate of almost double every season. Fresh Catnip leaves can be simmered in water to promote a sense of peace and relaxation in the home.

Catsfoot—*Antennaria dioca/Gnaphalium dioicum*

Also known as Cudweed, Life Everlasting, Mountain Everlasting

See also Balsam, White and Ivy, Ground, as Catsfoot is also a common name for those plants.

MEDICAL: Astringent. A warm water infusion will extract the active ingredients.

PART USED: Herb

MAGICKAL: An infusion of Catsfoot consumed right after you wake every morning is said to promote health and long life.

Catshair—*See* Spurges

Cat's Valerian—*See* Valerian

Cattail—*Typha capensis*—Masculine, Mars, Fire

Also known as Tabua, Ibhuma, Balangot

ASTROLOGICAL: *Primary*: Aries, Scorpio; *Secondary:* Aries, Leo, Sagittarius

MAGICKAL: Cattails are one of the greatest herbs to serve as a phallic symbol to represent our Horned Lord. In a pinch, natural cattails make great wands.

Cauliflower—*Brassica spp.*—Feminine, Moon, Water

ASTROLOGICAL: *Primary*: Cancer; *Secondary*: Cancer, Pisces, Scorpio

MAGICKAL: Lends itself to protection.

Cayenne—*Capsicum minimum*—Masculine, Mars, Fire

Also known as African Pepper, Chili Pepper, Chilies, Bird Pepper

ASTROLOGICAL: *Primary*: Aries, Scorpio; *Secondary*: Aries, Leo, Sagittarius

GOD: Eleggua

MEDICAL: Febrifuge, Stimulant, Tonic. Relief from congestion can be had by using Cayenne pepper in cooking. It will also lend itself to easing stomach ulcers, high blood pressure, and improving blood circulation. Stimulates and eases tightness of the chest. Invigorates the body, strengthens the immune system, and acts as a good general tonic. A warm vinegar infusion of Cayenne works topically to relieve bursitis. Apple cider vinegar seems to be the best. Cayenne will cause sweating and lower fevers, but chances are a sick person won't want to eat much. So put Cayenne powder into empty jell caps. If using size 00 jell caps, the dose is 1 or 2 caps every three or four hours.

PART USED: Fruit

MAGICKAL: The words *Cayenne* and *capsicum* both find their root in the ancient Greek word for "to bite," and that is exactly what this friend does; it takes a bite out of baneful magick that has been worked against you. Sprinkle Cayenne around the entrance to your home, or hang it in the four corners to chomp down on baneful magick. In cooking, Cayenne will bring on physical passion and lustful thoughts. The body seems to respond to being bitten by releasing endorphins to numb the pain. When a goodly amount of Cayenne is doing the biting, the body tends to release enough of those natural intoxicants to lift the heart as well as bury a few inhibitions.

Cayenne

Cedar—*Cedrus atlantica / Cedrus libani / Cedrus spp.*—Masculine, Sun, Fire

Also known as Cedarwood

WARNING: Essential oil of Cedar may be dangerous to unborn children.

ASTROLOGICAL: *Primary*: Leo; *Secondary*: Aries, Leo, Sagittarius

GODS: Amun-Ra, Brahma, Babalu Aye, Shango, Indra, Jupiter, Obatala, Odin, Poseidon

GODDESS: Ochun

MAGICKAL: Cedar is one of the Old World trees whose story reminds us that even the ancients should have paid more attention to needs before desires. So praised was this wood for incense that it was virtually extinct in Lebanon due to over-harvesting. So bad was the carnage that even today the tree is a rarity there. In North America it was used by pre-Columbian Americans in ceremonial fires for purification. It was also burned with Sagebrush for the same purpose. This is probably why it is sometimes cited as one of the nine woods referred to in the Wiccan Rede, but that reference seems to be found only in the references of North American Wiccans who often borrow from indigenous cultures. Cedar in the wallet attracts money. Cedar powder in a sachet attracts love. But Cedar is better suited for purification rites. Fresh Cedar twigs are often placed on top of the hot rocks in a sweat lodge; the resulting steam was considered the best way to purify mind, body, and spirit. Many other cultures burned it in bonfires for the same purpose. Add Wood Betony for an extra effect. Cedar powder is often added to incense to produce a similar effect. Essential oil of Cedar promotes the sensation of positive connections with our Lord and the masculine half of Divinity.

Cedar, Red—*Juniperus virginiana*—Masculine, Mars, Fire

WARNING: Essential oil of Red Cedar may be dangerous to unborn children.

ASTROLOGICAL: *Primary*: Aries, Scorpio; *Secondary*: Aries, Leo, Sagittarius

MAGICKAL: Red Cedar powder is used in sachets and incenses intended to promote love. Essential oil of Cedar promotes the sensation of positive connections with our Lord and the masculine half of Divinity. It can be diffused to promote physical love by furthering the apparent masculinity of a male partner.

Cedarwood—*See* Cedar

Cedron—*See* Lemon Verbena

Celandine—*See* Celandine, Greater

☠Celandine, Greater —*Chelidonium majus*—Masculine, Sun, Fire

Also known as Celandine, Celydoyne, Chelidonium, Devil's Milk, Garden Celandine, Kenning Wort, Swallow Herb, Swallow-Wort,

Tetterwort

ASTROLOGICAL: *Primary*: Leo; *Secondary*: Aries, Leo, Sagittarius

MEDICAL: Alterative, Diuretic, Purgative

PART USED: Herb

MAGICKAL: To understand the magickal properties of Greater Celandine, you will need a tarot deck. Almost any deck will do, but some have strayed so far from the point of this exercise that you should use the Rider-Waite deck. From that deck, draw The Lovers card and The Devil card. The magickal properties of this herb are those properties that transform the Devil card into the Lovers card. Typically, it is worn in a sachet close to the heart for this purpose. Change both herb and sachet daily, and discard the old with your bondage.

☠Celandine, Lesser—*Ranunculus ficaria*

Also known as Small Celandine, Figwort, Smallwort, Pilewort

GOD: Chandra

MEDICAL: Astringent. A warm water infusion is created for topical use only.

PART USED: Herb

Celery—*Apium graveolens*—Masculine, Mercury, Fire

Also known as Aipo, Karafs, Elma, Smallage, Wild Celery

ASTROLOGICAL: *Primary*: Gemini, Virgo; *Secondary*: Aries, Leo, Sagittarius

MEDICAL: Carminative, Diuretic, Nervine, Stimulant, Tonic. Fresh or in a hot water infusion Celery will act as a mild sedative and settles the stomach.

PARTS USED: Herb, Root, Seed

MAGICKAL: Chewing Celery seeds reportedly helps concentration, but when placed in one's pillow, they reportedly promote sleep. I haven't found either to be true. Burned over charcoal with equal amounts of Orris root and Gum Arabic improves divinatory skills. Celery stalks are a good bet for appetizers before a romantic meal, as they stir lust in women. Celery juice seems to have the same effect, so I do not at all believe this property is due to its obvious phallic shape as many have implied. Powdered Celery seeds can be kept in a sachet next to the bed to promote sleep.

Centaury—*Erythraea centaurium*—Masculine, Sun, Fire

Also known as Century, Centory, Christ's Ladder, Feverwort, Filewort, Red Centaury

ASTROLOGICAL: *Primary*: Leo; *Secondary*: Aries, Leo, Sagittarius

MEDICAL: Stomachic, Tonic. A warm water infusion is an excellent daily preventative against kidney dysfunction. Also helps keep the blood pure, acts as a good tonic, and settles the digestive system.

PARTS USED: Herbs, Leaves

MAGICKAL: Reportedly, burning Centaury on a campfire will keep away snakes. I have observed that burning anything on a campfire will attract snakes, as they like the warmth.

Celydoyne—*See* Celandine, Greater

Century—*See* Centaury

Centocchiio—*See* Periwinkle

Centory—*See* Centaury

Centinode—*See* Knotgrass

Ceterach—*See* Fern

Cetraria—*See* Moss, Iceland

Ceylon cinnamon—*See* Cinnamon

Ceylon Tree—*See* Oleander

Chagareltin—*See* Fig

Chamaemelon—*See* Chamomile, German and Chamomile, Common

Chamomile, Common—*Chameamelum nobile/ Anthemis nobilis*—Feminine, Venus, Water

Also known as Camomyle, Chamaimelon, Ground Apple, Heermannchen, Manzanilla, Maythen, Whig Plant

WARNING: Some folk are highly allergic to Chamomile.

ASTROLOGICAL: *Primary*: Libra, Taurus/Leo (flower); *Secondary:* Cancer, Pisces, Scorpio

GODS: Shango, Olocun

GODDESS: Ochun

MEDICAL: Anodyne (mild), Antispasmodic, Diuretic, Nervine, Tonic

PARTS USED: Flowers, Herb, Oil. Calms and soothes the mind. Use in a warm water infusion, but do not allow the plant material to contact boiling water as that will destroy many of its relaxing properties. Also used to treat mild depression and insomnia. Acts as a mild diuretic. A warm water infusion is an excellent topical treatment for chapped skin.

MAGICKAL: The Saxon name for Common Chamomile is Maythen, which is where this wonderful flower obtains much of its magickal lore and why if you see a recipe calling for Chamomile, it is probably asking for this variety. A strong but unsweetened infusion of Chamomile is said to be one of the best aids in sleep a person could choose. Add a few drops of Lavender oil to your pillow, drink a cup of Chamomile infusion before bed, and it is lights out when the

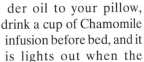

Chamomile

lights go out. That same infusion is said to draw love when mixed with the bath water or luck at gambling when used to wash the hands. Try mixing some baking soda into your Chamomile infusion, then use the mix in your bath prior to a romantic evening. In the home, an infusion of Chamomile can be mixed into mop water or sprinkled in the flower bed. Dried whole flowers can be scattered the night before and then swept up in the morning. The scent is divine and is said to bless the home as well as remove spells cast against both home and inhabitants. Essential oil of Common Chamomile is precious and expensive. It is diffused to bring on sleep. Mixed with equal amounts of Lavender oil, it makes an even better oil for this purpose.

GENERAL: Chamomile is a plant whose attributes are not at all agreed upon. Most commonly, they are listed as Masculine, Sun, Water; my oldest notes cite them as Feminine, Venus, Water. It appears as if, in natural form, the attributes Masculine and Sun are made from the look of the plant, but from its smell in any state we recognize it as associated with the Element Water. Thus, the essential oil, which no longer retains the look of the plant, takes on the attributes of the scent, which are Feminine, Venus, Water. This applies to both Common Chamomile and German Chamomile.

Chamomile, German—*Matricaria recutita/ Matricaria chamomilla*—Feminine, Venus, Water

Also known as Ground Apple, Camomyle, Chamaimelon, Heermannchen, Wild Chamomile

See Chamomile, Common for a note on the attributes of this plant.

ASTROLOGICAL: *Primary*: Libra, Taurus/Leo (herb); *Secondary*: Cancer, Pisces, Scorpio

MEDICAL: Carminative, Sedative, Tonic. As a sedative, German Chamomile is much more effective than Common Chamomile. A warm water infusion is also useful in relieving headaches and intestinal cramps/gas.

PARTS USED: Flowers, Oil

GENERAL: If a recipe calls for Chamomile, chances are this is not the one it is calling for unless it was written in German and calls for the ingredient as Heermannchen Chamaimelon. If it is calling for this one, it will probably induce sleep. My advice, substitute common

chamomile (especially if it is to be consumed). Generally speaking, essential oil of German Chamomile is even more expensive than its cousin (Common Chamomile). It is generally used in meditation.

Chamomile, Roman—*See* Chamomile, Common

Chamomile, Stinking—*Anthemis cotula*—Masculine, Sun, Fire

Also known as Mayweed, Maruta Cotula, Dog Chamomile, Maruta Foetida, Dog-Fennel

ASTROLOGICAL: *Primary*: Leo; *Secondary*: Aries, Leo, Sagittarius

MEDICAL: Antispasmodic, Emetic, Emmenagogue, Tonic. A typical preparation is an infusion of 1 ounce of the dried herb in 1 pint of water. This is served 4 ounces at a time.

PART USED: Herb

MAGICKAL: If you wild craft your herbs, you may have come upon a cropping of beautiful Chamomile flowers, bundled them together, and inhaled deeply. If you had mistaken this plant for Common Chamomile, you had a big surprise. Listed here to fight confusion, this plant is rarely used in spellcraft, but does live up to its name.

Chanvre—*See* Marijuana

Charlock—*See* Mustard, Field

Chelidonium—*See* Celandine, Greater

Chervil—*Anthriscus cerefolium*—Masculine, Mercury, Air

ASTROLOGICAL: *Primary*: Gemini, Virgo; *Secondary:* Aquarius, Gemini, Libra

MEDICAL: Astringent, Diuretic, Expectorant, Nervine, Stimulant. This herb is good as an expectorant and stimulant of the body. Invigorates the body and acts as a mild diuretic. A warm water infusion is a good astringent. Note that while Chervil will stimulate the body, it will also relax the mind. Reportedly, it will aid in weight loss.

PART USED: Herb

Chestnut—*See* Chestnut, Sweet

☠**Chestnut, Horse**—*Aesculus hippocastanum/ Hippocastanum vulgare*—Masculine, Jupiter, Fire

Also known as Buckeye

ASTROLOGICAL: *Primary*: Pisces, Sagittarius; *Secondary:* Aries, Leo, Sagittarius

MEDICAL: Febrifuge, Narcotic. Although the entire plant is considered poisonous, the bark is sometimes used for its narcotic and febrifuge properties.

PARTS USED: Bark, Fruit

MAGICKAL: Introduced to England in the 16th century, the Horse Chestnut shares many of the same properties of the Sweet Chestnut, except that it is poisonous. Generally speaking, Horse Chestnuts are carried for good luck.

Chestnut, Sweet—*Castanea sativa*—Masculine, Jupiter, Fire

Also known as Fagus Castanea, Sardian Nut, Jupiter's Nut, Husked Nut, Spanish Chestnut

ASTROLOGICAL: *Primary*: Pisces, Sagittarius; *Secondary*: Aries, Leo, Sagittarius

MEDICAL: Astringent, Febrifuge, Tonic. The leaves are used in a decoction or warm water infusion as an astringent, febrifuge, and general tonic. Also treats coughs and respiratory complaints.

PARTS USED: Leaves, Fruit

MAGICKAL: Sweet Chestnuts are carried or worn to attract love. Serve as an appetizer to enhance the feelings of a romantic dinner. Also improves cognitive abilities. Hint: Grind them and serve on top of chocolate dishes as a dessert.

Chickweed—*Stellaria media*—Feminine, Moon, Water

Also known as Adder's-Mouth, Alsine Media, Augentrosgras, Indian Chickweed, Passerina, Satin Flower, Star Chickweed, Starweed, Starwort, Stellaire, Stitchwort, Tongue Grass, Winterweed, Qoqobala

ASTROLOGICAL: *Primary*: Cancer; *Secondary*: Cancer, Pisces, Scorpio

GODDESS: Ochun

MEDICAL: Demulcent, Refrigerant. Used most often as a poultice to reduce inflammation. A decoction taken internally acts to lower temperature and stiffens the stool.

PART USED: Herb

MAGICKAL: Chickweed is added to sauce (particularly tomato) and served with a meal (particularly pasta) to encourage fidelity in a marriage or monogamous relationship. However, should you be the one to have strayed or should you become the one who strays, Chickweed will ensure that your lover does as well. Call it poetic justice, cause and effect, or common sense—whatever it is, this plant certainly seems to speed up the magickal observation that like attracts like. If you are thinking about following a recipe for fidelity or love that suggests using menstrual blood in the spaghetti sauce, better to substitute Chickweed. Oh, if he finds out about your manipulation he might be upset, but not nearly as upset as if he had found out you followed that original recipe.

Chickweed

Chicory—*Cichorium intybus*—Masculine, Sun, Air

Also known as Barbe de Capucin, Hendibeh, Succory, Wild Cherry, Wild Succory

ASTROLOGICAL: *Primary*: Leo; *Secondary:* Aquarius, Gemini, Libra

MEDICAL: Diuretic, Laxative, Nervine, Sedative (mild), Tonic. A weak infusion of Chicory flowers is a mild sedative; however, the roots may have stimulating properties. It is an excellent tonic and easy to use on a daily basis. Just mix it with your morning coffee.

PARTS USED: Flowers, Root

MAGICKAL: Mix Chicory with coffee grounds; brew

Chicory

and drink prior to a job interview or other exchange where you might need the blessings of a favor. While asking for that job or favor, be sincere and the Chicory will lend itself to both sincerity and good fate. Fresh Chicory is carried in the pockets for the same general purpose. Also promotes love.

Chives—*Allium schoenoprasum*—Masculine, Mars, Fire
Also known as Ail Civitte, Cives, Petit Poureau
ASTROLOGICAL: *Primary*: Aries, Scorpio; *Secondary*: Aries, Leo, Sagittarius
MEDICAL: Sprinkle uncooked Chives on meals to help in decreasing blood pressure and, reportedly, to assist in weight loss.
PART USED: Herb
MAGICKAL: Eating Chives is credited with easing a broken heart and encouraging a person to move on. It will also assist with breaking a bad habit.

Chocolate Flower—*See* Geranium

Chondrus—*See* Moss, Irish

Chongras—*See* Pokeweed

Christ's Ladder—*See* Centaury

Christe Herbe—*See* Hellebore, Black

Christmas Rose—*See* Hellebore, Black

Christ's Thorn—*See* Holly

☠ **Chrysanthemum**—*Chrysanthemum sinense*—Masculine, Sun, Fire
Also known as Mum
ASTROLOGICAL: *Primary*: Leo; *Secondary*: Aries, Leo, Sagittarius
MAGICKAL: Cunningham tells us that drinking an infusion of Chrysanthemums will cure us of drunkenness. He also points out that Chrysanthemums are poisonous. Being fond of drunkenness and not so fond of poison, I have yet to test this lore.

Chameleon Star—*See* Bromeliad

Chang Nao—*See* Camphor

Chatim—*See* Dita Tree

Chebbit—*See* Dill

Cheese Rennet—*See* Cleavers (A)

Cheese Renning—*See* Cleavers (A)

Cherry—*Prunus avium*—Feminine, Venus, Water
Also known as Cherry Stalks, Mazzard Cherry, Sweet Cherry
ASTROLOGICAL: *Primary*: Libra, Taurus; *Secondary*: Cancer, Pisces, Scorpio
MEDICAL: Astringent, Pectoral, Tonic. The stalks are used in decoction and infusion in a ratio of 1/2 ounce to 1 pint of water. This will soften stool and help with lung and breathing complaints. Relief from mild coughs may be had from syrup made with the fruit. This folk remedy is so popular that modern pharmaceutical cough syrups often contain artificial flavor and color to trick folk into thinking the relief comes from more natural sources.

Cherry

Cherry Cough Syrup
2 pints water
1 pint cherries
1 pint honey
1 lemon

Bring water to a boil; add cherries and sliced lemon. Lower heat, cover, and simmer until the cherries have become soft. Mash the solid ingredients; return to a boil and then strain through a screen or pasta strainer. Discard the solids and put the liquid aside to cool. Once cool, check consistency. If it is between a thick and thin maple syrup, refrigerate for future use. If it is too thick, warm again and add water. Too thin, evaporate off some of the liquid. Take 1 or 2 tablespoons to relieve coughs. Unlike pharmaceutical cough syrups, this one can be taken as needed as no one has ever overdosed on cherries, honey, or lemon.

PARTS USED: Fruit, Stalks

MAGICKAL: In love spells, Cherry juice substitutes for both Dove's Blood and one's own. However, many suppliers of spellcraft components offer Dove's Blood Ink, which works as well or better (and contains no actual blood). A simple love spell can be made by dipping a Cherry in whipped cream or powdered sugar and feeding it to your lover by its stem.

Cherry Stalks—*See* Cherry

☠Cherry Laurel—*Prunus laurocerasus*
MEDICAL: Narcotic, Sedative
PART USED: Leaves

Cherry Pie—*See* Heliotrope

Cherry, Wild—*Prunus serotina*—Feminine, Venus, Water
Also known as Virginian Prune, Black Cherry
ASTROLOGICAL: *Primary*: Libra, Taurus; *Secondary*: Cancer, Pisces, Scorpio
MEDICAL: Astringent, Expectorant, Pectoral, Sedative, Tonic. A good expectorant and one of the most common ingredients in natural cough syrups.
PARTS USED: Bark, Bark of Root
MAGICKAL: Wild Cherries make an excellent love-drawing tincture/perfume for women who prefer the affections of other women.

Cherry, Winter—*Physalis alkekengi*
Also known as Alkekengi Officinale, Coqueret, Judenkirsche, Schlutte, Cape Gooseberry, Strawberry Tomato
MEDICAL: Aperient, Diuretic. A typical dose is 10 berries.
PART USED: Fruit

Chèvre-Feuille—*See* Honeysuckle

Chewing John—*See* Galangal

China Root—*See* Galangal

Chili Pepper—*See* Cayenne

Chilies—*See* Cayenne

China Rhubarb—*See* Rhubarb

Chinese Anise—*See* Star Anise

Chinese Cinnamon—*See* Cinnamon, Chinese

Chinese Lovage—*See* Lovage

Chinese Parsley—*See* Coriander

Christ's Spear—*See* Fern

Chun Pi—*See* Ailanthus

Church Steeples—*See* Agrimony

Cilantro—*See* Coriander

Cilentro—*See* Coriander

Cimicifuga—*See* Cohosh, Black

China Aster—*See* Aster

Cingulum Sancti Johannis—*See* Mugwort

☠Cinnamon, Chinese—*Cinnamomum cassia*—Masculine, Sun, Fire
Also known as Bastard Cinnamon, Canton Cassia, Cassia Aromaticum, Cassia Bark, Cassia Linnea
WARNING: The extract/concentrate is poisonous.
ASTROLOGICAL: *Primary*: Leo; *Secondary*: Aries, Leo, Sagittarius
MEDICAL: Astringent, Carminative, Emmenagogue (mild), Stimulant, Stomachic. Large amounts can be fatal. The oil is greatly antiseptic; however, it is also very dangerous. Best to avoid.
PARTS USED: Bark, Oil

Cinnamon, Common—*Cinnamom zeylanicum*—Masculine, Sun, Fire

Also known as Ceylon Cinnamon, Sweet Wood, Laurus Cinnamomum

WARNING: Essential oil often burns when placed on the skin.

ASTROLOGICAL: *Primary*: Leo; *Secondary*: Aries, Leo, Sagittarius

GODS: Aeacus, Babalu Aye, Helios, Orunla, Ra, Surya

GODDESSES: Aphrodite, Ochun, Oya, Venus

MEDICAL: Astringent, Antiseptic, Carminative, Pectoral, Stimulant, Tonic. For relief of the symptoms of the common cold, boil 5 Cinnamon sticks in 1 pint of water for 30 minutes. Allow the scent to fill the house. Sweeten with honey, and serve with one of the Cinnamon sticks as a stir rod should more honey be desired. Works on the young and the old, but let kids mix in their own honey with the Cinnamon stick and they will love this folk remedy. Tastes like a red-hot candy. This will also stimulate blood flow, open the respiratory system, invigorate the body, and act as a good tonic. Cinnamon is a very powerful astringent. However, it should never be used in high concentration. Instead, a mild warm water infusion is best. If it is too strong, it will sting.

Cinnamon

PART USED: Bark

MAGICKAL: One can document the use of Cinnamon oil to times before its well-known inclusion in the oil of Abramelin the Mage. It was used in Egyptian mummification rites and offered to the Egyptian deities by pharaohs. Included in much ancient incense, Cinnamon was burned in Greek, Roman, and Egyptian temples. Burn 1 part Cinnamon with 3 parts Gum Arabic for a simple money-drawing incense. It is a major component of incenses intended to attract love and money, as well as those to inspire lust and heighten psychic energy. Cinnamon is sometimes used in love- and lust-inducing recipes. Essential oil of Cinnamon is often used in oil blends intended to enhance psychic abilities. It is also sometimes used as a primary ingredient of Initiation oils. However, the main reason that is done is to remind the initiate of the mark one receives by joining a certain group. Although most of these oils are blended such that a permanent mark is not left from the oil, it may certainly feel as if one is.

Cinnamon Root—*See* Cinnamon and Spikenard, Ploughman's

Cinnamon Sedge—*See* Calamus

Cinnamon, White—*Canella alba*

Also known as Canella, Canellae Cortex, White Wood, Wild Cinnamon

MEDICAL: Stomachic. A typical dose is 20 grains of powdered inner bark.

PART USED: Inner bark

Cinnamon Wood—*See* Sassafras

Cinquefoil—*See* Five-Finger Grass

Circeium—*See* Mandrake

Circoea—*See* Mandrake

Citron—*Citnus medica*—Masculine, Sun, Air

Also known as Forbidden Fruit, Rough Lemon, and Sukake

ASTROLOGICAL: *Primary*: Leo; *Secondary*: Aquarius, Gemini, Libra

GODS: Babalu Aye, Obatala, Orunla

GODDESS: Yemaya

MAGICKAL: When eaten, Citron enhances natural psychic powers and empathy in particular. It is most often available as a candied fruit. Sometimes used in conjunction with Camphor for healing spells. Some speculate that it was the Citron and not the Apple that is referred to in the story of Adam and Eve. The curse that came with that meal was more of cause and effect: They ate of the forbidden fruit and suffered the pain of empathy. Indeed, I have included this in my creation myth because as an adopted child who was witness to the birth of his own child, I can tell you firsthand that the pain of childbirth could not possibly measure to the pain of raising a child.

Citrus Medica—*See* Lemon

Citrus Limonum—*See* Lemon

Citronnier—*See* Lemon

Cittim Bark—*See* Buckthorn, Californian

Cives—*See* Chives

Clappedepouch—*See* Shepherd's Purse

Clary—*See* Sage, Clary

Clary Sage—*See* Sage, Clary

Cleavers—Could be a reference to *Galium verum* or *Galium aparine*. *See* Cleavers (A) and Cleavers (B).

Cleavers (A)—*Galium verum*—Feminine, Venus, Water
Also known as Cheese Renning, Cheese Rennet, Fragrant Bedstraw, Lady's Bedstraw, Our Lady's Bedstraw, Madder's Cousin, Maid's Hair, Petty Mugget, Yellow Bedstraw
ASTROLOGICAL: *Primary*: Libra, Taurus; *Secondary*: Cancer, Pisces, Scorpio
MEDICAL: *Galium verum* and *Galium verum* have the same medical uses. *See* Cleavers (B)
MAGICKAL: Cleavers is worn in pink sachets to attract purity in love. Typically this is the herb of choice when looking for love unclouded by lust.

Cleavers (B)—*Galium aparine*—Feminine, Saturn, Air
Also known as Barweed, Catchweed, Clivers, Eriffe, Everlasting Friendship, Goosebill, Goosegrass, Grip Grass, Hayriffle, Hedgeheriff, Loveman, Mutton Chops, Robin-Run-In-the-Grass, Scratweed

ASTROLOGICAL: *Primary*: Aquarius, Capricorn; *Secondary*: Aquarius, Gemini, Libra
MEDICAL: Alterative, Aperient, Diuretic, Tonic. An ounce of the dried herb is infused into a pint of water and consumed 4 to 8 ounces at a time.
PART USED: Herb
MAGICKAL: Used for all forms of bindings, especially bindings of friendship and love. This lore comes from the plants tendency to cleave or bind to fabric when contacted.

Clear Eye—*See* Sage, Clary

Clivers—*See* Cleavers (B)

Cloron's Hard—*See* Spikenard, Ploughman's

Clot—*See* Mullein

Clot-Bur—*See* Burdock

Cloth of Gold—*Crocus angustifolia*—Masculine, Sun, Fire
Also known as Turkey Crocus, and sometimes listed as "Cloth of God," but I believe that folk name is a typo.
ASTROLOGICAL: *Primary*: Leo; *Secondary*: Aries, Leo, Sagittarius
MAGICKAL: If you sleep the night in a field of these most beautiful flowers without disturbing them, you will awake with a renewed sense of the relationship humanity shares with nature. Disturb them and you will cause the opposite unless you do so with both sacrifice and permission.

Cloudberry—*See* Blackberry

Clove—*Syzygium aromaticum, Caryophyllus aromaticus, Eugenia carophyllus*—Masculine, Jupiter, Fire
Also known as Carenfil, Mykhet, Eugenia Aromatica.
ASTROLOGICAL: *Primary*: Pisces, Sagittarius; *Secondary*: Aries, Leo, Sagittarius
GODS: Babalu Aye, Shango, Eleggua, Obatala, Ochosi, Oggun, Oko

GODDESSES: Ochun, Oya

MEDICAL: Anodyne, Carminative, Stimulant. A warm water infusion acts as a mild stimulant. When used to gargle, the same infusion will sooth a sore throat. A paste made from powdered Cloves and water will temporarily relieve a toothache. Chewing a few Cloves will relieve motion and seasickness. When consumed, Clove acts as a mood elevator. Now, why was it that your grandma stuck them into your holiday ham? This is another excellent example of operational Witchcraft (a.k.a. spellcraft) being practiced even when the person casting the spell had no idea what they were doing. Hey, it's a "family tradition."

Clove

PARTS USED: Flower bud, Oil

MAGICKAL: This is one of my absolute favorites. Mixed with a few other ingredients, Clove is an excellent base to promote prosperity while at the same time creating pleasant vibrations and driving out the unpleasant. A sachet of Clove will attract a mate, especially when mixed with Cinnamon. During the dark half of the year, push Cloves into an orange, dust lightly with powdered Galangal root, and hang it in your home. This simple talisman will bring the blessings of all the wondrous things that one should be prosperous in. Cloves also fight depression and are the perfect ingredient to help a friend who is depressed, especially depression brought on by the loss of a loved one. However, the Clove will not work on its own; instead, it should be baked into your favorite recipe. Add with Nutmeg to cider and serve warm to fight back the winter blues. Invite friends over to share in the blessing. Rum is a pleasant addition. Essential oil of Clove is sometimes blended with other oils to promote courage and sometimes prosperity. More often, it is diffused to promote healing and a sense of family and home.

Clover, Red—*Trifolium pratense*—Masculine, Mercury, Air

Also known as Trefoil, Purple Clover

ASTROLOGICAL: *Primary*: Gemini, Virgo; *Secondary:* Aquarius, Gemini, Libra

GOD: Babalu Aye

GODDESSES: Ochun, Venus

MEDICAL: Alterative, Antispasmodic, Nervine, Pectoral, Stimulant, Tonic. A warm water infusion is made with 1 ounce of the dried flowers in 1 pint of water. A dose of 2 drams is useful in calming the mind and as a general tonic. Used topically, it eases skin irritation and mild rashes. Great for treating cold sores. Used internally, it is said to cure pimples.

PART USED: Flower

MAGICKAL: Red Clover is the flower of choice for bathing prior to meeting to make handfasting/wedding arrangements. Adds luck to the union.

Clove Root—*See* Avens

Clown's Lungwort—*See* Mullein

Club Moss—*See* Moss, Common Club and Moss, American Club

Coakum—*See* Pokeweed

☠**Coca, Bolivian**—*Erythroxylon Coca*

Also known as Cocaine, Cuca

MEDICAL: Anesthetic (local), Astringent, Stimulant. The leaves and extract are a powerful stimulant of mind and body. In Bolivia, native people routinely use them. Typically, the leaves are chewed for their stimulating effect. However, extended use in this manner destroys not only the teeth, but also the body. Its most attractive medical use is as a local anesthetic.

PART USED: Leaves

MAGICKAL: If there is a tarot card relationship to this plant, it is The Devil card. Although Wiccans do not generally believe in the existence of such a manifestation of evil as the Devil or Satan, that tarot card describes this plant to a T. Coca leaves and their concentrate (cocaine) are highly addictive. As Wiccans seek a symbiotic relationship with the Green World rather than a relationship of slavery and servitude, the use of this plant and its extract should be avoided except that use stipulated by accredited medical professionals.

Cocaine—*See* Coca, Bolivian

Cocklebur—*See* Agrimony and Burdock

Cockle Buttons—*See* Burdock

Cocks—*See* Plantain, Ribwort

Coconut—*Cocos nucifera*—Feminine, Moon, Water

Also known as Niyog, Ranedj

ASTROLOGICAL: *Primary*: Cancer; *Secondary*: Cancer, Pisces, Scorpio

GODS: Ganymede, Mars, Oko, Olocun, Orunla

GODDESSES: Athena, Nut, Yemaya

MAGICKAL: In lore found where Coconut trees grow, they are used much the way Europeans used "Witches Bottles" for protection. Either whole or split and filled with other items of protection, they were hung in the home. It is said that lovers who drink from the same Coconut will forever have their relationship protected by the spirit that previously inhabited it. Curiously enough, it was while I was in Germany that I found this lore. The subject came up while I was pondering the fact that one simply cannot purchase a reportedly traditional German chocolate cake while in Germany. Why? No Coconut trees.

Coconut

Coffee—*Coffea arabica*—Masculine, Mars, Fire

ASTROLOGICAL: *Primary*: Scorpio, Aries; *Secondary:* Aries, Leo, Sagittarius

GOD: Eleggua

MEDICAL: Stimulant. Some forms of asthma respond well to a good strong cup of Coffee. Generally speaking, it is used as a cognitive stimulant. Incidentally, if you have heard of Coffee enemas and thought they were ridiculous, you will love to hear that such procedures have historically been prescribed to combat narcotic overdose. You see, *narcotics* are bad.

PARTS USED: Leaves, Seeds

MAGICKAL: Instant Coffee will work in spellcraft, but freshly brewed is much better. Coffee is the author's beverage of choice as it heightens the cognitive abilities and frees one's mind from writer's block. It is also useful for clearing the mind of blocks in all creative activities. The scent of freshly ground or brewed Coffee has the effects listed above, but will not result in restless sleep or excess physical energy.

Cohosh, Black—*Cimicifuga racemosa*—Masculine

Also known as Actaea, Black Snakeroot, Bugbane, Cimicifuga, Rattle Root, Squawroot

MEDICAL: Alterative, Astringent, Diuretic, Emmenagogue, Expectorant. Reportedly, the root is an antidote to rattlesnake bites. My advice: Always go to the emergency room when bitten by a rattlesnake.

PART USED: Root

MAGICKAL: An infusion of Black Cohosh can be added to the bath to relieve impotency as well as drive away negative energy. Also used as a floor wash.

Cohosh

Cohosh, Blue—*Caulophyllum thalictroides*—Masculine

Also known as Blueberry Root, Squawroot, Papoose Root

MEDICAL: Anthelmintic, Antispasmodic, Diuretic, Diaphoretic, Emmenagogue, Nervine, Stimulant. Sometimes listed as a general and uterine stimulant. A warm water infusion of the leaves and stems tends to calm the mind.

However, this will typically increase blood pressure and cause blood vessel constriction.

PART USED: Root

Cokan—*See* Pokeweed

Cola—*See* Kola Nut

Cole Seed—*See* Mustard, Rape

Colewort—*See* Avens

Colic Root—*See* Galangal; Snakeroot, Button; and Yam, Wild

Coll—*See* Hazelnut

Coltsfoot—*Tussilago farfara*—Feminine, Venus, Water

Also known as Ass's Foot, British Tobacco, Bull's Foot, Butterbur, Coughwort, Donnhove, Hallfoot, Horsehoof, Pad'ane, Pas d'ane, Sponnc, Foal's Foot, Fieldhove, Foalswort

ASTROLOGICAL: *Primary*: Libra, Taurus; *Secondary*: Cancer, Pisces, Scorpio

MEDICAL: Demulcent, Expectorant, Tonic. A decoction is made with 1 ounce of the herb and 1 quart of water. Decrease volume by boiling to 1 pint. Strain and serve in 8-ounce doses. Will aid breathing, rid the body of toxins, and act as an expectorant. Coltsfoot is also used in cough syrups and other preparations to relieve the symptoms of the common cold and flu.

PARTS USED: Herb, Flowers, Leaves, Root

MAGICKAL: Sometimes called British Tobacco, the leaves are often smoked in a pipe to induce visions and a sense of tranquility. Some report a mild aphrodisiac effect. Coltsfoot is also carried on the person for these same attributes.

Coltstail—*See* Fleabane, Canadian

☠**Columbine**—*Aquilegia vulgaris*—Feminine, Venus, Water

Also known as Culverwort and Lion's Herb

ASTROLOGICAL: *Primary*: Libra, Taurus; *Secondary*: Cancer, Pisces, Scorpio

MEDICAL: Astringent. Historically used as an astringent; however, this plant has been abandoned due to its toxicity.

PARTS USED: Leaves, Roots, Seeds

MAGICKAL: The Saxons, who called this wildflower the Culverwort, rubbed the fresh flowers between their hands before battle to gain courage. The crushed seeds are rubbed into the palms to attract women.

Colza—*See* Mustard, Rape

Comfrey—*Symphytum officinale*—Feminine, Saturn, Water

Also known as Assear, Blackwort, Boneset, Bruisewort, Consohda, Consound, Gavez, Gum Plant, Healing Herb, Knitback, Knit Bone, Miracle Herb, Slippery Root, Wallwort, Smeerwartel, Karakaffes, Yulluc, Ztworkost

WARNING: Should never be taken internally by women who are pregnant or nursing.

ASTROLOGICAL: *Primary*: Aquarius, Capricorn; *Secondary*: Cancer, Pisces, Scorpio

MEDICAL: Astringent (mild), Demulcent, Diuretic, Expectorant, Stimulant, Tonic. A decoction is made with 1 ounce of the chopped root in 1 quart of water. Reduce by boiling to 1 pint and strain. Serve 4 ounces at a time for relief from common congestion and minor aches and pains. It works as an expectorant, mild diuretic, and calms the mind. As an infusion, the leaves and root are both good for cuts and scratches as it cleans and kills bacteria. Acts as a mild stimulant and topical astringent. Substitute milk for water in the above decoction as a treatment for diarrhea. The diarrhea will become more prevalent an hour after consumption and then taper off. Drink one glass every couple of hours until symptoms stop. Comfrey leaves are an excellent poultice material for sprains and sore muscles.

Comfrey

PARTS USED: Leaves, Root

MAGICKAL: The Saxons called this plant Yulluc and believed it would protect them in their travels. Sachets of comfrey were sometimes given to bards and entertainers to protect them as they traveled from town to town.

Common Bamboo—*See* Bamboo

Common Barberry—*See* Barberry, Common

Common Club Moss—*See* Moss, Common Club

Common Daisy—*See* Daisy, Common

Common Fleabane—*See* Fleabane, Common

Common Gorse—*See* Gorse

Common Groundsel—*See* Groundsel, Common

Common Heather—*See* Heather

Common Hedge Mustard—*See* Mustard, Common Hedge

Common Henbane—*See* Henbane

Common Hydrangea—*See* Hydrangea

Common Lilac—*See* Lilac

Common Lime—*See* Lime Tree

Common Maidenhair—*See* Fern

Common Mallow—*See* Mallow, Blue

Common Mulberry—*See* Mulberry, Common

Common Nettle—*See* Nettle, Lesser

Common Oak—*See* Oak

Common Plantain—*See* Plantain, Common

Common Polypody—*See* Fern

Common Sage—*See* Sage, Common

Common Scullcap—*See* Scullcap

Common Shrubby Everlasting—*See* Gnaphalium Stoechas

Common Spleenwort—*See* Fern

Common Thyme—*See* Thyme

Common Wayside Dock—*See* Dock, Round-leaved

Compass Plant—*Silphium laciniatum/ Silphium paciniatum*
See also Rosemary, as they share many of the same common names.
Silphium laciniatum and *Silphium paciniatum* are actually two closely related plants. However, they share so many common names that these plants seem to be indistinguishable in lore and reference. Generally speaking, *Silphium laciniatum* is listed as having the common names Compass Plant, Compass Weed, Polar Plant, and Rosin Weed, but it is also sometimes known as Bumweed and Compass Point. However, Rosin Weed is sometimes listed as only a folk name for *Silphium paciniatum*. *Silphium paciniatum* is listed as having the common names Compass Plant, Compass Weed, Polar Plant, and Rosin Weed. So then, the names Bumweed and Compass Point seem unique to *Silphium laciniatum*; the name Rosin Weed might be more or less unique to *Silphium Paciniatum*. Chances are if you are in Ohio and happen to think you have found the Compass Plant, this is the one you have found.
MEDICAL: (*Silphium perfoliatum and Silphium paciniatum*)—Alterative, Diaphoretic, Tonic
MAGICKAL: The roots of the Compass Plant (whichever variety) were once believed to ward off lightning when burned, and the rest of the plant was used in other forms of weather magick.

Compass Point—*See* Compass Plant

Compass-weed—*See* Compass Plant and Rosemary

Cornu Cervinum—*See* Plantain, Buck's Horn

Consohda—*See* Comfrey

Consound—*See* Comfrey

Consumptive's Weed—*See* Yerba Santa

Copal—*Bursera odorata*—Masculine, Sun, Fire
ASTROLOGICAL: *Primary*: Leo; *Secondary*: Aries, Leo, Sagittarius
GODS: Babalu Aye, Eleggua, Obatala, Oggun,
GODDESS: Ochun
MAGICKAL: There are many different types of Copal resin. But two different categories stick out. The first is the white to yellow variety. These vary from white to a deep yellow. The other is black (see Copal, Black). The white/yellow Copal is often burned over charcoal for protection and the drawing of Sun energy. It is sometimes used in recipes to attract love but seems to work only for men attempting to attract women. Even then, there are much better choices. True essential oil of Copal is available, but it is rare, costly, and unusual to find in the Western marketplace. However, if you are fortunate enough to find it, then you are truly blessed as almost nothing can overcome general depression like a room in which true essential oil of Copal has been diffused. Failing the availability of essential oil, the aroma of Copal can be added to the air by slowly burning over charcoal. Its aroma is similar to Frankincense, but with a slight hint of citrus. The aroma is uplifting and cleansing.

Copal, Black—*Bursera fugaroides*—Masculine, Sun, Fire
Also known as Copal Negro, Food of the Gods
ASTROLOGICAL: *Primary*: Leo; *Secondary*: Aries, Leo, Sagittarius
GOD: Obatala
GODDESS: Ochun
MAGICKAL: Aztecs called Black Copal the "Food of the Gods." It is burned to gain the blessings of the native deities of South America. I have never seen essential oil of Black Copal available either in the Western world or on the world market. Its rich pine scent is dispersed into the air by burning over charcoal. It smells like Frankincense with a strong hint of Pine. The aroma is uplifting and cleansing.

Copal Negro—*See* Copal, Black

Coriander—*Coriandum sativum*—Masculine, Mars, Fire
Also known as Chinese Parsley, Cilantro, Cilentro, Culantro, Uan-Suy, Stinkdillsamen, Hu-Suy, Hu-Sui
ASTROLOGICAL: *Primary*: Aries, Scorpio; *Secondary*: Aries, Leo, Sagittarius
GODS: Babalu Aye, Obatala, Oko, Ochosi
GODDESS: Ochun
MEDICAL: Carminative, Stimulant
PARTS USED: Leaves, Oil, Seeds

When used in cooking, Coriander seeds will aid digestion. A warm water infusion acts as a mild stimulant. Mix with your favorite coffee.
MAGICKAL: Send your lover off to work with a pinch of powdered Coriander brewed into his or her coffee each morning. After a full work week of this treatment, greet them at the door with a bottle of plum wine that has spent the day

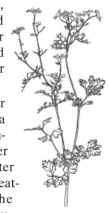

Coriander

soaking in powdered Coriander. You will have a lust-filled evening. Essential oil of Coriander can be diffused to relieve the common headache and may cause a shift in consciousness conducive to healing.

Corn—*Zea Mays*—Feminine, Venus, Earth
Also known as Giver of Life, Maize, Sacred Mother, Seed of Seeds
ASTROLOGICAL: *Primary*: Libra, Taurus; *Secondary*: Capricorn, Taurus, Virgo
GODS: Cinteotl, Gwion, Oko

GODDESSES: Corn Goddess/Mother

MEDICAL: Diuretic (silk), Tonic (silk, husk)

PARTS USED: Husk, Seeds, Silk

To relieve a stuffed-up nose and headache, a decoction of Corn husks and water is often the trick. Boil for 30 minutes, strain, and sweeten with honey. A warm water infusion of Corn silk will act as a diuretic, a urinary tract cleanser, kidney cleanser, and general tonic.

Corn

MAGICKAL: Laced on a necklace or ground into a powder, blue Corn is used to bring the blessings of Mother Earth in her incarnation as Corn Mother. Red Corn is ground and mixed with incense to aid childbirth. Interestingly enough, the color associations with the four cardinal directions by today's Wiccans may have been influenced by pre-Columbian people. Similar color associations were made by some of the Pueblo people of Western New Mexico (the Zuni in particular). Generally, Wiccans use green for North (Earth), but the other three are strikingly similar to modern convention:

East (Air)—White Corn

South (Fire)—Red Corn

West (Water)—Blue Corn

North (Earth)—Yellow Corn

GENERAL: Contrary to popular belief, Maize is not a pre-Columbian American name. The word's origin is Spanish, *maiz*. The word simply migrated into the Arawakan (*mahiz* and *mahis*) via Cuba. In the great majority of the English-speaking world, the name *Corn* is a general name meaning "grain." Hence the widespread attack on modern Pagan authors who made reference to pre-Christian European Pagans making Corn dolls as what is now called Corn in the United States was not present in pre-Christian Europe. Now if the author said "corn husk" dolls, attack away as it is probably close to impossible to create a doll of most other grains (too small).

Corn Flower—*See* Bachelor's Buttons

Corn Rose—*See* Poppy, Red

Corn Poppy—*See* Poppy, Red

Cornish Lovage—*See* Lovage

Corn Mint—*See* Mint

Corsican Moss—*See* Moss, Corsican

Cortex Granati—*See* Pomegranate

Cortezade Granada—*See* Pomegranate

Coneflower—*See* Echinacea

Convallaria—*See* Lily of the Valley

Convall-Lily—*See* Lily of the Valley

Costa Canina—*See* Plantain, Ribwort

Costmary—*Tanacetum balsamita*—Masculine, Mercury, Air

Also known as Bible Leaf

ASTROLOGICAL: *Primary*: Virgo, Gemini; *Secondary*: Aquarius, Gemini, Libra

MEDICAL: Emmenagogue, Expectorant, Tonic. Expression from fresh plant material is useful in mending cuts. Both fresh herb and a warm water infusion act as an expectorant and general tonic.

PART USED: Leaves

MAGICKAL: A strong infusion of the dried leaves can be used in mop water to clean kitchen and bath during the Spring Equinox to bring on the energy needed for spring cleaning and the launching of new projects. Simmering the fresh leaves will bring on a feeling of refreshment, causing hidden physical and emotional energy to rise for whatever purpose you intend.

Cotton—*Gossypium barbadense*—Feminine, Moon, Earth

Astrological: *Primary*: Cancer; *Secondary*: Capricorn, Taurus, Virgo

Medical: Abortifacient. For reference purpose only, the root of the Cotton plant was used by slaves in the United States to bring on abortion. As with most abortifacients, this is accomplished by bringing on contractions of the uterus. An infusion of the seeds reportedly increases the production of milk in nursing women.

Parts used: Root, Seeds

Magickal: Generally speaking, Cotton is the best material to make sachets and bags used in magick.

Cotton

Cottonweed—*See* Cudweed

Coughwort—*See* Coltsfoot

Coumaria Nut—*See* Tonka

Cowbane—*See* Hemlock, Water

Cowcucumber—*See* Cucumber

Cowcumber—*See* Cucumber

Cow-Flop—*See* Foxglove

Cowgrass—*See* Knotgrass

Cowslip—*Primulas veris*—Feminine, Venus, Water

Also known as Arthritica, Artetyke, Buckles, Crewel, Cuy, Cuy Lippe, Drelip, Fairy Cups, Frauenschlussel, Herb Peter, Key Flower, Key of Heaven, Lady's Key, Lippe, Mayflower, Our Lady's Keys, Paigle, Paralysio, Palsywort, Password, Peggle, Petty Mulleins, Plumrocks

In their gold coats spots you see;
Those be rubies, fairy favours,
In those freckles live their savours:

I must go seek some dewdrops here
And hang a pearl in every cowslip's ear.

—William Shakespeare, *A Midsummer Night's Dream*

Astrological: *Primary*: Libra, Taurus; *Secondary*: Cancer, Pisces, Scorpio

Goddess: Freya

Medical: Antispasmodic, Sedative

Part used: The yellow center portion of the flower.

Magickal: The Saxons called it Cuy Lippe. Ancient Greeks called it Paralysio. Both used it to make a mildly narcotic and aphrodisiacal wine with recipes such as the one found in Chapter 6.

Coyne—*See* Quince

Cramp Bark—*Viburnum opulus*

Also known as Black Haw, Crampweed, Dog Rowan Tree, Gaitre Berries, Guelder Rose, High Cranberry, King's Crown, May Rose, Red Elder, Silver Bells, Snowball Tree, Water Elder, Whitsun Bosses, Witsun Rose

Medical: Antispasmodic, Diuretic, Nervine. A decoction is made with 1/2 ounce powdered bark in 1 pint of water. Reduce by one half. Strain and serve in tablespoon doses. May be used as tea, but not as effectively as decoction.

Part used: Bark

Crampweed—*See* Cramp Bark and Five-Finger Grass

Cranberry—*Vaccinium oxycoccus*—Feminine, Moon, Water

Astrological: *Primary*: Cancer; *Secondary:* Cancer, Pisces, Scorpio

Medical: Tonic

Part used: Fruit

Drinking Cranberry juice will lower the acidity level of urine within the body. This will ease the pain associated with kidney infections, allow the kidneys to heal, and lessen diaper

Cranberry

rash in children. Children who drink 4 ounces of Cranberry juice right before sleep are less likely to wet the bed.

MAGICKAL: Cranberry lends itself to protection.

NOTE: Some folk list the planetary association of cranberry as Mars, due to its red color.

Cranesbill Root, American—*See* Geranium

Crocus—*Crocus vemus*—Feminine, Venus, Water

See also Saffron, Spanish, as it shares this folk name.

ASTROLOGICAL: *Primary*: Libra, Taurus; *Secondary*: Cancer, Pisces, Scorpio

GODS: Oko, Olocun

MAGICKAL: Crocus is grown to attract love.

Cross-leaved Gentian—*See* Gentian

Crosswort—*See* Boneset

Crowberry—*See* Pokeweed

Crowdy Kit—*See* Figwort, Water

Crown Corn—*See* Ague Root

Crown of Thorns—*See* Spurges

Crowsfoot—*See* Geranium

Crewel—*See* Cowslip

Cuca—*See* Coca, Bolivian

Cubeb—*Piper cubeba*—Masculine, Mars, Fire
Also known as Tailed Pepper

ASTROLOGICAL: *Primary*: Aries, Scorpio; *Secondary*: Aries, Leo, Sagittarius

MEDICAL: Carminative, Stimulant. Historically, used to treat gonorrhea.

PART USED: Unripe Fruit

MAGICKAL: Dried Cubeb berries are often ground and used in sachets and incense recipes to attract and heighten lust. This is mildly amusing, as the same plant has been used to treat gonorrhea.

Cuckoo's Bread—*See* Plantain, Common

Cuckowe's Meat—*See* Sorrel, Wood

Cucumber—*Cucumis sativus*—Feminine, Moon, Water

Also known as Agurk, Cowcucumber, Cowcumber, Gurka, Haswey, Kheyar, Lekiti

ASTROLOGICAL: *Primary*: Cancer; *Secondary*: Cancer, Pisces, Scorpio

MEDICAL: Diuretic. Cucumber slices placed over the eyes will relieve minor signs of fatigue. Drinking Cucumber juice will relieve many kidney problems. Sliced and placed on the eyes, cucumbers are also said to relieve tension and promote concentration.

Cucumber

PARTS USED: Fruit, Seeds

MAGICKAL: The plant that proves that plant genders were not always assigned because of the look of the plant. Interestingly enough, if a man eats the fruit of a Cucumber, it will decrease lust, but if a woman eats the seeds, they will promote both lust and fertility.

Cucumber Tree—*See* Magnolia

Cuddle Me—*See* Heartsease

Cuddy's Lungs—*See* Mullein

Cudweed—*Graphalium uliginosum*

Also known as Cottonweed, March Everlasting

See also Catsfoot, Life Everlasting (Perl Flowered)

MEDICAL: Astringent. A warm water infusion makes a fine mouthwash and combats infections of the mouth.

PART USED: Herb

MAGICKAL: Carried or worn, Cudweed reportedly restores youthfulness.

Culantro—*See* Coriander

Cull Me—*See* Heartsease

Culverwort—*See* Columbine

Cumin—*Cumimum cyminum*—Masculine, Mars, Fire

Also known as Cumino, Cumino Aigro, Sanoot, Kimoon, Passion Seed

ASTROLOGICAL: *Primary*: Aries, Scorpio; *Secondary*: Aries, Leo, Sagittarius

GODS: Babalu Aye, Shango, Eleggua, Obatala, Ochosi, Oggun, Oko, Olocun

GODDESSES: Ochun, Yemaya

MEDICAL: Antispasmodic, Carminative, Stimulant. Generally added to food or taken in powdered form.

PART USED: Fruit

MAGICKAL: While in Germany, I noticed that a lot of the cottage industry breads sold on the street contained just a hint of Cumin. Though I asked many merchants why this was, the only answer I ever received was that it was in the recipe. Much later, while reading herb lore, I found that the Cumin was baked into the bread to keep it from being stolen off their stands. During the Middle Ages, Cumin was one of the most popular spices grown in Europe. Although commonly mixed with all orders of food, Cumin is also found in great amounts of folklore. Ground and scattered on the floor, it guards the home and brings the blessings of love. In a fine white sachet, it was carried by brides to ensure that baneful forces did not attack her wedding, and then the sachet was given to her husband to ensure his fidelity. Lore states that if a new husband wears a sachet of Cumin around his neck as he makes love to his bride, the scent of the Cumin will ensure her conception. For a quick and easy lust potion, serve it to your lover on a cold night in front of a warm fire. Pour two glasses of wine and sprinkle equal amounts of powdered Cumin in each glass, warm by the fire, and drink together. Passion and lust will certainly follow. If it does not, repeat. Crushed Cumin seeds are added to potpourri and simmered to fill the home with a sense of security. The scent will mildly elevate existing lust.

Cumino—*See* Cumin

Cumino Aigro—*See* Cumin

Cup Moss—*See* Moss, Cup

Curled Dock—*See* Dock, Yellow

Curled Mint—*See* Mint

Currant, Black—*Ribes nigrum*

Also known as Quinsy Berries, Squinancy Berries

MEDICAL: Diaphoretic, Diuretic, Febrifuge. A warm water infusion of the leaves acts as a diuretic and treats gout. Gargle with it to relieve sore throats. Juice of the berry is both diuretic and diaphoretic in nature. A decoction is made of the bark.

PARTS USED: Bark, Fruit, Leaves, Root

Currant, Red—*Ribes rubrum*

Also known as Reps, Ribs, Risp

MEDICAL: Antiscorbutic, Aperient, Laxative, Refrigerant. An expression of the fruit works well to sooth burns and prevent blisters. A jelly made with equal amounts of sugar is a great spread for toast on hot summer mornings. The expression of the berry mixed with equal amounts of water and served over ice will cool the body.

PART USED: Fruit

Curry, Black—*Murraya koenigii*—Masculine, Mars, Fire

ASTROLOGICAL: *Primary*: Aries, Scorpio; *Secondary*: Aries, Leo, Sagittarius

MAGICKAL: When you see a reference to Curry outside of a cookbook, you are probably looking for the specific plant *Murraya koenigii* and not the blend of spices called for in cookbooks by the same name. Reportedly, if one burns Curry at night, it will keep away evil spirits. I have never found the burning of Curry to do anything other than stink up the house.

Cutweed—*See* Bladderwrack

Cuy—*See* Cowslip

Cuy Lippe—*See* Cowslip

Cyclamen, Ivy-leaved—*Cyclamen hederaefolium*—Feminine, Venus, Water

Also known as Groundbread, Pain de Porceau, Passion Ivy, Sow-Bread, Swine Bread

ASTROLOGICAL: *Primary*: Libra, Taurus; *Secondary*: Cancer, Pisces, Scorpio

GODDESS: Hecate

MAGICKAL: Grown in the ritual area or around the home, Cyclamen is said to protect the area from baneful spells cast against the property owner or his/her guests. The act of love when surrounded by Cyclamen is said to heighten passion and promote conception. Using small amounts of the taproot in sweet breads and similar desserts is said to cause a person to fall deeply in love with the person with whom it is shared. However, there is some information indicating that overconsumption may be dangerous. The problem is that references are not specific as to what a safe dose is.

Cypress—*Cupressus sempervirens*—Feminine, Saturn, Earth

Also known as Tree of Death

ASTROLOGICAL: *Primary*: Aquarius, Capricorn; *Secondary*: Capricorn, Taurus, Virgo

GODS: Apollo, Babalu Aye, Brahma, Shango, Cupid, Jupiter, Mithras, Oggun, Pluto, Saturn

GODDESSES: Aphrodite, Astarte, Artemis, Athena, Bhavani, Cybele, Demeter, Heket, Hebe, Mut, Nephthys, Rhea

MAGICKAL: If you purchase Cypress at the store and it seems just a little bit too green to be natural, chances are that it is not. Soaking it in warm water will generally remove the artificial green coloring agent. You will then have to dry it for a week or so before using it. Cypress is strongly associated with death. It was used in ancient Egypt to make coffins and is still used today to

Cypress

ease the passage of both the departed and his or her loved ones. A Cypress flower arrangement is an excellent gift at a wake, when sitting shivah, or sent to the home of one who is grieving. A home built without disturbing surrounding Cypress trees is well-protected by the magickal properties of the trees. A branch of Cypress waved over the sick is said to absorb the sickness. Burn the branch after use to destroy the sickness that was removed. For this reason, Cypress is often included in incense recipes. A small sprig of Cypress gently tied to a rose will bless the deceased and help him or her to move on. Essential oil of Cypress is diffused to ease grief and transition.

Daphne—*See* Bay

☠ **Daffodil**—*Narcissus Pseudo-narcissus*—Feminine, Venus, Water

Also known as Asphodel, Daffy-Down-Dilly, Fleur de Coucou, Goose Leek, Lent Lily, Narcissus, Porillon

ASTROLOGICAL: *Primary*: Libra, Taurus; *Secondary*: Cancer, Pisces, Scorpio

GODS: Adonis, Attis

GODDESSES: Ceres, Yemaya

MAGICKAL: A Daffodil in the lapel of a fine suit will attract love and increase luck in all matters. Fresh (preferably planted) daffodils in the bedroom will increase the chances of conception, especially when watered by both lovers just prior to the act of love. Fresh Daffodil flowers are simmered to encourage a sense of contented love.

Daffodil

GENERAL: The attributes are sometimes cited as Masculine, Mars, Fire.

Daffy-Down-Dilly—*See* Daffodil

Daggers—*See* Iris

Daisy, American—*See* Daisy, Common

☠Daisy, Common—*Bellis perennis*—Feminine, Venus, Water

Also known as American Daisy, Bruisewort, Bairnwort, Eye of the Day, Llygad y Dydd

ASTROLOGICAL: *Primary*: Libra, Taurus; *Secondary*: Cancer, Pisces, Scorpio

GODS: Thor, Oko

MAGICKAL: The Scotts called it Bairnwort. The Welsh called Llygad y Dydd (Eye of the Day). Worn to attract love, but the Ox-eye Daisy has a much better effect, causing your tongue to become silver so you will attract affections to yourself.

NOTE: Many references intermix the magickal properties and folk names of the Common Daisy (*Bellis perennis*) and the Ox-Eye Daisy (*Chrysanthemum leucanthemum*), making distinction in lore difficult.

Daisy, European—See Daisy, Ox-eye

☠Daisy, Ox-eye—*Chrysanthemum leucanthemum, Leucanthemum vulgare*—Feminine, Venus, Water

Also known as European Daisy, Great Ox-eye, Goldens, Marguerite, Moon Daisy, Horse Gowan, Maudlin Daisy, Field Daisy, Dun Daisy, Butter Daisy, Horse Daisy, Maudlinwort, Gowan

ASTROLOGICAL: *Primary*: Libra, Taurus; *Secondary*: Cancer, Pisces, Scorpio

GOD: Thor

GODDESSES: Artemis, Freya

MEDICAL: Antispasmodic, Diuretic. The flowers and herb are used as tea. One ounce of the root is made into a decoction with 1 quart of water. Reduce by boiling to 1 pint. Strain and serve by the tablespoon.

PARTS USED: Flower, Herb, Root

MAGICKAL: Like Freya, to whom the Daisy is sacred, wearing the first Ox-eye Daisies of spring will give the gift of flirtation, attracting love, and inspiring lust with your silver tongue. The Scotts called it Gowan.

*NOTE: Many references intermix the magickal properties and folk names of the Common Daisy (*Bellis perennis*) and the Ox-eye Daisy (*Chrysanthemum leucanthemum*), making distinction in lore difficult.

Damiana —*Turnera aphrodisiaca/Turnera diffuse*—Masculine, Mars, Fire

ASTROLOGICAL: *Primary*: Aries, Scorpio; *Secondary*: Aries, Leo, Sagittarius

GODS: Ganesha, Kurma, Shu, Vishnu, Zeus

GODDESSES: Artemis, Diana

MEDICAL: Diuretic, Purgative (mild), Stimulant, Tonic. Served as tea for a general tonic. A decoction of 1 ounce in 1 quart of water is reduced by boiling to 1 pint. Strain and serve in 4-ounce doses as a stimulant of the reproductive organs.

PART USED: Leaves

MAGICKAL: An infusion of Damiana can be used as a simple lust potion. The decoction described above is better. However, it seems to have a cumulative effect, causing the person who consumes it to be sought after. Drink a cup of Damiana tea with each meal for a month for this potion to have strong effect. I believe this works by enhancing natural empathy. Adding Saw Palmetto berries (*Serenoa repens*) in an equal amount by weight will greatly enhance the potion's effect on women, but will make little difference in men. Damiana is sometimes added to incense to aid in obtaining visions; it is smoked for this purpose as well. Smoking Damiana reportedly acts on the body as a mild euphoric. When encountering a recipe that calls for Hashish, an extract of the volatile oils in Damiana can be mixed back into the dry leaves to form a magickal substitute.

Dandelion—*Taraxacum officinale*—Masculine, Jupiter, Air

Also known as Blowball, Cankerwort, Lion's Tooth, Piss-a-Bell, Priest's Crown, Puffball, Swine Snout, White Endive, Wild Endive

ASTROLOGICAL: *Primary*: Pisces, Sagittarius; *Secondary*: Aquarius, Gemini, Libra

MEDICAL: Diuretic, Tonic. Vegetarians and diabetics will benefit from including Dandelion flowers in their diet. Dandelions aid in anemia and stabilizing blood sugar. Fresh Dandelion flowers and greens act as a mild diuretic (mix them into your salad). Eating fresh Dandelions with large amounts of water will quicken recovery from hangovers. The fresh juice expressed from their stems is said to remove warts. A warm water infusion of Dandelion is a good tonic for the liver and gallbladder.

Dandelion

PARTS USED: Leaves, Roots

MAGICKAL: Mix equal amounts of coffee grinds and roasted Dandelion root. Brew as you would coffee and drink an hour prior to divination for added vision. Neither sweeten, nor add milk.

GENERAL: You have not lived until you have had homemade Dandelion wine. Dandelion wine brings a quick intoxication that leaves the head clear after a short period of time. It's simple chemistry at its finest. The diuretic properties of Dandelion drive fluids from the body such that the alcohol is absorbed quickly. However, the same properties drive the alcohol out as well.

Darlahad—*See* Barberry, Indian and Barberry, Nepal

Date—*See* Palm, Date

Datura—*See* Thornapple

Dayyap—*See* Lime

Deadly Nightshade—*See* Belladonna

Dead Men's Bells—*See* Foxglove

Dead Nettle—*See* Nettle, Purple Dead; Nettle, White Dead; and Nettle, Yellow Dead

Deaf Nettle—*See* Nettle, White Dead

Death Angel—*See* Agaric Mushroom

Death Cap—*See* Agaric Mushroom

Death Flower—*See* Yarrow

Death's Herb—*See* Belladonna

Deerstongue—*Liatris odoratissima*—Masculine, Mars, Fire

Also known as Hound's-Tongue, Trilissia odorata, Vanilla Leaf, Wild Vanilla

ASTROLOGICAL: *Primary*: Aries, Scorpio; *Secondary*: Aries, Leo, Sagittarius

GODS: Shango, Ochosi, Oko

GODDESS: Ochun

MEDICAL: Demulcent, Diaphoretic, Febrifuge. Both decoction and infusion are employed.

PART USED: Leaves

MAGICKAL: Deerstongue is used by women to attract men. Carry in a pink sachet; burn with Gum Arabic by an open window. Simmered in water, dried leaves of Deerstongue will release a gentle vanilla scent. This scent stimulates the intuitive portions of the brain. This is an excellent herb to simmer during tarot readings. Will also cause a heightened sense of lust in men.

Deilen Ddu—*See* Figwort, Knotted

Delicate Bess—*See* Valerian, Red-Spur

Delight of the Eyes—*See* Ash, Mountain

Desert Tea—*See* Ma Huang

Deus Caballinus—*See* Henbane

Devil's Apple—*See* Thornapple

Devil's Bit—*See* Ague Root; Scabious, Field; Scabious, Lesser; and Scabious, Devil's Bit

Devil's Bite—*See* Snakeroot, Button

Devil's Dung—*See* Asafoetida

Devil's Eye—*See* Henbane and Periwinkle

Devil's Cherries—*See* Belladonna

Devil's Flower—*See* Bachelor's Buttons

Devil's Guts—*See* Dodder

Devil's Milk—*See* Celandine, Greater

Devil's Nettle—*See* Yarrow

Devil's Oatmeal—*See* Parsley

Devil's Shoestring—*Vibumum alnifolium*
Also known as Lucky Money Root
MAGICKAL: The root is carried for prosperity when gambling or looking for employment.

Devil's Tree—*See* Dita Tree

Devil's Trumpet—*See* Thornapple

Dewberry—*See* Blackberry

Dew of the Sea—*See* Rosemary

Dhan—*See* Rice

Didin—*See* Myrrh

Didthin—*See* Myrrh

Digitalis—*See* Foxglove

Dill—*Anethum graveolens/Peucedanum graveolens*—Masculine, Mercury, Fire

Also known as Aneton, Buzzalchippet, Chebbit, Dill Weed, Dilly, Garden Dill, Fructus Anethi, Hulwa, Keper, Sowa
ASTROLOGICAL: *Primary*: Gemini, Virgo; *Secondary*: Aries, Leo, Sagittarius
GODS: Shango, Eleggua
GODDESS: Ochun
MEDICAL: Carminative, Stimulant, Stomachic. Increases milk production in breastfeeding women.

Dill

Settles the stomach and relieves gas pain. Generally speaking, it is used in cooking for its medical properties.
PART USED: Seeds
MAGICKAL: An infusion of Dill added to the bath attracts love. Used in cooking, it inspires lust. Although Dill acts as an aphrodisiac when consumed, its scent is one of cleansing. Simmer fresh Dill during spring-cleaning and after the home has been closed for some time to rid it of that sick home feeling.

Dill Weed—*See* Dill

Dilly—*See* Dill

Dita Tree—*Alstonia scholaris*
Also known as Alstonia, Bitter Bark, Devil's Tree, Pale Mara, Chatim
MEDICAL: Vermifuge. The bark is used to make an infusion that has been said to relieve menstrual cramps, treat parasitic worms, and resolve chronic diarrhea.
PART USED: Bark
MAGICKAL: Dita Tree seeds were once thought to be mildly aphrodisiac. From their use in that capacity, they have been found to enhance the pleasure of sexual intercourse by slightly depressing the central nervous system, thus delaying male orgasm and prolonging erection. Prepare an infusion of Damiana and allow to cool. Add 2 grams of crushed Dita Tree seed to 2 cups Damiana infusion. Mix thoroughly. Shake every 4 hours for 24 hours; strain and serve. Any single batch of seeds will have varying amounts of the active ingredient and every man will respond differently, so you will have to experiment.
GENERAL: In the East, the bark of the Dita Tree was once used much the way paper is today.

Dioscorea—*See* Yam, Wild

Dittany of Crete—*Dictamus origanoides/ Dictamus albus*—Feminine, Venus, Water
ASTROLOGICAL: *Primary*: Libra, Taurus; *Secondary*: Cancer, Pisces, Scorpio
GODS: Osiris, Orunla

GODDESSES: Oya, Persephone, Psyche

MAGICKAL: Dittany of Crete is a base ingredient for astral projection incense as well as incense intended to bring about the manifestation of spirits.

Divale—*See* Belladonna

Divine Root—*See* Ginseng, American

Dreamer's Tree—*See* Beech

Drelip—*See* Cowslip

Dock, Red—*Rumex aquaticus*

Also known as Water Dock

MEDICAL: Alterative, Deobstruent, Tonic. Used as a warm water infusion.

PART USED: Root

MAGICKAL: When a love spell calls for the blood of a dove, mix a strong infusion of Red Dock with the juice of red grapes and use it instead.

Dock, Round-leaved—*Rumex obtusifolius*

Also known as Common Wayside Dock, Butter Dock

MEDICAL: Fresh leaves are a folk remedy for mild burns and blisters. The leaves are often applied as a rustic remedy for burns and scalds and used for dressing blisters, serving also as a popular cure for Nettle stings.

Dock, Yellow—*Rumex crispus*—Masculine, Jupiter, Air

Also known as Curled Dock

ASTROLOGICAL: *Primary*: Pisces, Sagittarius; *Secondary*: Aquarius, Gemini, Libra

MEDICAL: Alterative, Laxative, Tonic

PART USED: Root

MAGICKAL: An infusion of Yellow Dock root is useful in drawing money to a business. Simply sprinkle it about the place, but be careful, as it stains.

Dog Chamomile—*See* Chamomile, Stinking

Dog's Finger—*See* Foxglove

Dodder—*Cusseta European/Cusseta glomurata*—Feminine, Saturn, Water

Also known as Beggarweed, Devil's Guts, Fireweed, Hellweed, Lady's Laces, Love Vine, Scaldweed, Strangle Tare, Witches' Hair

ASTROLOGICAL: *Primary*: Aquarius, Capricorn; *Secondary*: Cancer, Pisces, Scorpio

MAGICKAL: Dodder is used in cord and knot magick. It is especially useful in cord/knot magick for love in accordance with Will, but it is a very poor choice for bindings. Never use it for binding your love in a relationship, or it will have the opposite effect.

GENERAL: Dodder is a parasitic plant that forms no leaves. Instead, the bulk of the plant is stems that grow like laces.

☠**Dogbane**—*Apocynum androsaemifolium*

Also known as Amyroot, Bitterroot, General Marion's Weed, Indian Hemp, Rheumatism Weld, Wild Cotton, Wild Ipecac

GODDESS: Vesta

MAGICKAL: While some lore exists that this plant is used in love mixtures, such practices are not advised. While there are exceptions, if it is poisonous (bane) to a dog, it is not too good for humans. The folk name Indian Hemp comes from its strong fibers in the stalk and not any other property similar to Marijuana. Although the confusion has certainly made a few people rather sick, as skin contact with the fresh leaves may cause blistering.

Dogbane

Doffle—*See* Mullein

Dog-Fennel—*See* Chamomile, Stinking

Dog Tooth Violet—*See* Adder's-Tongue

Dove's Foot—*See* Geranium

Dulcamara—*See* Woody Nightshade

Dun Daisy—*See* Daisy, Ox-eye

Dutch Rushes—*See* Horsetails

Dog Bane—*See* Oleander

Dog-Bur—*See* Hounds Tongue

Dog's Tongue—*See* Hounds Tongue

Dolloff—*See* Meadowsweet

Dollor—*See* Meadowsweet

Donnersbart—*See* Houseleek

Donnhove—*See* Coltsfoot

Dracontium—*See* "Cabbage, Skunk"

Draconis Resina—*See* Dragon's Blood

Dragon's Blood—*Daemomorops Draco/ Daemomorops propinquos*—Masculine, Mars, Fire

Also known as Blood, Blume, Calamus Draco, Draconis Resina, Sanguis Draconis, Dragon's Blood Palm

ASTROLOGICAL: *Primary*: Aries, Scorpio; *Secondary*: Aries, Leo, Sagittarius

GODS: Agni, Ares, Shango, Eleggua, Horus the Elder, Horus the Younger, Mars, Montu, Obatala, Ochosi, Oggun, Olocun, Orunla, Shiva

GODDESSES: Athena, Minerva, Ochun, Oya

MEDICAL: Astringent, Disinfectant. Historically, it is a key ingredient in ancient cures for syphilis, but it probably did not work.

PART USED: Resin

MAGICKAL: When burned as incense, the smoke is mildly relaxing. It was carried by Roman soldiers to clean wounds, stop bleeding and provide relief from pain. However, the relief that it offered those soldiers was most likely due to its use as a topical disinfectant, not a narcotic value. Often, Dragon's Blood is a key ingredient in love and lust inspiring incenses. This is amusing, as historically it has been used to treat syphilis. Burn by an open window to cause a loved one to return. More than any other use, small amounts of Dragon's Blood are mixed with other incense to add forceful intent. While it is sometimes used in love spells, it is better it be used in matters where a firm hand is needed. I have found that although its smoke is a mild aphrodisiac to men, it should not be used in a place of business as it drives sales down. Odd, as Patchouli (an aphrodisiac for women) drives sales up.

GENERAL: In public high schools, this relatively inexpensive incense is sold as of "Red Opium" and with a more traditional name "Red Rock" for prices of about a dollar per gram, which is rather ridiculous because it is sold in herb shops for between three and five dollars (depending on market conditions) an ounce (about 28 grams). As with just about any smoke, if you concentrate it and inhale it, you will effectively asphyxiate yourself. In my store, this resin from a palm tree gives me hours of joy when unlearned people ask, "Is this real?" I answer, "Why, yes, it is. We keep the dragon in the basement and tap him regularly. Of course, the price of fire insurance when you have a dragon in your basement is outrageous."

Dragon's Blood Palm—*See* Dragon's Blood

Dragon Flower—*See* Iris

Dropberry—*See* Solomon's Seal

Drunken Sailor—*See* Valerian, Red-Spur

Drunken Soldier—*See* Valerian, Red-Spur

Duck's Foot—*See* Mandrake, American

Duffle—*See* Mullein

Dulse—*Rhodymenia palmatta*—Feminine, Moon, Water

ASTROLOGICAL: *Primary*: Cancer; *Secondary*: Cancer, Pisces, Scorpio

MAGICKAL: Reportedly, Dulse induces lust; I have not found this to be the case.

Dumb Nettle—*See* Nettle, White Dead

Dummy Nettle—*See* Nettle, Yellow Dead

Durmast Oak—*See* Oak

Dutch Honeysuckle—*See* Honeysuckle

Dutchman's Breeches—*Dicentra cucullaria*
MAGICKAL: Reportedly attracts love.

Dwale—*See* Belladonna

Dwaleberry—*See* Belladonna

Dwarf Flax—*See* Flax, Mountain

Dwarf Gorse—*See* Gorse

Dwarf Mallow—*See* Mallow, Dwarf

Dwayberry—*See* Belladonna

Dyer's Alkanet—*See* Alkanet

Dyer's Bugloss—*See* Alkanet

Dyer's Madder—*See* Madder

Dyer's Saffron—*See* Saffron, Mexican

Earth Smoke—*See* Fumitory

Earth Star—*See* Bromeliad

East India Catarrh Root—*See* Galangal

East Indian Rhubarb—*See* Rhubarb

Ebil—*See* Cardamom

Ebony—*Diospyros lotus*
Also known as Lama, Obeah Wood
MAGICKAL: Lore states that the Ebony tree attracts lightning and retains its power after struck. For this reason, Ebony wands are said to be particularly powerful.

Ebony

Amulets made of Ebony are used for protection. Dark Ebony is an ideal choice for the hilt of an athame or sword.
GENERAL: Do not even consider purchasing Ebony from any source that is not reputable. This is an endangered wood. Post-consumer Ebony, deadfall, and trees grown specifically for harvest are acceptable and legal sources of this wood. However, it is common for this wood to be illegally harvested and sold.
NOTE: Some will take issue with my approval of using endangered woods such as Ebony for magickal tools. Ecology is important. In fact, it is the core of what I hope this book will convey. However, understanding the importance of why a plant should be preserved is served by understanding its many uses. If something is seen as having no value, chances are it will be treated as if it has no value.

Echinacea—*Echinacea augustifolia/Echinacea purpurea*
Also known as Black Sampson, Coneflower, Niggerhead, Rubeckia
MEDICAL: (*Echinacea augustifolia*) Alterative, Antiseptic. *Echinacea augustifolia* is used as an immune system builder. Typically it is taken as a warm water infusion or powdered and encased in capsules. It is also used in the treatment of illness where an internal antiseptic is beneficial to treatment.
PART USED: Root
MAGICKAL: *Echinacea augustifolia* was used by pre-Columbian people as an offering. It also has the reputation of acting as an aphrodisiac. For the latter purpose, it is made into a warm water or warm wine infusion.

Echinacea

GENERAL: *Echinacea purpurea* has similar medical and magickal properties; however, it is not the preferred variety as the active chemical properties of the plant are not nearly as prevalent. If *Echinacea purpurea* is the only variety available, it is useful. But don't think you are getting a deal based on its lower price.

NOTE: When purchasing Echinacea, pay extra attention to the Latin name. If the merchant is selling it simply as Echinacea, chances are that he is selling *Echinacea purpurea*, not *Echinacea augustifolia*. If the merchant offers both, chances are that if your reference calls for Echinacea, it is referring to *Echinacea augustifolia*. Unethical merchants have caused this confusion by selling *Echinacea purpurea* (a less expensive herb) and marketing it simply as Echinacea so that their prices look better than their competition—who are probably selling the more expensive herb.

Ecore de Granade—*See* Pomegranate

Ecorce Sacree—*See* Buckthorn, Californian

Eddo—*See* Allspice

Edellebere—*See* Liverwort, American

Edelweiss—*Leontopodium alpinum*

MAGICKAL: Grow in your home with plenty of care. Tell it your heart's desire each and every day and how you intend on achieving that desire. It may well help you to achieve your goal within 13 moons. If it does not, continue to care for it, but give it to a friend who might help you with your goal.

Eerie—*See* Yarrow

Eggplant—*Solanum melogena*—Feminine, Jupiter, Earth

Also known as Aubergine, Terong, Oriental Eggplant, Garden Eggplant, Italian Eggplant, Berenjena, Nasu, Ngagwa, Talong, Brinjal, Melongene, Guinea Squash.

ASTROLOGICAL: *Primary*: Pisces, Sagittarius; *Secondary*: Capricorn, Taurus, Virgo

MEDICAL: Historically, the roots have been used to treat asthma and the leaves to treat dysentery. However, as a member of the Nightshade family the only part of this plant that should be consumed is the fruit.

Egyptian Gum—*See* Arabic, Gum

Egyptian Lotus—*See* Lotus

Egyptian Mint—*See* Mint

Egyptian Privet—*See* Henna

Egyptian Thorn—*See* Acacia

⚲Elder—*See List*—Feminine, Venus, Water
    English Elder—*Sambucus nigra*
    American Elder—*Sambucus canadensis*

ASTROLOGICAL: *Primary*: Libra, Taurus; *Secondary*: Cancer, Pisces, Scorpio

GOD: Olocun

GODDESSES: Hel, Hulda, Ochun, Venus

CELTIC TREE CALENDAR (Ruis)—November 25th thru December 21st—The thirteenth month of the year

MEDICAL: (*Sambucus nigra*) Diuretic (ripe berries), Purgative (bark). American Elder berries act as a diuretic. The leaves help wounds to heal quickly. English lore warns against burning the Elder. Although the ripe berries are used to make wine and the flowers are used to make tea, the bark, leaves, roots, and unripened berries are poisonous.

PARTS USED: Bark, Flowers, Leaves

MAGICKAL: Elder is the one wood warned against inclusion in ritual fires as cited in both the Wiccan Rede and its most cited source, the Rede of the Wiccae. Pendants and talismans made of Elder offer protection and encourage one to be faithful to his or her spouse. Elder berries and flowers are scattered to the Four Quarters during the opening of Wiccan rites to call the blessings of the Four Quarters upon the magick that is to be worked. Elder trees planted in the Four Quarters of a property also lend protection, prosperity, and call forth blessings.

Elecampane—*Inula helenium*—Masculine, Mercury, Air

Also known as Alantwurzel, Alycompaine, Aunee, Elf Dock, Elfwort, Horseheal, Marchalan, Nurse Heal, Scabwort, Velvet Dock, Wild Sunflower

ASTROLOGICAL: *Primary*: Gemini, Virgo; *Secondary*: Aquarius, Gemini, Libra

MEDICAL: Alterative, Antiseptic, Astringent, Diaphoretic, Diuretic, Expectorant, Stimulant (mild), Tonic. Often used in cough syrups. Works as an expectorant. Elecampane is sometimes used as a substitute for ephedra in relieving bronchial problems.

PART USED: Root

MAGICKAL: The Welsh called it Marchalan. The Germans called it Alantwurzel. Both agreed that it attracts love when worn. Try carrying it in a pink sachet. Mixed with equal amounts of Gum Arabic, it makes fine incense to aid in scrying (especially with a magick mirror or water).

Elf Dock—*See* Elecampane

Elf Leaf—*See* Lavender and Rosemary

Elfwort—*See* Elecampane

Elm, Common—*Ulmus campestris*—Feminine, Saturn, Water

Also known as Broad-leaved Elm, Elven, English Elm, European Elm, Ulmi Cortex

GOD: Odin

MEDICAL: Astringent, Demulcent, Diuretic, Tonic. A warm water infusion of the flowers has been employed as a tonic and diuretic.

PARTS USED: Dried inner bark, Flowers

Elm

MAGICKAL: Planted around the home to protect from lightning strikes. A wand made of Elm is said to be particularly useful in love spells. For the same reason, amulets of Elm are worn to attract love.

Elm, Slippery—*Ulmus fulva/Ulmus fulvus*—Feminine, Saturn, Air

Also known as Indian Elm, Moose Elm, Red Elm

ASTROLOGICAL: *Primary*: Aquarius, Capricorn; *Secondary*: Aquarius, Gemini, Libra

MEDICAL: Demulcent, Diuretic, Emollient, Expectorant. Slippery Elm bark is a common component in the treatment of congestion, as it is a mild expectorant. A teaspoon of the powdered inner bark is the typical dose. It is typically boiled in a 1/2 pint of water and served hot.

PART USED: Inner bark

MAGICKAL: To halt gossip, knot a cord of Dodder three times; with each knot say:

And never shall they speak out loud
Of things they do not know
Nor whisper softly to themselves
But watch the dodder grow

Then burn in a safe container over coals stoked with incense made of 1 part Slippery Elm and 3 parts Gum Arabic.

Elma—*See* Celery

Elven—*See* Elm, Common

El-Tour—*See* Borage

Enchanter's Plan—*See* Vervain

Endive—*Cichorium endivia*—Masculine, Jupiter, Air

ASTROLOGICAL: *Primary*: Pisces, Sagittarius; *Secondary*: Aquarius, Gemini, Libra

MAGICKAL: Fresh and uncooked Endive is served with a romantic dinner to raise lust and physical strength.

Endive, Green—*See* Lettuce, Wild

Enebro—*See* Juniper

English Adder's Tongue—*See* Fern

English Cowslip—*See* Primrose

English Elm—*See* Elm, Common

English Lavender—*See* Lavender

English Liverwort—*See* Liverwort, English

English Mandrake—*See* White Bryony

English Rhubarb—*See* Rhubarb

Englishman's Foot—*See* Plantain, Common

Ephedrine—*See* Ma Huang

Erba Santa Maria—*See* Spearmint

Eriffe—*See* Cleavers (B)

Eryngo—*See* Holly, Sea

Eternal Flower—*See* Gnaphalium Stoechas

Eucalyptus—*Eucalyptus globulus*—Feminine, Moon, Water
Also known as Blue Gum Tree, Stringy Bark Tree
WARNING: May cause skin irritation, especially in small children.
ASTROLOGICAL: *Primary*: Cancer; *Secondary*: Cancer, Pisces, Scorpio
GODS: Babalu Aye, Eleggua, Obatala, Oggun
GODDESS: Yemaya
MEDICAL: Antiseptic, Disinfectant, Stimulant. Boiling Eucalyptus leaves in water is a wonderful treatment for the common cold and day-to-day illnesses. But don't drink it. The steam rising from the pot makes for great relief. After being strained and allowed to cool, the water works well in most humidifiers. Diffusing essential oil of Eucalyptus or simmering the leaves in a room that has seen conflict will clear the air of hostile intent and help calm the participants. The scent is also used to heal and to maintain health.
PARTS USED: Leaves, Oil

Eugenia Aromatica—*See* Clove

Euphrasia—*See* Eyebright

Euphrosyne—*See* Eyebright

Euphorbia—*See* Spurges

European Bittersweet—*See* Woody Nightshade

European Daisy—*See* Daisy, Ox-Eye

European Elm—*See* Elm, Common

European Mistletoe—*See* Mistletoe, European

European Pennyroyal—*See* Pennyroyal

European Raspberry—*See* Raspberry

☠**European White Bryony**—*Bryonia alba*—Masculine, Mars, Fire
Also known as Black-Berried White Bryony
ASTROLOGICAL: *Primary*: Aries, Scorpio; *Secondary*: Aries, Leo, Sagittarius
MEDICAL: Diuretic. Used only in miniscule amounts in homoeopathic tinctures.
PART USED: Root
MAGICKAL: For magickal use, see White Bryony, as they have the same limited uses.

Even of the Star—*See* Horehound, White

Everlasting Friendship—See Cleavers (B)

Eye Balm—See Goldenseal

☠**Eyebright**—*Euphrasia officinalis*—Masculine, Sun, Air
Also known as Augentrost, Casse-Lunnette, Euphrasia, Euphrosyne, Red Eyebright
ASTROLOGICAL: *Primary*: Leo; *Secondary*: Aquarius, Gemini, Libra
MEDICAL: Antiasthmatic, Astringent, Diaphoretic, Expectorant. A warm water infusion consumed once a day will improve memory and help to rid the kidneys of stones. Used topically, it is a good astringent.
PARTS USED: Herb (harvested while flowering), Seeds

Eyebright

MAGICKAL: A warm water infusion consumed once a day will increase psychic abilities.

NOTE: Lobelia is sometimes called Eyebright as well.

Eye of the Day—*See* Daisy, Common

Eye Root—*See* Golden Seal

Faggio—*See* Beech

Fagos—*See* Beech

Fagus Castanea—*See* Chestnut, Sweet

Fake Saffron—*See* Saffron, Mexican

Fakouha—*See* Caper

Fairy Bells—*See* Sorrel, Wood

Fairy Caps—*See* Foxglove

Fairy Flax—*See* Flax, Mountain

Fairy Fingers—*See* Foxglove

Fairy Petticoats—*See* Foxglove

Fairy Thimbles—*See* Foxglove

Fairy Weed—*See* Foxglove

Fair Lady—*See* Belladonna

Fairy Cups—*See* Cowslip

False Bittersweet—*See* American Bittersweet

False Hellebore—*See* Hellebore, False

False Jacob's Ladder—*See* Abscess Root

False Sarsaparilla—*See* Sarsaparilla

False Wintergreen—*See* Pipsissewa

Faya—*See* Beech

Fear's Grape—*See* Pokeweed

Featherfew—*See* Feverfew

Featherfoil—*See* Feverfew

Febrifuge Plant—*See* Feverfew

Felon Herb—*See* Mugwort

Felonwort—*See* Woody Nightshade

Feltwort—*See* Mullein

Felwort—*See* Gentian

Female Fern—*See* Fern

Fenkel—*See* Fennel

Fennel—*Foeniculum vulgare*—Masculine, Mercury, Fire

Also known as Fenkel, Samar, Sweet Fennel, Sheeh, Wild Fennel

ASTROLOGICAL: *Primary*: Gemini, Virgo; *Secondary*: Aries, Leo, Sagittarius

GODS: Bacchus, Babalu Aye, Dionysus, Obatala, Pan, Prometheus

MEDICAL: Carminative, Pectoral. Increases milk production of nursing women, settles colic, and improves digestion. Especially useful for gastritis. Served as tea, Fennel seeds are said to help relieve the symptoms of asthma and cleanse both kidneys and urinary tract.

PARTS USED: Leaves, Roots, Seeds

MAGICKAL: A wand or staff (thyrsus) made of Fennel

Fennel

stalk, wound clockwise from bottom to top with ivy and terminated with a pinecone, is one of the most sacred symbols to Dionysus, perhaps even more than wine itself. This tool is well worth the effort of growing your own Fennel, as it aids in the exploration of the Mysteries of Dionysus and all Mysteries where the feminine sides of men are to be raised. When consumed, it lends itself to a sense of well-being and increases physical strength. Essential oil of Fennel is diffused to stir bravery.

Fenugreek—*Foenum-graecum/Trigonella foenum-graecum*—Masculine, Mercury, Air

Also known as Bird's Foot, Greek Hayseed, Hilba, Watu

WARNING: Should not be used if pregnant.

ASTROLOGICAL: *Primary*: Gemini, Virgo; *Secondary*: Aquarius, Gemini, Libra

GODS: Apollo, Ganesh

MEDICAL: Stomachic. Fenugreek is often recommended by herbalists to increase a mother's milk production but should never be taken by a pregnant woman. Some of those same herbalists generally recommend it to cure impotency in men. Oddly enough, and perhaps an urban legend, Fenugreek consumed regularly will increase the breast size of both women and men. A typical preparation is made by decoction of 1 ounce of the seed in 1 quart of water. Reduce volume to 1 pint by boiling. Strain and serve in 4-ounce doses.

PART USED: Seeds

MAGICKAL: It is interesting to note the connection between Fenugreek and the Hindu elephant god Ganesh as he is often described as having breasts, soft skin, and has been connected to homoerotic worship. An infusion of Fenugreek can be added to mop water to bring money. Living seeds (non-culinary) can be scattered in the backyard or garden for the same purpose.

Fern—*See List*—Masculine, Mercury, Air

The varieties of plants that have been called Ferns include (but are not limited to):

> **Adder's-Tongue, English**—*Ophioglossum vulgatum*
>
> Also known as Christ's Spear
>
> **Bracken**— *Pteridium aquilinum*
>
> Also known as Brake Fern, Female Fern
>
> Burn large amounts of last year's harvest of this herb on a spring bonfire to bring on rain and to bless the new season's seeds. Seems to work best in April.

> **Hart's-Tongue**—*Scolopendrium vulgare/ Asplenium scolopendrium*
>
> Also known as Hind's-Tongue, Buttonhole, Horse Tongue, God's-Hair, Lingua Cervina
>
> **Lady Fern**—*Asplenium Felix-foemina*
>
> Also known as Athyrium Filix-Foemina
>
> **Maidenhair, Common**—*Asplenium trichomanes*
>
> **Maidenhair, True**—*Adiantum Capillus-veneris/Adiantum pedatim*
>
> Also known as Rock Fern, Hair of Venus, Venus Hair
>
> This is an exception to the general attributes of the fern; here they are Feminine, Venus, and Water
>
> GODDESSES: Venus
>
> ☙ **Male Fern**—*Dryopteris Felix-mas/Aspidium Filix-mas*
>
> Also known as Male Shield Fern
>
> When grown in the home, Male Fern is said to attract women to it. When it is necessary to trim, carry the fresh trimmings with you; but do not over-trim, or it will act in the opposite manner.
>
> **Moonwort**—*Botrychium lunaria*
>
> **Polypody, Common**—*Polypodiurn vulgare*
>
> Also known as Polypody of the Oak, Wall Fern, Brake Root, Rock Brake, Rock of Polypody, Oak Fern
>
> **Prickly-Toothed Shield Fern**—*Aspidium spinulosum*
>
> **Royal Fern**—*Osmunda regalis*
>
> Also known as Osmund the Waterman, Heart of Osmund, Water Fern, Bog Onion
>
> **Spleenwort, Black**—*Asplenium Adiantum-nigrum*
>
> Also known as Black Maidenhair
>
> **Spleenwort, Common**—*Asplenium ceterach*
>
> Also known as Ceterach, Finger Fern, Scaly Fern, Miltwaste
>
> **Wall Rue**—*Asplenium Ruta-muraria*
>
> Also known as White Maidenhair, Tentwort

ASTROLOGICAL: *Primary*: Gemini, Virgo; *Secondary*: Aquarius, Gemini, Libra

GODS: Babalu Aye, Obatala

NOTE: The attributes listed above are general opinion. Those exceptions that I found are listed with the specific type of Fern. This was the hardest plant to order because so many different plants have been called Ferns. Many are poisonous, and I will admit to not having much luck either growing or using this plant for magickal purposes.

Feslien—*See* Basil

Female Fern—*See* Fern and Moss, Hair Cup

Female Fern Herb—*See* Moss, Hair Cup and Fern

Feverfew—*Chrysanthemum Parthenium/ Tanacetum parthenium*—Masculine, Venus, Water

ASTROLOGICAL: *Primary:* Libra, Taurus; *Secondary:* Cancer, Pisces, Scorpio

Also known as Febrifuge Plant, Featherfew, Featherfoil, Flirtwort, Bachelor's Buttons

MEDICAL: Aperient, Carminative, Sedative (mild). An excellent herb for relief from colds and chest complaints associated with all forms of illness. Bring 1 pint of water to a boil, reduce to a simmer, and add 1 ounce of Feverfew; remove from heat. Once cool, strain, reheat the liquid, dissolve enough honey to improve the taste, and serve to the sick one. Also good in the treatment of insomnia.

PART USED: Herb

MAGICKAL: Folklore tells us that Feverfew is carried for protection, especially against illness.

Feverwort—*See* Boneset and Centaury

Fico—*See* Fig

Fiddlewood—*See* Figwort, Water

Fiddler—*See* Figwort, Water

Field Daisy—*See* Daisy, Ox-Eye

Field Gentian—*See* Gentian

Field Hops—*See* Yarrow

Fieldhove—*See* Coltsfoot

Field Mustard—*See* Mustard, Field

Fig, Common—*Ficus carica*—Masculine, Jupiter, Fire

Also known as Chagareltin, Fico, Mhawa

ASTROLOGICAL:
Primary: Pisces, Sagittarius; *Secondary:* Aries, Leo, Sagittarius

GODS: Brahma, Dionysus, Jupiter, Pluto, Zeus

MEDICAL: Laxative (mild)

MAGICKAL: Eating Figs reportedly increases reproductive fertility in women, vitality in men, and potential for prosperity in both.

Fig

PART USED: Fruit

Figwort—*See* Celandine, Lesser; Figwort, Wate; and Figwort, Knotted

Figwort, Knotted—*Scrophularia nodosa*—Feminine, Venus, Water

Also known as Deilen Ddu, Rose Noble, Herbe du Siege, Throatwort, Carpenter's Square, Kernelwort

ASTROLOGICAL: *Primary:* Libra, Taurus; *Secondary:* Cancer, Pisces, Scorpio

MEDICAL: Anodyne. A decoction is made with 1 ounce of the herb in 1 quart of water. Reduce by boiling to 1 pint. Strain and use topically on burns and minor injuries.

PART USED: Herb

MAGICKAL: The Irish called it Rose Noble and hung it to smoke and dry beside Summer Solstice fires. When dried, it was hung indoors for protection and for the very unique odor it emits after being smoke-dried. This was probably not originally an Irish tradition, migrating perhaps from the Norse tribes.

Figwort, Water—*Scrophularia aquatica*—Feminine, Venus, Water

Also known as Water Betony, Fiddlewood, Fiddler, Crowdy Kit, Brownwort, Bishops' Leaves

ASTROLOGICAL: *Primary:* Libra, Taurus; *Secondary:* Cancer, Pisces, Scorpio

MEDICAL: Anodyne. A decoction is made with 1 ounce of the leaves in 1 quart of water. Reduce by boiling to 1 pint. Strain and use topically to decrease the pain of sunburn and bruises.

PART USED: Leaves

MAGICKAL: A pillow filled with Water Figwort leaves is said to prevent nightmares.

Finger Fern—*See* Fern

Fingerhut—*See* Foxglove

Fir

One of the nine woods cited in the Wiccan Rede as best for use in ritual fires.

Fireweed—*See* Dodder

Fish Mint—*See* Spearmint

Five Fingers—*See* Five-Finger Grass and Ginseng, American

Five-Finger Blossom—*See* Five-Finger Grass

Five-Finger Grass—*Potentilla reptans*—Masculine, Jupiter, Fire

Also known as Cinquefoil, Crampweed, Five Finger Blossom, Five Fingers, Goosegrass, Goose Tansy, Moor Grass, Pentaphyllon, Silver Cinquefoil, Silverweed, Sunkfield, Synkefoyle

ASTROLOGICAL: *Primary:* Pisces, Sagittarius; *Secondary:* Aries, Leo, Sagittarius

GODS: Ochosi, Orunla

GODDESS: Ochun

MEDICAL: Astringents (herb), Febrifuge (herb), Styptic (root). An infusion of 1 ounce of the herb in 1 pint of water is simmered for 30 minutes, strained, and served 4 ounces at a time to resolve diarrhea and lower fever. An expression of the fresh root will slow bleeding when used topically. If dried root is the only thing available, a decoction can be made with 2 ounces of the dried root in 1 quart of water. Reduce by boiling to 1/2 pint and use topically.

PARTS USED: Herb, Root

MAGICKAL: As you can well imagine, Five-Finger Grass is one of the more popular herbs in the modern Wiccan's kitchen. It just has one of those names that people like. With its associations to the pentagram itself in addition to lore that each point on each leaf represents love, money, health, power, and wisdom, it is often carried in sachets or mixed into incenses for either or all of those purposes. As an infusion, it is sprinkled about the home, added to the bath, and used to mop floors to wash away baneful magick and curses. Reportedly, washing your hands with its infusion will wash away hexes. Like Chicory, Five-Finger Grass is often used to win favors. A tincture of Chicory and Five-Finger Grass is often used to win court cases. Prior to going to court, bathe with an infusion of Five-Finger Grass, wear your best outfit, and top it off with an appropriate perfume or cologne. Cut that perfume or cologne with 10 percent tincture of Chicory and Five-Finger Grass.

GENERAL: Because the flowers of Five-Finger Grass resemble that of Silverweed, the plants have often been confused. Silverweed thus became a common name (as many do) out of confusion. So if you are looking for Silverweed, make sure it is not *Potentilla anserina*, or you might be looking for something other than Five Finger Grass.

Five-Flowered Gentian—*See* Gentian

Five-leaved Ivy—*See* Ivy, American

Filewort—*See* Centaury

Flaggon—*See* Iris

Flag Lily—*See* Blue Flag

Flannel Plant—*See* Mullein

Flax—*Linum usitatissimum*—Masculine, Mercury, Fire

Also known as Linseed, Linaza, Sib Muma

ASTROLOGICAL: *Primary:* Gemini, Virgo; *Secondary*: Aries, Leo, Sagittarius

GODDESS: Hulda

MEDICAL: Demulcent, Emollient, Laxative (oil), Pectoral. Crushing and simmering 1 ounce of the seed in 1 pint of water for 30 minutes makes an infusion. Strain and serve 4 ounces at a time. The oil is used by the teaspoon as a mild laxative.

PARTS USED: Seeds, Oil

MAGICKAL: Flax is sacred to Hulda, who first shared the magick of spinning and weaving cloth. Flaxseed in a linen sachet is often left near the sewing machine in her honor.

Flax

Flax, Mountain—*Linum catharticum*—Masculine, Mercury, Fire

Also known as Dwarf Flax, Fairy Flax, Mill Mountain, Purging Flax

See also Senega

ASTROLOGICAL: *Primary:* Gemini, Virgo; *Secondary*: Aries, Leo, Sagittarius

MEDICAL: Purgative

PART USED: Herb

Flax, Perennial—*Linum perenne*—Masculine, Mercury, Fire

ASTROLOGICAL: *Primary:* Gemini, Virgo; *Secondary*: Aries, Leo, Sagittarius

MEDICAL: A decoction of the fresh herb is consumed to combat the pain of arthritis. A few drops of the tincture made from the fresh herb and seeds treats diarrhea.

PARTS USED: Herb (fresh), Seeds.

Fleabane, Canadian—*Erigeron Canadense*

Also known as Fleawort, Coltstail, Prideweed

MEDICAL: Astringent, Diuretic, Tonic. Served as tea.

PARTS USED: Herb, Seeds

Fleabane, Common—*Inula dysenterica*—Feminine, Venus, Water

Also known as Middle Fleabane, Rarajeub

ASTROLOGICAL: *Primary*: Libra, Taurus; *Secondary*: Cancer, Pisces, Scorpio

MEDICAL: Astringent. Both decoction and water infusion are employed.

PARTS USED: Herb, Root

MAGICKAL: Fleabane seeds encourage chastity. The leaves are used in protection from negative forces, especially the plague. I am sure this comes from its ability to drive away fleas, but Damiana seems to work much better for that task.

Fleabane

Fleabane, Great—*See* Spikenard, Ploughman's

Fleaseed—*See* Plantain, Psyllium

Fleawort—*See* Fleabane, Canadian

Fleur de Coucou—*See* Daffodil

Fleur de Luce—*See* Iris

Fleur-de-Lys—*See* Blue Flag

Fliggers—*See* Iris

Flirtwort—*See* Feverfew

Flixweed Mustard—*See* Mustard, Flixweed

Floppy-Dock—*See* Foxglove

Floptop—*See* Foxglove

Floramon—*See* Amaranth

Flor Del Peru—*See* Be-Still

Florentine Iris—*See* Orris

Flores Carthami—*See* Saffron, Mexican

Flores Rhoeados—*See* Poppy, Red

Flower of Immortality—*See* Amaranth

Flower O'Luce—*See* Heartsease

Flowering Sally—*See* Loosestrife, Purple

Fluffweed—*See* Mullein

Flukes—*See* Potato

Fly Agaric—*See* Agaric Mushroom

Fly Fungus—*See* Agaric Mushroom

Foal's Foot—*See* Coltsfoot

Foalswort—*See* Coltsfoot

Folk's Gloves—*See* Foxglove

Food of the Gods—*See* Asafoetida and Copal, Black

Forbidden Fruit—*See* Citron

Fo-Ti-Tieng—*See* Gotu Kola

Fox Bells—*See* Foxglove

Foxes Glofa—*See* Foxglove

☠**Foxglove**—*Digitalis purpurea*—Feminine, Venus, Water
Also known as Bloody Fingers, Cow-Flop, Dead Men's Bells, Digitalis, Dog's Finger, Fairy Caps, Fairy Fingers, Fairy Petticoats, Fairy Thimbles, Fairy Weed, Fingerhut, Floppy-Dock, Floptop, Folk's Gloves, Fox Bells, Foxes Glofa, Gloves of Our Lady, Great Herb, Lion's Mouth, Lusmore, Lus Na Mbau Side, Our Lady's Gloves, Revbielde, Virgin's Glove, Witches' Bells, Witches' Thimbles

ASTROLOGICAL: *Primary*: Libra, Taurus; *Secondary*: Cancer, Pisces, Scorpio

MEDICAL: Very old herbals list this as diuretic and beneficial to heart problems. In fact, this is the original natural source for the powerful heart medicine digitalis. The plant works on the heart by contracting the blood circulatory system, thus raising blood pressure tremendously. However, it should never be used internally by one who is not learned in modern medicine, as it is rather easy to cause death.

Foxglove

PART USED: Leaves

MAGICKAL: A strong infusion of Foxglove can be used for protection. Paint on the path entering your home in a solar cross, but be careful when preparing and handling it. Even the steam rising from this brew should be considered dangerous. Brew only outdoors with a good breeze. Although this plant is deadly, it is beautiful. If you have no children or animals that can reach it, grow in a window box to protect your home.

GENERAL: Despite urban legend, this herb will not get you high. It will, however, make the entire world look blue right before it kills you. Yes, I did say it makes the world look blue.

Fox's Clote—*See* Burdock

Foxtail—*See* Moss, American Club

Frangipangi—*See* Frangipani

☠**Frangipani**—*Plumeria acutifolia*—Feminine, Venus, Water
Also known as Frangipangi, Graveyard Flowers, Melia, Plumeria, Temple Tree

ASTROLOGICAL: *Primary*: Libra, Taurus; *Secondary*: Cancer, Pisces, Scorpio

GOD: The Buddha

GODDESS: Ochun

MAGICKAL: Frangipani is used in love-drawing spellcraft. This beautiful flower promotes calm romantic love in the order of peace, love, and... Well, you get the idea. Its common name, Temple Tree, comes from the Far East, where it was grown for the peace, love, and tranquility it would bring to a spiritual location. This is why its scent was so popular during the mid- and late 60s when folk were beginning to once again experiment more openly with alternative spirituality and lifestyles.

Fragrant Bedstraw—*See* Cleavers

Fragrant Everlasting—*See* Balsam, White

Frangula Bark—*See* Buckthorn, Alder

Frank—*See* Frankincense

Frankincense—*Boswellia Thurifera/Boswellia carterii*—Masculine, Sun, Fire

Also known as Frank, Incense, Olibans, Olibanum, Olibanus

ASTROLOGICAL: *Primary*: Leo; *Secondary*: Aries, Leo, Sagittarius

GODS: Aeacus, Amun Ra, Baal, Babalu Aye, Shango, Hades, Helios, Krishna, Narasinha, Obatala, Pluto, Surya, Vishnu, Vulcan

GODDESSES: Demeter, Mut, Venus

MEDICAL: Stimulant

PART USED: Resin

MAGICKAL: Burn at sunrise to honor Ra, the new day, and the masculine principle of the soul itself. If you should greet the sun on the morning after Winter Solstice, best to drum it up with clouds of Frankincense smoke. Frankincense is one of the oldest magickal incenses. It is burned for purification, cleansing, general spirituality, uplifting, and for the consecration

Frankincense

of ritual tools by smoke. A necklace of Frankincense (or alternating Frankincense and Myrrh) makes an excellent talisman of protection. Unfortunately, these are very difficult to make, and the source that once brought them in from Africa seems to have dried up. Carry Frankincense tears in a sachet for the same purpose; but if you ever see a string of Frankincense at a reputable bead shop, purchase them without questioning the cost (especially if their origin is Africa). Magickally speaking, you will not regret your purchase. If Frankincense is not available, you can substitute equal amounts of Rosemary and Gum Arabic for most recipes. Essential oil of Frankincense is very expensive. As such, the resin is often burned over charcoal for its therapeutic value. If you can afford the oil, it is better for aromatherapy uses, but the resin/charcoal method will do. The scent of Frankincense is uplifting and causes a shift from thoughts of the material world to the etheric world.

Frauenmantle—*See* Lady's Mantle

Frauen Munze—*See* Spearmint

Frauenschlussel—*See* Cowslip

Freixo—*See* Ash

French Honeysuckle—*See* Rue, Goat's

French Lavender—*See* Lavender

French Tarragon—*See* Tarragon

French Wheat—*See* Buckwheat

Freesia—*Freesia spp.*—Feminine, Venus, Water

ASTROLOGICAL: *Primary*: Libra, Taurus; *Secondary*: Cancer, Pisces, Scorpio

MAGICKAL: If you find yourself in the first stages of a relationship during the spring but have a nervous heart, then pick this herb's fresh flowers and carry in a pink sachet. They will ease your nerves and help you to move forward with the relationship.

Frey—*See* Gorse

Friar's Cap—*See* Aconite

Fructus Anethi—*See* Dill

Fruit of the Gods—*See* Apple

Fruit of the Underworld—*See* Apple

Fruit Plantain—*See* Banana

Fumiterry—*See* Fumitory

Fumitory—*Fumaria officinalis*—Feminine, Saturn, Earth

Also known as Beggary, Earth Smoke, Fumiterry, Fumus, Fumus Terrae, Kaphnos, Nidor, Scheiteregi, Taubenkropp, Vapor, Wax Dolls

ASTROLOGICAL: *Primary*: Aquarius, Capricorn; *Secondary*: Capricorn, Taurus, Virgo

MEDICAL: Aperient, Diaphoretic (mild), Diuretic, Tonic (mild)

PART USED: Herb

MAGICKAL: Fumitory is burned in the home to rid it of unwelcome spirits. A white vinegar infusion of Fumitory can be used for this same purpose, but a water infusion creates a fast money wash for hands or floor.

Fumitory

Fumus—*See* Fumitory

Fumus Terrae—*See* Fumitory

Furze—*See* Gorse

Fuzzy Fruit—*See* Peach

Fuzzyweed—*See* Tarragon

Fyrs—*See* Gorse

Gagroot—*See* Lobelia

Galangal—*Alpina officinalum/Alpina galanga*—Masculine, Mars, Fire

Also known as Chewing John, China Root, Colic Root, East India Catarrh Root, Galingal, Galingale, Gargaut, India Root, Kaempferia Galanga, Lesser Galangal, Low John, Low John the Conqueror, Rhizoma Galangae

ASTROLOGICAL: *Primary*: Aries, Scorpio; *Secondary*: Aries, Leo, Sagittarius

GODS: Shango, Obatala, Ochosi, Oggun, Oko

GODDESS: Ochun

MEDICAL: Carminative, Stimulant. A typical dose of the powdered root is 15 grains. As a decoction, 30 grains are boiled in 1 pint of water. Reduce volume by boiling to 1/3; strain and serve. In larger amounts, Galangal is sometimes listed as a hallucinogen.

PART USED: Root

MAGICKAL: A charm of Galangal root worn around the neck draws good luck. Strung with silver beads or carried in a green sachet with coinage, it draws luck with money and gambling. Powdered Galangal root sprinkled lightly over the bed will inspire lust. Simmering Galangal root will stimulate the conscious mind and help one to complete tasks even though sleep is nipping at the eyes.

Galgenmannchen—*See* Mandrake

Galingal—*See* Galangal

Galingale—*See* Galangal

Gallitricum—*See* Sage, Clary

Gallows—*See* Mandrake

Ganeb—*See* Marijuana

Ganja—*See* Marijuana

Garclive—*See* Agrimony

Garden Eggplant—*See* Eggplant

Gardenia—*Gardenia jasminoides*—Feminine, Moon, Water

ASTROLOGICAL: *Primary*: Cancer; *Secondary*: Cancer, Pisces, Scorpio

GODS: Babalu Aye, Obatala

GODDESS: Yemaya

MAGICKAL: When given as a gift, the living plant speeds healing. Simple love incense can be had by mixing 1 part finely powdered Gardenia petals with 3 parts Gum Arabic. Fresh Gardenia flowers are grown in the home such that its scent will elevate the mood and strengthen the sense of family love.

Garden Angelica—*See* Angelica

Garden Celandine—*See* Celandine, Greater

Garden Dill—*See* Dill

Garden Heliotrope—*See* Valerian

Garden Lettuce—*See* Lettuce

Garden Mint—*See* Spearmint

Garden Patience—*See* Rhubarb, Monk's

Garden Purslane—*See* Purslane, Golden

Garden Rhubarb—*See* Rhubarb

Garden Rue—*See* Rue

Garden Sage—*See* Sage, Common

Garden Savory—*See* Savory, Summer

Garden Thyme—*See* Thyme

Garden Violet—*See* Heartsease

Garde Robe—*See* Southernwood

Gargaut—*See* Galangal

Garget—*See* Pokeweed

Garlic—*Allium sativum*—Masculine, Mars, Fire

Also known as Ajo, Poor Man's Treacle, Stinkweed

ASTROLOGICAL: *Primary*: Aries, Scorpio; *Secondary*: Aries, Leo, Sagittarius

GODS: Babalu Aye, Eleggua, Obatala

GODDESS: Hecate

MEDICAL: Antiseptic, Astringent, Diaphoretic, Diuretic, Expectorant, Stimulant. Relief from the common cold and mild chest complaints can be had by cooking with fresh Garlic. Fresh Garlic acts as an expectorant when consumed and as an astringent when used topically. Grind a fresh clove and apply to corns at night; bandage and repeat for a few weeks to remove the corn. A fresh clove of Garlic will ease tooth pain when chewed or pressed into a cavity. Eating it regularly will aid sinus problems.

PART USED: Bulb

MAGICKAL: Although there are probably several hundred recipes for "Four Thieves Vinegar," they all originate with the story of the four thieves who claimed to use a vinegar infusion of Garlic to defeat the plague while they stole from the bodies of the plague's victims. Fresh Garlic is the perfect offering for Hecate, especially when asking her to watch over childbirth. It is also a good idea to leave it at the crossroads, with no favors asked, on your way to and from

Garlic

volunteering at a senior citizen function. Remember that respecting the elderly is the first step in receiving respect when you are elderly. Garlic is worn and eaten for protection from all things. Who hasn't seen a vampire movie where Garlic was hung from someone's bedposts or the entrance to the home? Although Dracula might not be lurking in the dark of your closet, psychic/social vampires abound in this world. Eating Garlic regularly will help keep you well-protected against their energy-draining ways. Brides can carry a clove of Garlic for good luck and to protect her wedding. At the reception, Garlic in the sauce will ensure her husband's lust that night. Best served with tomato or other mildly acidic sauce.

Garlic Mustard—*See* Mustard, Garlic

Garlic Shallot—*See* Shallot

Gavez—*See* Comfrey

Gaxels—*See* Hawthorn

Gay Feather—*See* Snakeroot, Button

Gazels—*See* Hawthorn

Gearwe—*See* Yarrow

Geisblatt—*See* Honeysuckle

Gelso—*See* Mulberry, Common

Gemeiner Wachholder—*See* Juniper

General Marion's Weed—*See* Dogbane

Geneva—*See* Juniper

Genevrier—*See* Juniper

Genista Green Broom—*See* Broom

Gentian—*See List*—Masculine, Mars, Fire
ASTROLOGICAL: *Primary*: Aries, Scorpio; *Secondary*: Aries, Leo, Sagittarius

Gentian, Autumn— *Gentiana amarella*
Also known as Bitterwort, Felwort, Baldmoney

Gentian, Cross-leaved— *Gentiana cruciata*

Gentian, Field—*Gentiana campestris*
Also known as Bitter-root, Felwort

Gentian

Gentian,   Five-Flowered—*Gentiana quinqueflora*

Gentian, Japanese—*Gentiana scabrae*
Also known as Ryntem Root

Gentian, Marsh—*Gentiana Pneumonanthe*

Gentian, Spring—*Gentiana Verna*

Gentian, White—*Laserpitum latifolia*
Also known as Bastard Lovage

Gentian, Yellow— *Gentiana lutea*
Also known as Bitterroot, Hochwurzel

GENERAL: Each of the Gentian varieties will add power to an incense or sachet mix. Yellow Gentian has the extra quality of attracting love. An infusion of Yellow Gentian added to a bath will attract love.

Geranium—*Geranium maculatum*—Feminine, Venus, Water

Also known as Alum Bloom, Alum Root, American Cranesbill Root, Chocolate Flower, Crowsfoot, Dove's Foot, Old Maid's Nightcap, Spotted Cranesbill, Wild Cranesbill, Wild Geranium, Shameface, Storksbill

ASTROLOGICAL: *Primary*: Libra, Taurus; *Secondary*: Cancer, Pisces, Scorpio

GODS: Shango, Eleggua, Mars, Montu, Obatala, Oko, Shiva

GODDESSES: Athena, Minerva

MEDICAL: Astringent, Styptic, Tonic. An infusion is made with 1 ounce of the herb to 1 pint of water.
Part used: Leaves

Geranium

MAGICKAL: Grown in and around the home, Geraniums are an excellent way of protecting the home and yard against negative energy of all kinds.

Geranium, Rose—*Pelargonium graveolens*—Feminine, Venus, Water

ASTROLOGICAL: *Primary*: Libra, Taurus; *Secondary*: Cancer, Pisces, Scorpio

GOD: Obatala

MAGICKAL: Used in spells intended to heighten romance; however, it may reduce sexual desire in men. Carried and grown for protection. Essential oil of Rose Geranium is diffused to heighten the sense of romance in women.

German Chamomile—*See* Chamomile, German

Germander—*Teucrium chamaedrys*

MEDICAL: Diaphoretic, Diuretic, Stimulant, Tonic. Served as tea, Germander is a mild pain reliever. Helps sore throats and the general aches and pains of a hard day at work.

PART USED: Herb

German Rue—*See* Rue

Ghost Flower—*See* Thornapple

Gillies—*See* Carnation

Gillyflower—*See* Carnation

Gill-Go-by-the-Hedge—*See* Ivy, Ground

Gill-Go-Over-the-Ground—*See* Ivy, Ground

Gin Berry—*See* Juniper

Ginger—*Zingiber officinale*—Masculine, Mars, Fire

Also known as African Ginger

ASTROLOGICAL: *Primary*: Aries, Scorpio; *Secondary*: Aries, Leo, Sagittarius

GODS: Babalu Aye, Shango, Eleggua, Ochosi, Oko, Orunla

GODDESS: Ochun

MEDICAL: Anticoagulant, Carminative, Expectorant, Stimulant, Tonic. Relief from the common cold can be had by eating Ginger candy (available in many Asian grocery stores). If you

do not have access to this treat, try simmering an ounce of fresh Gingerroot in a pint of orange juice. Remove from heat, strain, and serve chilled. Ginger will encourage perspiration, serve as a cooling influence on the body, and act as an expectorant. If you ever have a chance to drink real Ginger ale on a hot summer day, you are in for a real treat. A warm water infusion of Gingerroot works as a mild stimulant and tonic. It will also help with seasickness and inner ear problems. If you ever find yourself ready to visit the side rails of an ocean liner, try to find some real Ginger ale. However, including Gingerroot with your favorite meals can have this same effect. A warm alcohol infusion is an excellent evening tonic.

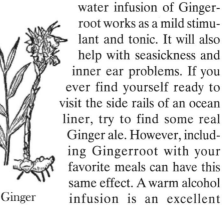

Ginger

PART USED: Root

MAGICKAL: A hot Ginger sauce will greatly increase your chances of a romantic evening being just that—a romantic evening. Crystallized Ginger (available in Asian groceries) lends itself to this endeavor well. Eating Ginger yourself before love spells will increase the chances of those spells working. Fresh Ginger is always better to use in cooking for magickal intents. Essential oil of Ginger is diffused to promote sexual desire in men.

Ginger, White—*Hedychium coronarium*—Feminine, Venus, Water

ASTROLOGICAL: *Primary*: Libra, Taurus; *Secondary*: Cancer, Pisces, Scorpio

GENERAL: White Ginger wood resembles bamboo. It is used to make talismans for protection.

MAGICKAL: If you are fortunate enough to have access to White Ginger flowers, you have an excellent scent to stimulate love. Either inhale the fresh flowers or simmer dried flowers in water.

Ginger, Wild—*Asarum canadense*

MEDICAL: Carminative, Diaphoretic, Diuretic, Stimulant. An infusion of 1/2 ounce of powdered root in 1 pint of water is simmered for 30 minutes and served warm to treat chronic congestion of the chest and to assist in breathing.

PART USED: Root

MAGICKAL: When consumed, acts as an aphrodisiac for men.

Ginepro—*See* Juniper

Gin Plant—*See* Juniper

Ginseng, American—*Panax quinquefolium*— Masculine, Sun, Fire

Also known as Aralia Quinquefolia, Divine Root, Five Fingers, Man Root, Redberry, Root of Life, Sang, Tartar Root, Red Berry, Man's Health, Wonder of the World Root

ASTROLOGICAL: *Primary*: Leo; *Secondary*: Aries, Leo, Sagittarius

GODS: Shango, Oko, Vishnu

GODDESSES: Artemis, Diana, Ochun

MEDICAL: Stimulant (mild), Tonic. The whole root or infusion of root is consumed by men to increase and maintain vitality and a healthy sexual appetite. Acts as a good tonic and immune system

Ginseng

booster for both men and women. Often listed as a stimulant; however, as such it seems to have a cumulative rather than an immediate effect. Despite its reputation, I have not found this to inspire lust above or beyond the norm. A curative in that department, perhaps.

PART USED: Root

MAGICKAL: An excellent and safe substitute for Mandrake. I do not advise that you wild craft this herb unless you do so on your own land.

The root is generally considered of very low quality until it is at least five years old. Harvesting a plot that someone else had their eyes on for a couple of years may result in some rather undesired outcomes. Further, due to its value, it has been almost stripped from National Parks and other public property. Adding to the carnage could land you in jail or paying very heavy fines.

Giver of Life—*See* Corn

Gladdon—*See* Calamus

Gladyne—*See* Iris

Gloves of Our Lady—*See* Foxglove

Gnaphaliums—See List
See also Gnaphalium Stoechas

Gnaphalium Arenarium—Also known as Branching Everlasting

Gnaphalium Cymosum—Used by some pre-Columbian Americans after rituals where a person is bitten by a rattlesnake to recover from that bite.

Gnaphalium Citrinum—*See* Gnaphalium Stoechas

Gnaphalium Stoechas—*Helichrysum Stoechas*

Also known as Common Shrubby Everlasting, Eternal Flower, Gnaphalium Citrinum, Goldilocks, Stoechas Citrina

MEDICAL: Deobstruent, Expectorant

Goat Root—*See* White Bryony

Goat's Leaf—*See* Honeysuckle

Goat's Rue—*See* Rue, Goat's

Goat Weed—*See* St. John's Wort

Godfathers and Godmothers—*See* Heartsease

God's-Hair—*See* Fern

Golden Maidenhair—*See* Moss, Hair Cup

Goutberry—*See* Blackberry

Gowan—*See* Daisy, Ox-Eye

Goldenrod—*Solidago virgaurea*—Feminine, Venus, Air

Also known as Aaron's Rod, Blue Mountain Tea, Goldruthe, Gonea Tea, Sweet-Scented Goldenrod, Solidago, Verge d'Or, Wound Weed, Woundwort

ASTROLOGICAL: *Primary*: Libra, Taurus; *Secondary*: Aquarius, Gemini, Libra

MEDICAL: Carminative, Stimulant. Served as tea, Goldenrod will aid in healing wounds when applied to the damaged area.

PART USED: Leaves

MAGICKAL: The flowers of the Goldenrod, picked in the morning, are dried and used in money drawing incense, powders, and other herbal mixtures.

Goldens—*See* Daisy, Ox-eye

Golden Groundsel—*See* Groundsel, Golden

Golden Purslane—*See* Purslane, Golden

☠**Goldenseal**—*Hydrastis canadensis*—Masculine, Sun, Fire

ASTROLOGICAL: *Primary*: Leo; *Secondary*: Aries, Leo, Sagittarius

Also known as Eye Balm, Eye Root, Ground Raspberry, Indian Dye, Indian Paint, Jaundice Root, Orange Root, Turmeric Root, Warnera, Wild Curcuma, Yellow Root, Yellow Puccoon

MEDICAL: Alterative, Laxative (mild), Stomachic, Tonic. A very good immune system builder and general tonic in small amounts. In large amounts it is poisonous.

PART USED: Root

MAGICKAL: Some tribes of pre-Columbian Americans made a strong infusion of the Goldenseal root to be used as a dye for clothing, tools, and weapons. Goldenseal root is used in sparing amounts in money-drawing incense, powders, and herbal blends.

Golden Senecio—*See* Groundsel, Golden

Golden Star—*See* Avens

Goldilocks—*See* Gnaphalium Stoechas

Goldruthe—*See* Goldenrod

Goldy Star—*See* Avens

Gonea Tea—*See* Goldenrod

Goosebill—*See* Cleavers (B)

Goosegrass—*See* Five-Finger Grass and Cleavers (B)

Goose Leek—*See* Daffodil

Goose Tansy—*See* Five-Finger Grass

Gotu Kola—*Hydrocotyl asiatica*

Also known as Asian Marsh Pennywort, Bevilacqua, Boilean, Fo-Ti-Tieng, Indian Pennywort, Hydrocotyl

MEDICAL: Tonic. Gotu Kola was used by the ancients to obtain clarity and to rejuvenate brain and nerve cells. In recent times it has found its way back into herbal medicine for the same purpose and is commonly sold in fashionable nutrition centers and "smart bars."

PART USED: Leaves

MAGICKAL: Gotu Kola is used in incenses to improve meditation. However, it is better used as an infusion. To improve meditation as well as concentration, drink an infusion of 1 teaspoon Gotu Kola every morning or afternoon. It will take about a week for the cumulative effects to be realized. Increasing the daily dose to 2 or 3 tablespoons a day will improve male sexual appetite if weak prior to its use. In this aspect, Gotu Kola should not be considered an aphrodisiac because it acts more as a fortification.

Gorse—*See List*—Masculine, Mars, Fire

Also known as Broom, Frey, Furze, Fyrs, Gorst, Goss, Prickly Broom, Ruffett, Whin

    Dwarf Gorse—*Ulex minor*

Common Gorse—*Ulex euopaeus*
Western Gorse—*Ulex gallii*

ASTROLOGICAL: *Primary*: Aries, Scorpio; *Secondary*: Aries, Leo, Sagittarius

GODS: Jupiter, Lugh, Thor

CELTIC TREE CALENDAR (Onn)—Spring Equinox

MAGICKAL: Grown around the home as a hedge line, Gorse lends itself to both physical and psychic protection.

Gorse

NOTE: Some references cite the associations as Feminine, Sun, Air.

Gorst—*See* Gorse

Gort—*See* Ivy, Common

Goss—*See* Gorse

Grains of Paradise—*Aframomum melequeta/ Amomum melegeuta*—Masculine, Mars, Fire

Also known as African Pepper, Guinea Grains, Guinea Pepper, Mallaquetta Pepper, Melequeta

ASTROLOGICAL: *Primary*: Aries, Scorpio; *Secondary*: Aries, Leo, Sagittarius

GODS: Shango, Eleggua, Oko

GODDESSES: Ochun, Yemaya

MAGICKAL: A handful of this herb thrown into the air at each Quarter is said to bring a wish into manifestation.

Granatwurzelrindle—*See* Pomegranate

Granadilla—*See* Passion Flower

Grape—*See* Vine

Grapefruit—*Citrus paradisa*—Feminine, Moon, Water

ASTROLOGICAL: *Primary*: Cancer; *Secondary*: Cancer, Pisces, Scorpio

MAGICKAL: Aids in purification. Drink Grapefruit juice when you feel spiritually icky.

*NOTE: Some references cite the planetary association as Sun.

Grape Hyacinth—*See* Hyacinth, Grape

Grape Vine—*See* Vine

Gravelroot—*See note*

Listed variously as *Eupatorium purpureum, Eupatorium trifoliatum, Eupatorium maculatum, Eupatorium verticillatum, Eupatorium ternifolium*

Also known as Gravelweed, Hempweed, Joe Jie, Joe-Pye Weed, Jopi Weed, Purple Boneset, Queen of the Meadow, Queen of the Meadow Root, Trumpet Weed

MAGICKAL: A few leaves of this plant in the mouth will increase the effectiveness of sexual advances. I have seen this cited as love-drawing, but have found it to help only with sex.

*NOTE: Each of the following plants share the common name Gravelroot: Meadowsweet, Trumpet Weed, and to some extent Queen of the Meadow/Queen of the Meadow Root.

Gravelweed—*See* Gravelroot

Graveyard Dust—*See* Mullein

Graveyard Flowers—*See* Frangipani

Great Burdock—*See* Burdock

Greater Scullcap—*See* Scullcap

Great Fleabane—*See* Spikenard, Ploughman's

Great Herb—*See* Foxglove

Great Morel—*See* Belladonna

Great Raifort—*See* Horseradish

Great Wild Valerian—*See* Valerian

Grecian Laurel—*See* Bay

Greek Hayseed—*See* Fenugreek

Greek Nuts—*See* Almond

Green Endive—*See* Lettuce, Wild

Green Ginger—*See* Wormwood

Green Hellebore—*See* Hellebore, Green

Green Mint—*See* Spearmint

Green Purslane—*See* Purslane, Green

Green Spine—*See* Spearmint

Grenadier—*See* Pomegranate

Grenadille—*See* Passion Flower

Grip Grass—*See* Cleavers (B)

Ground Apple—*See* Chamomile, German and Chamomile, Common

Groundbread—*See* Cyclamen, Ivy-leaved

Groundeswelge—*See* Groundsel, Common

Ground Glutton—*See* Groundsel, Common

Ground Holly—*See* Pipsissewa

Ground Moss—*See* Moss, Hair Cup

Groundsel, Common—*See List*—*Senecio vulgaris*—Feminine, Venus, Water
Also known as Ground Glutton, Grundy Swallow, Groundeswelge, Sention, Simson

    Groundsel, Golden—*Senecio aureus*—Feminine, Venus, Water
    Also known as Golden Senecio, Life Root, Squaw Weed
    ASTROLOGICAL: *Primary*: Libra, Taurus; *Secondary*: Cancer, Pisces, Scorpio
    MEDICAL: Astringent, Diuretic, Emmenagogue, Pectoral
    PARTS USED: Herb, Root

    Groundsel, Hoary—*Senecio erucifolius*—Feminine, Venus, Water
    ASTROLOGICAL: *Primary*: Libra, Taurus; *Secondary*: Cancer, Pisces, Scorpio

    Groundsel, Mountain—*Senecio sylvaticus*—Feminine, Venus, Water
    ASTROLOGICAL: *Primary*: Libra, Taurus; *Secondary*: Cancer, Pisces, Scorpio

    Groundsel, Viscid—*Senecio viscosus*—Feminine, Venus, Water
    Also known as Stinking Groundsel
    ASTROLOGICAL: *Primary*: Libra, Taurus; *Secondary*: Cancer, Pisces, Scorpio

ASTROLOGICAL: *Primary*: Libra, Taurus; *Secondary*: Cancer, Pisces, Scorpio
MEDICAL: Anthelmintic, Antiscorbutic, Diaphoretic, Diuretic, Emetic, Purgative. A mild infusion acts as a purgative. A strong infusion acts as an emetic. Unfortunately, the strength of the infusion will vary greatly with the patient.
PART USED: Herb
NOTE: Most often a reference to Groundsel is calling for Common Groundsel (*Senecio vulgaris*), but it could also be calling for any of the various varieties listed.

Ground Raspberry—*See* Goldenseal

Guado—*See* Woad

Guava—*Psidium guajava*—Feminine, Venus, Water
ASTROLOGICAL: *Primary*: Libra, Taurus; *Secondary*: Cancer, Pisces, Scorpio
MAGICKAL: Drinks made from Guava juice work as magickal and spiritual cleansers. Great for getting rid of psychic sludge. Unfortunately, it is very hard to find. Check gourmet shops and Mexican grocery stores.

Guava

Guede—*See* Woad

Guelder Rose—*See* Cramp Bark

Guinea Grains—*See* Grains of Paradise

Guinea Pepper—*See* Grains of Paradise

Guinea Squash—*See* Eggplant

Gum Mastic—*Pistacia lentiscus / Pistacia galls*—Masculine, Sun, Air
Also known as Mastic, Masticke
ASTROLOGICAL: *Primary*: Leo; *Secondary*: Aquarius, Gemini, Libra
GODS: Hanuman, Hermes, Parashurama, Vishnu
MEDICAL: Diuretic, Stimulant. A teaspoon of the tincture can be used to treat diarrhea or added to your favorite tea for use as a stimulant.
PART USED: Resin
MAGICKAL: Gum Mastic is a frequently used ingredient found in spirit-drawing incense recipes. A simple recipe is 1 part Gum Mastic and 2 parts Lavender powder. It is also used to stimulate the intuitive portions of the brain. The tincture is an aphrodisiac. It is typically mixed with sweet sauces and then added to confections and candy in the amount of a teaspoon to a tablespoon of the tincture.

Grundy Swallow—*See* Groundsel, Common

Grouts—*See* Oats

Gizri—*See* Carrot

Graxa—*See* Hibiscus

Greater Periwinkle—*See* Periwinkle

Great Ox-eye—*See* Daisy, Ox-eye

Ground Ivy—*See* Ivy, Ground

Guarana—*Paullinia cupana/Panela supana*
Also known as Brazilian Cocoa, Uabano
WARNING: Abuse may result in changes to the way your body processes blood sugar.

MEDICAL: Febrifuge, Narcotic (mild), Nervine, Stimulant, Tonic. Guarana contains about three times the amount of caffeine as coffee beans. Its other active ingredients are similar to Cocaine, making this one of the strongest stimulants commonly available. Generally speaking, Guarana is prepared and served as one would coffee.
PART USED: Seeds
MAGICKAL: For a mildly stimulating aphrodisiac, modify cooking recipes to include Guarana whenever Cocoa powder is called for. Substitute 1 part Guarana and 3 parts Cocoa; that is to say, if the recipe calls for 4 tablespoons Cocoa, use 1 tablespoon Guarana and 3 tablespoons Cocoa. The result is heightened alertness and blood flow to the sexual organs.

Guardrobe—*See* Rosemary

Guatemalan Oak—*See* Oak

Gujatatti Elachi—*See* Cardamom

Gum Arabic—*See* Arabic, Gum

Gumamela—*See* Hibiscus

Gum Benzoin—*See* Benzoin

Gum Bush—*See* Yerba Santa

Gum Camphor—*See* Camphor

Gum Myrrh Tree—*See* Myrrh

Gum Plant—*See* Comfrey

Gurka—*See* Cucumber

Gypsy Flower—*See* Hounds-Tongue

Hagdorn—*See* Hawthorn

Hag's Tapers—*See* Mullein

Hagthorn—*See* Hawthorn

Hair Cap Moss—*See* Moss, Hair Cap

Hair of Venus—*See* Fern

Hairy Mint—*See* Mint

Hallelujah—*See* Sorrel, Wood

Hallfoot—*See* Coltsfoot

Halves—*See* Hawthorn

Hand of Power—*See* Lucky Hand

Hand Root—*See* Lucky Hand

Hanf—*See* Marijuana

Hare's Beard—*See* Mullein

Haw—*See* Hawthorn

Haya—*See* Beech

Happy Major—*See* Burdock

Hardock—*See* Burdock

Harebell—*See* Bluebell

Harefoot—*See* Avens

Harran—*See* Horehound, White

Hart's Thorn—*See* Buckthorn, Alder

Hart's-Tongue—*See* Fern

Haswey—*See* Cucumber

Hawthorn—*Crataegus oxacantha*—Masculine, Mars, Fire
Also known as Bread and Cheese Tree, Gaxels, Gazels, Hagdorn, Hagthorn, Halves, Haw, Hazels, Huath, Ladies' Meat, Le Pine Noble, May, Mayblossom, May Bush, Mayflower, Quick, Thorn, Tree of Chastity, Whitethorn
ASTROLOGICAL: Aries, Scorpio; *Secondary*: Aries, Leo, Sagittarius
GOD: Hymen
GODDESSES: Blodeuwedd, Cardea, Flora, Olwyn, Virgin Mary

CELTIC TREE CALENDAR (Huath)—May 13th thru June 9th—The sixth month of the year
MAGICKAL: Hawthorn is one of the nine woods that the Wiccan Rede says is best for ritual fires. It reportedly promotes both fertility and chastity (not celibacy, unless one is without their love). A Hawthorn hedge in the garden or around the home will lend protection. Some state that it should be the centerpiece of a Wiccan's garden. The Hawthorn is referred to as "Thorn" in the British Tree Fairy Triad as well as the many that have sprouted up elsewhere citing three sacred trees as Oak, Ash, and Thorn.

Hawthorn

NOTE: Hawthorn is sometimes cited as feminine, but masculine is more often its association.

Haymaids—*See* Ivy, Ground

Hayriffle—*See* Cleavers (B)

Hazels—*See* Hawthorn

Hazel—*See* Hazelnut

Hazelnut—*Corylus avellana*—Masculine, Sun, Air
Also known as Coll, Hazel
ASTROLOGICAL: *Primary*: Leo; *Secondary*: Aquarius, Gemini, Libra
GODS: Aengus mac Og, Chandra, Hermes, Mercury, Thor
GODDESSES: Artemis, Diana, Ochun
CELTIC TREE CALENDAR (Coll)—August 5th thru September 1st—The ninth month of the year
MAGICKAL: The wood of the Hazelnut tree is one of the nine woods referenced in the Wiccan Rede. It is also an excellent wood from which to make the hilt of an athame as well as

the body of a general-purpose wand. However, if used for the hilt of an athame, it should be stained much darker. It is also a fond choice for the construction of dowsing rods, both straight and forked. Eaten, Hazelnuts heighten reproductive fertility and cognitive abilities.

Headache—*See* Poppy, Red

Healing Herb—*See* Comfrey

Heart of Osmund—*See* Fern

Heartsease—*Viola tricolor*—Feminine, Saturn, Water

Also known as Banewort, Banwort, Bird's Eye, Bonewort, Bouncing Bet, Bullweed, Call-Me-to-You, Cuddle Me, Cull Me, Flower O'Luce, Garden Violet, Godfathers and Godmothers, Herb Constancy, Herb Trinitatis, Horse Violet, Jack-Jump-up-and-Kiss-Me, Johnny Jumper, Johnny Jump-ups, Kit-Run-About, Kit-Run-in-the-Fields, Kiss-Her-in-the-buttery, Kiss-Me-at-the-Garden-Gate, Little Stepmother, Live-in-Idleness, Loving Idol, Love-in-Idleness, Love-Lies-Bleeding, Meet-Me-in-the-Entry, Pansy, Pensee, Pink-Eyed-John, Pink-O'-the-Eye, Stepmother, Tickle-My-Fancy, Tittle-My-Fancy, Three-Faces-Under-a-Hood, Wild Pansy

ASTROLOGICAL: *Primary*: Aquarius, Capricorn; *Secondary*: Cancer, Pisces, Scorpio

MEDICAL: Diuretic (herb), Emetic (root and seeds), Expectorant (herb), Nervine, Purgative (root and seeds), Tonic (herb). A warm water infusion of the herb will aid with asthma, bronchitis, and congestion, and will act as a mild diuretic, tonic, and expectorant. Topically, fresh herb is ground up and applied to the skin to treat eczema and boils. But its most common use is said to be in mend-

Heartsease

ing a broken heart and calming the mind. A warm water or red wine infusion of Heartsease calms the mind and makes heartache diminish.

PARTS USED: Herb, Root, Seeds

MAGICKAL: Heartsease, or Pansy, is worn and given to promote romance and love. It is said that carrying Heartsease flowers will mend a broken heart and leave it ready for new love. This lore is probably due to the historic use to treat medical ailments of the heart.

GENERAL: Heartsease is an excellent example of how medical and magickal uses were once merged. As anyone who has ever suffered from a broken heart will tell you, anything that can medically treat this condition will seem as if it is magick.

Hartshorne—*See* Plantain, Buck's Horn

Heath—*See* Heather

Heather—*Calluna vulgaris*—Feminine, Venus, Water

Also known as Common Heather, Heath, Ling, Scottish Heather

ASTROLOGICAL: *Primary*: Libra, Taurus; *Secondary*: Cancer, Pisces, Scorpio

GODS: Shango, Dagda, Eleggua, Obatala, Oggun, Oko

GODDESSES: Cybele, Isis, Ochun, Uroica, Venus

CELTIC TREE CALENDAR (Ura)—Summer Solstice

MAGICKAL: Carried to guard against violent crime, but should not be used in place of common sense. Ccarry it in a dark colored sachet. When you feel you might be entering harm's way, stop, inhale its mild scent, and see if there is not a better route around the trouble.

Heather

Hebenon—*See* Henbane

Hedgeheriff—*See* Cleavers (B)

Hedgemaids—*See* Ivy, Ground

Hedge Taper—*See* Mullein

Heemst—*See* Mallow, Marsh

Heermannchen—*See* Chamomile, German and Chamomile, Common

He Huan Pi—*See* Albizia

Heidekorm—*See* Buckwheat

☠ **Heliotrope**—*Heliotropium Peruviana/Heliotropium europaeum/Heliotropium arborescens*—Masculine, Sun, Fire
Also known as Cherry Pie, Hindicum, Tumsole
ASTROLOGICAL: *Primary*: Leo; *Secondary*: Aries, Leo, Sagittarius
GODS: Apollo, Babalu Aye, Eleggua, Obatala, Orunla, Ra
GODDESS: Ochun
MAGICKAL: In a dream pillow, Heliotrope encourages prophecy. When carried, it will help one to go unnoticed. Used in conjunction with other banishing herbs, Heliotrope is used to cleanse a home and drive out undesired spirits and ghosts.

☠**Hellebore, Black**—*Helleborus niger*—Feminine, Saturn, Water
Also known as Christe Herbe, Christmas Rose, Melampode, Winter Rose
ASTROLOGICAL: *Primary*: Aquarius, Capricorn; *Secondary*: Cancer, Pisces, Scorpio
GODDESS: Athena
MEDICAL: Anthelmintic, Emmenagogue, Narcotic (violently), Purgative (major). Black Hellebore is so dangerous that skin contact with the fresh root may produce major irritation. Historically, a tincture of the root has been used; however, such use has been abandoned due to the easy potential of overdose and death.

PART USED: Root
MAGICKAL: Black Hellebore has no magickal property that makes it of enough interest to use despite its poisonous properties.

☠**Hellebore, False**—*Adonis autumnalis/Adonis vernalis*
Also known as Adonis, Pheasant's Eye, Red Chamomile, Red Mathes, Red Morocco, Rose-a-Rubie, Sweet Vernal Hellebore
MAGICKAL: False Hellebore has no magickal property that makes it of enough interest to use despite its poisonous properties.

☠**Hellebore, Green**—*Veratrum viride*
Also known as American Hellebore, Indian Poke, Itch-Weed, Swamp Hellebore
MEDICAL: Diaphoretic, Emetic, Sedative
PART USED: Root
MEDICAL: Use of this plant has been abandoned due to its extremely poisonous nature.
MAGICKAL: Green Hellebore has no magickal property that makes it of enough interest to use despite its poisonous properties.

☠**Hellebore, White**—*Veratrum album/Veratrum Lobelianium/Veratrum Californicum*
Also known as Weiszer Germer, Weisze Nieszwurzel
GODS: Saturn
MEDICAL: Use of this plant has been abandoned due to its extremely poisonous nature.
PART USED: Root
MAGICKAL: White Hellebore has no magickal property that makes it of enough interest to use despite its poisonous properties.

Hellweed—*See* Dodder

Helmet Flower—*See* Scullcap

Helping Hand—*See* Lucky Hand

Hemidesmus—*See* Sarsaparilla

☠**Hemlock**—*Conium maculatum*—Feminine, Saturn, Water

Also known as Beaver Poison, Herb Bennet, Kex, Kecksies, Musquash Root, Poison Hemlock, Poison Parsley, Spotted Corobane, Spotted Hemlock, Water Parsley

GODDESS: Hecate

ASTROLOGICAL: *Primary*: Aquarius, Capricorn; *Secondary*: Cancer, Pisces, Scorpio

MEDICAL: Antispasmodic, Sedative, Paralyser. Drying Hemlock will destroy many of the active ingredients. Cooking or warming it in an infusion will further destroy the active ingredients. But neither of these should be considered a way to render it non-poisonous.

Hemlock

PARTS USED: Fruit, Leaves, Seeds (each fresh)

MAGICKAL: The juice of fresh Hemlock is used to purify the blade of ritual athames and swords; however, the risk of growing it in your home is far too great to bother with this practice.

☠**Hemlock, Water**—*Cicuta virosa*

Hemp—*See* Marijuana

Hempweed—*See* Gravelroot

Hen and Chickens—*See* Houseleek

Henbell—*See* Henbane

☠**Henbane**—*Hyosycamus niger*—Feminine, Saturn, Water

Also known as Black Nightshade, Cassilata, Cassilago, Common Henbane, Deus Caballinus, Devil's Eye, Hebenon, Henbell, Hog's Bean, Hyoscyamus, Isana, Jupiter's bean, Jusquiame, Poison Tobacco, Symphonica

ASTROLOGICAL: *Primary*: Aquarius, Capricorn; *Secondary*: Cancer, Pisces, Scorpio

GODDESS: Athena

MEDICAL: Antispasmodic, Diuretic, Hypnotic. Similar to the effects of Belladonna, but not as pronounced or strong. The use of this plant is best avoided due to its poisonous nature.

PARTS USED: Branches, Flowering tops, Leaves (fresh), Seeds

GENERAL: Another herb best left alone. I am sure this one kills many teenagers every year as it is often listed as an ingredient in so-called flying ointments and smokes.

Hendibeh—*See* Chicory

Henna—*Lawsonia alba/Lawsonia inermis*

Also known as Al-Khanna, Al-Henna, Egyptian Privet, Henne, Jamaica Mignonette, Mehndi, Mendee, Smooth Lawsonia

MEDICAL: Emmenagogue (fruit). Henna has primarily been used in cosmetics. It is used to dye the hair and skin.

PARTS USED: Flowers, Fruit, Leaves

MAGICKAL: Henna is most often used to stain the skin, effectively providing a painless tattoo that lasts about two weeks. Preparation is relatively simple, but it can be purchased ready to use in paste form. The ready-made mixtures often come in an applicator tube. Henna body art

Henna

is said to bless the wedding night. It provides hours of entertainment for the bridesmaids the night before (decorating the bride) and hours of exploration the night of the wedding (the husband's exploration of those designs).

Henne—*See* Henna

Hen Plant—*See* Plantain, Ribwort

Hepatica—*See* Liverwort, American

Herba Sacra—*See* Vervain

Herba John—*See* St. John's Wort

Herba Ruta Caprariae—*See* Rue, Goat's

Herba Stella—*See* Plantain, Buck's Horn

Herbe de la Croix—*See* Mistletoe, European

Herbe de la Laque—*See* Pokeweed

Herbe de St. Julien—*See* Savory, Summer

Herbe du Siege—*See* Figwort, Knotted

Herb Ivy—*See* Plantain, Buck's Horn

Herb-of-Grace—*See* Rue

Herb Trinity—*See* Liverwort, American

Herb Bennet—*See* Avens and Hemlock

Herb Constancy—*See* Heartsease

Herb of Circe—*See* Mandrake

Herb of Enchantment—*See* Vervain

Herb of Gladness—*See* Borage

Herb of Grace—*See* Vervain

Herb of the Cross—*See* Vervain

Herb Patience—*See* Rhubarb, Monk's

Herb Peter—*See* Cowslip

Herb of the Devil—*See* Thornapple

Herb Trinitatis—*See* Heartsease

Herbygrass—*See* Rue

Hetre—*See* Beech

Hexenmannchen—*See* Mandrake

Hibiscus—*Hibiscus sabdariffa/Hibiscus rosanensis*—Feminine, Venus, Water

Also known as Graxa, Gumamela, Kharkady, Shoeflower, Tulipan

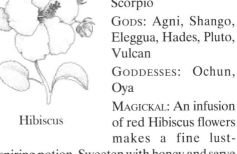
Hibiscus

ASTROLOGICAL: *Primary*: Libra, Taurus; *Secondary*: Cancer, Pisces, Scorpio

GODS: Agni, Shango, Eleggua, Hades, Pluto, Vulcan

GODDESSES: Ochun, Oya

MAGICKAL: An infusion of red Hibiscus flowers makes a fine lust-inspiring potion. Sweeten with honey and serve hot. Alternatively, the infusion can be blended with fruit punch and served cold.

High Blackberry—*See* Blackberry

High John—*See* High John the Conqueror

☠**High John the Conqueror**—*Ipomea purga/Ipomea jalapa*—Masculine, Mars, Fire

Also known as High John, Jalap, Jalap Bindweed

ASTROLOGICAL: *Primary*: Aries, Scorpio; *Secondary*: Aries, Leo, Sagittarius

MEDICAL: Cathartic, Purgative. Historically, High John has been used as a cathartic and purgative. As purgative, it has even been used to treat children and babies. However, modern medicine has found that it is poisonous and should not be consumed.

PART USED: Root

MAGICKAL: High John the Conqueror root is carried for general success, especially in gambling. But it is also very useful in protection spells. Crushing the High John root and soaking it in vegetable oil for one cycle of the moon makes a very general purpose anointing oil. An infusion of High John root can be mixed with mop water to provide a home with luck (and a wonderful BBQ smell).

Hilba—*See* Fenugreek

Hindebar—*See* Raspberry

Hindberry—*See* Raspberry

Hindbur—*See* Raspberry

Hindbeer—*See* Raspberry

Hindicum—*See* Heliotrope

Hind's-Tongue—*See* Fern

Hirtentasche—*See* Shepherd's Purse

Hochwurzel—*See* Gentian

Hog Apple—*See* Mandrake, American

Hog Fennel—*See* Masterwort

Hog's Bean—*See* Henbane

Hog Weed—*See* Broom and Knotgrass

Hoholi—*See* Sesame

Holly, American—*Ilex opaca*—Masculine, Mars, Fire

☙**Holly, Common**—*Ilex aquifolium*—Masculine, Mars, Fire

Also known as Aquifolius, Bat's Wings, Christ's Thorn, Holy Tree, Holm Chastle, Holm, Holme Chase, Hulm, Hulver Bush, Tinne

ASTROLOGICAL: *Primary*: Aries, Scorpio; *Secondary*: Aries, Leo, Sagittarius

GODS: Taranis, Thor, Jesus Christ, Lugh

CELTIC TREE CALENDAR (Tinne)—July 18th thru Aug 4th—The eighth month of the year.

MEDICAL: Diaphoretic (leaves), Emetic (berries), Purgative (berries). The berries are so purgative and emetic that they are generally considered poisonous.

PARTS USED: Bark, Berries, Leaves

MAGICKAL: A decoction of Holly leaves (not berries) makes a magickal calmative. However, it is not consumed. A couple of warm drops massaged gently on a child's back will calm the tike. This same potion (or even raw leaves) has a similar effect on wild animals when placed in their path.

Holly

GENERAL: Holly berries show us that the old saying that if a bird can eat it, then it is safe is complete hogwash. Thrushes and blackbirds routinely eat these berries, but if a human eats them they tend to curl up into a little ball due to the abdominal pains between bouts of projectile vomiting. Something occurred to me at a Winter Solstice celebration in which we dressed the Oak King with a crown of Oak and the Holly King with a crown of Holly. Our Holly King was remarkably uncomfortable. The thorn-like prickles of the Holly leaves scratched and teased at his skin. With the plant's connection to the Christian holiday of Christmas, its folk name "Christ's Thorn," and the Pagan lore of the Holly King's self-sacrifice, it does seem that a great deal of Pagan lore was hidden in Christian practices.

Hollyhocks—*Althea rosea*

MEDICAL: Expectorant, Pectoral. A warm water infusion of Hollyhock herb will relieve chest congestion and act as a mild expectorant. May help prevent kidney stones if used regularly.

PART USED: Herb

GENERAL: Hollyhock and Marshmallow are often used as substitutes for each other.

Holly-leaved Barberry—*See* Barberry, Holly-leaved

Holly, Sea—*Eryngium maritinum/Eryngium campestre*—Feminine, Venus, Water

Also known as Eryngo, Krausdistel, Panicaut, Sea Hulver, Sea Holme, Yerba del Sapo

ASTROLOGICAL: *Primary*: Libra, Taurus; *Secondary*: Cancer, Pisces, Scorpio

MEDICAL: Diaphoretic, Diuretic, Expectorant, Stimulant

PART USED: Root

MAGICKAL: Give Sea Holly to a couple that is quarreling. Ask them to put aside the quarrel for one meal, and the following evening ask them to prepare that meal together, mixing the Sea Holly into the sauce and salad in sparing amounts (no more than a handful). Have them scatter whatever is left on the bedroom floor and tell them that they don't have to make love that night, but they do have to sleep in the same room. By morning the quarrel might not be over, but it will be well on its way.

Holy Herb—*See* Vervain

Holy Thistle—*See* Thistle, Blessed

Holy Tree—*See* Holly

Holm Chastle—*See* Holly

Holm—*See* Holly

Holme Chase—*See* Holly

Holm Oak—*See* Oak

Holy Herb—*See* Yerba Santa

Holy Thorn—*See* Barberry, Common

Honey

MEDICAL: Honey is the base for many natural cough syrups. Locally harvested honey makes for a good preventative measure against allergies; however it may cause an allergic reaction itself. Give it a try and see if it helps or hurts.

Honeysuckle—*Lonicera caprifolium/Lonicera japonica/Lonicera Periclymenum*—Masculine, Jupiter, Earth

Also known as Capri-Foglio, Chèvre-Feuille, Dutch Honeysuckle, Geisblatt, Goat's Leaf, Woodbine

ASTROLOGICAL: *Primary*: Pisces, Sagittarius; *Secondary*: Capricorn, Taurus, Virgo

GODS: Babalu Aye, Shango, Eleggua, Obatala, Ochosi, Oggun, Orunla

GODDESS: Ochun

MEDICAL: Pectoral. An expression of the fresh vine is used to stop the itch and redness of insect bites. A warm water infusion of the root is a good treatment for asthma and excellent in a poultice for mild wounds. The fresh leaves and root also work as a good poultice.

PARTS USED: Flowers, Leaves

MAGICKAL: Grown in the home, the Honeysuckle will attract money. Outside the home it will bring general luck.

Hops—*Humulus lupulus*—Masculine, Mars, Air

Also known as Beer Flower

ASTROLOGICAL: *Primary*: Aries, Scorpio; *Secondary*: Aquarius, Gemini, Libra

GOD: Dagda

MEDICAL: Anodyne, Diuretic, Nervine, Tonic. A warm water infusion of Hops is used to assist sleep; however, they should not be used by folk who have trouble with depression as they tend to add to the depression. If depression is not present, Hops is good as an evening tonic.

Hops

Part used: Flowers

MAGICKAL: Hops is sown into dream pillows for both restful sleep and dream retention. Inhaling the scent of fresh Hops will relax mind, body, and soul.

Horse Violet—*See* Heartsease

Herb Willow—*See* Loosestrife, Yellow

Horehound—*See* Horehound, White

Horehound, Black—*Marrubium nigrum/ Ballota nigra*—Masculine, Mercury, Air
Also known as Stinking Horehound
ASTROLOGICAL: *Primary*: Gemini, Virgo; *Secondary*: Aquarius, Gemini, Libra
MEDICAL: Antispasmodic, Stimulant, Vermifuge. An infusion of Black Horehound is used as a mild stimulant, but it tastes nasty and should not be consumed if pregnant. Oddly enough, there is a great deal of lore that states that Black Horehound is a cure for the bite of a "mad dog."
PART USED: Herb

Horehound, White—*Marrubium vulgare*—Masculine, Mercury, Air
Also known as Bull's Blood, Even of the Star, Harran, Hoarhound, Horehound, Huran, Llwyd y cwn, Marrubium, Maruil, Seed of Horns, Soldier's Tea
ASTROLOGICAL: *Primary*: Gemini, Virgo; *Secondary*: Aquarius, Gemini, Libra
GODS: Eleggua, Horus the Elder, Obatala
MEDICAL: Expectorant, Tonic. Check the ingredients on one of those herbal cough drops. Chances are that one of the first herbs will be Horehound because it is that good at relieving coughs, sore throats, and chest congestion, as well as is very effective as an expectorant. A warm water infusion of Horehound will have the same effect. Mix with honey to taste. Called "Soldier's Tea," probably because it acts as a mind stimulant. Should not be consumed if you are pregnant.
PART USED: Herb
MAGICKAL: If you are making incense to honor Horus, this is the Horehound you are looking for. I cannot stress enough how horribly Black Horehound will make your house smell.

Horse Mint—*See* Mint

Horseradish—*Cochlearia Armoracia/ Armoracia rusticana*—Masculine, Mars, Fire
Also known as Great Raifort, Mountain Radish, Moutarde des Allemands, Red Cole
ASTROLOGICAL: *Primary*: Aries, Scorpio; *Secondary*: Aries, Leo, Sagittarius
MEDICAL: Antiseptic, Aperient, Diuretic, Expectorant, Rubefacient, Stimulant. Acts as a strong expectorant. A warm milk infusion of Horseradish is a good treatment for the symptoms of asthma. Best to use skim milk. In a poultice, the ground fresh root is good for pain relief when applied directly to the injury.

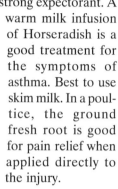

Horseradish

PART USED: Root
MAGICKAL: Horseradish is excellent for purification and cleansing of psychic sludge. Drying fresh roots in the kitchen will help keep the house free of negative energy, but in my home I have to use other herbs. Any fresh Horseradish always winds up in my belly long before it is dry.
GENERAL: When I was younger, I was observing Seder (a Jewish rite) with some friends. During the rite, slavery was explained as both bitter and sweet. I was served a beautifully sweet paste (I don't remember the name) as an example of sweetness and then the freshest horseradish in the world as an example of the bitterness of slavery. After tasting both, I asked, "Could I have more bitterness of slavery please?" Fortunately, my host and hostess were amused.

Horsetails—Feminine, Saturn, Earth
Also known as Bottle Brush, Dutch Rushes, Paddock Pipes, Pewterwort, Shavegrass

ASTROLOGICAL: *Primary*: Aquarius, Capricorn; *Secondary*: Capricorn, Taurus, Virgo

MAGICKAL: The act of love in a room or area filled with Horsetails is said to be particularly fertile.

NOTE: There are many plants in this category, including: Equisetum arvense, Equisetum hyemale, Equisetum maximum, Equisetum sylvaticum

Horsetails

Horse Tongue—*See* Fern

Hoary Groundsel—*See* Groundsel, Hoary

Hoary Plantain—*See* Plantain, Hoary

Hoodoo Herb—*See* Vervain

Hoodwort—*See* Scullcap

Horminum—*See* Sage, Clary

Horse Chestnut—*See* Chestnut, Horse

Horse Daisy—*See* Daisy, Ox-eye

Horseheal—*See* Elecampane and Spikenard, Ploughman's

Horsehoof—*See* Coltsfoot

Horsemint—See Bergamot, Wild

Horse Gowan—See Daisy, Ox-eye

Hound's-Tongue—*Cynoglossum officinale/Lindefolia spectabilis*—Masculine, Mars, Fire

Also known as Dog-Bur, Dog's-Tongue, Gypsy Flower, Sheep Lice, Tongue of Dog, Woolmat

See also Deerstongue, which is also called Hound's-Tongue

ASTROLOGICAL: *Primary*: Aries, Scorpio; *Secondary*: Aries, Leo, Sagittarius

MAGICKAL: A sachet of Hound's-Tongue placed close but out of the reach of a domestic puppy will cause its cries to lessen. In the wild, slipping some into your shoe will reportedly keep dogs from barking at you. I have found the former to be a bit useful but the latter to be without any truth.

Houseleek—*Sempervivum tectorum*—Masculine, Jupiter, Air

Also known as Ayron, Ayegreen, Bullock's Eye, Donnersbart, Hen and Chickens, Joubarbe des Toits, Jupiter's Beard, Jupiter's Eye, Sengren, Thor's Beard, Welcome-Home-Husband-Thou-Never-So-Drunk, Welcome-Home-Husband-Thou-Never-So-Late

ASTROLOGICAL: *Primary*: Pisces, Sagittarius; *Secondary*: Aquarius, Gemini, Libra

GOD: Thor

MEDICAL: Astringent, Diuretic, Emetic (in large doses), Purgative (in large doses), Refrigerant

MAGICKAL: The Houseleek will bring love to a house if grown indoors, but its best use will take a bit of work. Take a road trip to Monroe County Indiana (or another area rich in geodes) with everyone that lives in your house (especially a spouse). Take some hiking boots and a couple of heavy hammers. Make a picnic of it and have fun searching for the perfect geodes (two feet across or larger), then crack them open and hope you find them to be mostly hollow with a slight interior covering of rusty quartz. On your way home, stop at a gardening store and ask for Hen and Chickens and the right potting soil. When you get home, give your new plants their new homes (the geodes). As they grow, they will remember and keep the love that you shared that day.

PART USED: Fresh leaves

Hreow—*See* Rue

Huath—*See* Hawthorn

Huckleberry—*Vaccinium myrtillus / Vaccinium Frondosum*—Feminine, Venus, Water

Also known as Airelle, Bilberry, Black Whortles, Bleaberry, Blueberries, Hurts,

Hurtleberry, Trackleberry, Whinberry, Whortleberry

ASTROLOGICAL: *Primary*: Libra, Taurus; *Secondary*: Cancer, Pisces, Scorpio

MAGICKAL: One part Huckleberry and 2 parts Gum Arabic ground into a powder makes fine incense for meditative sleep. The process takes two people; one sleeps and the other tends the coals and stokes them with this incense. The one remaining awake should hold a clear mental image of that which the two hope to manifest and then describe it over and over in perfect detail to their sleeping partner. After the partner wakes, they trade places and repeat. Do not wake the sleeper unless there is an emergency.

Huckleberry

Hulm—*See* Holly

Hulver Bush—*See* Holly

Huauhtli—*See* Amaranth

Hulwa—*See* Dill

Humble Plant—*See* Mimosa

Hundred Eyes—*See* Periwinkle

Hundred-leaved Grass—*See* Yarrow

Huo Xiang—*See* Agastache

Hu Po—*See* Amber

Huran—*See* Horehound, White

Hurrburr—*See* Burdock

Hurtlesickle—*See* bachelor's Buttons

Hurtleberry—*See* Huckleberry

Hurts—*See* Huckleberry

Hurtsickle—*See* Bachelor's Buttons

Hu-Suy—*See* Coriander

Hu-Sui—*See* Coriander

Husked Nut—*See* Chestnut, Sweet

Hyacinth, Grape—*Muscari racemosum*
Also known as Starch Hyacinth
MEDICAL: Diuretic, Stimulant
PART USED: Herb

Hyacinth, Wild—*Hyacinthus nonscriptus / Scilla nonscriptus / Hyacinthus orientalis*—Feminine, Venus, Water
Also known as Bluebell, Nodding Squill
ASTROLOGICAL: *Primary*: Libra, Taurus; *Secondary*: Cancer, Pisces, Scorpio
GODS: Babalu Aye, Shango, Eleggua, Oggun, Oko
GODDESS: Ochun
MAGICKAL: Growing Hyacinth will help prevent spring depressions. The beautifully scented flower shows itself around the Spring Equinox. Its dried flowers are sometimes used in love sachets and incense

Hyacinth

blends. Fresh flowers are used to prevent nightmares. Inhale prior to sleep and leave the fresh flower beside the bed. The dried flower can also be used for this purpose by simmering it in water, but this method is not nearly as effective.

Hydrangea—*Hydrangea arborescens/Hydrangea vulgaris*
Also known as Common Hydrangea, Seven Barks, Wild Hydrangea
MEDICAL: (*Hydrangea arborescens*)—Diuretic, Cathartic, Tonic. The exact strength of a decoction is hard to determine, as it will vary with the patient.
PARTS USED: Leaves, Roots

MAGICKAL: A strong infusion of Hydrangea is used as a floor wash to drive negative magick from your home and to protect it against future invasions. Powder and scatter into your carpet at night, then vacuum your home thoroughly and dispose of the vacuum bag immediately. If you believe you have a hex placed on you by someone you know, use a clean vacuum bag. Then after vacuuming up the scattered Hydrangea, scatter it in the person's front yard as you walk by to casually return the attack.

Hydrocotyle—*See* Gotu Kola

Hyoscyamus—*See* Henbane

Hyssop—*Hyssopus officinalis*—Masculine, Jupiter, Fire

Also known as Isopo, Ysopo, Yssop

ASTROLOGICAL: *Primary*: Pisces, Sagittarius; *Secondary*: Aries, Leo, Sagittarius

GODS: Babalu Aye, Brahma, Shango, Eleggua, Jupiter, Obatala, Ochosi, Oggun, Pluto, Zeus

GODDESSES: Ochun

MEDICAL: Astringent, Carminative, Diaphoretic, Expectorant, Pectoral, Stimulant. Relief from common colds and mild breathing disorders can be had with a warm water infusion of hyssop. Acts as an expectorant. This is most common with the treatment of winter-month colds and mild upper respiratory infections. Mix 1 teaspoon per measuring cup of warm water, simmer, and sweeten with honey. Given three times a day (between each meal), this tea will greatly speed recovery from the common cold. Seems to improve the function of the immune system. Also acts as a mild stimulant and astringent. A warm water

Hyssop

infusion of the herb may help to increase blood pressure of those who suffer from low blood pressure. Acts as a good tonic for vegetarians.

PART USED: Herb

MAGICKAL: Hyssop is the number one choice for a lustral bath or other bathing for purification. A strong infusion of Hyssop can also be added to mop water to purify the kitchen and hearth areas of the home. Essential oil of Hyssop is diffused to clear the cognitive mind; however, it must always be diluted prior to use because, in its concentrated form, its scent alone can cause medical problems.

Ibhuma—See Cattail

Iboga—*Tabernanthe iboga*

Also known as Ibogaine

GENERAL: Boar, gorilla, and porcupine have all been seen to repeatedly eat this plant and then later show its powerful effect. Boar will go so far as to dig up the root to get at the highest concentration of the active ingredient. In repeating this behavior, there seems to be an indication that animals enjoy its intoxicating effects. This dispels one of the many false differences between humanity and other forms of the animal kingdom. We are not the only creatures that deliberately become intoxicated.

MAGICKAL: Iboga bark is consumed as part of initiatory rites and ceremonies of several of the secret societies in the area of the Congo (approximately where humanity first walked the earth). Typically, it is used for seeking vision and advice from ancestors. When one considers the chemical effects on the body, it becomes easy to see why such traditions would form. In its natural form, Iboga is a strong stimulant and mild hallucinogen. Be warned that this is a very powerful plant. It is also illegal in many parts of the world. The amount of active ingredients (mainly Ibogaine) will vary greatly from one plant to the next. Even the time of day that this plant is harvested will greatly influence chemical constancy. Mild amounts will cause a stimulating effect bordering on euphoria. However, too much will cause convulsions and perhaps paralysis. If that paralysis is of the respiratory system, the outcome might be death. So why do I include it here? Well, if you think you have heard about Iboga or Ibogaine before, chances are that you have. Although it is currently considered part of Grey (maybe even Black) science, research has shown that in clinical conditions this plant can be used to cure many addictions, especially heroin, morphine, and other drugs created from the Poppy. The reason many have already heard about this plant is that it was splattered all over the evening news when the first research results were released. That research stated that a single dose of Iboga, given as part of clinical research being conducted on active heroin addicts, resulted in 80 percent of those who participated in the study never returning to the use of heroin. I believe these results are a factor of both the vision quest provided by Iboga as well as the desire to improve one's life, demonstrated by participation in the study. In this research, we see vision quest as a very powerful tool, but only after years of preparation. In this case, that preparation was living life addicted to heroin and finally reaching bottom. Hence, I believe the 80 percent cure rate is just as much because the patients wanted to be cured as it was due to their vision quest. On the other hand, Iboga and Ibogaine have made their way into the illicit drug market. When I experimented with it, it was very popular among the "Shaman in a Pill" types. I no longer associate with many of the folk I knew back then because they have continued to abuse this and other sacraments. While it may be pompous to say, I feel I have matured beyond that point in my life. This translates into modern vision quest by telling us that taking a hallucinogen for vision quest will only provide you with true answers and help if that is what you are truly looking for. In other words, using chemicals for intoxication while justifying it by claiming you are on a vision quest will result in exactly what you were truly after: nothing but intoxication. Why bother deluding yourself?

Iceland Lichen—*See* Moss, Iceland

Iceland Moss—*See* Moss, Iceland

Imperatoria—*See* Masterwort

Incense—*See* Frankincense

Incensier—*See* Rosemary

Indian Barberry—*See* Barberry, Indian

Indian Dye—*See* Golden Seal

Indian Chickweed—*See* Chickweed

Indian Elm—*See* Elm, Slippery

Indian Fig Tree—*See* Banyan

Indian God Tree—*See* Banyan

Indian Gum—*See* Arabic, Gum

Indian Hemp—*See* Dogbane

Indian Paint—*See* Golden Seal

Indian Pennywort—*See* Gotu Kola

Indian Poke—*See* Hellebore, Green

Indian Posy—*See* Balsam, White

Indian Root—*See* Spikenard, American

Indian Sage—*See* Boneset

Indian Sarsaparilla—*See* Sarsaparilla

Indian Spikenard—*See* Spikenard, American

Indian-Tobacco—*See* Lobelia

Indian Valerian—*See* Valerian, Indian

India Root—*See* Galangal

Intoxicating Pepper—*See* Kava Kava

Iris—*See List*—Feminine, Venus, Water
See also Orris

Yellow Iris—*Iris Pseudacorus*
Also known as Iris Aquatica, Daggers, Dragon Flower, Fleur de Luce, Gladyne, Iris Lutia, Jacob's Sword, Myrtle Flower, Fliggers, Flaggon, Levers, Livers, Meklin, Segg, Shalder, Sheggs, Yellow Flag

Iris Minor—*Iris tenax*
ASTROLOGICAL: *Primary*: Libra, Taurus; *Secondary*: Cancer, Pisces, Scorpio
GOD: Oko
MAGICKAL: Iris is simmered to promote an uplifting feeling in the home.

Iris Versicolor—*See* Blue Flag

Iris Aquatica—*See* Iris

Iris Lutia—*See* Iris

Iris Minor—*See* Iris

Irish Broom—*See* Broom

Irish Moss—*See* Moss, Irish

Irish Tops—*See* Broom

Isana—*See* Henbane

Isopo—*See* Hyssop

Ispaghul Plantain—*See* Plantain, Ispaghul

Italian Eggplant—*See* Eggplant

Italian Lovage—*See* Lovage

Italian Parsley—*See* Lovage

Italian Sarsaparilla—*See* Sarsaparilla

Itch-wWed—*See* Hellebore, Green

Itm—*See* Olive

Iuliole—*See* Sorrel, Wood

Ivy, American—*Vitis Hederacea/Ampelopsis Quinquefolia/Cissus Hederacea/Ciccus Quinquefolia*
Also known as Five-leaved Ivy, Virginia Creeper, Wood Vine
MAGICKAL: Growing on the outside walls and surrounding area of a home, American Ivy protects and helps fortify the home against negative energy. Unfortunately, with time it will also cause damage to building material.

Ivy, Common—*Hedera Helix*—Feminine, Saturn, Water
Also known as Gort
ASTROLOGICAL: *Primary*: Aquarius, Capricorn; *Secondary*: Cancer, Pisces, Scorpio
GODS: Bacchus, Brahma, Dionysus, Osiris
GODDESSES: Ariadne, Artemis, Arianrhod, Pasiphae, Persephone, Psyche
CELTIC TREE CALENDAR (Gort)—September 30th thru October 27th)—The eleventh month of the year
MAGICKAL: A wand or staff (thyrsus) made of Fennel stalk and wound clockwise from bottom to top with ivy and terminated with a pinecone is one of the most sacred symbols to Dionysus, perhaps even more than wine itself. This tool is well worth the effort of growing your own Fennel as it aids in the exploration of the Mysteries of Dionysus and all Mysteries where the feminine side of men is to be raised.

Ivy, Ground—*Glechoma Hederacea*
Also known as Alehoof, Catsfoot, Gill-Go-By-the-Hedge, Gill-Go-Over-the-Ground, Haymaids, Hedgemaids, Lizzy-Run-up-the-Hedge, Nepeta Glechoma, Robin-Run-in-the-Hedge, Tun-Hoof

☙ Ivy, Poison—*Rhus Toxicodendron*
Also known as Poison Vine

Ivy, Poison

Ivy-leaved Cyclamen—*See* Cyclamen

Jacaranda Caroba—*See* Carob

Jack-by-the-Hedge—*See* Mustard, Garlic

Jack-Jump-up-and-Kiss-Me—*See* Heartsease

Jackstraw—*See* Plantain, Ribwort

Jacob's Ladder—*See* Lily of the Valley

Jacob's Staff—*See* Mullein

Jacob's Sword—*See* Iris

Jalap—*See* High John the Conqueror and Pokeweed

Jalap Bindweed—*See* High John the Conqueror

Jamaica Sarsaparilla—*See* Sarsaparilla

Jamestown-Weed—*See* Thornapple

Japanese Gentian—*See* Gentian

Jasen Beli—*See* Ash

Jasmine—*See Note*—Feminine, Moon, Water
Also known as Anbar, Jessamin, Moonlight-on-the-Grove, Peote's Jessamine, Yasmin
ASTROLOGICAL: *Primary*: Cancer; *Secondary*: Cancer, Pisces, Scorpio
GODS: Ganesa, Shu, Oko, Olocun, Orunla, Vishnu, Zeus
GODDESSES: Artemis, Diana, Ochun, Yemaya
MAGICKAL: Jasmine is often scattered or burned with sandalwood when conducting "coven calls" or when attempting to find spiritual connections. The same is true of drawing prosperity, but to a lesser degree. Fresh Jasmine will encourage restful sleep and increase psychic abilities. Jasmine absolute is one of the most expensive oils on the market today and for good reason. It takes huge amounts of the plant to produce even the smallest amount of

oil. As a result, the great majority of what is on the market is synthetic and virtually useless for aromatherapy. Diffusing true Jasmine absolute into the air will greatly ease the pain of childbirth as well as regular monthly pain associated with a woman's reproductive system. It provides relaxation to the body of both men and women.

Jasmine

*NOTE: Jasmine belongs to the genus *Jasminum* in the natural order *Oleaceae*, which numbers about 150 species. The most common are *Jasminum grandiflorum, Jasminum officinale,* and *Jasmininum odoratissimum.*

Jat—*See* Alfalfa

Jaundice Root—*See* Goldenseal

Jamaica Mignonette—*See* Henna

Jessamin—*See* Jasmine

Jewelweed—*Impatiens aurea / Impatiens biflora*
MEDICAL: Cathartic, Diuretic, Emetic. Internal use of this plant has been found to be dangerous. Today, its only use is topical. An expression of the stems makes a good immediate treatment for Poison Oak / Poison Ivy. A warm water infusion works to relieve the itch after it has set in.
PART USED: Herb

Jimson-Weed—See Thornapple

Job's Tears—*Coix lachryma-jobi*
Also known as Tear Grass
MAGICKAL: A string of Job's Tears around the neck will reportedly remove the pain of a sore throat as well as bring good luck.

Joe Jie—*See* Gravelroot

Joe-Pye Weed—*See* Gravelroot

Johimbe—*See* Yohimbe

Johnny Jumper—*See* Heartsease

Johnny Jump-Ups—*See* Heartsease

John's Bread—*See* Carob

John's Wort—*See* St. John's Wort

Jojoba—*Simmondsia Chinenis*
GOD: Adonis
GENERAL: Jojoba usually refers to the oil made from this plant. It is not actually oil, but more of a wax that is liquid at room temperature. This is the ideal material from which to create magickal oils for gifts or for commercial use. Although other base oils are often more appropriate to the specific purpose, they will go rancid with time. Jojoba will not. So if you have no idea when you will use a preparation requiring base oil, reach for Jojoba.

Jopi Weed—*See* Gravelroot

Joubarbe des Toits—*See* Houseleek

Joulaf—*See* Oats

Jove's Flower—*See* Carnation

Joy-on-the-Ground—*See* Periwinkle

Joy-of-the-Mountain—*See* Oregano

Juglans—*See* Oak

Juniper—*Juniperus communes*—Masculine, Sun, Fire
Also known as Enebro, Gemeiner Wachholder, Geneva, Genevrier, Gin Berry, Ginepro, Gin Plant
ASTROLOGICAL: *Primary*: Leo; *Secondary*: Aries, Leo, Sagittarius

GODS: Asclepius, Babalu Aye, Shango, Cupid, Dionysus, Eleggua, Hymen, Oggun, Silvanus
MAGICKAL: A strong tincture of Juniper berries on your ankles will calm wild animals that otherwise may not allow you to pass. It also lets you sneak up on frogs when you have forgotten your telephoto lens, but it seems to make snakes hide. The tincture also attracts love, especially when prepared with equal amounts of Sandalwood. Essential oil of Juniper is diffused for cleansing purposes. It is believed that the scent acts as a disinfectant for the air. Juniper berries provide an uplifting scent that relieves stress and battles mental fatigue.

Juniper

Juno's Tears—*See* Vervain

Jupiter's Bean—*See* Henbane

Jupiter's Beard—*See* Houseleek

Jupiter's Eye—*See* Houseleek

Jupiter's Nut—*See* Chestnut, Sweet

Jupiter's Staff—*See* Mullein

Jusquiame—*See* Henbane

Kablin—*See* Patchouli

Kaempferia Galanga—*See* Galangal

Kafoor—*See* Camphor

Kakelah Seghar—*See* Cardamom

Kaphnos—*See* Fumitory

Karafs—*See* Celery

Karakaffes—*See* Comfrey

Karan—*See* Myrrh

Karcom—*See* Saffron, Spanish

Kasui—*See* Cashew

Kauayan-Kiling—*See* Bamboo

Kava Kava—*Piper Methysticum*—Feminine, Saturn, Water

Also known as Ava, Ava Pepper, Ava Root, Awa Root, Intoxicating Pepper

ASTROLOGICAL: *Primary*: Aquarius, Capricorn; *Secondary*: Cancer, Pisces, Scorpio

GODS: Lono, Kane, Kanaloa, Tane

MEDICAL: Anesthetic, Narcotic, Stimulant (initially), Sedative (later). Some cite the active ingredient in Kava Kava as narcotic in nature and second only to opium in effect. However, such levels of intoxication come only when consuming huge amounts. Those amounts, like opium, can be dangerous (especially to the kidneys), and even mild amounts can cause an upset stomach. When using huge amounts or an extraction/concentrate, the potential for respiratory paralysis is present.

PART USED: Root

MAGICKAL: There is perhaps no better known lust-inspiring intoxicant than Kava Kava. Like Damiana, Kava Kava increases the pleasure in lovemaking by improving the psychic connection between lovers. It also relieves anxiety, aids in sleep, and may bring visions. A Kava Kava milk shake sounds great right now. That's right, a milk shake. You see, if you chew the root, it will numb your mouth and provide a generally poor experience. If you boil it in tea, not only will you have a lousy tasting tea, but also you will remove most of the active ingredients when you strain the mixture. The result will be a tea no more stimulating than a weak cup of coffee. (Most of the active ingredients are not water soluble). See Chapter 6 for a recipe.

Kava Kava

Kecksies—*See* Hemlock

Kelp—*See* Bladderwrack

Kemps—*See* Plantain, Ribwort

Kenning Wort—*See* Celandine, Greater

Keper—*See* Dill

Kermesbeere—*See* Pokeweed

Kernelwort—*See* Figwort, Knotted

Kex—*See* Hemlock

Key Flower—*See* Cowslip

Key of Heaven—*See* Cowslip

Kharkady—*See* Hibiscus

Kheyar—*See* Cucumber

Kidney Beans—*Phaseolus vulgaris*

MEDICAL: Diuretic. A warm water infusion of dried beans and pods provides a diuretic action, which may be used to cleanse the kidneys. May encourage the passing of stones.

PART USED: Fruit

Kidneywort—*See* Liverwort, American

Kif—*See* Marijuana

Kikwata—*See* Acacia

Kimoon—*See* Cumin

King Root—*See* Bloodroot

King's Cure—*See* Pipsissewa

Kiss-Her-in-the-Buttery—*See* Heartsease

Kiss-Me-at-the-Garden-Gate—*See* Heartsease

Kit-Run-About—*See* Heartsease

Kit-Run-in-the-Fields—*See* Heartsease

Klamath Weed—*See* St. John's Wort

Knight's Milfoilv—*See* Yarrow

Knitback—*See* Comfrey

Knit Bone—*See* Comfrey

Knotted Figwort—*See* Figwort, Knotted

Knotgrass—*Polyganum aviculare*—Feminine, Saturn, Earth

Also known as Allseed, Armstrong, Bird's Tongue, Centinode, Cowgrass, Hog Weed, Knotweed, Nine-Joints, Ninety-Knot, Pigweed, Pigrush, Red Robin, Sparrow Tongue, Swynel Grass, Swine's Grass

ASTROLOGICAL: *Primary*: Aquarius, Capricorn; *Secondary*: Capricorn, Taurus, Virgo

MEDICAL: Astringent, Emetic (fruit), Purgative (fruit). Served as tea to treat diarrhea.

PARTS USED: Herb, Fruit

MAGICKAL: Knotgrass is an excellent herb for use in the Outsider Offering and Challenge of Wiccan Rituals. The central theme is that the herb will absorb the Outsiders, so they can be disposed of outside of the sacred ritual space. Keeping a basket of Knotgrass outside the front door of your home is an excellent way to keep problems at work, at work. Whenever you come home, run your fingers through the loose herb, and visualize the stress and tension from work leaving your fingers and being absorbed by the herb. Discard the herb in a stream or creek during the waning moon. Fish love it and will carry away your stress to where it can do no harm.

Knotweed—*See* Knotgrass

Knyghten—*See* Yarrow

Kola Nut—*Cola nitida*
Also known as Cola
MEDICAL: Stimulant. Powdered Kola Nut is sometimes chewed prior to meals to improve appetite and digestion.
PART USED: Nut
GENERAL: When Coca-Cola was forced to stop their use of Cocaine in their popular beverage, they replaced it with Cola/Kola. Today, it contains neither.

Kouroubaga—*See* Allspice

Krapp—*See* Madder

Krausdistel—*See* Holly, Sea

Krokos—*See* Saffron, Spanish

Kumquat—*Fortunella spp.*—Masculine, Sun, Air
ASTROLOGICAL: *Primary*: Leo; *Secondary*: Aquarius, Gemini, Libra
MAGICKAL: Eating Kumquat will increase prosperity and bring the opportunity for riches into your life.

Kummel—*See* Caraway

Kunkuma—*See* Saffron, Spanish

Kush Kush—*See* Vetivert

Lacris—*See* Licorice

Lactucarium—*See* Lettuce, Wild

Ladder to Heaven—*See* Lily of the Valley

Ladies' Meat—*See* Hawthorn

Ladies' Seal—*See* White Bryony

Lad's Love—*See* Southernwood

Lady Fern—*See* Fern

Ladykins—*See* Mandrake

Lady-of-the-Meadow—*See* Meadowsweet

Lady's Foxglove—*See* Mullein

Lady's Key—*See* Cowslip

Lady's Laces—*See* Dodder

Lady's Mantle—*Alchemilla vulgaris*—Feminine, Venus, Water

Also known as Bear's Foot, Frauenmantle, Leontopodium, Lion's Foot, Nine Hooks, Pied-de-Lion, Stellaria

See also Yarrow, as Lady's Mantle is one of the folk names for Yarrow.

ASTROLOGICAL: *Primary*: Libra, Taurus; *Secondary*: Cancer, Pisces, Scorpio

MEDICAL: Astringent, Styptic. A typical preparation is 1 ounce of the dried herb in an infusion of 1 pint of water. Simmer for 30 minutes, strain, and serve 4 ounces at a time. Indicated for excess menstruation.

PARTS USED: Herb, Root

MAGICKAL: To attract a sincere love interest, carry Lady's Mantle in a pink sachet and visit your favorite interests club. What do I mean by an "interests club"? Well, if you like computers, go to a computer club; if you like animals, then volunteer at the Humane Society or zoo.

Lady's Purse—*See* Shepherd's Purse

Lady's Seal—*See* Solomon's Seal

Lady's Slipper—*See* Valerian, American

Lady's Thistle—*See* Thistle

Lady-of-the-Woods—*See* Birch

Laitue Vireuse—*See* Lettuce, Wild

Lama—*See* Ebony

Lamb Mint—*See* Spearmint

Lamb's Tongue—*See* Plantain, Ribwort

Lammint—*See* Peppermint

Lapstones—*See* Potato

Lappa—*See* Burdock

Lasafa—*See* Caper

Lattouce—*See* Lettuce

Laurel—*See* Bay

Laurel Camphor—*See* Camphor

Laurier d' Apollon—*See* Bay

Laurier Sauce—*See* Bay

Laurus Cinnamomum—*See* Cinnamon

Laurus Sassafras—*See* Sassafras

Lavamana—*See* Rue, Goat's

Lavender—*See list*—Masculine, Mercury, Air
Also known as Elf Leaf, Nard, Nardus, Spike

  English Lavender—*Lavandula officinalis/ Lavendula angustifolia/Lavendula vera*

  French Lavender—*Lavande Stoechas*

  Spike Lavender—*Lavendula spica*

ASTROLOGICAL: *Primary*: Gemini, Virgo; *Secondary*: Aquarius, Gemini, Libra

GODS: Babalu Aye, Shango, Eleggua, Mercury, Obatala, Olocun

GODDESS: Ochun

MEDICAL: Nervine, Sedative, Tonic. A warm water infusion of Lavender (*Lavandula officinalis*) will aid sleep. However, it seems to cause heartburn in many that consume it. Sometimes used as a general tonic. Lavender tea is an excellent choice for relaxing after a hard day. Lavender flowers or a few drops of

Lavender

the essential oil in the bath will relax and relieve minor aches and pains.

PARTS USED: Flowers, Oil

MAGICKAL: The scent of Lavender attracts men, holds their attention, and loosens their grip on money. It also causes women to think of romance. I am sure you have heard the expression "smells like a French whore." That expression comes from people who observed that French prostitutes once used Lavender oil and perfume to attract customers. If your business is dependent on men spending money, this will work for you without respect to what you are selling. Lavender paper is the perfect material on which to write a love letter or spell. Unfortunately, it is very difficult to find. Failing a skilled papermaker, you can rub French Lavender flowers onto a piece of parchment paper until the paper picks up the scent. An infusion of Lavender is an excellent floor wash and bath, as it will bring with it a sense of peace and restfulness to your home. If you are fortunate enough to have access to fresh Lavender flowers, try sprinkling them on your bed prior to preparing a romantic dinner for your mate, but let the Lavender be a surprise for dessert. Lavender mixed with Rosemary strengthens a woman's chastity; but it does so by reminding her of her partner's love, so it heightens the romantic feeling between the two. Lavender mixed with Sandalwood and burned over charcoal will attract helpful spirits. Add Sweetgrass to the mix and burn for this purpose, and you will certainly feel the presence of positive, but usually unseen, visitors. Essential oil of Lavender promotes relaxation and sleep. Diffused into the room prior to sleep will ensure a restful night. English Lavender seems to be the best choice for this use. It also promotes calm lovemaking.

GENERAL: Lavindin is a hybrid that was manipulated such that less growing time and material could be used in the creation of essential oils. Its use in matters of love seems to be fine, but when using Lavindin for sleep or rest, it does not seem to be as effective.

*NOTE: Spike Lavender (*Lavendula spica*) is on very rare occasion referred to as Lesser Lavender, Minor Lavender, and sometimes Spikenard. There is some speculation that the "Spikenard" of the Christian Bible is most likely a reference to Spike Lavender.

Le Blé Noir—*See* Buckwheat

Leek—*Allium porrum*—Masculine, Mars, Fire

ASTROLOGICAL: *Primary*: Aries, Scorpio; *Secondary*: Aries, Leo, Sagittarius

MAGICKAL: Eating Leeks with your lover will strengthen mutual bonds of the heart. Rubbed on the body, it invigorates and heightens physical prowess.

Leemoo—*See* Lemon

Lekiti—*See* Cucumber

Lemon—*Citrus limon*—Feminine, Moon, Water

Also known as Citrus Medica, Citrus Limonum, Citronnier, Leemoo, Limoun, Limone, Neemoo, Pucker Fruit, Ulamula

ASTROLOGICAL: *Primary:* Cancer; *Secondary*: Cancer, Pisces, Scorpio

GOD: Oko

GODDESSES: Oya, Yemaya

MEDICAL: Antiscorbutic, Astringent, Carminative (oil), Diaphoretic (juice), Diuretic (juice), Refrigerant, Stimulant (oil). Used topically, Lemon juice treats eczema, athlete's foot, gout, and decreases the itching of many skin problems. Apply at night. To treat boils and corns, soak a cloth in Lemon juice and apply overnight. To treat gout, apply the fresh fruit to the affected joint. Relief from a minor cold can be had by blending water, honey, and Lemon juice to taste and drinking hot/warm. To keep colds at bay as well as to treat them at

Lemon

their onset, an infusion can be made by mixing 1 part Lemon peel with 1 part crushed Rose hips. Sweeten with honey and drink anytime you might want the extra vitamin C in your diet. I add Lemon juice to many of my herbal teas for this purpose. Lemonade, sweetened with honey, helps with the common cold. Lemon juice may be added to virtually any tea or other beverage to fight congestion and provide a vitamin-C boost.

PARTS USED: Juice of fruit, Oil, Peel

MAGICKAL: An infusion of fresh Lemon peel can be used to cleanse magickal tools. It can also be used as a floor wash for the same purpose. In the bath, it is used for the lustral bath prior to full moon rituals. You can substitute a bit of Lemon juice or dried peel if you have to, but the fresh peel works best. Served to your lover or spouse at dessert time, Lemon will strengthen your bonds. This is especially the case when added to Oriental tea with honey or pie. Essential oil of Lemon is diffused to bring energy to the body.

Lemon Balm—*Melissa officinalis*—Feminine, Moon, Water

Also known as Bee Balm, Lemon Balsam, Melissa, Sweet Balm, Sweet Melissa, Tourengane, Oghoul

ASTROLOGICAL: *Primary*: Cancer; *Secondary*: Cancer, Pisces, Scorpio

GODS: Eleggua, Obatala

MEDICAL: Astringent, Carminative, Diaphoretic, Diuretic, Expectorant, Febrifuge, Stimulant, Tonic. A warm water infusion of Lemon Balm makes a good cleanser of cuts and scrapes as well as an expectorant and general tonic. For daily use, it can be blended with your favorite tea. Lemon Balm herb is useful in treating mild heart palpitations brought on by stress and tension. It is also used topically to ease mosquito bites, but be warned that it will also attract bees. Boil Lemon Balm in water and allow the scent to fill the house. Then sweeten with honey and drink to invigorate the body. Lemon Balm acts as a mild stimulant and

diuretic. Used topically, the fresh leaves will help stop bleeding. A poultice made from a warm water infusion also works, however the fresh leaves work better.

PART USED: Herb

MAGICKAL: Ah, the herb that has started many loving relationships. Soak a sweet red wine in Lemon Balm, add a bit of local honey to taste, and serve with candlelight. You will probably find out exactly why Arabian legend praises this herb as the bringer of physical pleasures as well as spiritual delights. Some folklorists add that it is often carried in a pink sachet for the same purpose, but I've always had better luck with the wine method. Lemon Balm may be used in virtually any tea preparation instead of Lemon to provide the same flavor. Consuming such a tea will add the attribute of love to the tea's effect. As an example, one might flavor Chamomile (which encourages sleep) with Lemon Balm to encourage lover's dreams. Essential oil of Lemon Balm is diffused to relax the body and to relieve sore muscle pain. Its scent is also uplifting and calming to the mind.

Lemon Balsam—*See* Lemon Balm

Lemongrass—*Cymbopogon citratus*—Masculine, Mercury, Air

ASTROLOGICAL: *Primary*: Gemini, Virgo; *Secondary*: Aquarius, Gemini, Libra

GODS: Mercury, Olocun, Orunla

GODDESS: Ochun

MAGICKAL: An infusion of Lemongrass reportedly promotes lust and increases psychic abilities. It is often an integral part of incense recipes for these purposes. Grown outside the home, it repels snakes; but don't forget that snakes repel several animals baneful to the garden. If you do not live in an area where dangerous snakes are fond of showing up in strange places, best to let them be—or you might discover a rodent problem and want the snakes back. Essential oil of Lemongrass is diffused to promote activity in the intuitive and creative portions of the brain.

Lemon Verbena—*Aloysia triphylla/Lippia citriodora*—Masculine, Mercury, Air

Also called Cedron, Yerba Louisa

ASTROLOGICAL: *Primary*: Gemini, Virgo; *Secondary*: Aquarius, Gemini, Libra

GOD: Olocun

MEDICAL: (*Lippia citriodora*)—Diaphoretic, Expectorant, Febrifuge, Sedative. A warm water infusion will encourage perspiration, relax the mind, and act as an expectorant. It is thus used on a cool day to defeat the heat, as well as to break fevers. The same infusion is good for cleaning small cuts and scrapes. Concentrated extractions are used in the creation of cough drops and syrups.

PARTS USED: Leaves, Flowering Tops

MAGICKAL: An infusion of Lemon Verbena will prevent the memory of dreams. Carried, it will increase your ability to attract the opposite sex but only on a strictly physical level. For anything else, you will have to take it from there. Essential oil of Lemon Verbena is diffused for purification and a sense of spring.

NOTE: Cedron is sometimes listed as *Simaba Cedron*, but I am unclear if this is a different plant with the same common name or if it is a plant with several Latin names/subcategories.

Lavose—*See* Lovage

Leather Jackets—*See* Potato

Leontopodium—*See* Lady's Mantle

Le Pine Noble—*See* Hawthorn

Lentil—*Lens culinaris*—Feminine, Moon, Water

ASTROLOGICAL: *Primary*: Cancer; *Secondary*: Cancer, Pisces, Scorpio

MAGICKAL: Roman Pagan lore states that eating Lentils will aid in staying awake and attentive. However, most lore cites it as having a calming effect when consumed.

GENERAL: Lentil is sometimes a reference to the plant *Lens culinaris*. However, in cooking it is most often a reference to the seed alone.

Lent Lily—*See* Daffodil

Lesser Galangal—*See* Galangal

Lesser Lavender—*See* Lavender

Lesser Periwinkle—*See* Periwinkle

Lesser Scullcap—*See* Scullcap

Lettuce—*Lactuca sativa/Lactuca saliva* (2)—Feminine, Moon, Water

Also known as Garden Lettuce, Lattouce, Sleep Wort

ASTROLOGICAL: *Primary*: Cancer; *Secondary*: Cancer, Pisces, Scorpio

GOD: Min

MEDICAL: Nervine, Sedative (mild). Cooked Lettuce acts as a sedative. Fresh Lettuce prevents seasickness.

PARTS USED: Leaves

MAGICKAL: Lettuce after dinner, not before, will ensure a good night's sleep. Before travel it will guard against motion sickness, and on a trip away from your love it will promote chastity. Because Lettuce contains virtually no nutritional value, if you eat nothing but Lettuce you will quickly lose energy because your metabolism adjusts as if starving. If you should happen to tend iguana, never even think about giving it to them as anything more than a treat.

Lettuce Opium—*See* Lettuce, Wild

Lettuce, Wild—*Lactuca virosa*—Feminine, Moon, Water

Also known as Acrid Lettuce, Green Endive, Lactucarium, Laitue Vireuse, Lettuce Opium, Prickly Lettuce, Lopium, Strong-Scented Lettuce

WARNING: May be addictive. May be illegal in some areas.

ASTROLOGICAL: *Primary*: Cancer; *Secondary*: Cancer, Pisces, Scorpio

GOD: Min

MEDICAL: Expectorant, Narcotic, Sedative. The extracted and concentrated resin of Wild Lettuce has been prescribed as a substitute for opium when opium was prescribed to be smoked or eaten. While not as strong as opium, it does not upset the stomach as opium will.

PARTS USED: Leaves, Milk of Leaves

MAGICKAL: Magickally speaking, it can be used as a substitute for opium (often called for in flying ointments and the like). If you want to experiment with the concentrate, a simple Web search will show that a thousand Websites offer the concentrated resin for sale. However, a water extraction can easily be done at home. Warm gently in water, but do not boil. Low heat should be applied for at least 12 hours, adding additional water as needed. Strain the liquid, and allow to evaporate. The remaining resin can be used as a substitute for opium. You will recover approximately a gram of extract per ounce of herb.

Leucanthemum Vulgare—*See* Daisy, Ox-eye

Levant Salep—*See* Lucky Hand

Levers—*See* Iris

Libanotis—*See* Rosemary

Licorice—*Glycyrrhiza glabra/Liquiritia officinalis*—Feminine, Venus, Water

Also known as Lacrisse, Lacris, Licourice, Lycorys, Reglisse, Regolizia, Sweet Root

WARNING: Although we all grew up with this as a flavor of candy, those chews probably did not contain the actual herb. It certainly does not today, as the list of health warnings for this herb is quite surprisingly lengthy. Check with a credible medical reference, preferably a doctor, before using this herb regularly or in large amounts.

Licorice

ASTROLOGICAL: *Primary*: Libra, Taurus; *Secondary*: Cancer, Pisces, Scorpio

MEDICAL: (*Glycyrrhiza glabra*) Demulcent, Emollient, Pectoral (mild). Chewing the root or drinking a warm water infusion of the root helps with breathing. Licorice has been used successfully in programs to quit smoking. Instead of lighting up, chew on the end of a Licorice root. Licorice is often recommended to raise estrogen levels. While it does not in fact raise those levels, it provides substances that mimic estrogen and might act as if estrogen levels were increased. Reportedly eases the symptoms of menopause.

PART USED: Root

MAGICKAL: Chewing Licorice root prior to making love will greatly increase your passion and your body's ability to keep up with it. Friends have told me that chewing on Licorice when you feel the urge to smoke a cigarette will help you quit.

Licourice—*See* Licorice

Lilac—*Syringa vulgaris*—Feminine, Venus, Water

Also known as Common Lilac

ASTROLOGICAL: *Primary*: Libra, Taurus; *Secondary*: Cancer, Pisces, Scorpio

GODS: Shango, Eleggua, Obatala, Oggun, Orunla

MEDICAL: Antiperiodic, Febrifuge, Tonic, Vermifuge

MAGICKAL: Grown in and around the home, Lilacs are protective. Fresh flowers are simmered to produce an uplifting feeling and to lighten the atmosphere of a room.

PARTS USED: Fruit, Leaves

Little Stepmother—*See* Heartsease

Live-in-Idleness—*See* Heartsease

Lacrisse—*See* Licorice

Levant Salep—*See* Lucky Hand

Life Everlasting—*See* Balsam, White; Catsfoot; Cudweed; Gnaphaliums; Life Everlasting, Perl Flowered

Life Everlasting, Perl Flowered—*Antennaria Margaritaceum*

Also known as American Everlasting, Cudweed

Life Everlasting, Sweet-Scented—*See* Balsam, White

Life of Man—*See* Spikenard, American

Life Root—*See* Groundsel, Golden

⚥**Lily**—*See List*—Feminine, Moon, Water
See also Lily, BlueWater and Lily of the Valley

   Tiger Lily—*Lilium tigrinum*
   White Lily—*Lilium candidum*

Also known as Madonna Lily

ASTROLOGICAL: *Primary*: Cancer; *Secondary*: Cancer, Pisces, Scorpio

GODS: Adonis, Attis, Kuan Yin*, Montu

GODDESSES: Athena (tiger), Ceres, Venus, Juno, Minerva (tiger), Nephthys, Persephone, Psyche

MAGICKAL: Grown in and around the home, the Lily protects the landowner from unwanted human guests as well as visitations by ghosts without respect to their welcome. The fresh flowers are simmered to ease heartache during and after failed matters of the heart.

GENERAL: Sometimes the primary astrological associations for Lily are listed as Gemini and/or Virgo. When this occurs, the citation is correct, but it is a reference to Lily of the Valley (*Convallaria majalis*), which is also called Lily.

NOTE: The family *Liliaceae* contains over 100 varieties with the same attributes. The two most common are those listed previously. *Kuan Yin is typically listed as goddess/female. See Liber ab Clementia in *A Wiccan Bible* for further explanation

Lily Constancy—*See* Lily of the Valley

Lily of the Valley—*Convallaria majalis*—Masculine, Mercury, Air

Also known as Convallaria, Convall-Lily, Jacob's Ladder, Ladder to Heaven, Lily, Lily Constancy, Male Lily, May Lily, Our Lady's Tears

ASTROLOGICAL: *Primary*: Gemini, Virgo; *Secondary*: Aquarius, Gemini, Libra

GODS: Apollo, Asclepius

MEDICAL: Diuretic. Generally not used in modern herbal medicine. A tincture was used during World War I to treat those who had been exposed to mustard gas and other chemical weapons.

Lily of the Valley

PARTS USED: Flowers, Herb

MAGICKAL: Lily of the Valley is an ideal gift for someone who has been feeling under the weather or depressed. It will greatly elevate the mood of its recipient. Fresh flowers are simmered to promote calmness and to relax the emotions.

Lily, Blue Water—*Nymphaea caerula*—Masculine, Sun, Fire

Also known as Blue Lotus

ASTROLOGICAL: *Primary*: Leo; *Secondary*: Aries, Leo, Sagittarius

GODS: Amun Ra, Hapi, Atum, Horus the Elder, Horus the Younger, Neptune*, Poseidon*

MAGICKAL: This flower was so valued by the Egyptians that they often used it in their most sacred of rites. When King Tut's mummy was first discovered in 1922, it was covered with the flowers of the Blue Water Lily (a.k.a. Blue Lotus). But its praise did not stop in Egypt. In India it was praised as the flower that gave birth to Brahma. Moving a bit more down the coast, we find the Buddhist prayer: "Om! Mani padme hum," which translates into English as "Oh! The jewel of the lotus flower!" Each of these cultures most likely associated the Blue Lotus with their religious Mysteries because it is a mildly intoxicating plant. When used in an infusion of warm sweet wine (water will do), the effects of even a small glass can produce a pure uplifting feeling and sense of well-being that rivals some of the most expensive pharmaceuticals. However, its most noted property has been a relatively closely guarded secret until recently. Today, it is often considered the Viagra of the plant world, and rightly so.

GENERAL: Do not confuse with Blue Lily (*Agapanthus Africanus*). I choose to list this herb as Blue Water Lily rather than Blue Lotus because that is how it appears most often within the Pagan community. However, if you feel this plant may be of particular value to your health or spiritual practices, you should research it under its more common name, Blue Lotus.

*NOTE: The associations with Neptune and Poseidon are most likely correct for Blue Water Lily; however, they are typically listed with Lotus but not Blue Water Lily. I believe it is most correct to list these gods with Lotus, as it seems more of the folk name Lotus that was used to refer to the Blue Water Lily.

Lignum Aloes—*See* Wood Aloes

Lignum Crucis—*See* Mistletoe, European

Lime—*Citrus limetta*—Masculine, Sun, Fire
Also known as Calmouc, Dayyap, Loomi

ASTROLOGICAL: *Primary*: Leo; *Secondary*: Aries, Leo, Sagittarius

GODS: Babalu Aye, Shango, Eleggua, Obatala, Oggun

GODDESS: Oya

MAGICKAL: Lime is used for purification and to promote love. Essential oil of Lime is uplifting and cleansing.

NOTE: This is the Lime that bears the Lime fruit. *See also* Lime Tree, as its common name is also Lime.

Lime Tree—*Tilia europaea/Tilia vulgaris*—Masculine, Jupiter, Air
Also known as Common Lime, Lime, Linden, Linden Flowers, Linn Flowers

ASTROLOGICAL: *Primary*: Pisces, Sagittarius; *Secondary*: Aquarius, Gemini, Libra

GODDESSES: Lada, Venus

MAGICKAL: Honey from hives that gathered their goods from this tree is a sure-bet ingredient for love potions. Good luck finding it as it is some of the most expensive and rare honey in the world. Your best bet is a gourmet supplier. If you are lucky, you may be able to find honey liquor made from this plant. If so, the label will most likely read Linden Flower Honey, and the price tag will not be slight. Ah, but what price love? Its wood can be carved into protective and luck-drawing beads or talismans. Its flowers encourage restfulness. Grown around the home, it provides protection. But good luck finding the plant, wood, or flower outside of Europe.

GENERAL: Not to be confused with the tree that bears the fruit by a similar name, the Lime Tree can reach 130 feet in height as opposed to the tree, which bears the Lime fruit and generally reaches only 8 feet in height. The juice of the fruit is simmered with water to cleanse a room.

Limoun—*See* Lemon

Limone—*See* Lemon

Linden—*See* Lime Tree

Linden Flowers—*See* Lime Tree

Link—*See* Broom

Ling—*See* Heather

Lingua Cervina—*See* Fern

Linn Flowers—*See* Lime Tree

Linseed—*See* Flax

Linaza—*See* Flax

Lion's Foot—*See* Lady's Mantle

Lisan Selvi—*See* Borage

Little Dragon—*See* Tarragon

Little Queen—*See* Meadowsweet

Liverleaf—*See* Liverwort, American

Livers—*See* Iris

Liverweed—*See* Liverwort, American

Liverwort, American—*Anemone hepatica/ Hepatica triloba*—Masculine, Jupiter, Fire

Also known as Edellebere, Hepatica, Herb Trinity, Kidneywort, Noble Liverwort, Liverleaf, Liverweed, Trefoil

ASTROLOGICAL: *Primary*: Pisces, Sagittarius; *Secondary*: Aries, Leo, Sagittarius

MEDICAL: Astringent, Demulcent, Tonic, Vulnerary. An infusion of 1 ounce of the leaves and or flowers is made with 1 pint of water. Simmer for 30 minutes and serve 4 ounces at a time. Topically, an infusion or the fresh leaves are used to clean minor wounds.

Liverwort

PARTS USED: Flowers, Leaves

MAGICKAL: A woman may bring the blessings of love by keeping on her person a pink sachet of Liverwort from sunup until sundown.

Liverwort, English—*Peltigera Canina*—Masculine, Jupiter, Fire

Also known as Ash-Colored Ground Liverwort

ASTROLOGICAL: *Primary*: Pisces, Sagittarius; *Secondary*: Aries, Leo, Sagittarius

MAGICKAL: English Liverwort has the same magickal properties as American Liverwort.

Lizzy-Run-up-the-Hedge—*See* Ivy, Ground

Lesan—*See* Borage

Lion's Herb—*See* Columbine

Lion's Mouth—*See* Foxglove

Lion's Tooth—*See* Dandelion

Lippe—*See* Cowslip

Liquid Amber—*Liquidambar orientis*—Masculine, Sun, Fire

Also known as Amber, Amber Resin

ASTROLOGICAL: *Primary*: Leo; *Secondary*: Aries, Leo, Sagittarius

GENERAL: Not to be confused with Amber resin or Amber. Liquid Amber is but one of the ingredients of that mixture commonly sold under each of those names. To make matters a bit more confusing, Amber is often listed as a gemstone. As a gemstone, it is a petrified tree sap. When you get right down to the heart of the matter, Liquid Amber comes from the Amber resin tree. Typically, it is used for protection. The commercial product made with Liquid Amber and marketed as either Amber resin, Liquid Amber, or just Amber is usually a combination of this resin, beeswax, and Benzoin Gum. Although much cheaper products litter the modern marketplace, this mixture should always be made with beeswax and contain absolutely no synthetic ingredients. If you should happen upon the real thing, you will forever recognize its penetrating scent. This Amber resin mixture is often sold in small cubes. It can be worn or burned in incense. The result of both has been proven to relax the body and heighten reception of sensual pleasures. While it might seem tempting to purchase pure Liquid Amber and attempt to make blends similar to the commercially available mixes, true Liquid Amber is very difficult to acquire. If you find a recipe that calls for it, your best bet is to use the commercially available Amber resin in twice the quantity listed in the recipe.

Liver Lily—*See* Blue Flag

Llygad y Dydd—*See* Daisy, Common

Llwyd y Cwn—*See* Horehound, White

☠ **Lobelia**—*Lobelia inflata/Rapuntium inflatum*—Feminine, Saturn, Water

Also known as Asthma Weed, Bladderpod, Eyebright, Gagroot, Indian Tobacco, Vomitwort, Pukeweed

WARNING: Although I have used this herb many times, it is often listed as poisonous in large doses. Even small amounts can reportedly cause nausea and vomiting.

ASTROLOGICAL: *Primary*: Aquarius, Capricorn; *Secondary*: Cancer, Pisces, Scorpio

MEDICAL: (*Lobelia inflata*) Antiasthmatic, Diaphoretic, Expectorant, Nervine, Stimulant. If you are not concerned about the folk names Pukeweed and Vomitwort, a mild infusion of Lobelia (just a pinch) sweetened with Chamomile and honey seems to work as a body stimulant, expectorant, and mind calmer. Larger amounts seem to work as a depressant. However, it is sometimes listed as poisonous and should never be taken by anyone who is pregnant. With the same warnings but without the Chamomile, the infusion has helped many friends who suffer from asthma. Use with EXTREME caution and much more education than is provided here.

PARTS USED: Flowering Herb, Seeds

MAGICKAL: To bring a lover into your life, pick the tiny Lobelia flowers one at a time with your left hand, placing them into your right hand, palm up, until the pile is as high as possible. With each one picked, say as you place it into your right hand: "Violet and blue, A love that is new." When you can no longer carry any more, place them in a widemouthed bottle to dry until the next new moon; then place them into a blue sachet and carry in your pocket. Each day, go to a public place, take one flower carefully out of the sachet and repeat to yourself the above line. Then give the flower to someone who catches your eye. If something develops of the following conversation, save the rest in case it does not work out. You will have love in your life before you run out of flowers.

Locust Pod—*See* Carob

Logowe—*See* Sesame

Lolu—*See* Wood Aloes

Long Plantain—*See* Plantain, Ribwort

Loomi—*See* Lime

Loosestrife, Purple—*Lythrurn salicaria*—Feminine, Moon, Earth

Also known as Blooming Sally, Braune Weiderich, Flowering Sally, Lysimaque Rouge, Lythrum, Partyke, Purple Willow Herb, Rainbow Weed, Rother Weiderich, Sage Willow, Salicaire, Spiked Loosestrife

ASTROLOGICAL: *Primary*: Cancer; *Secondary*: Capricorn, Taurus, Virgo

MAGICKAL: An infusion of Purple Loosestrife used in mop water will "loose the strife" in a home. It can also be scattered to the floor, left overnight, and then swept or vacuumed.

Loosestrife, Yellow—*Lysimachia vulgaris*

Also known as Herb Willow, Willow-Wort, Yellow Willow Herb, Wood Pimpernel

MEDICAL: Astringent, Expectorant

PART USED: Herb

MAGICKAL: Yellow Loosestrife has the same magickal properties as Purple Loosestrife.

Lopium—*See* Lettuce, Wild

Love-in-Winter—*See* Pipsissewa

Love Fruit—*See* Orange, Sweet

Love Orange—*See* Orange, Sweet

Low John—*See* Galangal

Low John the Conqueror—*See* Galangal

Lorbeer—*See* Bay

Lotus—*Nelumbium nelumbo/Nelumbium speciosum/Nelumbo speciosa*—Feminine, Moon, Water

See also Lily, Blue Water, as Lotus was incorrectly identified as Blue Water Lily for some time.

Also known as Baino, Sacred Lotus, Water Lotus, Egyptian Lotus

ASTROLOGICAL: *Primary*: Cancer; *Secondary*: Cancer, Pisces, Scorpio

GODS: Apollo, Babalu Aye, Shango, Eleggua, Kephra, Mercury, Neptune*, Obatala, Oggun, Olocun, Poseidon*

GODDESSES: Dolma, Yemaya

Lotus

MAGICKAL: Fresh flowers and oil are used for protection.

*NOTE: The associations with Neptune and Poseidon are most likely correct for Blue Water Lily; however, they are typically listed with Lotus but not Blue Water Lily. I believe it is most correct to list these gods with Lotus, as it seems more of the folk name Lotus that was used to refer to the Blue Water Lily.

Lotus, Blue—*See* Lily, Blue Water

Lotus, Sacred—*Nelumbo nucifera*—Feminine, Moon, Water

MAGICKAL: Sacred Lotus has been used widely in conjunction with religious ritual in Central Asia and the Far East. Apart from the celebration of its sheer beauty, the Sacred Lotus was considered sacred due to the mystical effects it produces when smoked or made into tea. Reportedly, the use of Sacred Lotus produces a feeling of joy and personal well-being that is experienced by folk who use the street drug ecstasy. Having never used ecstasy, I cannot compare the two. The flower was mentioned in Homer's *The Odyssey* when Ulysses and his crew visited the Island of the "Lotus Eaters."

Lousewort—*See* Wood Betony

Lovage—*Levisticum officinale/Ligusticum Levisticum*—Masculine, Sun, Fire

Also known as Chinese Lovage, Cornish Lovage, Italian Lovage, Italian Parsley, Lavose, Love Herbs, Love Rod, Love Root, Loving Herbs, Lubestico, Old English Lovage, Sea Parsley

ASTROLOGICAL: *Primary*: Leo; *Secondary*: Aries, Leo, Sagittarius

MEDICAL: Carminative, Diuretic, Stimulant. Generally consumed in decoction or infusion.

PARTS USED: Leaves, Roots, Seeds

MAGICKAL: A strong infusion will aid in attracting and promoting love when it is used in a bath prior to meeting new people. A tincture can be worn on the pulse points as a quick and easy love-drawing perfume. Add a few drops of essential oil of Patchouli to attract the love of a woman. If attempting to attract the love of a man, make the tincture from equal amounts of Lovage root and Vanilla bean.

Lovage, Bastard—*See* Gentian, White

Lovage, Black—*Smyrnium Olisatrum*

Also known as Alexanders, Alisanders, Black Pot-Herb

Lovage, Scotch—*Ligusticum Scoticum*—Masculine, Sun, Fire

Also known as Sea Lovage

ASTROLOGICAL: *Primary*: Leo; *Secondary*: Aries, Leo, Sagittarius

MEDICAL: Carminative. Generally used as an infusion.

PART USED: Root

MAGICKAL: Scotch Lovage can be used as a substitute for Lovage (*Levisticum officinale/ Ligusticum Levisticum*) for making tinctures and sachets to attract love, but should not be used in the bath.

☠**Lovage, Water**—*Cenanthe fistulosa*

Love Herbs—*See* Lovage

Loving Idol—*See* Heartsease

Love-in-Idleness—*See* Heartsease

Loveman—*See* Cleavers (B)

Love Rod—*See* Lovage

Love Root—*See* Lovage

Loving Herbs—*See* Lovage

Love-Will—*See* Thornapple

Love Leaves—*See* Burdock

Love-Lies-Bleeding—*See* Amaranth and Heartsease

Love Vine—*See* Dodder

Lubigan—*See* Calamus

Lucerne—*See* Alfalfa

Lucky Bean—*See* Be-Still and Tonka

☠**Lucky Hand**—Feminine, Venus, Water

Also known as Hand of Power, Hand Root, Helping Hand, Orchid, Salep, Saloop, Sahlep, Satyrion, Levant Salep

ASTROLOGICAL: *Primary*: Libra, Taurus; *Secondary*: Cancer, Pisces, Scorpio

GOD: Castor

GODDESS: Ochun

MAGICKAL: If ever there was a classic New Orleans root, this one is it. The root of the Lucky Hand is carried for luck and for success at gambling. In a pink sachet, it is carried to attract love. You can "charge" Lucky Hand root by anointing it with essential oil of Rose, or use it as is. A tincture of Lucky Hand root with a drop or two of Rose oil makes excellent luck oil. Now for a little bit of occult (meaning hidden) knowledge: Although Lucky Hand seems to be one of those mystical herbs that you can only find in an occult shop, the term Lucky Hand is often used to refer to any plant in the Orchid family. It can usually be had at your local florist. To acquire its roots, simply raise the plant yourself.

NOTE: Today the name "Lucky Hand Root" is used to refer to such a wide variety of roots that cross with Adam and Eve Root that separating the two is impossible. I believe the separate terms originally referred to separate plants, but today it seems that the difference between Adam and Eve Root and Lucky Hand Root is based only on the look of the root. Lucky Hand refers to several plants in the same family, including: *Orchis conopea, Orchis coriphora, Orchis latifolia, Orchis maculata, Orchis mascula, Orchis Morio, Orchis militaris, Orchis pyrimidalis, Orchis saccifera*

Lucky Money Root—*See* Devil's Shoestring

Lucky Nut—*See* Be-Still

Lurk-in-the-Ditch—*See* Pennyroyal

Lusmore—*See* Foxglove

Lus Na Mbau Side—*See* Foxglove

Lubestico—*See* Lovage

Lycopod—*See* Moss, American Club

Lycorys—*See* Licorice

Lysimaque Rouge—*See* Loosestrife, Purple

Lythrum—*See* Loosestrife, Purple

Macadamia—*Macadamia spp.*—Feminine, Jupiter, Earth

ASTROLOGICAL: *Primary*: Pisces, Sagittarius; *Secondary*: Capricorn, Taurus, Virgo

MAGICKAL: Used in prosperity rituals and meals intended to open the pathways to prosperity.

Mace—*See* Nutmeg

Mackerel Mint—*See* Spearmint

Mad Apple—*See* Thornapple

Mad-Dog Scullcap—*See* Scullcap

Mad Dog Weed—*See* Plantain, Water

Madherb—*See* Thornapple

Madere—*See* Allspice

Mad Root—*See* White Bryony

Madweed—*See* Scullcap

Madwort—*See* Alyssum

Magic Mushroom—*See also* Agaric Mushroom
WARNING: The term "magic mushroom" has been used to describe a variety of mushrooms which reportedly have psychedelic properties. Most of these are illegal and dangerous, if not deadly.

Maia—*See* Banana

Maize—*See* Corn

Madagascar Periwinkle—See Periwinkle

Madder—*Rubia tinctorum*—Feminine, Venus, Water
Also known as Dyer's Madder and Krapp
ASTROLOGICAL: *Primary*: Libra, Taurus; *Secondary*: Cancer, Pisces, Scorpio
MEDICAL: Historically, Madder root has been used to treat rachitis. However, it is most likely the treatment was only given because the root has been observed to dye the bones red. It also tends to color milk and urine. Why anyone thought red bones were stronger is unknown.
PART USED: Root
MAGICKAL: The leaves of the Madder are used to clean and polish magickal tools that are made of metal. Make sure you give this book to a student before telling them to clean their athame with Krapp, or they might misunderstand.

Madder's Cousin—*See* Cleavers

Madonna Lily—*See* Lily

Magnolia—*Magnolia grandifolia/Magnolia acuminata/Magnolia virginiana*—Feminine, Venus, Earth
Also known as Blue Magnolia, Cucumber Tree, Magnoliae Cortex, Magnolia Tripetata, Swamp Sassafras
ASTROLOGICAL: *Primary*: Libra, Taurus; *Secondary*: Capricorn, Taurus, Virgo
GODS: Oko, Olocun
GODDESS: Yemaya
MEDICAL: Diaphoretic, Laxative, Tonic. Used as an infusion. One ounce of the chopped root to 1 pint of water. Simmer for 30 minutes, strain, and serve 4 ounces at a time.
PART USED: Root

Magnolia

MAGICKAL: The scent of Magnolia is said to strengthen a monogamous relationship. The flowers are said to attract a faithful man to a woman.

Magnoliae Cortex—*See* Magnolia

Magnolia Tripetata—*See* Magnolia

Maidenhair, Common—*See* Fern

Maidenhair, True—*See* Fern

Maid's Ruin—*See* Southernwood

☠ **Mahogany, Mountain**—*Cercocarpus ledifolius*—Masculine, Mars, Fire
ASTROLOGICAL: *Primary*: Aries, Scorpio; *Secondary*: Aries, Leo, Sagittarius
GENERAL: Both the Planetary and Primary astrological association of Mountain Mahogany are disputed often. Listed here are the most often cited and those that appear to be most accurate. Charms of Mountain Mahogany are reportedly great gifts for mountain climbers as lore tells us the Mountain Mahogany protects from lightning strikes. Although I am absolutely sure there are exceptions, I have read that lightning will not strike the tree itself.
MAGICKAL: Mahogany is a great material for hilt and scabbard of both athames and swords. It is available at most woodworking shops.
NOTE: Seeds and leaves are poisonous.

Ma Huang—*Ephedra vulgaris*

Also known as Bringham Weed, Desert Tea, Mormon Tea, Popotillo, Squaw Tea, Stick Tea

WARNING: Will likely increase blood pressure and heart rate in proportion to amount consumed. Consult a doctor before using.

MEDICAL: Antispasmodic, Expectorant, Stimulant. Ma Huang has been used to improve breathing and treat respiratory problems in China for almost 5,000 years. It has been used in conjunction with alcohol in Tantric rites and can be found today in almost every supermarket and many gas stations. Mixed with alcohol and other ingredients, its active ingredient is marketed as NyQuil. A synthetic version is commonly sold as Sudafed. For a time, it was one of the major ingredients in products marketed as herbal alternatives to the street drug ecstasy. To be a bit more accurate, most of the commercial products contain either the primary active ingredient in Ma Huang, ephedrine, or a manmade version of the drug commonly called pseudoephedrine. In both its natural and synthetic form, this substance has received a great deal of bad press. Due to its great potential for abuse and the sometimes devastating results of that abuse, the herb has become illegal in some areas. The synthetic form of ephedrine is one of the ingredients in the creation of the street drug crystal meth. But make no mistake, ephedrine alone can be dangerous and has been responsible for at least one death in my home state. Where legal and in small doses, an infusion of Ma Huang acts as a strong decongestant and stimulant. I have used it often to battle illnesses that attack the lungs.

PART USED: Herb

GENERAL: The name "Ma Huang" and "ephedra" are used to indicate *Ephedra vulgaris*, *Ephedra geradiana*, *Ephedra sinica*, and *Ephedra equisentina*, as well as others that contain large amounts of the chemical ephedrine.

Maid's Hair—*See* Cleavers (A)

Makula Kula—*See* Castor

Malicorio—*See* Pomegranate

Malt—*See* Barley

Male Lily—*See* Lily of the Valley

Male Shield Fern—*See* Fern

Mallaquetta Pepper—*See* Grains of Paradise

Malum Punicum—*See* Pomegranate

Mamona—*See* Castor

Mandrake, English—*See* White Bryony

Mangel—*See* Beet

Mango—*Mangifera indica*—Masculine, Mars, Fire

ASTROLOGICAL: *Primary*: Aries, Scorpio; *Secondary*: Aries, Leo, Sagittarius

MAGICKAL: Consumed, the meat (not the skin) increases sexual desire in both men and women. Also lends itself to protection.

Mangold—*See* Beet

Manicon—*See* Thornapple

Man Root—*See* Ginseng, American

Man's Health—*See* Ginseng, American

Manzanilla—*See* Chamomile, Common

March Everlasting—*See* Cudweed

Marsh Mint—*See* Mint

Mastic—*See* Gum Mastic

Masticke—*See* Gum Mastic

May Lily—*See* Lily of the Valley

Melequeta—*See* Grains of Paradise

Malicorio—*See* Pomegranate

Mallow, Blue—*Malva sylvestris*—Feminine, Moon, Water

Also known as Common Mallow, Return-to-Me

ASTROLOGICAL: *Primary*: Cancer; *Secondary*: Cancer, Pisces, Scorpio

GODS: Eleggua, Obatala

GODDESS: Venus

MAGICKAL: The folk name Return-to-Me says it all. If your love has left, bring Blue Mallow into your home to cause the strayed love to reconsider his or her departure. However, if you are attempting to secure the return of a same-sex partner, I am told Dwarf Mallow works better.

Mallow, Dwarf—*Malva rotundifolia*—Feminine, Moon, Water

ASTROLOGICAL: *Primary*: Cancer; *Secondary*: Cancer, Pisces, Scorpio

GODDESS: Venus

MEDICAL: Expectorant. A warm water infusion acts as an expectorant.

PART USED: Leaves

MAGICKAL: The Dwarf Mallow is used as is the Blue Mallow, but to cause a same sex partner to return. An infusion of Dwarf Mallow flowers will reportedly attract same-sex lovers as well when worn as a perfume.

Mallow, Marsh—*Althaea officinalis*—Feminine, Moon, Water

Also known as Athea, Heemst, Mortification Root, Slaz, Sweet Weed, Wymote Mallow

ASTROLOGICAL: *Primary*: Cancer; *Secondary*: Cancer, Pisces, Scorpio

MEDICAL: Demulcent, Emollient, Expectorant. One ounce of the root is decocted in 1 pint of water. Reduce to half by boiling. Strain and serve 4 ounces at a time. Simmering 1 ounce of the herb in 1 pint of water for 30 minutes can make a warm water infusion of the flowers and leaves. Serve 4 ounces at a time. Either decoction of root or infusion of herb will relieve a congested chest and sooth both sore throats and irritations of the urinary tract.

PARTS USED: Herb, Roots

MAGICKAL: Mixed into incenses and sachet mixtures to promote psychic powers. Grown in and around a ritual area, the living plant lends itself to protection. Voodoo traditions sometimes use the cut or dried plants to attract desired spirits.

GENERAL: Hollyhock and Marshmallow are often used as substitutes for each other.

Mallow, Musk—*Malva meschata*—Feminine, Moon, Water

ASTROLOGICAL: *Primary*: Cancer; *Secondary*: Cancer, Pisces, Scorpio

GODDESSES: Venus

MAGICKAL: Musk Mallow is used to make oils and ointments for protection. Many use it to create the New Orleans style oil "Protection from the Black Arts." To do so, gently warm a base oil (vegetable oil will do) with Musk Mallow for several hours, cool, strain, and use to anoint self, candles, or as a part of a protection spell. This oil is a magickal substitute for true musk oil.

Mallow, Sea Tree—*Lavatera arborea*

Mamao—*See* Papaya

Mandragen—*See* Mandrake

Mandragor—*See* Mandrake

☠**Mandrake**—*Atropa mandragora/Mandragora officinale*—Masculine, Mercury, Fire

Also known as Alraun, Anthropomophon, Baaras, Brain Thief, Circeium, Circoea, Galgenmannchen, Gallows, Herb of Circe, Hexenmannchen, Ladykin Mandragen, Mandragor Mannikin, Raccoon Berry, Satan's Apple, Semihomo, Sorcerer's Root, Wild Lemon,

Mandrake

Witches' Mannildn, Womandrake, Zauberwuzel

See also White Bryony and Mandrake, American (especially if the reference calls for Raccoon Berry)

ASTROLOGICAL: *Primary*: Gemini, Virgo; *Secondary*: Aries, Leo, Sagittarius

GODS: Eleggua, Kurma, Vishnu

GODDESSES: Artemis, Diana, Hathor, Hecate

MEDICAL: Anesthetic (root), Emetic (root), Intoxicant (leaves and root), Purgative (root), Sedative (sleep). The leaves are boiled in whole milk and used as a cooling poultice. In large amounts, the root is said to bring on delirium. A wine infusion of powdered bark of root is useful in treating pain with sleep.

PARTS USED: Leaves, Root

GENERAL: Mandrake root was prescribed for relaxation. Larger amounts were used as anesthetic during operations and sometimes used to render the patient unconscious. An amount somewhere between relaxation and unconsciousness reportedly enhances the act of love as well as bringing out dormant insanity. Too much and it reportedly kills. Now for the really strange part of its legend, I have consumed a mandrake (bark of root and whole root) as an infusion/tincture of brandy and of wine, drank great amounts of this mixture indeed, and found it to be of little or no difference in effect than that of brandy or wine. So if you are looking for an intoxicant, please don't waste your time and risk your life. All medical references I can find state loosely that I should be dead as a result of my youthful ignorance.

NOTE: Not to be confused with American Mandrake (*Podophyllum peltatum*). The Latin name *Mandragora officinale* predates *Atropa mandragora*. The newer name reflects its close relation to Belladonna (*Atropa belladonna*).

☠ **Mandrake, American**—*Podophyllum peltatum*—Masculine, Mercury, Fire

Also known as May Apple, Duck's Foot, Hog Apple, Raccoon Berry, Wild Lemon

ASTROLOGICAL: *Primary*: Gemini, Virgo; *Secondary*: Aries, Leo, Sagittarius

GODS: Shango, Obatala, Oggun, Olocun

MEDICAL: Cathartic, Diuretic, Purgative. In large doses, will cause vomiting, damage to the digestive system, and death.

MAGICKAL: Although the American Mandrake is not closely related to Mandrake *(Atropa mandragora/Mandragora officinale)* it has the approximately same magickal properties. Having never tried, I find the root of the American Mandrake to be useful only in creating money-drawing powders and poppets for use in both money and love spells. The fruit of the May Apple is sometimes eaten to promote love and to empower a person to become prosperous, but the root and leaves are never consumed, as they are poisonous.

Mannikin—*See* Mandrake

Maple—*Acer saccharum*—Feminine, Jupiter, Earth

ASTROLOGICAL: *Primary*: Pisces, Sagittarius; *Secondary*: Capricorn, Taurus, Virgo

GODS: Ochosi

MAGICKAL: Promotes love and prosperity. When its syrup is consumed, it brings a sense of well-being and love.

Maple

Marigold—*See* Calendula

May Apple—*See* Mandrake, American

Mapou—*See* Wood Aloes

Maracoc—*See* Passion Flower

Marchalan—*See* Elecampane

Marguerite—*See* Daisy, Ox-eye

Marijuana—*Cannabis sativa/Cannabis Indica/ Cannabis Rudelius*—Feminine, Saturn, Water

Also known as Cannabis, Cannabis Chinese, Chanvre, Ganeb, Ganja, Hemp, Hanf, Kif, Tekrouri, and a variety of street names too long to list.

ASTROLOGICAL: *Primary*: Aquarius, Capricorn; *Secondary*: Cancer, Pisces, Scorpio

MEDICAL: Anodyne, Intoxicant, Nervine, Sedative. In pain relief and as a sedative, it has an advantage over opium as it is not addictive, does not cause constipation, and does not decrease appetite as all opiates do.

One wonders why it is that those suffering from wasting away syndrome are still given opiates at all. Dose will vary greatly with the particular plant and the age of the dried material. The active ingredients oxidize quickly, thus age and improper storage will decrease the drug's action. The active ingredients are alcohol and fat soluble.

PARTS USED: Flowering tops of the female, leaves

Marijuana

MAGICKAL: Intoxicants do have a legitimate place in spiritual development, but recreation for the sake of recreation should be presented as just that, so we can be clear in our discussion and dissemination of information. As recreational drug use is not the subject of this book, I will not dally on the subject. Marijuana has gone through many changes since the time when it was acceptably used for spiritual exploration. Due to hybridizing for THC content, the smallest amounts of the herb now produce immense intoxication. While everyone should have the right to explore their own sense of spirituality, sitting on the couch, watching *Jerry Springer,* and eating pizza just doesn't strike me as very religious. Small amounts of Marijuana in oil-bearing foods are an effective tool in addressing a great many inhibitions. When smoked, the modern variety tends to produce an almost instant intoxication, which can approach hallucination. In small amounts, I have found it to be useful in relieving the pain of physical therapy when one is recovering from injuries that require painful stretching of the tendons. However, it is entirely possible that overmedication will mask the pain that reminds you that you might be overdoing the rehabilitation. However, all these uses and, in particular, the recreational uses pale in light of how much power this plant has to address wasting away syndrome. Speaking as one who sat with his father as he changed from a strong, proud man into a living skeleton because doctors are not at this time legally allowed to prescribe it as medicine, I tell you this plant is not only sacred, it is magickal. The war against its sacred and medical use is yet another Witch-hunt causing the unnecessary suffering of thousands.

NOTE: There are many varieties of Marijuana and one should not think that either is *cannabis sativa*, *cannabis indica*, or *cannabis rudelius* as the cultivation of this plant is illegal in most areas. As a result, both price and demand are high, so underground hybridization has resulted in an inability to separate the potentially different varieties. As a result, virtually all varieties of Marijuana are commonly classified as *cannabis sativa*.

Marjoram—*Origanum marjorana*—Masculine, Mercury, Air

ASTROLOGICAL: *Primary*: Gemini, Virgo; *Secondary*: Aquarius, Gemini, Libra

GODS: Parashurama, Vishnu

GODDESSES: Ochun, Venus

MEDICAL: Pectoral. A decoction of Marjoram aids as a regular treatment for mild asthma. In powdered form, it is sometimes sniffed to bring on sneezing. For

Marjoram

this purpose, it is more often compounded with other herbs.

PART USED: Herb

MAGICKAL: In the bath, Marjoram promotes both romantic love and celibacy, reminding us that romance and sex is not the same thing. In meals, it promotes a sense of peace and calm. Marjoram was used by ancient Egyptians to scent mummies. While that might not be very practical today, diffuse essential oil of Marjoram into the bedroom and you will probably sleep like a mummy.

Marrubium—*See* Horehound, White

Maruil—*See* Horehound, White

Marsh Gentian—*See* Gentian

Marshmallow—*See* Mallow, Marsh

Maruta Foetida—*See* Chamomile, Stinking

Masterwort—*Imperatoria ostruthium*—Masculine, Mars, Fire

Also known as Hog Fennel, Imperatoria

See also Angelica, as Masterwort is also a common name for Angelica

ASTROLOGICAL: *Primary*: Aries, Scorpio; *Secondary*: Aries, Leo, Sagittarius

MEDICAL: Antispasmodic, Carminative, Stimulant. A wine decoction of the root is an excellent treatment for asthma.

PART USED: Root

MAGICKAL: Masterwort is used in spirit evocation. Mixed with Sandalwood and Lavender in equal amounts, it is sometimes used as an incense in conjunction with the instructions found in *The Key of Solomon the King*; however, this incense blend is a postmodern creation and was never recommended in that book.

Matonia Cardamomum—*See* Cardamom

Maudlin Daisy—*See* Daisy, Ox-eye

Maudlinwort—*See* Daisy, Ox-eye

May—*See* Hawthorn

Mayblossom—*See* Hawthorn

May Bush—*See* Hawthorn

Mayflower—*See* Cowslip and Hawthorn

Maythen—*See* Chamomile, Common

Mayweed—*See* Chamomile, Stinking

Maruta Cotula—*See* Chamomile, Stinking

Maypop—*See* Passion Flower

Mazzard Cherry—*See* Cherry

Mbiba—*See* Cashew

Mbono—*See* Castor

Mdogo—*See* Castor

Meadow Anemone—*See* Anemone

Meadowsweet—*Spiraea Ulmaria/Filipendula Ulmaria/Spiraea Filipendula*—Masculine, Jupiter, Air

Also known as Bridewort, Dolloff, Dollor, Gravel Root, Lady-of-the-Meadow, Little Queen, Meadowwort, Meadsweet, Queen-of-the-Meadow, Steeplebush, Trumpet Weed

See also Gravelroot, as they both share the common names Gravelroot, Trumpet Weed, and to some extent Queen-of-the-Meadow/Queen-of-the-Meadow Root.

ASTROLOGICAL: *Primary*: Pisces, Sagittarius; *Secondary*: Aquarius, Gemini, Libra

GODS: Eleggua

GODDESSES: Blodeuwedd, Ochun, Yemaya

MEDICAL: Astringent, Diuretic. A warm water infusion of the flowers or herb (1 ounce in 1 pint of water) acts as a good diuretic as well as a good source for iron and magnesium. It is also very useful in treating diarrhea, helps to lower blood pressure, and acts as a good tonic for vegetarians.

PARTS USED: Flowers, Herb

MAGICKAL: Sometimes called Meadsweet, its flowers were often used in the creation of honey wine. If you are not a skilled brewer and are fortunate enough to find mead, a mead infusion can be made with Meadowsweet flowers for an excellent love potion. Simply soak 1 ounce of Meadowsweet in 2 pints of mead for a moon and then serve over a romantic dinner.

GENERAL: Meadowsweet has been cited as one of the three herbs sacred to the Druids. The other two in the same citations are Vervain and Water Mint (listed here under Mint). The problem with this cite is that there were certainly other herbs sacred to the Druids.

Meadowwort—*See* Meadowsweet

Meadsweet—*See* Meadowsweet

Mecca Balsam—*See* Balm of Gilead

Medicine Plant—*See* Aloe

Meet-me-in-the-Entry—*See* Heartsease

Mehlige Aletria—*See* Ague Root

Mehndi—*See* Henna

Meklin—*See* Iris

Melampode—*See* Hellebore, Black

Melia—*See* Frangipani

Melissa—*See* Lemon Balm

Melogranato—*See* Pomegranate

Melongene—*See* Eggplant

Milfoil—*See* Yarrow

Militaris—*See* Yarrow

Military Herb—*See* Yarrow

Milkwort—*See* Senega

Millefolium—*See* Yarrow

Millet—*Panicum milaiceum*—Feminine, Jupiter, Earth

ASTROLOGICAL: *Primary*: Pisces, Sagittarius; *Secondary*: Capricorn, Taurus, Virgo

MAGICKAL: When consumed, Millet will reportedly increase one's wealth.

NOTE: References to Millet may be referring to any of several similar or related grasses.

Mimosa—*Mimosa Pudica*—Feminine, Saturn, Water

Also known as Humble Plant, Sensitive Plant, Shame Plant, Sleeping Plant

ASTROLOGICAL: *Primary*: Aquarius, Capricorn; *Secondary*: Cancer, Pisces, Scorpio

GODS: Shango, Eleggua

MAGICKAL: The word *Mimosa* is sometimes used to describe a broad range of plants, but none is more magickal than the Sensitive Plant. Easily grown at home from readily available seeds, the Sensitive Plant will attract gentle love into the home and encourage prophetic dreams. This beautiful child of summer and winter gets its name from its reaction to the slightest touch when it is young. The leaves will almost instantly close up and droop. This plant should never be picked. If it should become necessary to trim, do so with your sharpest knife or swiftest scissors. Never use trimmings for magickal purposes. Should leaves drop on their own, they can be used for purification and protection baths.

Mimosa

Meadow Cabbage—*See* Cabbage, Skunk

Mechoacan du Canada—*See* Pokeweed

Mendee—*See* Henna

Menthe de Notre Dame—*See* Spearmint

Mesquite—*Prosopis juliflora*—Feminine, Moon, Water

Also known as Mizquitl

ASTROLOGICAL: *Primary*: Cancer; *Secondary*: Cancer, Pisces, Scorpio

MAGICKAL: Mesquite is added to ritual fires for its healing properties and to barbecues for its great taste.

Mexican Damiana—*See* Damiana

Mexican Saffron—*See* Saffron, Mexican

Miltwaste—*See* Fern

Middle Fleabane—*See* Fleabane, Common

Minarta—*See* Avens

Mitan—*See* Olive

Mizquitl—*See* Mesquite

Mkwatia—*See* Acacia

Mgunga—*See* Acacia

Mhawa—*See* Fig

Michaelmas Daisy—*See* Aster

Mill Mountain—*See* Flax, Mountain

Minor Lavender—*See* Lavender

Mint—*See List*—Masculine, Mercury, Air

See also Bergamot, Peppermint, Spearmint

ASTROLOGICAL: *Primary*: Gemini, Virgo; *Secondary*: Aquarius, Gemini, Libra

GODS: Eleggua, Pluto

GODDESSES: Hecate, Minth

Mint, Corn—*Mentha arvensis*

MEDICAL: Astringent, Stimulant, Tonic

PART USED: Herb

Mint, Curled—*Mentha acrispa*

MEDICAL: Astringent, Stimulant, Tonic

PART USED: Herb

Mint, Egyptian—*Mentha rotundifolia*

Also known as Round Leaved Mint

MEDICAL: Astringent, Stimulant, Tonic

PART USED: Herb

Mint, Horse—*Mentha sylvestris*

MEDICAL: Astringent, Stimulant, Tonic

PART USED: Herb

Mint, Wild—*Mentha sativa*

Also known as Hairy Mint, Marsh Mint, Water Mint, Whorled Mint

MEDICAL: Astringent, Stimulant (mild), Stomachic, Tonic. A warm water infusion of the herb acts as a mild stimulant, a general tonic, and topical astringent. Chewing the fresh leaves will relieve nausea.

PARTS USED: Herb

MAGICKAL: Wild Mint has been cited as one of the three herbs sacred to the Druids. The other two in the same citations are Vervain and Meadowsweet. The problem with this reference is that there were certainly other herbs sacred to the Druids. Sprigs of Mint are used for asperging (sprinkling with blessed water). Some folk choose to use an infusion of Mint rather than pure water for this rite of cleansing. Mint is also used in lust incenses, but the smell of burning Mint leaves much to be desired.

Miracle Herb—*See* Comfrey

Mirra Balsam—*See* Myrrh

Mismin—*See* Spearmint

☙ **Mistletoe, American**—*Phoradendenaron macrophyllum*—Masculine, Sun, Air

ASTROLOGICAL: *Primary*: Leo; *Secondary*: Aquarius, Gemini, Libra

GODS: Babalu Aye, Shango, Eleggua, Obatala, Ochosi, Oggun

MAGICKAL: American Mistletoe is often listed as a magickal substitute for European Mistletoe; however, generally speaking, the folk names and deity associations are not shared. I do not believe such substitution is sensible.

☠ **Mistletoe, Euro-pean**—*Viscum al-bum*—Masculine, Sun, Air

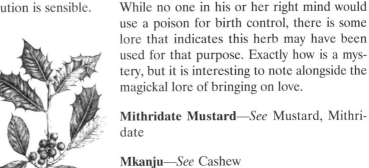

Mistletoe

Also known as Bird-lime Mistletoe, Herbe de la Croix, Mystyldene, Lignum Crucis

ASTROLOGICAL: *Primary*: Leo; *Secondary*: Aquarius, Gemini, Libra

GODS: Apollo, Odin

GODDESSES: Freya, Frigga, Venus

MEDICAL: Antispasmodic, Narcotic, Nervine, Tonic

PARTS USED: Berries, Leaves

MAGICKAL: Reportedly, the Druids felt Mistletoe was so sacred that very special care was given to its harvest. According to several references, on the sixth day of the waxing moon they would dress in all white and find the Mistletoe guided by visions. At ground level, they would spread large white sheets, holding it between them, not touching the ground, with the reverence one might a flag. One person would be sent up the Oak tree to slice the Mistletoe with a golden knife or sickle. If it fell and was caught in the white fabric, all was fine; but should it not be discovered or fall to the ground, legend had it that it was a very bad omen. Who doesn't know the blessings of Mistletoe on lovers and friends? Reportedly, kissing under the Mistletoe will strengthen a relationship; however, hanging a sprig of it in your home and kissing is not exactly what was intended by the old tradition, which was more along the lines of walking through the woods hand in hand with your lover, happening to notice that you have walked under the Mistletoe, and kissing to strengthen the relationship. It was never intended to be the trap, trickery, or social blackmail that it has become today.

While no one in his or her right mind would use a poison for birth control, there is some lore that indicates this herb may have been used for that purpose. Exactly how is a mystery, but it is interesting to note alongside the magickal lore of bringing on love.

Mithridate Mustard—*See* Mustard, Mithridate

Mkanju—*See* Cashew

Mokala—*See* Acacia

Monadra—*See* Bergamot, Wild

Moon Daisy—*See* Daisy, Ox-eye

Moonlight-on-the-Grove—*See* Jasmine

Moonwort—*See* Fern

Moor Grass—*See* Five-Finger Grass

Moose Elm—*See* Elm, Slippery

Morelle a Grappes—*See* Pokeweed

Morera—*See* Mulberry, Common

Mormon Tea—*See* Ma Huang

☠**Morning Glory**—*See Note*—Masculine, Saturn, Air

GODS: Castor

ASTROLOGICAL: *Primary*: Aquarius, Capricorn; *Secondary*: Aquarius, Gemini, Libra

MAGICKAL: All Morning Glories are *Ipomoea*, like High John the Conqueror root. This is why the root of the Morning Glory is a substitute for the High John the Conqueror root and why you should see High John the Conqueror for additional uses of the root. Bush Morning Glory (*Ipomoea lepthophylla*) is used to stop bad dreams. For this purpose, the seedpods (not just the seeds) are placed under the pillow or included in dream pillow blends. The root is burned an hour prior to sleep for the same reason. Heavenly Blue Morning Glory (*Ipomoea violacea*) seeds have been used in vision quest. However, too many can reportedly cause internal injury and even death. To make matters worse, commercially available seeds are often coated with a substance, which will induce vomiting. This is a very powerful hallucinogen. In fact, the illicit drugs sold under the names "Purple Jesus," "Purple Windowpane," and simply "Windowpane" are often made from these seeds. Like most powerful drugs, using Morning Glory seeds for vision quest can be dangerous and even fatal.

Morning Glory

Morr—*See* Myrrh

Mortification Root—*See* Mallow, Marsh

Mosquito Plant—*See* Pennyroyal

Moss, American Club—*Lycopodium complanatum*—Feminine, Moon, Water

Also known as American Ground Pine, Club Moss

ASTROLOGICAL: *Primary*: Cancer; *Secondary*: Cancer, Pisces, Scorpio

MAGICKAL: Diuretic. Used as a decoction or infusion, American Club Moss makes a powerful diuretic.

PART USED: Herb

MAGICKAL: American Club Moss is an excellent material to use in the creation of poppets to represent a person born with the sun sign Cancer.

Moss, Common Club—*Lycopodium clavatum*—Feminine, Moon, Water

Also known as Foxtail, Lycopod, Muscus Terrestris Repens, Selago, Vegetable Sulphur, Wolf's Claw

ASTROLOGICAL: *Primary*: Cancer; *Secondary*: Cancer, Pisces, Scorpio

MAGICKAL: Reportedly provides general blessings when uprooted with a silver knife. Common Club Moss is an excellent material to use in the creation of poppets to represent a person born with the sun sign Cancer.

Moss, Corsican—*Fucus Helminthocorton*—Feminine, Mercury, Earth

Also known as Alsidium Helminthocorton

ASTROLOGICAL: *Primary*: Gemini, Virgo; *Secondary*: Capricorn, Taurus, Virgo

MEDICAL: Anthelmintic, Febrifuge. Used as a decoction.

PART USED: Herb

MAGICKAL: Used in the construction of poppets for all uses, especially when those poppets represent someone born with the sun sign Virgo.

Moss, Cup—*Cladonia Pyxidata*—Feminine, Mercury, Earth

ASTROLOGICAL: *Primary*: Gemini, Virgo; *Secondary*: Capricorn, Taurus, Virgo

MEDICAL: Expectorant. Two ounces is decocted in 1 quart of water. Reduce by boiling to 1 pint, strain, and sweeten with honey. This decoction is served 4 ounces at a time.

PART USED: Herb

MAGICKAL: Carried to attract prosperity in all orders of the word. Used in the construction of poppets for all uses, especially when those poppets represent someone born with the sun sign Virgo.

Moss, Hair Cap—*Polytrichium Juniperum*—Feminine, Mercury, Earth

Also known as Bear's Bed, Golden Maidenhair, Female Fern Herb, Ground Moss, Robin's Eye, Rockbrake Herb

ASTROLOGICAL: *Primary*: Gemini, Virgo; *Secondary*: Capricorn, Taurus, Virgo

MEDICAL: Diuretic. Used as a tea.

PART USED: Herb

MAGICKAL: Used in the construction of poppets for all uses, especially when those poppets represent someone born with the sun sign Virgo.

Moss, Iceland—*Cetraria islandica*—Feminine, Mercury, Earth

Also known as Cetraria, Iceland Lichen

ASTROLOGICAL: *Primary*: Gemini, Virgo; *Secondary*: Capricorn, Taurus, Virgo

MEDICAL: Demulcent, Tonic

PARTS USED: Whole plant

MAGICKAL: Ground and scattered on the roof of a home, Iceland Moss is said to protect the home from storms and illness. Used in the construction of poppets for all uses, especially when those poppets represent someone born with the sun sign Virgo.

Moss, Irish—*Chondrus crispus*—Feminine, Moon, Water

Also known as Carrageen, Carrahan, Chondrus, Pearl Moss

ASTROLOGICAL: *Primary*: Cancer; *Secondary*: Cancer, Pisces, Scorpio

GODDESS: Ochun

MEDICAL: Demulcent, Emollient, Expectorant (mild). Used as tea.

PARTS USED: Whole plant

MAGICKAL: Irish Moss is the choice for the main ingredient in poppet stuffing if you intend the poppet to attract love, luck, or money. Choose a second herb to compliment the intent. In business, rub Irish Moss between your hands, allowing the herb to fall into your cash register as you grind it. Visualize money entering your business.

Moss, Spanish—*Tillandsia usneoides*—Feminine, Mercury, Earth

ASTROLOGICAL: *Primary*: Gemini, Virgo; *Secondary*: Capricorn, Taurus, Virgo

MAGICKAL: A tincture of Spanish Moss works as a protection perfume. Used as stuffing, Spanish Moss is perfect for poppets when those poppets are made for protection or healing.

Moss, Sphagnum—*Sphagnum Cymbifolium*—Feminine, Mercury, Earth

Also known as Bog Moss

ASTROLOGICAL: *Primary*: Gemini, Virgo; *Secondary*: Capricorn, Taurus, Virgo

MEDICAL: Antiseptic, Astringent. A warm water infusion is used topically to cleanse wounds.

PARTS USED: Whole plant

MAGICKAL: Used in the construction of poppets for all uses, especially when those poppets represent someone born with the sun sign Virgo.

Mother-of-the-Herbs—*See* Rue

Mother-of-the-Wood—*See* Sloe

Mother's Heart—*See* Shepherd's Purse

Motherwort—*Leonurus cardiaca*

MEDICAL: Antispasmodic, Diaphoretic, Emmenagogue, Nervine, Tonic. Used as a warm water infusion. Typically, 1 ounce of the herb to 1 pint of water served 4 ounces at a time.

PART USED: Herb

Mountain Ash—*See* Ash, Mountain

Mountain Balm—*See* Yerba Santa

Mountain Everlasting—*See* Catsfoot

Mountain Flax—*See* Flax, Mountain and Senega

Mountain Groundsel—*See* Groundsel, Mountain

Mountain Mahogany—*See* Mahogany, Mountain

Mountain Radish—*See* Horseradish

Moutarde des Allemands—*See* Horseradish

Muggons—*See* Mugwort

Mugwort—*Artemisia vulgaris*—Feminine, Venus, Earth

Also known as Artemis Herb, Artemisia, Cingulum Sancti Johannis, Felon Herb, Muggons, Naughty Man, Old Man, Old Uncle Henry, Sailor's Tobacco, St. John's Plant

See also Tarragon which is sometimes called Mugwort

WARNING: Should not be used if pregnant or nursing.

ASTROLOGICAL: *Primary*: Libra, Taurus; *Secondary*: Capricorn, Taurus, Virgo

GODS: Babalu Aye, Chandra, Eleggua, Obatala, Oggun,

GODDESSES: Artemis, Diana, Yemaya

MEDICAL: Diaphoretic, Diuretic, Emmenagogue, Nervine, Stimulant (mild). An infusion is made with the leaves. One ounce to 1 pint of water, simmered for 30 minutes. It is strained and served 1/2 teaspoon at a time.

PARTS USED: Leaves, Root

MAGICKAL: As described for medical purposes, in similar dose the infusion of Mugwort will aid in spirit communication and divination if consumed an hour before such an attempt. The same infusion is an excellent wash and

Mugwort

will charge scrying tools. In a dream pillow, it will promote nocturnal visits from lost loved ones as well as prophetic dreams, but used as an infusion it will not yield these results as it acts as a mild stimulant. Grown in or around the home, Mugwort is protective.

Muira-Puama—*Liriosma ovata*

GENERAL: Consuming the bark of Muira-Puama heightens physical sensation and brings on those wonderful tingles in the base of one's neck that are associated with light touch. This is an excellent plant for use in conjunction with light massage, when the massage is for the purpose of pleasure (as opposed to physical therapy). I have read that the powdered root has the same effect, but I have no personal experience with this.

Mulberry, Common—*Morus nigra/Morus rubra*—Masculine, Mercury, Air

Also known as Black Mulberry, Gelso, Morera

ASTROLOGICAL: *Primary*: Gemini, Virgo; *Secondary*: Aquarius, Gemini, Libra

MAGICKAL: Some Wiccans prefer their Circle cast with a wand or staff rather than an athame or a sword. For that purpose, Mulberry wood makes an excellent wood. It is also used for protection talismans. Eating ripe Mulberry (*Morus rubra*) berries will increase psychic awareness and reproductive fertility in women.

Mullein—*Verbascum thapsus*—Feminine, Saturn, Fire

Also known as Aaron's Rod, Adam's Flannel, Beggar's Blanket, Beggar's Stalks, Blanket Herb, Blanket Leaf, Bullock's Lungwort, Candlewick Plant, Clot, Clown's Lungwort, Cuddy's Lungs, Doffle, Duffle, Feltwort, Flannel Plant, Fluffweed, Graveyard Dust, Golden Rod, Hag's Tapers, Hare's Beard, Hedge Taper, Jacob's Staff, Jupiter's Staff, Lady's Foxglove, Mullein Dock, Old Lady's Flannel, Old Man's Fennel, Peter's Staff, Rag Paper, Shepherd's Clubs, Shepherd's Herb, Shepherd's Staff, Torches, Velvet Dock, Velvetback, Velvet Plant, White Mullein, Wild Ice Leaf, Woollen

ASTROLOGICAL: *Primary*: Aquarius, Capricorn; *Secondary*: Aries, Leo, Sagittarius

GODS: Jupiter

MEDICAL: Astringent, Demulcent, Diuretic, Emollient, Expectorant, Narcotic (mild), Sedative (mild), Tonic. Served as tea and sweetened with honey, Mullein is an excellent treatment to relieve coughs and sore throats. Serving this beverage hot will also help cleanse the throat of excess mucus, and it can also be prepared the night before and then consumed cold to keep one from coughing if unable to warm liquid. In the workplace, it can be rewarmed in the microwave or consumed cold or at room temperature. A poultice of Mullein herb is a good treatment for cuts and bruises. Mullein is a fantastic daily tonic and is especially useful in strengthening the immune system against cold weather illness.

PARTS USED: Flowers, Leaves

Mullein

MAGICKAL: A blanket made of Mullein is said to protect the sleeper from nightmares and bad dreams. Making such a blanket may be beyond your skill (I know it is mine), so use mullein in a dream pillow or sachet for the same purpose. Mullein is said to protect from wild animals when carried. However, I have found that it causes animals to avoid the person carrying it rather than to calm them. Scattering Mullein flowers about the garden seems to keep rabbits from showing the garden attention; however, for some reason it seems to attract burrowing critters. If you really feel crafty, I am told that the "fluff" from Mullein is the ideal material for spinning candlewicks. Not knowing how to spin thread, the best I have accomplished was twisting the fluff between my fingers to create a wick for a tea light.

Mullein Dock—*See* Mullein

Mum—*See* Chrysanthemum

Monk's Rhubarb—*See* Rhubarb, Monk's

Moras—*See* Vetivert

Murphies—*See* Potato

Muscus Terrestris Repens—*See* Moss, American Club

Musquash Root—*See* Hemlock

Muskateller Salbei—*See* Sage, Clary

Musk Mallow—*See* Mallow, Musk

Mustard—*Properties vary based on variety*
See also Mustard, Black; Mustard, Brown; Mustard, Common Hedge; Mustard, Field; Mustard, Flixweed; Mustard, Garlic; Mustard, Mithridate; Mustard, Rape; Mustard, Treacle Hedge; and Mustard, White

GODS: Asclepius

MEDICAL: Pungent. An infusion of White/Yellow seed is an excellent foot wash. Incorporating it into foot massage offers tremendous relief from common colds as well as mild depression. The problem in using these for magickal purposes is that they are often confused and mislabeled in Pagan and occult shops. Most often this is in the sale of so-called Black Mustard, which is most properly *Brassica nigra*. However, one of the folk names for Black Mustard is Brown Mustard. As a result, although they are different plants, Brown Mustard (*Brassica juncea*) is very often sold as Black Mustard (*Brassica nigra*). Making matters even more confusing,

Mustard

Brown and White/Yellow Mustard are often colored black with artificial materials and then sold as Black Mustard in those same Pagan/occult shops. Due to all of this confusion, the most proper common and Latin names for these plants has become cited incorrectly so often that citing them incorrectly can easily be seen as the most correct. My solution: Ignore occult shops for this one and purchase these only at a grocery or culinary shop.

PART USED: Seeds

GENERAL: There are many varieties of Mustard available today. Three of these are the most commonly available, as they are often used for culinary purposes. These are: Black Mustard (*Brassica nigra*), which is the most pungent and used widely in recipes from India. However, this plant is listed in many references as "for external use only" or "for occasional internal use only." Brown Mustard (*Brassica juncea*) is the one most commonly used to make Dijon-style mustards. This one is less pungent than Black Mustard, but more so than White/Yellow Mustard. White/Yellow Mustard (*Brassica alba*) is the mildest of the three and is the one most commonly used to make Ball Park Mustard.

Mustard, Black—*Brassica nigra/Sinapis nigra/Brassica sinapioides*—Masculine, Mars, Fire

Also known as Brown Mustard, but do not confuse Black Mustard with Brown Mustard for culinary use. These are two distinctly different plants.

ASTROLOGICAL: *Primary*: Aries, Scorpio; *Secondary*: Aries, Leo, Sagittarius

GODS: Asclepius

MEDICAL: Diuretic, Emetic, Irritant, Stimulant

PART USED: Seeds

MAGICKAL: Carried in a red sachet, Black Mustard seed is said to protect against baneful spirits, illness, and psychic vampires as well as increase cognitive functions. Sprinkled outside the home, it is said to protect the inhabitants from baneful magick. Sprinkled between your property and your neighbors, it is said to be a substitute for black salt, which keeps bad neighbors at bay.

Mustard, Brown—*Brassica juncea*—Masculine, Mars, Fire

ASTROLOGICAL: *Primary*: Aries, Scorpio; *Secondary*: Aries, Leo, Sagittarius

MEDICAL: Ground and turned into a paste by mixing with small amounts of sweet white wine, this mixture can be used occasionally to increase human fertility and is often served with food during a romantic dinner, followed by the other activity necessary for human fertility. If you do not want to make it yourself, just buy it ready-made at the grocery store. Look for brown or sweet Mustard.

MAGICKAL: It can also be used as a substitute for Black Mustard and is often sold under that name. However, for the uses listed with Black Mustard you will have better results using the real thing rather than the substitute.

Mustard, Common Hedge—*Sisymbrium officinale/Erysimum officinale*

Also known as Singer's Plant, St. Barbara's Hedge Mustard

MEDICAL: A strong infusion is used to relieve sore throats.

PART USED: Herb

Mustard, Field—*Sinapis arvensis/Brassica Sinapistrum*—Masculine, Mars, Fire

Also known as Charlock

ASTROLOGICAL: *Primary*: Aries, Scorpio; *Secondary*: Aries, Leo, Sagittarius

Mustard, Flixweed—*Sisymbrium sophia*

MEDICAL: An infusion of the herb is useful in treating asthma.

PART USED: Herb

Mustard, Garlic—*Sisymbrium alliaria*

Also known as Jack-by-the-Hedge, Sauce Alone

MEDICAL: Deobstruent, Diaphoretic

PARTS USED: Herbs, Seeds

Mustard, Mithridate—*Thlaspi arvense*

Also known as Pennycress

MAGICKAL: During a time when poison was commonly used to rid oneself of an enemy, this plant was a key ingredient in the Mithridate confection, which was said to be an antidote to poison. The concoction fell from favor when it was discovered that if a person had actually been poisoned, a patient often died even with the antidote (of course, not before paying for the antidote). However, the most interesting note on this plant is that when King James included his own feelings of paranoia to influence his translation of the Christian Bible, he translated the word for "poisoner" into Witch. This translation and Mithridate Mustard's inclusion in the antidote for poison is probably why folklore states that Mustard of all kinds is protection against Witchcraft.

Mustard, Rape—*Brassica napus*—Masculine, Mars, Fire

Also known as Cole Seed, Colza

ASTROLOGICAL: *Primary*: Aries, Scorpio; *Secondary*: Aries, Leo, Sagittarius

Mustard, Treacle Hedge—*Erysimum Cheirantholdes*

Also known as Treacle Wormseed, Wormseed

Mustard, White—*Brassica alba/Sinapis alba*—Masculine, Mars, Fire

Also known as Yellow Mustard.

ASTROLOGICAL: *Primary*: Aries, Scorpio; *Secondary*: Aries, Leo, Sagittarius

MEDICAL: An infusion is good treatment for bronchitis. When gargled, the same infusion is good to relieve sore throats.

PART USED: Seed

GENERAL: This is the most common Mustard today, found in just about every refrigerator and restaurant under its more common name, Yellow Mustard. It is used in the same way Black and Brown mustard is, but it is less effective.

Mutton Chops—*See* Cleavers (B)

Mykhet—*See* Clove

Myrrh—*Commiphora myrrha/alsumodendron Myrrha/Commiphora Myrrha*—Feminine, Moon, Water

Also known as Didin, Didthin, Bowl, Gum Myrrh Tree, Karan, Mirra Balsam, Morr, Odendron

ASTROLOGICAL: *Primary*: Cancer; *Secondary*: Cancer, Pisces, Scorpio

GODS: Adonis, Amun Ra, Babalu Aye, Shango, Eleggua, Mars (sweet myrrh), Neptune, Obatala, Oggun, Oko, Olocun, Pan, Poseidon, Priapus, Set

GODDESSES: Bhavani, Cybele, Demiter, Isis, Marian, Mut, Nyphthys, Oya, Rhea, Yemaya

MEDICAL: Astringent, Expectorant, Stimulant, Tonic. Myrrh is used to stop gums from bleeding. Grind into a powder and mix with water to make a paste. Apply to gums prior to sleep.

PART USED: Resin

MAGICKAL: Burned at noon to honor Ra and to bless the temples of Isis, Myrrh has been used in conjunction with magickal and religious practices when magickal and religious practices were not the separate things that they are often viewed today. Myrrh is not very pleasant incense to burn alone. Its scent (as is its taste) is rather bitter. Instead, it is combined with other material to make incense. Often, this other ingredient is Frankincense or Copal. Used internally, Myrrh is a decongestant and a mild stimulant. Mixed with alcohol, it can act as a depressive and could, in large amounts, cause unconsciousness and death. I have not tried this because of that all-important "death" aspect. Some believe that the "bitter herb"/ "poison" reportedly given to the historic Jesus of Nazareth was Myrrh mixed with alcohol or that the vinegar reportedly given him was wine, which when mixed in his stomach with Myrrh, may have caused him to feign death. Essential oil of Myrrh is very expensive. However, burning the resin over charcoal does not have the same effect as diffusing the essential oil, used to bring on a sense of connectivity with the often unseen but very real portions of our world. Myrrh essential oil is an excellent choice for Samhain rites and other rituals intended to contact loved ones who have moved on to the next life. Also useful in contacting nature spirits.

Myrrh

Myrtle—*Myrtus communis*—Feminine, Venus, Water

ASTROLOGICAL: *Primary*: Libra, Taurus; *Secondary*: Cancer, Pisces, Scorpio

GODS: Oko, Olocun

GODDESSES: Venus, Artemis, Astarte, Aphrodite, Hathor, Marian, Ochun

MAGICKAL: Myrtle is sometimes used in money spells, but it is more appropriately used to bless the home. When grown in the four quarters of the home, it brings love and good luck to those who live within. Growing Myrtle in this way will strengthen the love and friendship between the master and mistress of that home.

Myrtle

Myrtle Flag—*See* Calamus

Myrtle Flower—*See* Iris

Myrtle Grass—*See* Calamus

Myrtle Sedge—*See* Calamus

Mystyldene—*See* Mistletoe, European

Mziwaziwa—*See* Spurges

Narcissus—*See* Daffodil

Nard—*See* Lavender; Spikenard, American; and Spikenard, Ploughman's

Nardus—*See* Lavender

Narren Schwamm—*See* Agaric Mushroom

Narrow-leaved White Sage—*See* Sage, Common

Nasturtium—*Tropaeolum majus*

MEDICAL: Diuretic, Stimulant (mild), Tonic. A mild stimulant and diuretic with a peppery taste. Cooking will decrease its effects, so mix with salads and serve fresh. Nasturtium acts as a tonic and general immune system builder.

Nasturtium   PART USED: Leaves

Nasu—*See* Eggplant

Naughty Man—*See* Mugwort

Navet du Diable—*See* White Bryony

Nectarine—*Prunus spp.*—Feminine, Venus, Water

ASTROLOGICAL: *Primary*: Libra, Taurus; *Secondary*: Cancer, Pisces, Scorpio

MAGICKAL: Eating fresh Nectarine will bring on a sense of love and strengthen the love bonds between members of an established relationship.

Neemoo—*See* Lemon

Nelka—*See* Carnation

Nepal Barberry—*See* Barberry, Nepal

Nepeta Glechoma—*See* Ivy, Ground

Neroli—*See* Orange, Bitter

Nerve Root—*See* Valerian, American

Nettle—Most references to Nettle are asking for Greater Nettle (*see* Nettle, Greater), but they are sometimes looking for Nettle, Lesser. Generally speaking, a reference to Nettle is not referring to the other varieties by a similar name, but *see also* Nettle, Purple Dead; Nettle, White Dead; and Nettle, Yellow Dead.

Nettle, Greater—*Urtica dioica*—Masculine, Mars, Fire

Also known as Ortiga Ancha, Stinging Nettle

ASTROLOGICAL: *Primary*: Aries, Scorpio; *Secondary*: Aries, Leo, Sagittarius

GODS: Agni, Ares, Hades, Horus the Elder, Mars, Thor, Ochosi, Oko, Pluto, Varaha, Vishnu, Vulcan

GODDESSES: Nyphthys, Ochun

MEDICAL: Astringent. A warm water infusion is an excellent astringent. A warm milk infusion provides some relief of migraines.

PART USED: Herb

MAGICKAL: Used in purification baths. An infusion of Greater Nettle can also be used as a floor wash to purify the home and drive out negative energy. Burned in honor of Thor, Greater Nettle is sometimes included in storm-drawing spells as well as in talismans and sachets to bring strength and bravery.

Nettle, Lesser—*Urtica urens*—Masculine, Mars, Fire

Also known as Common Nettle, Stinging Nettle

ASTROLOGICAL: *Primary*: Aries, Scorpio; *Secondary*: Aries, Leo, Sagittarius

GODS: Varaha, Vishnu

MEDICAL: Astringent, Stimulating (mildly) Tonic. An infusion of 1 ounce of the herb in 1 pint of water. Simmer for 30 minutes and serve 4 ounces at a time.

PARTS USED: Herb, Seeds

MAGICKAL: Use in a poppet of a person along with herbs that align to their sun sign when attempting to lend them strength and courage. Can also be used as a substitute for Greater Nettle, but it is less effective.

Nettle, Purple Dead—*Lamium purpureum*

Also known as Archangel, Purple Archangel, Dead Nettle

MEDICAL: Diaphoretic. Served as tea.

PARTS USED: Flowers, Leaves

Nettle, White Dead—*Lamium album*

Also known as Archangel, Bee Nettle, Blind Nettle, Dead Nettle, Dumb Nettle, Deaf Nettle, White Archangel

Nettle, Yellow Dead—*Lamium Galeobdolon*

Also known as Archangel, Dead Nettle, Dummy Nettle, Weazel Snout, Yellow Archangel

New Jersey Tea—*Ceanothus americanus*

Also known as Red Root, Wild Snowball

MEDICAL: Astringent, Antispasmodic, Antisyphilitic, Expectorant, Sedative. Served as tea. Unlike other herbs for this purpose, New Jersey Tea does not raise the blood pressure. In fact, it is sometimes used to treat high blood pressure.

PART USED: Root

MAGICKAL: Said to promote lust

Ngagwa—*See* Eggplant

Nidor—*See* Fumitory

Niggerhead—*See* Echinacea

Nightly Man's Cherries—*See* Belladonna

Nine Hooks—*See* Lady's Mantle

Nine-Joints—*See* Knotgrass

Ninety-Knot—*See* Knotgrass

Nion—*See* Ash

Nirvara—*See* Rice

Niu Xi—*See* Achyranthes

Njjlika—*See* Basil

Niyog—*See* Coconut

Noah's Ark—*See* Valerian, American

Noble Laurel—*See* Bay

Noble Liverwort—*See* Liverwort, American

Noble Yarrow—*See* Yarrow

Nodding Squill—*See* Hyacinth, Wild

No Eyes—*See* Potato

None-so-Pretty—*See* Balsam, White

Norfolk Island Pine—*See* Pine, Norfolk Island

Nosebleed—*See* Yarrow

Ntola—*See* Agrimony

Nurse Heal—*See* Elecampane

Nutmeg—*Myristica fragrans*—Masculine, Jupiter, Fire
Also known as Bicuiba Acu, Qoust, Sadhika, Wohpala
ASTROLOGICAL: *Primary*: Pisces, Sagittarius; *Secondary*: Aries, Leo, Sagittarius
GODDESSES: Ochun, Oya
MEDICAL: Narcotic (in large doses), Stimulant, Tonic. The outercoating of the Nutmeg nut is called Mace. Because it is a specific part of a plant, its associations shift as do the extracts and concentrates of some plants.
PART USED: Kernel of seed

> **Mace**—*Myristica fragrans*—Masculine, Mercury, Air
> ASTROLOGICAL: *Primary*: Gemini, Virgo; *Secondary*: Aquarius, Gemini, Libra
> GODS: (specifically Mace) Hanuman, Hermes, Parashurama, Vishnu

Small amounts of Nutmeg will settle the stomach and aid in digestion. Large amounts will act as a narcotic. To treat diarrhea, simmer 1 cup whole milk, 1 level teaspoon Nutmeg, and 2 teaspoons Honey. Serve warm. Drink one cup every hour until the symptoms subside. In all seriousness, I have not found that the narcotic effect of nutmeg provides a useful amount of pain relief for any serious medical concern. Instead, it seems to be very useful as a mood elevator in doses of about 1 teaspoon.

MAGICKAL: Nutmeg is an excellent example of classic operational Witchcraft (a.k.a. spellcraft) finding its way into our modern culture. Just why did Grandma load all that Nutmeg into those sweets during the holidays if not to induce a festive mood? Chances are great that Grandma didn't know she was practicing spellcraft, and chances are even if she did, she probably did not recognize the science involved. Nutmeg has long been associated with luck and the strength of a strong home. Although it is sometimes drilled and strung on a cord for these attributes, it far more effective to use Nutmeg in cooking, especially in the cold winter months when the lack of sunlight and outdoor activities brings on family strife. Surprise everyone with a rich Nutmeg treat.

GENERAL: Often listed in Pagan lore as "not recommended for internal use." If I took that warning seriously, I would have to throw away half of my recipes for wintertime goodies. On the other hand, when I was young, I heard large amounts of whole Nutmeg would bring on visions. After consuming entirely too much, I found out it would also cause severe abdominal pain. So there I was, lying on my side and bent at the waist, waiting for visions that never came and wishing someone had told me it wouldn't really work. Okay, I might not have listened to them, and you probably won't listen to me, but I should say it anyway: Don't try this one for visions. Use it in moderation for making snacks. Use too much, and the only vision you will receive is that of the bottom of your toilet. Both Nutmeg and Mace (its outer coating) are often used in incense and sachet recipes to increase psychic and cognitive abilities. Essential oil of Nutmeg is diffused to invigorate the body and to increase the flow of energy throughout both body and soul. The scent is warm, invigorating, and inviting.

Oak—*See List*—Masculine, Sun, Fire

The Oak has many varieties, which include:

Common Oak—*Quercus robur*

Also known as British Oak, Tanner's Bark

Durmast Oak—*Quercus sessiliflora*

Guatemalan Oak—*Quercus Skinneri*

Also known as Juglans

Holm Oak—*Quercus ilex*

White Oak—*Quercus alba*

ASTROLOGICAL: *Primary*: Leo; *Secondary*: Aries, Leo, Sagittarius

GODS: Brahma, Dagda, Dianus, Essus, Hades, Herne, Horus the Elder, Janus, Jupiter, Mars, Pan, Pluto, Taranis, Thor, Varaha, Vishnu, Zeus

GODDESSES: Blodeuwedd, Diana

CELTIC TREE CALENDAR (Duir)—June 10th thru July 17th—The seventh month of the year.

MEDICAL: Astringent. A decoction of Oak leaves can be used with a poultice to treat wounds.

PART USED: Leaves

MAGICKAL: Oak is one of the nine woods said to be best for ritual fires in the Wiccan Rede. The Oak is referred to in the British Tree Fairy Triad as well as the many that have sprouted up elsewhere citing three sacred trees as Oak, Ash, and Thorn. According to some references, the Druids so revered the Oak that they

Oak

would never meet or hold rituals without the presence of this majestic tree. As the great bulk of Druid lore was either invented long after the height of their culture or manufactured by Rome as misinformation and propaganda, I am not entirely sure this is correct. Certainly the tree was sacred, but forbidding religious services without it seems to be more of revisionist/romantic history. Equal length twigs of Oak used for the frame of an Eye of God makes for an excellent protective talisman, especially when hung in the home. The Oak's seeds, acorns, make great phallic symbols and are often placed on the Wiccan altar to symbolize the presence of our Lord. Sometimes used as the tip of a wand, the acorn lends itself to masculine operations and the use of magick to cause sudden change.

MAGICKAL: Oak is excellent for the hilt and scabbard of athame and sword. However, from a practical viewpoint, it is not the best selection if a pinning technique is used to affix it. Oak splits comparatively easily and does not wear well.

Oak Fern—*See* Fern

Oakmoss—*Evernia prusnatri*—Feminine, Jupiter, Earth

ASTROLOGICAL: *Primary*: Pisces, Sagittarius; *Secondary*: Capricorn, Taurus, Virgo

GODDESSES: Ochun, Oya

MAGICKAL: Oakmoss is used in prosperity incenses and sachets. Oakmoss absolute is diffused or placed on the temples to promote a consciousness shift favorable to Initiation rituals.

Oats—*Avena sativa*—Feminine, Venus, Earth

Also known as Grouts, Joulaf, Oatmeal

ASTROLOGICAL: *Primary*: Libra, Taurus; *Secondary*: Capricorn, Taurus, Virgo

MEDICAL: Antispasmodic, Stimulant (mild)

PART USED: Seeds

MAGICKAL: Oats are used in prosperity spells. Eating a breakfast of oatmeal flavored with cinnamon and sweetened with honey will greatly increase your chances of securing a job. If you are already employed, eat the mixture an hour before going to work and you will stand a better chance of receiving a raise. Do the same if you work on commission or a bonus base, and it will increase your chance of increasing those commissions or that bonus.

Oatmeal—*See* Oats

Ocanet—*See* Alkanet

Obeah Wood—*See* Ebony

Odendron—*See* Myrrh

Ofbit—*See* Scabious, Devil's Bit

Oghoul—*See* Lemon Balm

Ohe—*See* Bamboo

Oingnum—*See* Onion

Old English Lovage—*See* Lovage

Old Field Balsam—*See* Balsam, White

Old Lady's Flannel—*See* Mullein

Old Maid's Nightcap—*See* Geranium

Old Man's Mustard—*See* Yarrow

Old Man's Pepper—*See* Yarrow

Old Man's Root—*See* Spikenard, American. This one might also be a reference to the root of the Mugwort.

Old Man—*See* Mugwort and Southernwood

Old Man's Fennel—*See* Mullein

Old Uncle Henry—*See* Mugwort

☠ **Oleander**—*Nerium oleander*—Feminine, Saturn, Earth
Also known as Adelfa, Ceylon Tree, Dog Bane, Rose Bay, Rose Bay Tree
ASTROLOGICAL: *Primary*: Aquarius, Capricorn; *Secondary*: Capricorn, Taurus, Virgo
MAGICKAL: Like most poisonous herbs, lore states that this one will bring great misfortune and illness if kept in the home.
GENERAL: Oleander is occasionally listed as Periwinkle due to a bad cite made in the book titled *Grieves' Modern Herbal* and the books that later built on that cite.

Olibans—*See* Frankincense

Olibanum—*See* Frankincense

Olibanus—*See* Frankincense

Olive—*Olea europaea/Olea Oleaster/Olea lancifolia/Olea gallica*—Masculine, Sun, Fire
Also known as Itm, Mitan, Olivier
ASTROLOGICAL: *Primary*: Leo; *Secondary*: Aries, Leo, Sagittarius
GODS: Adonis, Amun Ra, Apollo, Aristaeus, Asclepius, Brahma, Cupid, Eros, Ganymede, Hades, Hermes, Hymen, Indra, Janus, Jupiter, Mars, Mercury, Minos, Neptune, Odin, Pan, Pluto, Poseidon, Priapus, Silvanus
GODDESSES: Athena, Irene, Minerva, Nut, Ochun
MEDICAL: Antiseptic (leaves), Astringent (leaves), Demulcent (oil of fruit), Febrifuge (bark and leaves), Laxative (oil of fruit). A decoction of 2 cups of the fresh leaves in 1 quart of water is reduced to 1/2 pint, strained, and allowed to cool. It is served to treat fevers. Olive oil is an excellent base for other herbal remedies. Alone, it is a relatively safe way to treat mild earaches. Gently warm the oil; add several drops to the affected ear. It is reportedly a good treatment for bursitis. Simply rub Olive oil into the affected place.
PARTS USED: Bark, Leaves, Oil of fruit
MAGICKAL: When beeswax candles are not available, using oil lamps fed by Olive oil is an alternative to using paraffin-based candles. Olive oil is used as a general anointing oil. Eating Olives brings on fertility in both men and women. They act as a mild aphrodisiac on men and promote love between a couple that shares them. If a woman has a particular man in mind, she can cast a simple love spell by asking him out for pizza (with Olive slices, of course) and insisting on paying, stating that since she asked she should pay.

Olivier—*See* Olive

Onion—*Allium cepa*—Masculine, Mars, Fire

Also known as Oingnum, Onyoun, Unyoun, Yn-leac

ASTROLOGICAL: *Primary*: Aries, Scorpio; *Secondary*: Aries, Leo, Sagittarius

MEDICAL: Antiseptic, Diuretic, Tonic. Regular consumption lowers blood pressure and may help with heart problems. When simmered in oil, Onions will reportedly prevent and dissolve blood clots. Relief from congestion can be had by using Onions liberally in cooking. This is especially useful during the cold months and seems to work best when the Onions are lightly fried rather than raw. Deep-fried Onions do not seem to work at all. A slice of Onion can be bandaged over a corn prior to sleeping. Repeat each night for a few of weeks, and the corn will be gone.

Onion

PART USED: Bulb

MAGICKAL: Grown in the garden or window box, Onions help to protect the home. Lore tells us that burning Onion peels in the fireplace will bless the home with health and prosperity, but allowing them to fall to the ground will cause the opposite effect. Fresh Onions promote lust and are often included in salads for this purpose. Red Onions are said to promote both love and lust. Cooking the Onion decreases its effect, but it seems to work just fine dried, chopped, or powdered (just not cooked). So sprinkle Onion powder on food after cooking if you wish to inspire lust, but before if you do not. Fresh Onions are used to purify ritual tools, especially the athame and sword. Using a different knife to cut the Onion in half, just rub the fresh Onion halves on the blade during the full moon. Burn the Onion after use; never eat it, as you will consume whatever potentially negative energies (and bacteria) that were removed from the blade.

Onion Shallot—*See* Shallot

Onyoun—*See* Onion

Ophthalmic Barberry—*See* Barberry, Nepal

Orange, Bitter—*Citrus aurantium/Citrus Bigardarier*—Masculine, Sun, Air

Also known as Bigardarier Orange

ASTROLOGICAL: *Primary*: Leo; *Secondary*: Aquarius, Gemini, Libra

GODS: Eleggua, Obatala, Oggun

MAGICKAL: Two essential oils are extracted from the Bitter Orange plant. Neroli oil is extracted from the flowers and diffused to improve sexual relations by removing doubt and relaxing concerns over performance. Generally speaking, Neroli enhances joy in all things where doubt and anxiety interfere. Also used to relieve stress. Petitgrain oil is extracted from the leaves and diffused to clear the cognitive mind. It is particularly sacred to the Orisha Eleggua.

NOTE: The common names for Sweet Orange are sometimes used to refer to Bitter Orange, so please *see also* Orange, Sweet.

Orange, Sweet—*Citrus sinesis*—Masculine, Sun, Air

Also known as Love Fruit, Love Orange, Portugal Orange

ASTROLOGICAL: *Primary*: Leo; *Secondary*: Aquarius, Gemini, Libra

GODS: Eleggua, Indra, Jupiter

GODDESS: Ochun

MAGICKAL: Sweet Orange flowers are used in the bath to draw love. Orange fruit and juice can be used for this same purpose, especially when consumed an hour before meeting a potential mate. Essential oil of Sweet Orange is diffused to increase physical energy. This oil makes a good substitute for the more expensive Neroli Oil.

Orange Bergamot—*See* Bergamot, Orange

Orange Mint—*See* Bergamot, Orange

Orange Root—*See* Goldenseal

Orchid—*See* Lucky Hand

Oregano—*Origanum vulgare*—Masculine, Mercury, Air

Also known as: Wild Marjoram, Joy-of-the-Mountain

ASTROLOGICAL: *Primary*: Gemini, Virgo; *Secondary*: Aquarius, Gemini, Libra

MEDICAL: Carminative, Diaphoretic, Stimulant, Tonic (mild). Simmer the herb in Olive oil for 30 minutes, strain and allow to cool. This is a good rub for arthritis.

PARTS USED: Herb, Oil   Oregano

MAGICKAL: Oregano is often a part of business- and money-drawing incense. In cooking, it promotes a sense of peace and calm. The smell of burning Oregano is similar to fresh sweat.

Oregon Grape—*See* Barberry, Holly-leaved

Oregon Grape Root—*See* Barberry, Holly-leaved

Organ Broth—*See* Pennyroyal

Organs—*See* Pennyroyal

Organ Tea—*See* Pennyroyal

Oriental Eggplant—*See* Eggplant

Orris—*Iris germanica/Iris florentina*—Feminine, Venus, Water

Also known as Florentine Iris, Queen Elizabeth Root

ASTROLOGICAL: *Primary*: Libra, Taurus; *Secondary*: Cancer, Pisces, Scorpio

GODS: Babalu Aye, Eleggua, Obatala, Oggun, Osiris, Orunla

GODDESSES: Aphrodite, Isis, Hera, Iris, Ochun

MAGICKAL: Powdered Orris root is a staple in the modern Witch's herb cabinet. So long has the power of Orris root been thought to draw love, that powdered Orris root without any other ingredients is often called Love-Drawing Powder. It is sprinkled lightly on the body after a thorough shower for that purpose, but it will only work if you interact with potential lovers. It is also used in incenses and sachets for this purpose; however, it works best if worn as talc on the body. A tincture of Orris root mixed equally with essential oil of Patchouli is a powerful love-drawing perfume. The scent also works as a mild aphrodisiac on women when worn by men. Do not try to use a tincture of Patchouli as a substitute; it will not work nearly as well as the essential oil of Patchouli/tincture of Orris root mix. Powdered Orris root is used to preserve talismans that were made of fresh fruit. Roll the talisman in the powder and then hang to dry. Simmer Orris root to promote a sense of warm love. If Orris root is simmered in the room where lovemaking occurs, it seems to encourage the furthering of a psychic link between partners.

Ortiga Ancha—*See* Nettle, Greater

Osier—*See* Willow

Osmund the Waterman—*See* Fern

Oval Bachu—*See* Buchu

Our Herb—*See* Basil

Our Lady's Bedstraw—*See* Cleavers (A)

Our Lady's Gloves—*See* Foxglove

Our Lady's Keys—*See* Cowslip

Our Lady's Mint—*See* Spearmint

Our Lady's Tears—*See* Lily of the Valley

Pad'ane—*See* Coltsfoot

Paddock Pipes—See Horsetails

Peony—*Paeonia officinalis/Paeonia Corallina*—Masculine, Sun, Air

Also known as Peaony, Piney

ASTROLOGICAL: *Primary*: Leo; *Secondary*: Aquarius, Gemini, Libra

GODS: Obatala, Oggun

GODDESSES: Yemaya

MEDICAL: (*Paeonia officinalis*) Antispasmodic, Tonic. An infusion is made with 1 ounce of the powdered root in 1 pint of water. Simmer for 30 minutes, strain, and serve 4 ounces at a time.

PART USED: Root

Peony

MAGICKAL: Grown in home or yard, Peony protects against negative energy and, reportedly, storms as well. The root of the Peony is carved into small beads, strung, and worn for these properties as well. Those beads are called "piney beads" because the tradition came from folk who called this plant by its common name, Piney. Reportedly, necklaces as mentioned above as well as carrying the root on one's person will either prevent or cure lunacy. I have found this to be entirely untrue as I have tried it on several nutty girlfriends with absolutely no effect. Maybe I needed a bigger root.

Paigle—*See* Cowslip

Pain de Coucou—*See* Sorrel, Wood

Pain de Porceau—*See* Cyclamen, Ivy-leaved

Pale Mara—*See* Dita Tree

Palmarosa—*Cymbopogon martini*—Feminine, Venus, Water

ASTROLOGICAL: *Primary*: Libra, Taurus; *Secondary*: Cancer, Pisces, Scorpio

GODS: Babalu Aye

MAGICKAL: Essential oil of Palmarosa is diffused to cause a person to be in the right mood to attract love. It does not promote love itself, but causes your mood to become more attractive to the opposite sex.

Palm, Date—*Phoenix datylifera/Phoenix roebelenii*—Masculine, Sun, Air

ASTROLOGICAL: *Primary*: Leo; *Secondary*: Aquarius, Gemini, Libra

GODS: Apollo, Amun Ra, Mercury, Parashurama, Vishnu

GODDESSES: Artemis, Ayizan, Hecate, Isis

MAGICKAL: Dates are eaten by men to improve masculine energies, especially in the realm of sexual energies. They are consumed by women to increase sexual fertility. Palm oil and wood is used for these purposes as well as for protection. Fresh Dates, without sugar, are an excellent treat for iguana. Most love them.

Palsywort—*See* Cowslip

Pank—*See* Agaric Mushroom

Pansy—*See* Heartsease

Papao—*See* Papaya

Papaw—*See* Papaya

Paralysio—*See* Cowslip

Pas d'ane—*See* Coltsfoot

Passion Ivy—*See* Cyclamen, Ivy-leaved

Passion's Dock—*See* Rhubarb, Monk's

Passion Seed—*See* Cumin

Password—*See* Cowslip

Palma Christi—*See* Castor

Palms Christi Root—*See* Castor

Panicaut—*See* Holly, Sea

Papaya—*Carica papaya / Catica papaya / Papya carica*—Feminine, Moon, Water

Also known as Mamao, Tree Melon, Papao, Papaya, Papaw, Paw Paw, Put

ASTROLOGICAL: *Primary*: Cancer; *Secondary*: Cancer, Pisces, Scorpio

MEDICAL: Antiseptic, Stomachic. Papaya juice helps digestion and prevents upset stomachs. Swishing it in your mouth as a gargle will reduce gum bleeding and speed the healing of gums. It is also used as a topical treatment for minor cuts and scrapes. Fresh Papaya can also be applied directly to wounds.

PARTS USED: Fruit, Leaves, Seeds

MAGICKAL: Serve Papaya to strengthen the bonds with those whom you share it with.

NOTE: Virtually every Pagan reference cites this as *Catica papaya* or *Papya carica*, but virtually every source outside of the Pagan community cites it as *Carica papaya*.

Papaya

Papoose Root—*See* Cohosh, Blue

Papyrus—*Cyperus papyrus*—Masculine, Mercury, Air

ASTROLOGICAL: *Primary*: Gemini, Virgo; *Secondary*: Aquarius, Gemini, Libra

MAGICKAL: Paper made from woven Papyrus will strengthen any spell calling on Egyptian gods and goddesses or when traditional Egyptian magick is being used in conjunction with the written word. Unfortunately, it is often costly and hard to find.

Parsley—*Petroselinum crispum/Petroselinum sativum*—Masculine, Mercury, Air

Also known as Devil's Oatmeal, Percely, Persele, Persil, Petersilie, Petroselinum, Rock Parsley

ASTROLOGICAL: *Primary*: Gemini, Virgo; *Secondary*: Aquarius, Gemini, Libra

GODDESSES: Ochun, Persephone

MEDICAL: Diuretic (mild), Stimulant, Tonic. Relief from bad breath can be had by chewing fresh Parsley. This may be why the tradition of including it with a meal has survived so many years. It also promotes weight loss, helps with kidney pain, and acts as a very mild stimulant. The weight loss is probably temporary because Parsley is a mild diuretic. Including Parsley in daily meals will strengthen the immune system and act as a mild tonic. Rubbing fresh Parsley on insect bites will lesson the itch, pain, and redness. To cleanse the kidneys, make a warm water infusion of fresh Parsley. Simmer for 30 minutes and then let stand until cool. Strain and serve over ice. Drink several cups per day for several days. This will also help with arthritis.

PARTS USED: Leaves

MAGICKAL: When eaten, Parsley promotes love, fidelity, and fertility. When worn, it is protective. The tradition of placing Parsley on a plate of food is not just for looks; it has long been believed that doing so will protect the food from both physical and magickal contamination. It is also placed there to promote tips, as the stirrings of lust often cause a person to be more generous. In the bath, Parsley is used for purification. It is also used in the lustral bath prior to Samhain rituals or the Rite of Persephone.

Parsley

Partyke—*See* Loosestrife, Purple

Pasque Flower—*See* Anemone

Passe Flower—*See* Anemone

Passerina—*See* Chickweed

Passion Flower—*Passiflora incarnata*—Feminine, Venus, Water

Also known as Apricot Vine, Granadilla, Grenadille, Maracoc, Maypop(s), Passion Vine

ASTROLOGICAL: *Primary*: Libra, Taurus; *Secondary*: Cancer, Pisces, Scorpio

MEDICAL: Nervine, Narcotic, Sedative. The chemical effects are primarily due to the content of harmine and similar alkaloids. A safer way to use it is in a warm water infusion. Provides mild relief from pain and brings on sleep.

PART USED: Dried Herb

MAGICKAL: Grown in the home, Passion Flower is calming. Dried and carried, it is used for the same purpose.

Passion Flower

GENERAL: Harvesting for medicinal purposes should only take place after the berries have matured.

Passion Fruit—*Passiflora endulis*—Feminine, Moon, Water

ASTROLOGICAL: *Primary*: Cancer; *Secondary*: Cancer, Pisces, Scorpio

MAGICKAL: Shared during a family meal, Passion Fruit will promote a feeling of warmth. Served as part of a romantic meal, it promotes a sense of spiritual union and passionate love.

Passion's Dock—*See* Rhubarb, Monk's

Passion Vine—*See* Passion Flower

Password—*See* Primrose

Pastel—*See* Woad

Patchouli—*Pogostemon cablin/Pogostemon patchouli*—Feminine, Saturn, Earth

Also known as Kablin, Patchouly, Pucha-Pot

ASTROLOGICAL: *Primary*: Aquarius, Capricorn; *Secondary*: Capricorn, Taurus, Virgo

GODS: Bacchus, Shango, Dionysus, Herne, Obatala, Oggun, Set

GODDESS: Ochun

MEDICAL: Stimulant (mild), Prophylactic. In the Middle and Far East, Patchouli herb has been prescribed as a preventative measure against disease. In the Middle East it has been recommended to prevent conception.

PART USED: Herb

MAGICKAL: The scent of Patchouli promotes lust in the physical order alone. Although often combined with other ingredients to draw love, the nature of Patchouli is such that it is also used in spells to cause separation. Such is the case in Voodoo rites where Patchouli is used to stir lust while one is parted from his or her love. The powdered leaf is a substitute for graveyard dust, but only in spells designed to bring money. In those spells, Patchouli is used for its rich connection to the Earth in both sight and smell. Essential oil of Patchouli has a rich, deep earthy scent. It is diffused to attract women and to heighten lust. In women, it seems to lower sexual inhibitions, and in men it seems to lower anxiety and concerns over performance, thus improving the enjoyment for both sexes. I believe this is why Patchouli is used in money-drawing oils, especially for people in sales. It does seem as if sex sells.

Patchouly—*See* Patchouli

Patience Dock—*See* Rhubarb, Monk's

Pausinystalia—*See* Yohimbe

Paw Paw—*See* Papaya

Pea—*Pisum sativum*—Feminine, Venus, Earth

MAGICKAL: Eating peas will reportedly open one's heart to new love.

Peach—*Prunus persica/Amygdalis Persica/Persica vulgaris*—Feminine, Venus, Water

Also known as Fuzzy Fruit

ASTROLOGICAL: *Primary*: Libra, Taurus; *Secondary*: Cancer, Pisces, Scorpio

MEDICAL: Demulcent, Diuretic, Expectorant, Sedative. An infusion is made with 1 pint of water and either 1 ounce of the leaves or 1/2 ounce of the root. Simmer for 30 minutes, strain, and serve 4 ounces at a time.

PARTS USED: Leaves, Root, Fruit

MAGICKAL: Peach, especially sweetened with honey or in a pie, will reportedly heighten love and increase a woman's fertility. Peach pits can be used as a personal talisman of protection. Dry three pits and drill a hole wide enough for a cord in each; string them on a black cord and wear as a necklace. The wood of a peach tree is sometimes used in the creation of wands in some traditions. However, their feminine nature makes this less than an ideal choice considering the symbolism usually associated with Wiccan ritual.

Peach

Peanut—*Arachea hypogaea*—Feminine, Jupiter, Earth

ASTROLOGICAL: *Primary*: Pisces, Sagittarius; *Secondary*: Capricorn, Taurus, Virgo

GODS: Ganesa

MAGICKAL: Eating Peanuts will open the pathways to prosperity and fortune.

Peanut

Pear—*Pyrus communis*—Feminine, Venus, Water

ASTROLOGICAL: *Primary*: Libra, Taurus; *Secondary*: Cancer, Pisces, Scorpio

MEDICAL: Diuretic. Pear fruit acts as a diuretic. Eating a diet rich in Pears will prevent gout.

PART USED: Fruit

MAGICKAL: Pear fruit is considered to be a mild aphrodisiac and prosperity enabler.

Pearl Moss—*See* Moss, Irish

Pear, Prickly—*Opuntia spp.*—Masculine, Mars, Fire

ASTROLOGICAL: *Primary*: Aries, Scorpio; *Secondary*: Aries, Leo, Sagittarius

MAGICKAL: Used and consumed in rites for protection.

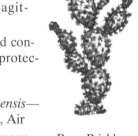

Pear, Prickly

Pecan—*Carya illinoensis*—Masculine, Mercury, Air

ASTROLOGICAL: *Primary*: Gemini, Virgo; *Secondary*: Aquarius, Gemini, Libra

MAGICKAL: Pecan shells are sometimes used in prosperity incense. Eaten, Pecan nuts are said to increase prosperity and help to secure current jobs against loss. Should your company be downsizing, eating Pecans might save a few of the hours your superiors think need to be cut or even your job itself.

Peepul Tree—*See* Bodhi

Peggle—*See* Cowslip

Pennyroyal—*Mentha pulegium/Hedeoma pulegiodes*—Masculine, Mars, Fire

Also known as European Pennyroyal, Lurk-in-the-Ditch, Mosquito Plant, Organ Broth, Organs, Organ Tea, Piliolerian, Pulegium, Run-by-the-Ground, Squaw Mint, Pudding Grass, Piliolerial, Tick Weed

WARNING: Pennyroyal or its smoke should never be handled by a woman who thinks she might be pregnant, is pregnant, or is nursing.

ASTROLOGICAL: *Primary*: Aries, Scorpio; *Secondary*: Aries, Leo, Sagittarius

GODS: Shango, Obatala

GODDESSES: Demeter, Yemaya

MEDICAL: (*Mentha pulegium*) Abortifacient, Antispasmodic, Carminative, Diaphoretic, Diuretic, Emmenagogue, Nervine, Stimulant. A warm water infusion of the herb is made with 1 ounce of the herb in 1 pint of water. Simmer for 30 minutes and serve 4 ounces at a time. Pennyroyal will cause uterine contractions and will aid in bringing on menstruation and labor. However, anyone who recommends it for inducing labor without a doctor's approval is a wing nut. Pennyroyal is probably the most commonly used abortifacient in the Pagan community. Ignore such references. Setting aside any reference to Wicca as a fertility religion, the truth is that while this plant may have been used to cause abortions when abortions were not legal, it was not without large risks. Today, there are legal and safer alternatives. I would never encourage a person to have an abortion, but if you are considering such an action, please consult a doctor at your local medical facility (not Super Wicca Man at your local coffee shop).

Pennyroyal

PART USED: Herb

MAGICKAL: Pennyroyal is an ingredient used for making incense to honor Demeter. Bundles of its fresh branches, tied as one would a smudge stick, are used to sprinkle Wiccan holy water in rights honoring Demeter. On occasion, similar bundles are burned as smudge sticks for the same purpose.

Pied-de-Lion—*See* Lady's Mantle

Pelican Flower—*See* Snakeroot

Pensee—*See* Heartsease

Pentaphyllon—*See* Five-Finger Grass

Peote's Jessamine—*See* Jasmine

Pepper-and-Salt—*See* Shepherd's Purse

Pepper, Black—*Piper nigrum*—Masculine, Mars, Fire

Also known as Piper

ASTROLOGICAL: *Primary*: Aries, Scorpio; *Secondary*: Aries, Leo, Sagittarius

GODS: Shango, Horus the Elder, Mars, Montu, Oko

MEDICAL: Carminative (fruit), Febrifuge (fruit), Stimulant (root), Tonic (root)

PARTS USED: Dried unripe fruit, Root

MAGICKAL: Pepper is used to drive out baneful energy, especially in food. Essential oil of Black Pepper is diffused to sharpen both cognitive and physical functions as well as to enhance and elevate personal courage. Although it might seem like you would sneeze if you do so, keeping the essential oil with you for a job interview will greatly enhance the outcome should you need a boost of courage. Simply inhale its scent a few times before the interview. Works great for first dates or to bring on the courage necessary to ask for that first date.

Peppermint—*Mentha piperita*—Masculine, Mercury, Fire

Also known as Brandy Mint, Lammint

ASTROLOGICAL: *Primary*: Gemini, Virgo; *Secondary*: Aries, Leo, Sagittarius

GODS: Babalu Aye, Shango, Eleggua, Obatala, Oko, Pluto

GODDESS: Ochun

MEDICAL: Antispasmodic, Astringent, Carminative, Stimulant, Stomachic, Tonic. Essential oil of Peppermint and Almond oil makes for a fantastic cure for congestion and sore feet. The trick is getting the ratio right. It will vary depending on skin sensitivity. Try 1/2 dram essential oil of peppermint to 1 cup of Almond oil. Increase or decrease the amount of Peppermint essential oil as needed. For congestion, rub into chest and back.

Peppermint

For sore feet, rub into the soles and backs of feet. Peppermint tea is an excellent choice for after-work relaxation. Will also settle the digestive system and fight back heartburn. A warm water infusion of Peppermint helps to clear the chest and eases the aches and pains of the common cold while settling the stomach. Works to relieve very mild headaches.

PARTS USED: Herb, Oil

MAGICKAL: A very strong infusion of Peppermint will strengthen love when used to wash your partner's feet after a long day on them. It is also a refreshing wash for sponge-bathing your partner, but do not use it near the genitals unless you and your partner are willing to experiment with infusion strengths. If you are both willing to experiment, it can be a very erotic experience. Essential oil of Peppermint is diffused to clear and focus the cognitive mind. It is also diluted and used as massage oil on the bottom of a person's feet to invigorate both mind and body.

Percely—*See* Parsley

☠ **Periwinkle**—*See List*—Feminine, Venus, Water

    Greater Periwinkle—*Vinca major*

    Lesser Periwinkle—*Vinca minor*

    Also known as Blue Buttons, Blue Dots, Centocchiio, Devil's Eye, Hundred Eyes, Joy on the Ground, Sorcerer's Violet

    Madagascar Periwinkle—*Vinca rosea/Lochnera rosea*

ASTROLOGICAL: *Primary*: Libra, Taurus; *Secondary*: Cancer, Pisces, Scorpio

MAGICKAL: By itself, Periwinkle is carried to attract money and to protect. It is sometimes scattered outside the home for the same purpose. However, this herb is rarely used alone and is instead just one of the ingredients found in much incense for money and protection.

GENERAL: Periwinkle is occasionally listed as Oleander, due to an incorrect citation made in the book *Grieve's Modern Herbal* and the books that later built on that reference. If you encounter a reference to Periwinkle, it will usually be referring to Lesser Periwinkle (*Vinca minor*).

Perennial Flax—See Flax, Perennial

Persea—*See* Avocado

Persele—*See* Parsley

Persil—*See* Parsley

Persimmon—*Diospyros virginiana*—Feminine, Venus, Water

ASTROLOGICAL: *Primary*: Libra, Taurus; *Secondary*: Cancer, Pisces, Scorpio

MEDICAL: Nervine. Eating the fruit will ease depression.

PART USED: Fruit

MAGICKAL: Persimmons are used in general luck-drawing mixtures. The fruit is consumed to promote contentedness.

Personata—*See* Burdock

Pestilenzkraut—*See* Rue, Goat's

Pesleporis—*See* Avens

Petersilie—*See* Parsley

Peter's Staff—*See* Mullein

Petitgrain—*See* Orange, Bitter

Petroselinum—*See* Parsley

Pettymorell—*See* Spikenard, American

Petty Mugget—*See* Cleavers (A)

Petty Mulleins—*See* Cowslip

Pewterwort—*See* Horsetails

Pheasant's Eye—*See* Hellebore, False

Philanthropium—*See* Burdock

Philanthropos—*See* Agrimony

Philtron—*See* Carrot

Phu—*See* Valerian

Phytolacca Berry—*See* Pokeweed

Phytolaque—*See* Pokeweed

Pick-Pocket—*See* Shepherd's Purse

Pick-Purse—*See* Shepherd's Purse

Pigeon Berry—*See* Pokeweed

Pigeon's Grass—*See* Vervain

Pigeonwood—*See* Vervain

Pigweed—*See* Knotgrass and Purslane, Golden

Pigrush—*See* Knotgrass

Pilot Weed—*See* Compass Plant

Pilewort—*See* Celandine, Lesser

Piliolerian—*See* Pennyroyal

Pill-Bearing Spurge—*See* Spurges

Pimpernel, Scarlet—*Anagallis arvensis*—Masculine, Mercury, Air
Also known as Adder's-Eyes, Bipinella, Poor Man's Weatherglass, Shepherd's Barometer
ASTROLOGICAL: *Primary*: Gemini, Virgo; *Secondary*: Aquarius, Gemini, Libra
MEDICAL: Diaphoretic, Diuretic, Expectorant. An infusion is made with 1 ounce of the herb in 1 pint of water. Simmer for 30 minutes, strain, and serve 4 ounces at a time. This infusion is sometimes given for relief from depression and similar ailments.
PART USED: Herb
MAGICKAL: Why was that do-gooder's name the Scarlet Pimpernel? Well, it could have had something to do with lore that states that if you rub the Scarlet Pimpernel against the blade of a sword or knife, that blade will refuse to do evil. Scarlet Pimpernel was also carried for protection, especially from bladed weapons that had not been rubbed with Scarlet Pimpernel. If you can find it, this is an excellent herb to rub the athame or sword for ritual purification. It can be used to make an infusion for floor wash, but is is not a great idea to use it in your bath. It tends to cause skin rash.

Pinang—*See* Betel Nut

Pine—*See List*—Masculine, Mars, Air
ASTROLOGICAL: *Primary*: Aries, Scorpio; *Secondary*: Aquarius, Gemini, Libra
GODS: Attis, Dionysus, Bacchus, Shango, Eleggua, Faunus, Green Man, Herne, Obatala, Pan, Priapus, Silvanus
GODDESSES: Artemis, Ariadne, Astarte, Cybele, Erigone, Fauna, Rhea, Venus, Yemaya
CELTIC TREE CALENDAR (Alim)—December 23
Some of the many kinds of pine include:

> **Scot's Pine**—*Pinus sylvestris*
> MEDICAL: Diuretic, Irritant, Rubefacient
> PARTS USED: Inner bark
> **Larch Pine**—*Pinus larix*
> MEDICAL: Astringent, Diuretic, Expectorant, Stimulant
> PARTS USED: Inner Bark
> **White Pine**—*Pinus strobus*

MEDICAL: Demulcent, Diuretic, Expectorant
PART USED: Inner bark
MAGICKAL: Pinecones are often used on the Wiccan altar to represent our Lord, the Masculine principle of our soul, and all things masculine. Should this Pinecone be wild crafted on the day of Summer Solstice, it is said to be of particular power. Eating Pine nuts is said to increase ones ability to practice projective/masculine magick. So eating Pine nuts is a common practice before attempting to cause sudden change or while working with

Pine

matters connected to both air and fire. Pine needles are sometimes used as purification incense. Essential oil of Pine is used to invigorate the body.

GENERAL: Pines are variously known as pitch, Pine nuts, or rosin depending on the part or concentration type. Pitch, rosin, and turpentine should not be taken internally. Although Pine needles and nuts are generally considered safe for human consumption in reasonable amounts, like so many extracts and concentrates, pitch, rosin, and turpentine are entirely too strong for consumption. Pine resin is used to make both oil of turpentine and rosin. It is sometimes mixed with Camphor and Beeswax to create a natural balm used much the way Vicks VapoRub is. When the oil of turpentine is distilled out of the tree resin, what remains is called rosin, from which pitch is made. You may run into references calling for pitch. Chances are you will not be able to purchase true pitch, but you can use either ground pine needles or rosin. Rosin is available at shops that sell musical instruments because it is used to treat the strings of several stringed instruments.

Pine, Norfolk Island—*Auricaria excela*—Masculine, Mars, Fire

ASTROLOGICAL: *Primary*: Aries, Scorpio; *Secondary*: Aries, Leo, Sagittarius

MAGICKAL: Grown near the home, the Norfolk Island Pine protects and blesses that home with prosperity. It is not used in money spells, but instead in the spells that bring plenty.

Piney—*See* Peony

Pineapple—*Ananas comusus*—Masculine, Sun, Fire

ASTROLOGICAL: *Primary*: Leo; *Secondary*: Aries, Leo, Sagittarius

MAGICKAL: Dried Pineapple fruit is carried to draw luck. It is also a tasty treat, so it is eaten for this same purpose in both dried and fresh form. Pineapple is an antiaphrodisiac, especially the juice. It is consumed to help distance the cognitive mind from the yearnings of the body such that intellectual decisions can be made. Although it decreases lust, it increases a sense of love and well-being.

Pine Nuts—*See* Pine

Ping Lang—*See* Betel Nut

Pinkaou—*See* Buchu

Pink-Eyed-John—*See* Heartsease

Pink-O'-the-Eye—*See* Heartsease

Pinks—*See* Potato

Piper—*See* Pepper, Black

Piperidge Bush—*See* Barberry, Common

Pipsissewa—*Chimaphila umbellata / Pyrola umbellata*

Also known as Butter Winter, False Wintergreen, Ground Holly, King's Cure, Love-in-Winter, Price's Pine, Princess Pine, Rheumatism Weed, Wintergreen

MEDICAL: Alterative, Astringent, Diuretic, Tonic. A decoction is made with 1 ounce of the dried leaves in 1 quart of water. Reduce by boiling to 1 pint, strain, and serve 4 ounces at a time.

PART USED: Leaves

MAGICKAL: Pipsissewa is carried to attract money and sometimes is an ingredient in spirit drawing incense. See Sweet Grass.

NOTE: Despite its folk names, Pipsissewa should not be confused with Wintergreen (*Gaultheria procumbens*).

Pipul—See Bodhi

Pistachio—*Pistachia vera*—Masculine, Mercury, Air

ASTROLOGICAL: *Primary*: Gemini, Virgo; *Secondary*: Aquarius, Gemini, Libra

MAGICKAL: Reportedly, eating Pistachios will break a love spell that has been cast upon you. I believe this is because Pistachios (like most nuts) fortify the body, thus strengthening cognitive functions and allowing one to think more clearly. I conclude that Pistachios do not break love spells, but they assist one in making an informed decision about the selection of a mate. Remember, love is sometimes thought to be a matter of the body and sometimes thought to be a matter of the soul, but true love is a matter of all three: mind, body, and soul. On the other hand, Pistachios reportedly encourage a sense of love when consumed. Perhaps the lore is that eating Pistachios will break the influence of a bad apple such that your heart will open to better options.

Pistachio

Pitch—*See* Pine

Petit Poureau—*See* Chives

Plum—*Prunus domesticus*—Feminine, Venus, Water

See also Plum, Wild

ASTROLOGICAL: *Primary*: Libra, Taurus; *Secondary*: Cancer, Pisces, Scorpio

MAGICKAL: Use Plums in home made meals and share with someone you love. They will strengthen and encourage all forms of love, including romantic love and kinship. Exceptionally good at strengthening the love shared by parents and children when prepared by the former and served to the latter, especially during the Yule season when warm treats are well received. Also works as a mild aphrodisiac.

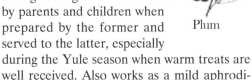

Plum

Plumeria—*See* Frangipani

Plumrocks—*See* Cowslip

Plum, Wild—*Prunus americana*—Feminine, Venus, Water

ASTROLOGICAL: *Primary*: Libra, Taurus; *Secondary*: Cancer, Pisces, Scorpio

MAGICKAL: Wild Plum wood is the ideal material to make prayer sticks and wands. Although the choice of wood is usually based on local trees, this practice is found in many cultures, including the pre-Columbian American Dakota and such seemingly faraway people as Tibetan Buddhists.

Pocan—*See* Pokeweed

☠ **Poison Lily**—*See* Blue Flag

☠**Poison Flag**—*See* Blue Flag

☠**Poison Hemlock**—*See* Hemlock

☠**Poison Ivy**—*See* Ivy, Poison

☠**Poison Parsley**—*See* Hemlock

☠**Poison Tobacco**—*See* Henbane

☠**Poison Vine**—*See* Ivy, Poison

Poke—*See* Pokeweed

Poke Berry—*See* Pokeweed

Pokeberry Root—*See* Pokeweed

☠**Pokeweed**—*See List*—Masculine, Mars, Fire

Latin names and varieties include *Phytolacca decandra, Blitum Americanum, Phytolacca Americana, Phytolacca Bacca, Phytolacca Phytolaccae Radix, Phytolacca Vulgaris*

Also known as American Nightshade, American Spinach, Amerikanische Scharlachbeere, Cancer Root, Chongras, Coakum, Cokan, Crowberry, Fear's Grape, Phytolacca Berry, Pigeon Berry, Garget, Herbe de la Laque, Jalap, Kermesbeere, Mechoacan du Canada, Morelle a Grappes, Phytolacca Root, Phytolaque, Pigeon Berry, Pocan, Poke, Poke Berry, Pokeberry Root, Poke Root, Polk Root,

Raisin d'Amerique, Red-Ink Plant, Scoke, Skoke, Virginian Poke

ASTROLOGICAL: *Primary*: Aries, Scorpio; *Secondary*: Aries, Leo, Sagittarius

GODDESS: Athena

MEDICAL: Emetic, Laxative, Purgative, Narcotic. An incredibly powerful laxative. Misuse may bring death. Now do you really want your obituary to state that you shit yourself to death?

PARTS USED: Berries, Root

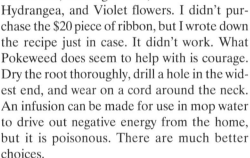

Pokeweed

MAGICKAL: In Salem, Mass., I once saw a ribbon that was said to bring back things that are lost, especially pets. I asked why I would believe such a thing, and they told me it was soaked in an infusion of Pokeweed, Galangal root, Hydrangea, and Violet flowers. I didn't purchase the $20 piece of ribbon, but I wrote down the recipe just in case. It didn't work. What Pokeweed does seem to help with is courage. Dry the root thoroughly, drill a hole in the widest end, and wear on a cord around the neck. An infusion can be made for use in mop water to drive out negative energy from the home, but it is poisonous. There are much better choices.

Poke Root—*See* Pokeweed

Polar Plant—*See* Compass Plant and Rosemary

Polecatweed—*See* Cabbage, Skunk

Polk Root—*See* Pokeweed

Polypody, Common—*See* Fern

Polypody of the Oak—*See* Fern

Poor Man's Parmacettie—*See* Shepherd's Purse

Poor Man's Treacle—*See* Garlic

Poor Man's Weatherglass—*See* Pimpernel, Scarlet

Poplar—*See* Aspen, American

Poplar Buds—*See* Balm of Gilead

NOTE: In the context of this reference, when a reference is made to Poplar Buds, that reference is referring to Balm of Gilead (*Populus balsamifera*) and not the bud of the Poplar (*Populus tremuloides*) or Aspen (*Populus grandidentata*). However, other references might not use the same terms.

Popotillo—*See* Ma Huang

Poppy, Red—*Papaver Rhoeas*—Feminine, Moon, Water

Also known as Corn Rose, Corn Poppy, Flores Rhoeados, Headache

ASTROLOGICAL: *Primary*: Cancer; *Secondary*: Cancer, Pisces, Scorpio

GODS: Agni, Babalu Aye (seed), Hades, Oko (seed), Olocun (seed), Pluto, Vulcan

GODDESSES: Yemaya (seed)

MEDICAL: Narcotic (mild), Sedative. An infusion of 1 ounce of the flowers in 1 pint of water is used. Simmer for 30 minutes, strain, and serve 4 ounces at a time.

PARTS USED: Flowers, Seeds

MAGICKAL: Both seeds and flower petals can be used in cooking for a simple lust potion without guilt, as the narcotic quality of Red Poppy is negligible. Poppy seeds promote reproductive fertility and love when eaten.

Poppy, Red

☠**Poppy, White**—*Papaver somniferum*—Feminine, Moon, Water

Also known as Mawseed, Opium Poppy

ASTROLOGICAL: *Primary:* Cancer; *Secondary*: Cancer, Pisces, Scorpio

GODS: Agni, Anubis, Hades, Kephra, Matsya, Neptune, Pluto, Saturn, Vishnu

GODDESSES: Bhavani, Cybele, Demeter, Mut, Nephthys, Rhea

MEDICAL: Anodyne, Antispasmodic, Astringent, Diaphoretic, Expectorant, Hypnotic, Narcotic, Sedative. Raw opium is extracted from the White Poppy. From that raw opium comes morphine, codeine, and heroin. With great amounts of conflict in the Middle East, this beautiful creature has become the subject of much controversy and propaganda. The truth behind the misinformation is that in the hands of a competent physician this is a powerful tool against pain.

PARTS USED: Capsules, Flowers.

MAGICKAL: Magickally speaking, if you encounter a reference to the White Poppy, try substituting Red Poppy. Not only is White Poppy legal and available, but aside from the strong narcotic effect, the two plants are relatively interchangeable.

GENERAL: Though history seems to favor the idea that it was introduced to the Western world by Arabic medicine, there is clear record that the Greek and Romans both harvested this valuable plant.

Porillon—*See* Daffodil

Portugal Orange—*See* Orange, Sweet

Potato—*Solanum tuberosum*—Feminine, Moon, Earth

Also known as Blue Eyes, Flukes, Lapstones, Leather Jackets, Murphies, No Eyes, Pinks, Red Eyes, Rocks, Taters, Tatties, Tubers

ASTROLOGICAL: *Primary*: Cancer; *Secondary*: Capricorn, Taurus, Virgo

MEDICAL: Slice in half and rub on the skin to stop the itching of eczema, mild burns, and other skin ailments.

MAGICKAL: Despite the ramblings of modern Pagan authors concerning ancient Irish Potato cults, the Potato was not introduced to Europe until the 16th century when it was praised as a cure-all (especially for impotency). It lost favor in the 18th century when the Church decided that it must be an abomination because it was not mentioned in the Christian Bible. One wonders why Corn (Maize) was not pronounced evil as well. Eating Potatoes lends protection and increases empathic abilities.

The Complete History of Medicine

2000 B.C.E.: Here, eat this root.

1000 C.E.: That root is Pagan. You will go to hell if you eat it. Say this prayer.

1800 C.E.: That prayer is superstition. Drink this potion.

1950 C.E.: Don't drink that snake oil. Take this pill.

1980 C.E.: That pill will just treat the symptoms. Here, take this antibiotic.

1995 C.E.: The germs are becoming resistant to antibiotics because they are overprescribed. Don't take anything.

2000 C.E.: The New Age rises: Here, eat this root.

Prickly Ash—*See* Ash, Prickly

Prickly-Toothed Shield Fern—Say that three times fast and then *see* Fern

Piliolerial—*See* Pennyroyal

Piss-a-Bell—*See* Dandelion

Plantain, Buck's Horn—*Plantago Coronopus*—Feminine, Venus, Earth

Also known as Buckshorne, Cornu Cervinum, Hartshorne, Herba Stella, Herb Ivy

ASTROLOGICAL: *Primary*: Libra, Taurus; *Secondary*: Capricorn, Taurus, Virgo

Plantain, Common—*Plantago major*—Feminine, Venus, Earth

Also known as Broad-leaved Plantain, Cuckoo's Bread, Englishman's Foot, Ripple

Grass, Slan-Lus, Snakeweed, Waybread, Weybroed, White Man's Foot

ASTROLOGICAL: *Primary*: Libra, Taurus; *Secondary*: Capricorn, Taurus, Virgo

MEDICAL: Astringent (mild), Deobstruent, Diuretic, Refrigerant. An infusion of the roots and leaves acts as a diuretic. Also helps in the treatment of diarrhea in children and young adults. A decoction of Plantain leaves is used topically to fight mild infection associated with cuts and scrapes.

PARTS USED: Leaves, Roots

Plantain, Fruit—See Banana

Plantain, Hoary—*Plantago media*—Feminine, Venus, Earth

ASTROLOGICAL: *Primary*: Libra, Taurus; *Secondary*: Capricorn, Taurus, Virgo

MEDICAL: Demulcent, Laxative. A decoction of whole milk is employed.

PART USED: Seeds

Plantain, Ispaghul—*Plantago ovata/Plantago decumbens/Plantago Ispaghula*—Feminine, Venus, Earth

Also known as Spogel Seed

ASTROLOGICAL: *Primary*: Libra, Taurus; *Secondary*: Capricorn, Taurus, Virgo

MEDICAL: Laxative (mild). A decoction of whole milk is employed.

PART USED: Seeds

Plantain, Psyllium—*Plantago Psyllium*—Feminine, Venus, Earth

Also known as Barguthi, Fleaseed, Psyllion, Psyllios, Psyllium Seeds

ASTROLOGICAL: *Primary*: Libra, Taurus; *Secondary*: Capricorn, Taurus, Virgo

Plantain, Ribwort—*Plantago lanceolata*—Feminine, Venus, Earth

Also known as Black Jack, Black Plantain, Cocks, Costa Canina, Hen Plant, Jackstraw, Kemps, Lamb's Tongue, Long Plantain, Quinquenervia, Ribwort, Ripple Grass, Snake Plantain, Wendles

ASTROLOGICAL: *Primary*: Libra, Taurus; *Secondary*: Capricorn, Taurus, Virgo

Plantain, Sea—*Plantago maritimo*—Feminine, Venus, Water

Also known as Sheep's Herb

ASTROLOGICAL: *Primary*: Libra, Taurus; *Secondary*: Cancer, Pisces, Scorpio

MEDICAL: Expectorant, Stomachic

PART USED: Herb

Plantain, Water—*Alisma Plantago*—Feminine, Venus, Water

Also known as Mad-Dog Weed

ASTROLOGICAL: *Primary*: Libra, Taurus; *Secondary*: Cancer, Pisces, Scorpio

MEDICAL: Astringent (seeds), Diaphoretic (leaves), Diuretic (leaves)

PARTS USED: Leaves, Seeds

GENERAL: If you have seen the modern herb blends intended to intoxicate, chances are you have seen one of the products reporting to contain "Mad-Dog Weed." Congratulations. You may have spotted one of the funniest marketing tools in the world. While "weed" is a common name for Marijuana, and Mad-Dog Weed might imply that it is intoxicating, the common name of this plant comes from its 19th century use in treating rabies/the bite of a mad dog.

Ploughman's Spikenard—*See* Spikenard, Ploughman's

Pomegranate—*Punica granatum*—Masculine, Mercury, Fire

Also known as Carthage Apple, Cortex granati, Cortezade Granada, Ecore de Granade, Granatwurzelrindle, Grenadier, Malicorio, Malum Punicum, Melogranato, Malicorio, Scorzo del Melogranati, Pound Garnet

Pomegranate

ASTROLOGICAL: *Primary*: Gemini, Virgo; *Secondary*: Aries, Leo, Sagittarius

GODDESSES: Ceres, Demeter, Hera, Persephone, Sekhmet

MEDICAL: Astringent (fruit), Demulcent (seeds), Refrigerant (fruit), Taeniafuge (bark)

PARTS USED: Bark, Fruit, Seeds

MAGICKAL: Pomegranate seeds are eaten to increase human fertility, but predominantly in women only. Before eating each seed, visualize yourself conceiving a healthy child. Perhaps it is this connection with life that also brings its connection to death. Pomegranate seeds are a favorite food at Samhain and during other rites intended to connect the living with those who have gone before (especially loved ones).

Pongo—*See* Agaric Mushroom

Pong—*See* Agaric Mushroom

Poor Man's Treacle—*See* Shallot

Pound Garnet—*See* Pomegranate

Pretty Betsy—*See* Valerian, Red-Spur

Prickly Broom—*See* Gorse

Prickly Pear—*See* Pear, Prickly

Priest's Crown—*See* Dandelion

Primrose—*Primula vulgaris*—Feminine, Venus, Earth

Also known as Butter Rose, English Cowslip, Password

ASTROLOGICAL: *Primary*: Libra, Taurus; *Secondary*: Capricorn, Taurus, Virgo

GODDESS: Freya

MEDICAL: Antispasmodic, Astringent, Emetic, Nervine, Vermifuge. To fight depression and relax the mind, make warm water infusion of 3 teaspoons of the herb, simmer for 30 minutes, strain, sweeten with honey, and serve hot.

Primrose

This infusion or the fresh flower helps to fight high blood pressure, especially when the high blood pressure was brought on by anxiety. High blood sugar is sometimes treated with either infusion or fresh flowers and leaves. However, make sure you check with your doctor before using this or any other herb to control diabetes.

PARTS USED: Herb, Root

MAGICKAL: When carried by women, Primrose will attract men. When grown in the garden, it will attract all orders of nature spirits, including fairies and sprites.

Primrose, Yellow Evening—*Oenothera hookeri*

MAGICKAL: The whole root of the Yellow Evening Primrose is an excellent charm for attracting deer. Scattering the chopped root will attract deer to the location of the scattering. Used as a hunting charm by primitive cultures, using the root for bow hunting is an excellent modern adaptation; however, using it as yet another edge with firearms might be going a bit too far.

Premorse Scabious—*See* Scabious, Devil's Bit

Prickly Lettuce—*See* Lettuce, Wild

Prideweed—*See* Fleabane, Canadian

Princess Flower—*See* Amaranth

Price's Pine—*See* Pipsissewa

Princess Pine—*See* Pipsissewa

Pseudosarsa—*See* Sarsaparilla

Psyllion—*See* Plantain, Psyllium

Psyllios—*See* Plantain, Psyllium

Psyllium Plantain—*See* Plantain, Psyllium

Psyllium Seeds—*See* Plantain, Psyllium

Pucha-Pot—*See* Patchouli

Pucker Fruit—*See* Lemon

Pudding Grass—*See* Pennyroyal

Puffball—*See* Dandelion

Pukeweed—*See* Lobelia

Pulegium—*See* Pennyroyal

Pumpkin—*Cucurbita pepo*—Feminine, Moon, Earth
ASTROLOGICAL: *Primary*: Cancer; *Secondary*: Capricorn, Taurus, Virgo
MEDICAL: Tonic. Eating Pumpkin seeds on a daily basis will help with problems of the prostate gland. A warm water infusion of the dried seeds is a good tonic for the prostate and bladder. For men who are healthy in this department, drinking a good stiff cup of Pumpkin seed tea is a good weekly tonic.
PART USED: Seeds
MAGICKAL: Eating Pumpkin seeds will increase a man's sexual desire. Eating any part of the Pumpkin will increase prosperity.

Purging Flax—*See* Flax, Mountain

Purple Archangel—*See* Nettle, Purple Dead

Purple Betony—*See* Wood Betony

Purple Boneset—*See* Gravelroot

Purple Clover—*See* Clover, Red

Purple Dead Nettle—*See* Nettle, Purple Dead

Purple Loosestrife—*See* Loosestrife, Purple

Purple Medic—*See* Alfalfa

Purple Willow Herb—*See* Loosestrife, Purple

Purslane—*See* Purslane, Golden and Purslane, Green

Purslane, Golden—*Portulaca sativa*—Feminine, Moon, Water
Also known as Garden Purslane, Pigweed
ASTROLOGICAL: *Primary*: Cancer; *Secondary*: Cancer, Pisces, Scorpio

MAGICKAL: Sewn into pillows to aid sleep and prevent nightmares. An infusion of Golden Purslane can be used in mop water to bring good fortune and luck to a home.

Purslane, Green—*Portulaca oleracea*—Feminine, Moon, Water
ASTROLOGICAL: *Primary*: Cancer; *Secondary*: Cancer, Pisces, Scorpio
MEDICAL: Diuretic. In a warm water infusion, the herb acts as a diuretic. It is often recommended for relieving mild kidney pains. Although it works in humans as a diuretic, the same infusion is said to relieve diarrhea in goats and other farm animals.
PART USED: Herb
MAGICKAL: Placed in the bottom of backpacks and rucksacks, Green Purslane protects soldier, camper, and hiker.

Pussy Pine—*See* Willow

Pussy Willow—*See* Willow

Put—*See* Papaya

Qadb—*See* Alfalfa

Qoqobala—*See* Chickweed

Quaking Aspen—*See* Aspen, American

Quassia—*Picraena excelsa/Quassia amara/Quassia Lignum*
Also known as Bitter Ash, Bitter Wood
MAGICKAL: Powdered Quassia is used in love-drawing incense.

Quince—*Cydonia vulgaris/Pyrus Cydonia*—Feminine, Saturn, Earth
Also known as Coyne

ASTROLOGICAL: *Primary*: Aquarius, Capricorn; *Secondary*: Capricorn, Taurus, Virgo
GODDESS: Venus

Quince

MAGICKAL: Dried seeds can be carried to protect a marriage. Place an equal number of seeds into a sachet for each member of the marriage. These sachets will protect the marriage. When one partner travels without the other, the other partner's seeds are placed in the sachet of the traveler who promises to return them safely. If a bride and groom share a single Quince at the wedding or reception, their union is said to be blessed. In marriage they are shared to ensure fertility and fidelity; however, always share the same fruit. You can eat more than one, but not so much as one by yourself. See Chapter 6 for a tasty marmalade recipe.

Quinsy Berries—*See* Currant, Black

Qoust—*See* Nutmeg

Queen Ann's Lace—*See* Carrot

Queen Elizabeth Root—*See* Orris

Queen of the Meadow—*See* Meadowsweet

Queen-of-the-Meadow Root—*See* Gravelroot
NOTE: Could also be a reference to the root of the Meadowsweet, which is sometimes called Queen-of-the-Meadow but is usually calling for Gravelroot. On the other hand, Gravelroot is also a common name for the Meadowsweet as well. Good luck figuring this one out without a Latin name!

Quick—*See* Hawthorn

Quickbane—*See* Ash, Mountain

Quinquenervia—*See* Plantain, Ribwort

Rabbit Root—*See* Sarsaparilla

Racznick—*See* Castor

Raccoon Berry—*See* Mandrake and Mandrake, American

Radish—*Raphanus sativus*—Masculine, Mars, Fire
Also known as Rapuns

Radish

ASTROLOGICAL: *Primary*: Aries, Scorpio; *Secondary*: Aries, Leo, Sagittarius
MAGICKAL: Include the Radish root in salad prior to a romantic dinner to stir lust. Will work in cooked dishes, but not as well. Also lends itself to protection.

Radix Viperina—*See* Snakeroot

Rainbow Weed—*See* Loosestrife, Purple

Rain Tree—*See* Ash, Mountain

Raisin d'Amerique—*See* Pokeweed

Ranedj—*See* Coconut

Ran Tree—*See* Ash, Mountain

Rapuns—*See* Radish

Rarajeub—*See* Fleabane, Common

Raspberry—*Rubus Idaeus/Rubus strigosus*—Feminine, Venus, Water
Also known as Bramble of Mount Ida, European Raspberry, Hindberry, Hindbur, Hindbeer, Hindebar, Raspbis, Red Raspberry
WARNING: Never to be used by pregnant women except with the permission of your doctor.
ASTROLOGICAL: *Primary*: Libra, Taurus; *Secondary*: Cancer, Pisces, Scorpio
MEDICAL: Astringent, Stimulant. A warm water infusion of the herb and/or fruit can be used to lessen menstruation pains and cleanse the kidneys. Juice will help as well. The same infusion can be frozen. With a doctor's permission, the resulting ice can be crushed or shaved and given

Raspberry

to a woman in labor to lessen the pain. Many hospitals will welcome this practice, but check with your doctor prior to following this suggestion. Be aware of the fact that Raspberry is a stimulant that may cause the uterus to contract. It should never be used during pregnancy except with a doctor's permission during labor. A warm water infusion of the root makes a fine astringent and antiseptic. It is useful in treating cuts and scrapes.

PARTS USED: Fruit, Leaves

MAGICKAL: Crushed, mixed with honey, and served on toast prior to spending the day with your partner will strengthen the bonds of love and protect the union. Raspberry can be turned into marmalade for the same purpose, but it is more effective (and easier) to simply crush them into honey.

Raspbis—*See* Raspberry

Rattle Pouches—*See* Shepherd's Purse

Rattle Root—*See* Cohosh, Black

Rattlesnake Root—*See* Senega

Rebs—*See* Currant, Red

Red Campion—*See* Bachelor's Buttons

Red Centaury—*See* Centaury

Red Chamomile—*See* Hellebore, False

Red Clover—*See* Clover, Red

Red Cole—*See* Horseradish

Red Cockscomb—*See* Amaranth

Red Dock—*See* Dock, Red

Red-Bearded Sarsaparilla—*See* Sarsaparilla

Red Berry—*See* Ginseng, American

Red Currant—*See* Currant, Red

Red Elm—*See* Elm, Slippery

Red Eyebright—*See* Eyebright

Red Eyes—*See* Potato

Red-Ink Plant—*See* Poke Weed

Red Mathes—*See* Hellebore, False

Red Morocco—*See* Hellebore, False

Red Poppy—*See* Poppy, Red

Red Raspberry—*See* Raspberry

Red River—*See* Snake Root

Red Robin—*See* Knotgrass

Red Root—*See* Bloodroot and New Jersey Tea

Red Sage—*See* Sage, Common

Red-Spur Valerian—*See* Valerian, Red-Spur

Red Valerian—*See* Valerian

Reglisse—*See* Licorice

Regolizia—*See* Licorice

Return-to-Me—*See* Mallow, Blue

Revbielde—*See* Foxglove

Rewe—*See* Rue

Rheumatism Root—*See* Yam, Wild

Rheumatism Weld—*See* Dogbane

Rhizoma Galangae—*See* Galangal

Rhubarb—*See List*—Feminine, Venus, Earth
   English Rhubarb—*Rheum Rhaponticum*
   Also known as Bastard Rhubarb, Garden Rhubarb, Sweet Round-leaved Dock
   MEDICAL: Astringent, Purgative (mild), Stomachic

PARTS USED: Root, Stalk

Turkey Rhubarb—*Rheum palmatum/ Rheum Rhaponticum*

Also known as China Rhubarb, East Indian Rhubarb

MEDICAL: Astringent, Aperient, Purgative, Stomachic, Tonic

PART USED: Root

ASTROLOGICAL: *Primary*: Libra, Taurus; *Secondary*: Capricorn, Taurus, Virgo

MAGICKAL: Rhubarb pie is served to strengthen the fidelity and bond between loving partners; however, it is not generally used to stir first love. Rhubarb root is one of the ingredients used to make Goofer Powder in Voodoo.

Rhubarb

Rhubarb, Monk's—*Rumex alpinus*—Feminine, Venus, Earth

Also known as Herb Patience, Garden Patience, Passion's Dock

ASTROLOGICAL: *Primary*: Libra, Taurus; *Secondary*: Capricorn, Taurus, Virgo

MAGICKAL: A tincture of Monk's Rhubarb root is useful in attracting love and in building passionate relationships that last. To draw a lover to you, place a drop on your left wrist after you bathe each morning, saying as you do:

Patience in my search
for a love that is new
Less in my search
and love won't be true.

Ribs—*See* Currant, Red

Ribwort—*See* Plantain, Ribwort

Ribwort Plantain—See Plantain, Ribwort

Rice—*Oryza sativa*—Masculine, Sun, Air

Also known as Bras, Dhan, Inari, Nirvara

ASTROLOGICAL: *Primary*: Leo; *Secondary*: Aquarius, Gemini, Libra

GODS: Agathos Daimon

GODDESS: Gauri

MAGICKAL: Served as a dish, Rice promotes fertility and a sense of security and calm. Eating Rice-based meals rather than those of other grains will greatly improve your ability to meditate or enter the astral. Rice is also said to increase reproductive fertility and lends itself to protection.

Ripple Grass—*See* Plantain, Common and Plantain, Ribwort

Risp—*See* Currant, Red

Robin-Run-in-the Grass—*See* Cleavers (B)

Robin's Eye—*See* Moss, Hair Cup

Rock Brake/Rockbrake Herb—*See* Fern or Moss, Hair Cup

NOTE: Generally speaking, Rock Brake is a variety of Fern, but Rockbrake Herb is Hair Cup Moss

Rock of Polypody—*See* Fern

Rock Parsley—*See* Parsley

Rocks—*See* Potato

Rocky Mountain Grape—*See* Barberry, Holly-Leaved

Roden-Quicken—*See* Ash, Mountain

Roden-Quicken-Royan—*See* Ash, Mountain

Roman Chamomile—*See* Chamomile, Roman

Roman Laurel—*See* Bay

Root of Life—*See* Ginseng, American

Rose—*Rosa damascena, Rosa centifolia, Rosa spp.*—*See List*

White Rose—Female, Moon, Water

Red Rose—Female, Jupiter, Water

Damascus Rose—Female, Venus, Water

ASTROLOGICAL: *Primary*: Cancer (White), Taurus (Damascus), Sagittarius (Red); *Secondary*: Cancer, Pisces, Scorpio

GODS: Adonis, Cupid, Eros, Harpa-Khruti, Harpocrates, Horus the Elder, Obatala (White), Oggun

GODDESSES: Aurora, Demeter, Hathor, Hulda, Isis, Nike, Ochun (Yellow), Venus

Rose

MEDICAL: A warm water infusion of the flowers (sweeten with honey) is good medicine for the common cold and helps with sinus problems. Rose hips (*Rosa canina*) have the added benefit of a natural shot of vitamin C. Rose hip tea is also good treatment for problems with the bladder.

PARTS USED: Buds, Flowers

MAGICKAL: Dried Rose hips can be drilled and strung on a necklace as a love-drawing charm. Red and pink petals are used in sachet and incense for the same purpose. However, while the scent of Roses does indeed stir feelings of love in both men and women, that same scent will decrease the feeling of lust in a man. An infusion of red and pink Rose petals can be used in the bath for the same purpose. An infusion of white or yellow Rose petals can be consumed to improve psychic and empathic abilities. Adding Rose petals to a dish is not only a great way to add color; it will promote love and a sense of well-being. Essential oil of Rose (called Otto of Rose/ Rose Attar) and Rose absolute are both used for many of the same purposes, but absolute is inferior. Diffuse Rose oil or absolute to encourage lust in women and to overcome some

Rose hips

sexual deficiencies in men. Although it does not act as an aphrodisiac on men, it is reported to increase sperm production and lesson anxiety related to sexual performance. In so doing, it is possible that the aroma of Rose may well cure anxiety-related impotence. Otto of Rose is used to overcome anxiety, and inhibition, and to relieve stress.

Rose-a-Rubie—*See* Hellebore, False

Rose Bay—*See* Oleander

Rose Bay Tree—*See* Oleander

Rose Geranium—*See* Geranium, Rose

Rose Hips—*See* Rose

Rosemary—*Rosemarinus officinalis/ Rosmarinus coronarium*—Masculine, Sun, Fire

Also known as Compass-weed, Compass Plant, Dew of the Sea, Elf Leaf, Guardrobe, Incensier, Libanotis, Polar Plant, Sea Dew

See also Compass Plant as they share many of the same common names.

ASTROLOGICAL: *Primary*: Leo; *Secondary*: Aries, Leo, Sagittarius

GODS: Babalu Aye, Eleggua, Ochosi, Oggun, Oko

GODDESS: Ochun

MEDICAL: (*Rosemarinus officinalis*) Astringent, Diaphoretic, Nervine, Stimulant, Tonic. An alcohol infusion is used to treat heart palpitations, to aid sleep, and decrease headaches. Daily use should not exceed 1/4 ounce of dried leaves or any extract thereof. A warm water infusion of the herb acts as both mild stimulant and muscle relaxer. Regular consumption of Rosemary serves as a general tonic and immune system booster. In large amounts, Rosemary may be toxic. Both alcohol and warm water infusions are good astringents. A good antidepressant can be had with a white wine infusion. Pour 1 pint of white wine over 1 ounce of Rosemary leaves. Allow to stand for three days at room temperature, strain, return to the bottle, and store in the refrigerator. It will be ready after three more days. Dose is one glass after dinner. When smoked in a water pipe, Rosemary assists in relieving a tight chest and helps the patient with breathing difficulties.

PARTS USED: Herb, Oil, Root

MAGICKAL: Rosemary is one of the most often and oldest herbs burned to cleanse a ritual site. For this reason, its quality in smudging Wiccan Circles and homes is rivaled only by Sage. An ideal blending of traditions would be to burn a blend of both Rosemary and Sage for smudging. Branches of Rosemary can be woven into Sage to create smudge sticks, or you can simply blend into loose incense. In the bath, an infusion of Rosemary calls forth the Maiden state in women of all ages as well as a bride's purification. It is the ideal infusion to add to a woman's lustral bath prior to a Beltane rite. Although the loss of virginity is not commonly planned from a religious viewpoint, it is a most sacred rite. With that said, should a woman plan this sacred occasion, Rosemary is an excellent lustral bath beforehand. Rosemary also stirs lust in both men and women. It is often used in cooking for this purpose. When consumed, it increases cognitive ability, opens the heart to love, and speeds both physical and emotional healing. Essential oil of Rosemary is diffused to clear the cognitive mind, improve memory, and soften conversations between men and women. The scent is uplifting, relieves stress, and battles mental fatigue.

Rosemary

Rose Noble—*See* Figwort, Knotted

Rother Weiderich—*See* Loosestrife, Purple

Rough Lemon—*See* Citron

Round-leaved Mint—*See* Mint

Rowan Tree—*See* Ash, Mountain

Roynetree—*See* Ash, Mountain

☠ **Rue**—*Ruta graveolens*—Masculine, Mars, Fire

Also known as Bashoush, Garden Rue, German Rue, Herb-of-Grace, Herbygrass, Hreow, Mother-of-the-Herbs, Rewe, Ruta

WARNING: Do not use if pregnant or nursing

ASTROLOGICAL: *Primary*: Aries, Scorpio; *Secondary*: Aries, Leo, Sagittarius

GODS: Ares, Babalu Aye, Shango, Eleggua, Horus the Elder, Mars, Montu, Obatala

GODDESSES: Aradia, Diana

MEDICAL: Antispasmodic, Emetic (in large doses), Emmenagogue, Stimulant, Stomachic (in small doses)

PART USED: Herb

MAGICKAL: New Orleans-style Voodoo indicates that an infusion of Rue is ideal for bath and floor wash to break spells cast against you. Inhaling the fragrance of fresh Rue clears the mind and assists in cognitive efforts.

Rue, Goat's—*Galega officinalis*—Masculine, Mercury, Air

Also known as French Honeysuckle, Herba Ruta Caprariae, Pestilenzkraut, Rutwica, Lavamana

ASTROLOGICAL: *Primary*: Gemini, Virgo; *Secondary*: Aquarius, Gemini, Libra

MEDICAL: Diaphoretic

PARTS USED: Flowering tops, Leaves

MAGICKAL: Goat's Rue is sometimes sprinkled under the sick bed to aid in healing.

Ruta—*See* Rue

Rag paper—*See* Mullein

Rape Mustard—*See* Mustard, Rape

Red Cedar—*See* Cedar, Red

Rheumatism Weed—*See* Pipsissewa

Rutwica—*See* Rue, Goat's

Robin-Run-in-the-Hedge—*See* Ivy, Ground

Rock Fern—*See* Fern

Rosin—*See* Pine

Round-leaved Dock—*See* Dock, Round-leaved

Royal Fern—See Fern

Rubeckia—*See* Echinacea

Ruffett—*See* Gorse

Run-by-the-Ground—*See* Pennyroyal

Rye—*Secale spp.*—Feminine, Venus, Earth

ASTROLOGICAL: *Primary*: Libra, Taurus; *Secondary*: Capricorn, Taurus, Virgo

MAGICKAL: Fresh Rye bread served to your family once a month will greatly improve your bonds by opening the heart to experiencing and offering love.

GENERAL: There is a growing belief that the Salem Witch trials were either started by or perpetuated by Ergot poisoning as a result of a particularly damp growing season. One of the staple crops in the area was Rye, a favorite host for Ergot during damp seasons. One of the symptoms of Ergot poisoning is hallucinations.

Ryntem Root—*See* Gentian

Sab—*See* Buchu

Sacred Bark—*See* Buckthorn, Californian

Sacred Herb—*See* Yerba Santa

Sacred Lotus—*See* Lotus

Sacred Mother—*See* Corn

Sacred Tree—*See* Bodhi

Sadhika—*See* Nutmeg

Saffer— *See* Saffron, Spanish

Safflower—*See* Saffron, Mexican

Saffron—*See* Saffron, Spanish and Saffron, Mexican

Saffron, Spanish—*Crocus sativus*—Masculine, Sun, Fire

Autumn Crocus, Crocus, Karcom, Krokos, Kunkuma, Saffer, Saffron, Zaffer

ASTROLOGICAL: *Primary*: Leo; *Secondary*: Aries, Leo, Sagittarius

GODS: Amun Ra, Brahma, Eros, Indra, Pluto, Zeus

GODDESS: Astarte

MEDICAL: Carminative, Diaphoretic, Emmenagogue. Used as a tincture. A typical dose is 10 drops.

PART USED: Flower pistils

MAGICKAL: In cooking, especially with Rice, Saffron stirs lust, strengthens the bonds of love, and brings joy. Green tea steeped with a pinch of finely ground Saffron will greatly improve divinatory practices of all types. This is probably the most expensive herb you will ever use, but its expense is well worth it. Do not confuse this with the much less expensive Mexican Saffron. Some retailers sell the cheaper herb under the name Saffron in an attempt to confuse the consumer.

Saffron

Saffron, Mexican—*Carthamus tinctorius*

Also known as American Saffron, Bastard Saffron, Dyer's Saffron, Fake Saffron, Flores Carthami, Safflower

GODS: Shango

GODDESSES: Ochun

MEDICAL: Diaphoretic, Laxative. An infusion is made with 1/2 ounce of the flowers in 1 pint of water. Simmer for 30 minutes, strain, and serve 4 ounces at a time.

PART USED: Flowers

MAGICKAL: Not a magickal substitute for Spanish Saffron. Mexican Saffron is an inexpensive material. The oil is sometimes used as a base oil for creating blends, but it is more often used as an inexpensive cooking oil. As such, it is commonly sold as Safflower.

Sage—*See* Sage, Clary; Sage, Common; Sage, White; and Sage, Vervain

Sagebrush—*See* Sage, White

Sage, Clary—*Salvia sclarea*—Masculine, Mercury, Air
Also known as Clear Eye, Clary, Gallitricum, Horminum, Muskateller Salbei, Sage, See Bright
WARNING: May have an adverse effect if used in conjunction with alcohol. Never use as a tincture.
ASTROLOGICAL: *Primary*: Gemini, Virgo; *Secondary*: Aquarius, Gemini, Libra
MEDICAL: Antispasmodic, Aperient, Astringent, Carminative, Pectoral, Tonic. Fresh leaves applied to burns, cuts, scratches, and insect bites will speed healing and sooth pain. An infusion will aid in treating colic.
PART USED: Herb
MAGICKAL: The leaves and seeds are sometimes burned to promote relaxation and to reduce anger. An infusion is made with 1 ounce of the herb in 1 pint of water. Simmer for 30 minutes, strain, and serve 4 ounces at a time. Essential oil of Clary Sage can and should be used as a substitute for essential oil of Common Sage as it shares the magickal properties but is nontoxic. When diffused or blended with carrier oil, its scent brings an uplifting feeling that will sometimes border euphoria. When used in pure form, its abuse will cause headaches. It will relax both body and mind, but has a lifting or energetic effect on the spirit.

Sage, Common—*Salvia officinalis/Salvia salvatrix*—Masculine, Jupiter, Air
Also known as Broad-leaved White Sage, Garden Sage, Narrow-leaved White Sage, Red Sage, Sage, Sawge
WARNING: Essential oil of Common Sage is toxic, especially to unborn children.

ASTROLOGICAL: *Primary*: Pisces, Sagittarius; *Secondary*: Aquarius, Gemini, Libra
GODS: Shango, Eleggua, Obatala, Orunla
MEDICAL: Astringent, Carmative, Diuretic, Nervine, Stimulant, Stomachic, Tonic. Common Sage *(Salvia officinalis)* is added to heavy meals; it settles the digestive system and aids in relaxation. Sage is best if grown at home. Its fresh leaves are used in cooking in a ratio of about 3 to 1 when a recipe calls for dried Sage. Relief from flu-like symptoms may be had by simmering Sage leaf in water for 1 hour, straining, and flavoring with orange and lemon juice. Okay to sweeten with honey. Fresh leaves and a warm water infusion act as a diuretic, help to cleanse the kidney, and act as a very mild stimulant and a topical

Sage

astringent. The infusion is also a good topical treatment for cold sores.
PART USED: Herb
MAGICKAL: Common Sage is used in healing and prosperity spellcraft, especially during winter. At the end of the season, it can be cut and hung in the home for protection and to be used throughout the winter. What is left when the new season produces more fresh Sage can be burned in the fireplace for a prosperous year. It is sometimes added to prosperity incense. When consumed, Sage provides a sense of well-being. Add it to wintertime meals to bring on a sense of well-being at home even when you are not able to be there in person.

Sage of Bethlehem—*See* Spearmint

Sage, Diviner's—*Salvia divinorum*—Masculine, Jupiter, Air
ASTROLOGICAL: *Primary*: Pisces, Sagittarius; *Secondary*: Aquarius, Gemini, Libra
GODS: Babalu Aye, Ochosi, Oggun

MAGICKAL: Diviner's Sage is often used for vision quest and assistance with scrying. If you are looking for an herb for recreational intoxication, this is not it. The effect this herb has on human consciousness is profound, but those effects are not in any order of recreation. Instead, it promotes very deep meditation and concentration. Without tremendous amounts of experience with meditation prior to its use, folk who use it tend to discover an inability to control the intent of that concentration and wind up thinking about, oh, let's say the flavor of milk for three hours. Those with extensive experience with controlled meditation and visualization will usually find that use of this herb will enhance their ability to visualize a thousand fold and then remain absolutely fixed on the object of their concentration. If you plan to use this sacrament, do so without distraction. No television, radio, or music. Do not plan on interacting with the public and, of course, do not plan on driving. Ensure that your environment is safe and always be accompanied by someone who will abstain during your use. When smoked in a pipe with constant flame during the inhalation, effects will take place almost instantly. The strong effects last about five to 10 minutes, taper off at about 30 minutes, and seem to be gone after an hour. When chewed for a prolonged time, the effects will decrease but last considerably longer. Diviner's Sage seems to have little or no effect when eaten or smoked without the use of a pipe and constant flame.

Sage, White—*See List*—Feminine, Venus, Earth

    Stiff Sagebrush—*Artemisia rigida*

    Tall Sagebrush—*Artemisia tridentata*

    Also known as Sagebrush, Smudge, White Desert Sage

ASTROLOGICAL: *Primary*: Libra, Taurus; *Secondary*: Capricorn, Taurus, Virgo

MAGICKAL: Although many other varieties of Sage are sold as smudge sticks (especially in eastern parts of the Midwest), this practice has come about by misunderstanding, misuse, and unscrupulous merchants. White Sage (Sagebrush) and not the other plants by similar name is the one that has been traditionally used by pre-Columbian Americans for cleansing. Yes, it costs a bit more in locations where it does not grow in the wild, but it is well worth the extra dollars. White Sage is bundled into sticks of various lengths and then burned at one end while weaving its smoke around objects, people, or any space (home or Circle). It is also ground into flakes, sometimes mixed with cedar, rosemary, tobacco, and other herbs, and then burned for the same purpose. A traditional way to burn this mixture is in an abalone shell, fanning the smoke with a feather that has been used only for that purpose.

Sage Willow—*See* Loosestrife, Purple

Sage, Vervain—*Salvia Verbenaca*—Masculine, Jupiter, Air

Also known as Christ's Eye, Oculus Christi, Wild English Clary

ASTROLOGICAL: *Primary*: Pisces, Sagittarius; *Secondary*: Aquarius, Gemini, Libra

MEDICAL: Stomachic

PART USED: Leaves

Sahlep—*See* Lucky Hand

Saille—*See* Willow

Sailor's Tobacco—*See* Mugwort

Salep—*See* Lucky Hand

Salicaire—*See* Loosestrife, Purple

Salicyn Willow—*See* Willow

Samar—*See* Fennel

Sandal—*See* Sandalwood, Yellow

Sandalwood—Usually a reference to Sandalwood, White but sometimes to Sandalwood, Red.

Sandalwood, White—*Santalum album*—Feminine, Moon, Water

Also known as Sandal, Sandalwood, Sander's Wood, Santal, White Saunders, Yellow Sandalwood

ASTROLOGICAL: *Primary*: Cancer; *Secondary*: Cancer, Pisces, Scorpio

GODS: Babalu Aye, Shango, Eleggua, Hanuman, Hermes, Obatala, Oko, Olocun, Orunla, Parashurama, Surya, Vishnu

GODDESSES: Oya, Venus, Yemaya

MAGICKAL: If a recipe related to love calls for Santal, it is probably calling for Red Sandalwood. If the recipe is for anything else, it is more likely that it is calling for Yellow Sandalwood. Powdered Sandalwood burning alone is a very pleasant scent that will aid in creative visualization. Mixed with Frankincense, it is a powerful general protection incense. Mix with equal amounts of Lavender to attract pleasant spirits. Sandalwood knives are sometimes used in place of the athame, especially when traveling. This practice is found in Hindu ritual, and you are more likely to get an athame of Sandalwood onto an airplane than one of metal. Sandalwood beads and talismans are protective. Sandalwood is one of the best wood incense bases. Mix true essential oils (dependant on intent) into powdered Sandalwood. Essential oil of Sandalwood is diffused to relax the conscious mind.

Sandalwood

Sandalwood, Red—*Pterocarpus santalinus*—Feminine, Venus, Water

Also known as Santal

ASTROLOGICAL: *Primary*: Libra, Taurus; *Secondary*: Cancer, Pisces, Scorpio

GODS: Vishnu

GODDESSES: Nike, Venus

MAGICKAL: If a recipe related to love calls for Santal, it is probably calling for Red Sandalwood. If the recipe is for anything else, it is more likely that it is calling for Yellow Sandalwood. Red Sandalwood is used as a wood base for love-drawing incense when used in conjunction with very strongly scented herbs and oils. It should not be used as a substitute for White Sandalwood or as the base for other incenses, as its scent when burned adds a harsh undertone that can distract from the other ingredients. Due to its color, Red Sandalwood is sometimes also associated with Fire and the sign Leo.

Sander's Wood—*See* Sandalwood, White

Sang—*See* Ginseng, American

Sanguinary—*See* Yarrow and Shepherd's Purse

Sanguis Draconis—*See* Dragon's Blood

Santal—*See* Sandalwood, White and Sandalwood, Red

Saloop—*See* Lucky Hand

Sardian Nut—*See* Chestnut, Sweet

Sarsaparilla—*See List*—Masculine, Jupiter, Fire

ASTROLOGICAL: *Primary*: Pisces, Sagittarius; *Secondary*: Aries, Leo, Sagittarius

American Sarsaparilla—*Aralia nudicaulis*

Also known as Bamboo Brier, False Sarsaparilla, Rabbit Root, Shot Bush, Small Spikenard, Wild Liquorice, Wild Sarsaparilla

MEDICAL: Alterative, Diaphoretic, Pectoral

PART USED: Root

Indian Sarsaparilla—*Hemidesmus Indica*

Also known as Hemidesmus, Pseudosarsa

MEDICAL: Alterative, Diuretic, Tonic

PART USED: Root

Italian Sarsaparilla—*Smilax aspera*

Jamaican Sarsaparilla—*Smilax ornata/ Smilax Medica*

Also known as Red-Bearded Sarsaparilla

MEDICAL: Alterative, Tonic

PART USED: Root

MAGICKAL: (all varieties) Sarsaparilla of all kinds is used in money-drawing incenses and love-drawing sachets.

Satan's Apple—*See* Mandrake

Satyrion—*See* Lucky Hand

Sauce Alone—*See* Mustard, Garlic

Saugh Tree—*See* Willow

Scaffold Flower—*See* Carnation

Scratweed—*See* Cleavers (B)

Scheiteregi—*See* Fumitory

Sanging—*See* Banana

Sanoot—*See* Cumin

Saqal—*See* Aloe

Saracen Corn—*See* Buckwheat

Sarrasin—*See* Buckwheat

Sassafrax—*See* Sassafras

 Sassafras—*Sassafras officinale/Sassafras varifolium/Sassafras albidum*—Masculine, Jupiter, Fire

Also known as Ague Tree, Cinnamon Wood, Laurus Sassafras, Sassafrax, Sassafras Radix, Saxifrax

WARNING: Although commonly sold in grocery stores, large amounts or habitual/ regular use can cause a host of health problems. Consult your doctor before

Sassafras

using. Pregnant women should not use it. Poisonous in large amounts. Contains Safrol.

ASTROLOGICAL: *Primary*: Pisces, Sagittarius; *Secondary*: Aries, Leo, Sagittarius

MEDICAL: Abortifacient, Alterative, Diaphoretic, Expectorant, Stimulant, Tonic. A warm water infusion of the root bark works as an expectorant and kidney cleanser. Over ice, the infusion will fight back the heat of summer. It is also used to relieve the symptoms of both menstrual and postpartum pains. Although sometimes listed as a tonic, there may be cumulative toxins from extended use.

PART USED: Bark of root

MAGICKAL: Sassafras is used in incense and sachets to draw money, especially when mixed with Cinnamon.

Sassafras Radix—*See* Sassafras

Satin Flower—*See* Chickweed

Savory, Summer—*Satureja hortesis/Satureia hortensis*—Masculine, Mercury, Air

Also known as Garden Savory, Herbe de St. Julien

ASTROLOGICAL: *Primary*: Gemini, Virgo; *Secondary*: Aquarius, Gemini, Libra

MEDICAL: (*Satureia hortensis*) Carminative, Diuretic. Small amounts used in cooking will increase cognitive functions, clear the mind, and settle the stomach. Acts as a mild diuretic.

PART USED: Herb

MAGICKAL: Said to work as an aphrodisiac when used in culinary preparations for a romantic dinner.

Savory, Winter—*Satureja montana/Satureia montana*—Masculine, Mercury, Air

ASTROLOGICAL: *Primary*: Gemini, Virgo; *Secondary*: Aquarius, Gemini, Libra

MAGICKAL: Carried in a sachet to improve cognitive functions and clear the mind.

Sawge—*See* Sage, Common

Saw Palmetto—*Serenoa repens*

Saxifrax—*See* Sassafras

Scabiosa Arvensis—*See* Scabious, Field

Scabious, Field—*Knautia arvensis*
Also known as Devil's Bit, Scabiosa arvensis

Scabious, Lesser—*Scabiosa Columbaria*
Also known as Devil's Bit

Scabious, Devil's Bit—*Scabiosa succisa*—Masculine
Also known as Devil's Bit, Ofbit, Premorse Scabious
MEDICAL: Diaphoretic, Demulcent, Febrifuge. 1 ounce of the herb is infused with 1 pint of water. Simmer for 30 minutes, strain, and serve 4 ounces at a time.
PART USED: Herb
GENERAL: If a recipe calls for Devil's Bit, it is probably calling for this variety of Scabious (*Scabiosa succisa*). There is some lore that says that a man who carries Devil's Bit in a white sachet will attract women who are pure of heart.

Scabwort—*See* Elecampane

Scaly Fern—*See* Fern

Scarlet Berry—*See* Woody Nightshade

Scaldweed—*See* Dodder

Scarlet Pimpernel—*See* Pimpernel, Scarlet

Scean de Solomon—*See* Solomon's Seal

Scoke—*See* Pokeweed

Scorzo del Melogranati—*See* Pomegranate

Scotch Broom—*See* Broom

Scottish—*See* Heather

Scullcap—*See List*—Feminine, Saturn, Water
  Common Scullcap—*Scutellaria galericulata*
  Also known as Greater Scullcap, Helmet Flower, Hoodwort, Toque
  Lesser Scullcap—*Scutellaria minor*
  Virginian Scullcap—*Scutellaria lateriflora*
  Also known as Blue Pimpernel, Hoodwort, Mad-Dog Scullcap, Madweed, Skullcap
WARNING: Do not consume in conjunction with any other drug, as the potential interactions are as yet unknown.
ASTROLOGICAL: *Primary*: Aquarius, Capricorn; *Secondary*: Cancer, Pisces, Scorpio
MEDICAL: (*Scutellaria lateriflora*) Antispasmodic, Astringent (mild), Nervine, Tonic
PART USED: Herb
MAGICKAL: If a woman makes love to her husband after consuming or bathing with this infusion, it is said that her husband's eye will not stray.
  1/2 ounce of Virginian Scullcap (*Scutellaria lateriflora*)
  1/2 ounce Common Chamomile
  1 pint fresh water
  Honey to taste
  Bring to boil, lower heat, add herbs, and simmer for one 30 minutes. Serve either warm or over ice.

Sea Buckthorn—*See* Buckthorn, Sea

Sea Dew—*See* Rosemary

Sea Holly—*See* Holly, Sea

Sea Hulver—*See* Holly, Sea

Sea Holme—*See* Holly, Sea

Sea Lovage—*See* Lovage, Scotch

Sealwort—*See* Solomon's Seal

Seamsog—*See* Sorrel, Wood

Sea Parsley—*See* Lovage

Sea Plantain—*See* Plantain, Sea

Sea Spirit—*See* Bladderwrack

Sea Tree Mallow—*See* Mallow, Sea Tree

Seawrack—*See* Bladderwrack

See Bright—*See* Sage, Clary

Seed of Seeds—*See* Corn

Seed of Horns—*See* Horehound, White

Seetang—*See* Bladderwrack

Segg—*See* Iris

Selago—*See* Moss, American Club

Semihomo—See Mandrake

Seneca—*See* Senega

Senega—*Polygala senega/Polygala Virginiana/ Senega officinalis*
Also known as Milkwort, Mountain Flax, Rattlesnake Root, Seneca, Senegae Radix, Seneka, Seneca Snakeroot, Seneca Rattlesnake Root
MEDICAL: (*Polygala senega*) Cathartic (large doses), Diaphoretic, Diuretic, Emetic (large doses), Expectorant. Anything larger than 15 grains of the powdered root is considered a large dose.
PART USED: Root
MAGICKAL: An infusion of Senega root is used in bath and floor wash for protection. An infusion is said to bring luck with money when a drop or two is rubbed into the palms.

Senegae Radix—*See* Senega

Seneka—*See* Senega

Seneca Snakeroot—*See* Senega

Seneca Rattlesnake Root—*See* Senega

Serpentary Radix—*See* Snakeroot

Serpentary Rhizome—*See* Snakeroot

Sesame—*Sesamum indicum/Sesamum Orientate*—Masculine, Sun, Fire
Also known as Bonin, Hoholi, Logowe, Til, Ufuta, Ziele
ASTROLOGICAL: *Primary*: Leo; *Secondary*: Aries, Leo, Sagittarius
GODS: Shango, Ganesa
GODDESS: Ochun
MAGICKAL: Sesame seeds promote lust, especially when sweetened and fed to your lover by hand. For this purpose, there is no better way to use sesame than the confection from the Middle East called halvah. Eating the seeds will also open paths to prosperity, increase reproductive fertility, and provide a sense of well-being.

Sesame

Sensitive Plant—*See* Mimosa

Sention—*See* Groundsel, Common

Serpent's Tongue—*See* Adder's-Tongue

Sete Wale—*See* Valerian

Setwall—*See* Valerian

Set Well—*See* Valerian

Set Wale—*See* Valerian

Seven Barks—*See* Hydrangea

Seven Year's Love—*See* Yarrow

Shafallah—*See* Caper

Shalder—*See* Iris

Shameface—*See* Geranium

Shame Plant—*See* Mimosa

Shavegrass—*See* Horsetails

Sheggs—*See* Iris

Sheeh—*See* Fennel

Sheep Lice—*See* Hound's-Tongue

Sheep's Herb—*See* Plantain, Sea

Sheep's Sorrel—*See* Sorrel, Sheep

Shepherd's Bag—*See* Shepherd's Purse

Shepherd's Barometer—*See* Pimpernel, Scarlet

Shepherd's Clubs—*See* Mullein

Shepherd's Herb—*See* Mullein

Shepherd's Purse—*Capsella bursa-pastoris*
Also known as Blindweed, Bourse de Pasteur (*French*), Case-Weed, Clappedepouch (*Irish*), Hirtentasche (*German*), Lady's Purse, Pepper-and-Salt, Pick-Pocket, Pick-Purse, Poor Man's Parmacettie, Mother's Heart, Rattle Pouches, Sanguinary, Shepherd's Bag, Shepherd's Scrip, Shepherd's Sprout, Witches' Pouches
MEDICAL: Astringent, Diuretic (mild), Stimulant, Tonic. Taken during menstruation, it will decrease flow. A strong decoction of the herb will slow bleeding when taken internally and act as an astringent when used externally. Although it acts as a diuretic and increases urine flow, it also has astringent properties and will help treat diarrhea.
PART USED: Herb

Shepherd's Scrip—*See* Shepherd's Purse

Shepherd's Staff—*See* Mullein

Shepherd's Sprout—*See* Shepherd's Purse

Shoeflower—*See* Hibiscus

Short Buchu—*See* Buchu

Shot Bush—*See* Sarsaparilla

Siam Benzoin—*See* Benzoin

Siamese Benzoin—*See* Benzoin

Sib Muma—*See* Flax

Stick Tea—*See* Ma Huang

Silver Branch—*See* Apple

Silver Bough—*See* Apple

Silver Cinquefoil—*See* Five-Finger Grass and Silverweed

Silver Leaf—*See* Balsam, White

Silverweed—*Potentilla anserina*—Masculine, Jupiter, Fire
ASTROLOGICAL: *Primary*: Pisces, Sagittarius; *Secondary*: Aries, Leo, Sagittarius
MEDICAL: Diuretic, Stomachic
PART USED: Herb
GENERAL: Although Silverweed and Five-Finger Grass are entirely separate plants, they have been confused so often that it is now impossible to separate their attributes. Most often, citations are referring to Five-Finger Grass, but I have found some exceptions.

Simpler's Joy—*See* Vervain

Simson—*See* Groundsel, Common

Singer's Plant—*See* Mustard, Common Hedge

Sirir—*See* Betel Nut

Skoke—*See* Pokeweed

Skunk Cabbage—*See* Cabbage, Skunk

Skunkweed—*See* Cabbage, Skunk

Skullcap—*See* Scullcap

NOTE: When you see a reference to this herb and the spelling is with a "k" (Skullcap) rather than with a "c" (Scullcap) the reference is most often calling for Virginian Scullcap (*Scutellaria laterifolia*) rather than the other varieties of Scullcap.

Steeplebush—*See* Meadowsweet

Sleeping Plant—*See* Mimosa

Sleep Wort—*See* Lettuce

Small Spikenard—*See* Sarsaparilla

Snagree—*See* Snakeroot

Snagrel—*See* Snakeroot

Snake Grass—*See* Yarrow

Snakeweed—*See* Snakeroot

Snapdragon—*Antirrhinum majus*—Masculine, Mars, Fire

Also known as Calf's Snout

ASTROLOGICAL: *Primary*: Aries, Scorpio; *Secondary*: Aries, Leo, Sagittarius

GODS: Eleggua, Obatala

MAGICKAL: Back in the day, this beautiful flower and its seeds were used to protect oneself against Witches. Today, it sometimes used by Witches to prevent being bewitched.

Snapdragon

Grown in the garden, Snapdragons lend protection from all forms of magick.

Soapwort—*Saponaria officinalis*

GENERAL: A strong decoction makes a great natural shampoo and liquid soap.

Soldier's Woundwort—*See* Yarrow

Solomon Seal—*See* Solomon's Seal

Solomon's Seal—*Polygonatum multiflorum/ Polygonatum officinale*—Feminine, Saturn, Water

Also known as Dropberry, Lady's Seal, St. Mary's Seal, Scean de Solomon, Sealwort, Solomon Seal, Weusswurz

ASTROLOGICAL: *Primary*: Aquarius, Capricorn; *Secondary*: Cancer, Pisces, Scorpio

MEDICAL: (*Polygonatum multiflorum*) Astringent, Demulcent, Tonic. A warm water infusion of the root acts as a diuretic.

PART USED: Root

MAGICKAL: For added protection, Solomon's Seal is sometimes placed at each of the Four Quarters prior to casting the Circle at Wiccan ritual.

Sopur Trefoil—*See* Sorrel, Wood

Sourgrass—*See* Sorrel, Wood

Soy—*Glycine max*—Feminine, Moon, Earth

ASTROLOGICAL: *Primary*: Cancer; *Secondary*: Capricorn, Taurus, Virgo

MAGICKAL: Eating Soy increases psychic abilities and opens one to empathy. It also lends itself to protection.

Squaw Mint—*See* Pennyroyal

Stanch Grass—*See* Yarrow

Stanch Griss—*See* Yarrow

Stanch Weed—*See* Yarrow

Stickwort—*See* Sorrel, Wood

Stiff Sagebrush—*See* Sage, White

Storksbill—*See* Geranium

Strangle Tare—*See* Dodder

Star Root—*See* Ague Root

Strawberry, Garden—*Fragaria vesca*—Feminine, Venus, Water

ASTROLOGICAL: *Primary*: Libra, Taurus; *Secondary*: Cancer, Pisces, Scorpio

MEDICAL: Astringent, Diuretic, Laxative. Both the fruit and leaves are laxatives, diuretics, and astringents. The leaves are most often cited for each of these purposes. They are typically mixed with other foods or simmered in a warm water infusion. This same warm water infusion was once prescribed to women in high-risk pregnancy to avoid miscarriages. However, such practices should be checked with your own obstetrician first. A warm water infusion of the leaves is a good source of iron and potassium and is sometimes cited as a treatment for gout. The fruit contains large amounts of vitamin C. Serves as a good tonic, especially for diabetics, as it seems to stabilize and normalize blood sugar levels.

PARTS USED: Fruit, Leaves

MAGICKAL: Eating Strawberries promotes a sense of romantic love.

Strawberry, Wild—*Fragaria virginiana*

MEDICAL: Diuretic

PART USED: Fruit

Stubwort—*See* Sorrel, Wood

Spiked Loosestrife—*See* Loosestrife, Purple

Spire Mint—*See* Spearmint

Sukake—*See* Citron

Sunflower—*Helianthus annuus*—Masculine, Sun, Fire

GODS: Apollo, Helios, Horus the Elder, Narasinha, Ra, Surya, Vishnu

GODDESSES: Demeter, Venus

MEDICAL: Diuretic, Expectorant

PARTS USED: Seeds, Oil

MAGICKAL: Sunflower

Sunflower

seeds and oil will increase energy and luck to propel one toward success at any endeavor. The key is to have a dream and then add Sunflower to your diet to bring that dream into manifestation.

Sunkfield—*See* Five-Finger Grass

Suntull—*See* Cabbage, Skunk

Supari—*See* Betel Nut

Surelle—*See* Sorrel, Wood

Slan-Lus—*See* Plantain, Common

Slaz—*See* Mallow, Marsh

Slippery Elm—*See* Elm, Slippery

Slippery Root—*See* Comfrey

Sloe—*Prunnus spinosa*—Masculine, Mars, Fire

Also known as Blackthorn, Mother of the Wood, Wishing Thorn

ASTROLOGICAL: *Primary*: Aries, Scorpio; *Secondary*: Aries, Leo, Sagittarius

GODDESSES: Morrigan

CELTIC TREE CALENDAR (Straif)—Samhain

MAGICKAL: Sloe is used in protection. On cold winter nights, warm Sloe gin is just the trick. Serve warm next to an open fire.

Smallage—*See* Celery

Small Celandine—*See* Celandine, Lesser

Smallwort—*See* Celandine, Lesser

Smeerwartel—*See* Comfrey

Smooth Lawsonia—*See* Henna

Smudge—*See* Sage, White

Snake Grape—*See* White Bryony

Snake Lily—*See* Blue Flag

Snake Plantain—*See* Plantain, Ribwort

☠**Snakeroot**—*Aristolochia serpentaria*

Snakeroot is also a common name for Senega. Also known as Pelican Flower, Radix Viperina, Red River, Serpentary Radix, Serpentary Rhizome, Snagree, Snagrel, Snakeweed, Texas Snakeroot, Virginian Snakeroot

MEDICAL: Diaphoretic, Stimulant, Tonic

PART USED: Root

MAGICKAL: Carry Snakeroot when looking for a job or when attempting to find necessary business contacts. It is also carried for general good luck.

Snakeroot, Black—*Sanicula marilandica*—Masculine, Mars, Fire

ASTROLOGICAL: *Primary*: Aries, Scorpio; *Secondary*: Aries, Leo, Sagittarius

MAGICKAL: An infusion of Black Snakeroot used in the bath will assist in finding new lovers. It is most appropriate in the lustral bath prior to a social Beltane celebration. The dried root may be carried to attract money.

Snakeroot, Button—*Liatris spicata*

Also known as Colic Root, Devil's Bite, Gay Feather

MEDICAL: Diuretic. A decoction is made with 1 ounce of the dried root in 1 quart of water. Reduce by boiling to 1 pint. Strain and serve 2 ounces at a time.

PART USED: Root

Snakeweed—*See* Plantain, Common

Soldier's Tea—*See* Horehound, White

Solidago—*See* Goldenrod

Sol Terrestris—*See* St. John's Wort

Soma—*See* Agaric Mushroom

Sops-in-Wine—*See* Carnation

Sorcerer's Berry—*See* Belladonna

Sorcerer's Root—*See* Mandrake

Sorcerer's Herb—*See* Thornapple

Sorcerer's Violet—*See* Periwinkle

Sorb Apple—*See* Ash, Mountain

Sorrel, Sheep—*Rumex acetosella*

MEDICAL: Diaphoretic, Diuretic, Refrigerant. A warm water infusion of the herb will reduce fevers and assist in cleansing the kidneys and urinary system. In respect to its action on the kidneys, it is kin to Cranberry juice cocktail, except that with an infusion you are able to determine the amount of added sugar.

PART USED: Herb

Sorrel, Wood—*Oxalis acetosella*—Feminine, Venus, Earth

Also known as Cuckowe's Meat, Fairy Bells, Hallelujah, Iuliole, Pain de Coucou, Seamsog, Sourgrass, Sopur Trefoil, Stickwort, Stubwort, Surelle, Three-leaved Grass

ASTROLOGICAL: *Primary*: Libra, Taurus; *Secondary*: Capricorn, Taurus, Virgo

MEDICAL: Antiscorbutic, Diuretic, Refrigerant. A decoction is made by boiling 1/2 ounce in 1 quart of water. Reduce by boiling to 1 pint. Strain and serve 4 ounces at a time.

PART USED: Herb

MAGICKAL: The dried leaves of the Wood Sorrel are carried to promote health.

Southernwood—*Artemisia abrotanum*—Masculine, Mercury, Air

Also known as Appleringie, Boy's Love, Garde Robe, Lad's Love, Maid's Ruin, Old Man

ASTROLOGICAL: *Primary*: Gemini, Virgo; *Secondary*: Aquarius, Gemini, Libra

MEDICAL: Anthelmintic, Antiseptic, Deobstruent, Emmenagogue, Tonic. An infusion is made with 1 ounce of herb to 1 pint of water.

Southernwood

Simmer for 15 minutes, strain, and serve 4 ounces at a time.

PART USED: Herb

MAGICKAL: Southernwood is a cousin to Wormwood. It is used to promote both lust and romance. Pick fresh Southernwood and place in a vase near the bed. Reportedly, young men love this plant because rubbing its ashes on one's face will promote beard growth. The recipe I was given when I was young said to burn dried Southernwood over a warming pot of Olive oil, allowing the ashes to fall into the oil. Rewarm the oil each morning and use as one would shaving cream, first rubbing it on, then shaving to remove it. Afterwards, shower and wash face thoroughly. Repeat this every morning until it works and then switch to shaving cream.

Sowa—*See* Dill

Sow-Bread—*See* Cyclamen, Ivy-leaved

Spanish Chestnut—*See* Chestnut, Sweet

Spanish Saffron—*See* Saffron, Spanish

Sparrow Tongue—*See* Knotgrass

Spearmint—*Mentha viridis/Mentha spicata*—Feminine, Venus, Water

Also known as Brown Mint, Erba Santa Maria, Fish Mint, Frauen Munze, Garden Mint, Green Mint, Green Spine, Lamb Mint, Mackerel Mint, Menthe de Notre Dame, Mismin, Our Lady's Mint, Sage of Bethlehem, Spire Mint, Yerba Buena

ASTROLOGICAL: *Primary*: Libra, Taurus; *Secondary*: Cancer, Pisces, Scorpio

GODS: Olocun

MEDICAL: Diuretic, Stomachic. A warm water infusion of the leaves and flowers makes a fine diuretic. Sweeten mildly with honey to calm colic.

Spearmint

PART USED: Herb

MAGICKAL: An infusion of Spearmint promotes and sharpens cognitive powers. Drink it warm as you study and cold prior to a test or a time when you must demonstrate your retention of your studies. Essential oil of Spearmint is diffused to ease a broken heart and to refresh the mind and body.

NOTE: My oldest record indicates that the attributes of Spearmint are Feminine, Venus, Water. However, I have found many references that state it is Masculine, Mercury, Air

Sphagnum Moss—*See* Moss, Sphagnum

Spleenwort, Common—*See* Fern

Spleenwort, Black—*See* Fern

Spignet—*See* Spikenard, American

Spike—*See* Lavender

Spike Lavender—*See* Lavender

Spikenard—*See* Lavender; Spikenard, American; Spikenard, Californian; and Spikenard, Ploughman's

Spikenard, American—*Aralia racemosa*—Feminine, Venus, Water

Also known as Spignet, Life-of-Man, Pettymorell, Old Man's Root, Indian Spikenard, Indian Root, Nard

ASTROLOGICAL: *Primary*: Libra, Taurus; *Secondary*: Cancer, Pisces, Scorpio

MEDICAL: Diaphoretic, Stimulant. An infusion is made with 1/2 ounce of powdered root and 1 pint of water. Simmer for 30 minutes, strain, and serve 4 ounces at a time.

PART USED: Root

MAGICKAL: A sachet of Spikenard helps keep absent lovers faithful. Scent it with your perfume or oil, carry it with you always, and then, when they must leave for a trip, give it to them telling them it will keep them safe from temptation.

Spikenard, Californian—*Aralia Californica*
NOTE: Californian Spikenard does not seem to share the magickal properties of American or Ploughman's Spikenard.

Spikenard, Ploughman's—*Inula Conyza/ Conyza Squarrosa*—Feminine, Venus, Water
Also known as Cloron's Hard, Horse Heal, Cinnamon Root, Great Fleabane, Nard
ASTROLOGICAL: *Primary*: Libra, Taurus; *Secondary*: Cancer, Pisces, Scorpio
GODS: Amathaon

Spinach—*Spinacea oleracea*—Feminine, Jupiter, Earth
ASTROLOGICAL: *Primary*: Pisces, Sagittarius; *Secondary*: Capricorn, Taurus, Virgo
MAGICKAL: Grown in the family garden, Spinach will increase communal prosperity. Eaten fresh, it will increase personal prosperity.

Spogel Seed—*See* Plantain, Ispaghul

Sponnc—*See* Coltsfoot

Spotted Cranesbill—*See* Geranium

Spotted Corobane—*See* Hemlock

Spotted Hemlock—*See* Hemlock

Spring Gentian—*See* Gentian

Spurge—*See* Spurges

☠**Spurges**—Applies to all *Euphorbias*—Feminine, Saturn, Water
Also known as Crown of Thorns, Euphorbia, Spurge, Wolf's Milk, Pill-Bearing Spurge, Catshair, Mziwaziwa
ASTROLOGICAL: *Primary*: Aquarius, Capricorn; *Secondary*: Cancer, Pisces, Scorpio
NOTE: There are over 3,000 species of this botanical. Listing each here is beyond the scope of this work.

Squash—*Curcurbita spp.*—Masculine, Sun, Fire
ASTROLOGICAL: *Primary*: Leo; *Secondary*: Aries, Leo, Sagittarius
MAGICKAL: Increases psychic, empathic, and cognitive abilities. In particular, eating Squash will allow one to better tune the senses to those things that are not generally considered a part of the natural world.

Squaw Root—See Cohosh, Blue and Cohosh, Black
NOTE: If you see a citation for Squaw Root, the reference is probably to Blue Cohosh (*Caulophyllum thalictroides*); however, some cites are referring to Black Cohosh (*Cimicifuga racemosa*). The more credible references seem to be pointing at Blue Cohosh for this folk name.

Squaw Tea—*See* Ma Huang

Squaw Weed—*See* Groundsel, Golden

Squinancy Berries—*See* Currant, Black

Star Anise—*Illicum verum*—Masculine, Jupiter, Air
Also known as Badiana, Chinese Anise
ASTROLOGICAL: *Primary*: Pisces, Sagittarius; *Secondary*: Aquarius, Gemini, Libra
GODDESS: Oya
MAGICKAL: A necklace of the seeds or seed pods of Star Anise are said to stimulate the intuitive portions of the brain. Simmering the seedpods provides the same effect. In Wiccan ritual, Star Anise is often scattered with the calling of each Quarter to seek the blessings of nature spirits.

Starch Hyacinth—*See* Hyacinth, Grape

St. Barbara's Hedge Mustard—*See* Mustard, Common Hedge

St. John's Wort—*Hypericum perforatum/Fuga daemonum*—Masculine, Sun, Fire

Also known as Amber, Goat Weed, Herba John, John's Wort, Klamath Weed, Sol Terrestris, Tiponweed

ASTROLOGICAL: *Primary*: Leo; *Secondary*: Aries, Leo, Sagittarius

GODS: Baldur

GODDESS: Ochun

MEDICAL: Astringent, Diuretic, Expectorant, Nervine, Stimulant. For internal use, 1 ounce of the herb is infused in 1 pint of water. Simmer for 30 minutes, strain, and serve 1 tablespoon as a dose. This is also a good topical treatment for burns. A warm Olive oil infusion of the flowers makes a good ointment for mild skin disorders. St. John's Wort is being researched for its treatment of HIV and cancer and the immune system problems that come with these killers. It is an excellent example of the symbiotic relationship between humanity and the Green World that has been entrusted to us.

St. John's Wort

PARTS USED: Flowers, Tops

MAGICKAL: Saint John's Wort is placed in the bottom of military gear to protect and lend bravery to the soldier. It is sometimes burned as protective incense and to drive out baneful energy, but its smell when burned is far less than pleasant. Sewn into a pillow and mixed with Lavender, Saint John's Wort will help a woman to dream of her husband even when she has not found him yet. Reportedly, during the Burning Times St. John's Wort was either force-fed or forced into the mouth of suspected Witches to cause them to confess. I believe this may have been an early form of chemically assisted brainwashing, which might be kin to the modern use of drugs and hypnosis to generate false memory syndrome.

St. Joseph's Wort—*See* Basil

St. Mary's Seal—*See* Solomon's Seal

Star Chickweed—*See* Chickweed

Star Flower—*See* Borage

Stargrass—*See* Ague Root

Starweed—*See* Chickweed

Starwort—*See* Ague Root, Aster, and Chickweed

Star of the Earth—*See* Avens

Stellaire—*See* Chickweed

NOTE: Stellaire is sometimes confused with Stellaria. I believe this may have started as a simple spelling error years ago as some French herbalist scribbled down his notes. As a result, if you see a reference today, you have to wonder if they are calling for Chickweed or Knotgrass.

Stellaria—*See* Knotgrass

NOTE: See Stellaire for information on a common mistake found in many herbal references.

Stepmother—*See* Heartsease

St. George's Herb—*See* Valerian

St. John's Plant—*See* Mugwort

Stinging Nettle—*See* Nettle, Greater and Nettle, Lesser

Stoechas Citrina—*See* Gnaphalium Stoechas

Stoechas Gnaphalium—*See* Gnaphalium Stoechas

Stringy Bark Tree—*See* Eucalyptus

Stinkdillsamen—*See* Coriander

Stinking Chamomile—*See* Chamomile, Stinking

Stinking Groundsel—*See* Groundsel, Viscid

Stinking Horehound—*See* Horehound, Black

Stinkweed—*See* Thornapple and Garlic

Sticklewort—*See* Agrimony

Stickwort—*See* Agrimony and Chickweed

Stramonium—*See* Thornapple

Strong-Scented Lettuce—*See* Lettuce, Wild

Succory—*See* Chicory

Sugarcane—*Saccharum officinarum*—Feminine, Venus, Water
ASTROLOGICAL: *Primary*: Libra, Taurus; *Secondary*: Cancer, Pisces, Scorpio
MAGICKAL: Chewing on Sugarcane or consuming small amounts of its extracts will promote a sense of love.

Sugar Pod—*See* Carob

Summer Savory—*See* Savory, Summer

Suterberry—*See* Ash, Prickly

Swallow Herb—*See* Celandine, Greater

Swallow-Wort—*See* Celandine, Greater

Swamp Cabbage—*See* Cabbage, Skunk

Swamp Hellebore—*See* Hellebore, Green

Swamp Sassafras—*See* Magnolia

Sweating Plant—*See* Boneset

Sweat Root—*See* Abscess Root

Sweet Almond—*See* Almond

Sweet Balm—*See* Lemon Balm

Sweet Basil—*See* Basil

Sweet Bay—*See* Bay

Sweet Cane—*See* Calamus

Sweet Cherry—*See* Cherry

Sweet Cicily—*Myrrhis odorata*
MEDICAL: Antiseptic (root), Carminative, Expectorant, Stomachic. As a topical antiseptic, a decoction is made by boiling 1 ounce of the root in 1 quart of water. Reduce by boiling to 1 pint and use topically. As a stomachic and carminative, 1 ounce of the herb is infused with 1 pint of water. Simmer for 30 minutes and serve 4 ounces at a time. A similar infusion is made with either seed or herb and red wine for its value as an expectorant.
PARTS USED: Herb, Root, Seeds
MAGICKAL: A strong tincture of Sweet Cicily is said to be an aphrodisiac perfume.

Sweet Cumin—*See* Anise

Sweet Fennel—*See* Fennel

Sweet Flag—*See* Calamus

Sweetgrass—*Hierochloe odorata*
See also Calamus, as Sweetgrass is one of its common names.
MAGICKAL: Sweetgrass is typically braided and then burned slowly one end to the other as an incense to call beneficial spirits. For this purpose, Sweetgrass is the ideal incense, but it is often hard to find. If you need a substitute, try mixing equal parts of Pipsissewa or Lavender with Rose hips and Violet flowers.

Sweet Melissa—*See* Lemon Balm

Sweet Orange—*See* Orange, Sweet

Sweet Potato—*Ipomoea batatas*—Feminine, Venus, Water
ASTROLOGICAL: *Primary*: Libra, Taurus; *Secondary*: Cancer, Pisces, Scorpio
MAGICKAL: Eating Sweet Potatoes with your lover will increase the ties of love and mildly enhance lust.

Sweet Rod—*See* Calamus

Sweet Root—*See* Licorice

Sweet Round-leaved Dock—*See* Rhubarb

Sweet Rush—*See* Calamus

Sweet-Scented Goldenrod—*See* Goldenrod

Sweet-scented Life Everlasting—*See* Balsam, White

Sweet Sedge—*See* Calamus

Sweet Vernal Hellebore—*See* Hellebore, False

Sweet Violet—*See* Violet

Sweet Weed—*See* Mallow, Marsh

Sweet Wood—*See* Cinnamon

Sweet Woodruff—*See* Woodruff

Swine Bread—*See* Cyclamen, Ivy-leaved

Swine's Grass—*See* Knotweed

Swine Snout—*See* Dandelion

Swynel Grass—*See* Knotgrass

Symphonica—*See* Henbane

Synkefoyle—*See* Five-Finger Grass

Tabua—*See* Cattail

Tag Alder—*See* Alder

Tanner's Bark—*See* Oak

Trackleberry—*See* Huckleberry

Tagar—*See* Valerian, Indian

Tailed Pepper—*See* Cubeb

Tall Sagebrush—*See* Sage, White

Talong—*See* Eggplant

Tamarind—*Tamarindus indicus*—Feminine, Saturn, Water

ASTROLOGICAL: *Primary*: Aquarius, Capricorn; *Secondary*: Cancer, Pisces, Scorpio

MAGICKAL: Consumed to promote romantic love.

Tamarind

Tamus—*See* White Bryony

Tangerine—*Citrus spp.*—Masculine, Sun, Air

ASTROLOGICAL: *Primary*: Leo; *Secondary*: Aquarius, Gemini, Libra

GODDESS: Oya

MAGICKAL: Promotes a sense of well-being. Consumed to ward off psychic and social vampires.

Tansy—*Tanacetum vulgare*—Feminine, Venus, Water

Also known as Buttons

See also Yarrow, as Tansy is a folk name for Yarrow

WARNING: This plant has been found to be dangerous when taken internally.

ASTROLOGICAL: *Primary*: Libra, Taurus; *Secondary*: Cancer, Pisces, Scorpio

MEDICAL: Anthelmintic, Astringent, Emmenagogue, Stimulant, Tonic

Part used: Herb

GENERAL: Powdered Tansy is used to keep ants away.

Tansy

Tarragon—*Artemisia dracunculus*—Feminine, Venus, Earth

Also known as French Tarragon, Fuzzyweed, Little Dragon, Mugwort

ASTROLOGICAL: *Primary*: Libra, Taurus; *Secondary*: Capricorn, Taurus, Virgo

GODDESS: Artemis

MEDICAL: Stomachic. A warm water infusion will settle the stomach, stimulate the appetite, and increase urine output. A warm wine infusion is an excellent choice to be served with appetizers.

PART USED: Herb

Tarragon

MAGICKAL: Hunters carry tarragon for good luck. It can be mixed with the morning coffee grinds for the same purpose. Brew and take with you in a Thermos; when your luck fails or your eyes falter, drink a cup. Be warned: Do not be foolish enough to think that you can get away with trickery in your hunting without being punished. Before using Tarragon or anything to improve your luck at hunting, I strongly suggest that you read up on Artemis.

Tartar Root—*See* Ginseng, American

Taters—*See* Potato

Tatties—*See* Potato

Taubenkropp—*See* Fumitory

Tear Grass—*See* Job's Tears

Teasel—*See* Boneset

Tein-Ching—*See* Woad

Tekrouri—*See* Marijuana

Temple Tree—*See* Frangipani

Tentwort—*See* Fern

Terong—*See* Eggplant

Tetterberry—*See* White Bryony

Tetterwort—*See* Bloodroot and Celandine, Greater

Texas Snakeroot—*See* Snakeroot

Thimbleberry—*See* Blackberry

Thistle—*Carduus spp.*—Masculine, Mars, Fire

Also known as Lady's Thistle, Thrissles

ASTROLOGICAL: *Primary*: Aries, Scorpio; *Secondary*: Aries, Leo, Sagittarius

GODS: Apollo, Bacchus, Shango, Eleggua, Obatala, Thor, Pan, Priapus, Set

GODDESSES: Minerva, Vesta

MAGICKAL: Thistle is grown in the garden and around the home for protection.

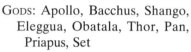

Thistle

Thistle, Blessed—*Centaurea benedicta/Cnicus Benedictus/Carbenia benedicta*—Masculine, Mars, Fire

Also known as Holy Thistle

ASTROLOGICAL: *Primary*: Aries, Scorpio; *Secondary*: Aries, Leo, Sagittarius

MAGICKAL: Blessed Thistle is carried for protection and has the same properties as Thistle.

Thorn—*See* Hawthorn

☠**Thornapple**—*Datura Stramonium*—Feminine, Saturn, Air

Also known as Apple of Peru, Datura, Devil's Apple, Devil's Trumpet, Ghost Flower, Herb of the Devil, Jamestown-Weed, Jimson-Weed, Love-Will, Mad Apple, Madherb, Manicon, Stinkweed, Stramonium, Sorcerer's Herb, Tulloch, Witches' Thimble

ASTROLOGICAL: *Primary*: Aquarius, Capricorn; *Secondary*: Aquarius, Gemini, Libra

MEDICAL: Anodyne, Antispasmodic, Narcotic, Sedative. Generally speaking, the leaves are not considered poisonous. This plant strongly resembles Belladonna in its actions and potential for abuse.

PARTS USED: Leaves, Seeds

MAGICKAL: Traditionally used to cause visions and sacred to the Aztecs, it is best you steer clear from this one or your vision may include that of a coffin door (from the inside) and your line may go the way of the Aztecs. When I was a teenager, I read a reference that spoke of the tremendous visions one could experience by eating the seeds of the Jimson-Weed. Because I had no one with real-world experience, I gave it a try. It is from that real-world experience that I tell you not to even think about putting any part of this plant into your body. A close friend reports equally frightening results from ingesting the seeds. To sum up her description, imagine not being sure who you were for three days and being honestly afraid you would never return to normal.

Thorny Burr—*See* Burdock

Thoroughwort—*See* Boneset

Thor's Beard—*See* Houseleek

Thor's Helper—*See* Ash, Mountain

Thousand Seal—*See* Yarrow

Three-Faces-Under-a-Hood—*See* Heartsease

Three-leaved Grass—*See* Sorrel, Wood

Thrissles—*See* Thistle

Throatwort—*See* Figwort, Knotted

Thyme—*Thymus vulgaris*—Feminine, Venus, Water
Also known as Common Thyme, Garden Thyme

ASTROLOGICAL: *Primary*: Libra, Taurus; *Secondary*: Cancer, Pisces, Scorpio

GODS: Babalu Aye, Obatala, Olocun

MEDICAL: Antispasmodic, Antiseptic, Astringent, Carminative, Diuretic, Tonic. Stimulates the thy-

Thyme

roid gland and acts as a mild diuretic. A warm water infusion of the leaves will help cleanse the kidneys and bladder. In large amounts, may overstimulate the thyroid gland and lead to poisoning. Topically, the fresh leaves or warm water infusion is an excellent astringent and can be used as a mouthwash to battle canker sores.

PART USED: Herb

MAGICKAL: Sewn into a pillow or simmered next to the bed, Thyme will encourage restful sleep. Fresh Thyme worn in a woman's hair will increase the desire of her gentlemen callers. Rubbing Thyme on the wrists and ankles will accomplish both of these. As an ingredient for incense, Thyme is cleansing. Dried sprigs are sometimes combined in smudge sticks with White Desert Sage. An infusion is a good cleansing mixture to add to the lustral bath prior to spring and summertime rituals. When consumed, it will improve psychic abilities, heighten empathy, and help cleanse the spiritual portions of ones being.

Tickle-my-Fancy—*See* Heartsease

Tickweed—*See* Pennyroyal

Tiger Lily—*See* Lily

Til—*See* Sesame

Tinne—*See* Holly

Tittle-my-Fancy—*See* Heartsease

Tiponweed—*See* St. John's Wort

Tlilxochitl—*See* Vanilla

☙Tobacco—*Nicotiana tabacum*
GODS: Oko, Ochosi

Toloache—*See* Thornapple

Tomato—*Lycopericon spp.*—Feminine, Venus, Water

ASTROLOGICAL: *Primary*: Libra, Taurus; *Secondary*: Cancer, Pisces, Scorpio

MEDICAL: To treat Poison Ivy, wash the area with water and then express the juice of a green Tomato on the affected area. One hour later, wash again and then apply a paste made from baking soda and water. Repeat as needed: water, Tomato juice, then baking soda.

Tomato

MAGICKAL: Mix Tomato sauce with Basil and a bit of Dill for a strong prosperity sauce. Grown in the home garden, they will lend themselves to both protection and prosperity. Eaten raw, they enhance feelings of love.

Tongue Grass—*See* Chickweed

Tongue of Dog—*See* Hound's Tongue

☠ **Tonka**—*Dipteryx odorata/Coumarouna odorata*—Feminine, Venus, Water

Also known as Coumaria Nut, Lucky Bean, Tonqua, Tonquin Bean

ASTROLOGICAL: *Primary*: Libra, Taurus; *Secondary*: Cancer, Pisces, Scorpio

GODDESS: Ochun

MEDICAL: Cardiac, Narcotic, Paralyser. Due to the tremendous chance of overdose, the use of this powerful medicine should be avoided. In large doses, it paralyses the heart.

PARTS USED: Seed/Bean

Tonka

MAGICKAL: Tonka beans are used in sachets to attract love and money, but never included in incense. A tincture of Tonka bean is sometimes added to essential oil of Patchouli to create a New Orleans-style quick money-drawing oil.

Tonqua—*See* Tonka

Tonquin Bean—*See* Tonka

Too—*See* Peach

Toothache Tree—*See* Ash, Prickly

Toque—*See* Scullcap

Torches—*See* Mullein

Tourengane—*See* Lemon Balm

Trail Grape—*See* Barberry, Holly-leaved

Trailing Grape—*See* Barberry, Holly-leaved

Treacle Hedge Mustard—*See* Mustard, Treacle Hedge

Treacle Wormseed—*See* Mustard, Treacle Hedge

Tree Melon—*See* Papaya

Tree of Chastity—*See* Hawthorn

Tree of Death—*See* Cypress

Tree of Enchantment—*See* Willow

Tree of Love—*See* Apple

Trefoil—*See* Clover, Red and Liverwort, American

Trembling Aspen—*See* Aspen, American

Trilissia odorata—*See* Deerstongue

True Maidenhair—*See* Fern

True Unicorn Root—*See* Ague Root

Truffles—*Tuber melanospermum*—Feminine, Venus, Water

ASTROLOGICAL: *Primary*: Libra, Taurus; *Secondary*: Cancer, Pisces, Scorpio

MAGICKAL: Truffles are so widely considered an aphrodisiac that their price is exorbitant, even in a world when magick is more often dismissed than valued. They also increase empathy.

Trumpet Flower—*See* Be-Still

Trumpet Weed—*See* Gravelroot and Meadowsweet

Tulipan—*See* Hibiscus

Tubers—*See* Potato

Tumsole—*See* Heliotrope

Turkey Crocus—*See* Cloth of Gold

Turmeric—*Curcurma domestica*—Masculine, Mercury, Air
ASTROLOGICAL: *Primary*: Gemini, Virgo; *Secondary*: Aquarius, Gemini, Libra
MAGICKAL: Consumption of Turmeric will help rid the spirit of psychic sludge.

Turmeric Root—*See* Goldenseal and Turmeric

Tun-Hoof—*See* Ivy, Ground

Turkey Rhubarb—*See* Rhubarb

Uabano—*See* Guarana

Uan-Suy—*See* Coriander

Ufuta—*See* Sesame

Ulamula—*See* Lemon

Ulmi Cortex—*See* Elm, Common

Umakhuthula—*See* Agrimony

Ungoozeh—*See* Asafoetida

Unicorn Root—*See* Ague Root

Unyoun—*See* Onion

Vada Tree—*See* Banyan

Valerian—*Valeriana officinalis*—Feminine, Venus, Water

Also known as All-Heal, Amantilla, Bloody Butcher, Capon's Tail, Capon's Trailer, Cat's Valerian, Garden Heliotrope, Great Wild Valerian, Phu, Red Valerian, Sete Wale, Setwall, Set Well, Set Wale, St. George's Herb, Vandal Root

WARNING: Habitual use may be habit-forming. I know that when I use it regularly, I just hate to run out. Most references say to use Valerian root no more often than once a day for no longer than three weeks.

ASTROLOGICAL: *Primary*: Libra, Taurus; *Secondary*: Cancer, Pisces, Scorpio

GODS: Eleggua

Valerian

GODDESS: Yemaya

MEDICAL: Antispasmodic, Carminative, Nervine, Stimulant. A great example of the difference between decoctions and infusions. A warm water infusion of the root will aid sleep. Bring that water to a boil, and you will destroy its medicinal effect. Valerian is also a good example of how dose will vary from patient to patient. In small doses, Valerian root acts as a depressant; in larger doses, a stimulant. In too large a dose it will make you sick. If it sounds impossible for one herb to have so many different effects on the same person and such dose variance depending on the person who uses it, consider what you have observed about how alcohol affects different people in different quantities. An infusion of Valerian root is the only working remedy that I have found for back pain. As a tincture, it works better. Typically, 1 ounce of an infusion made with high-proof vodka will do the trick.

PART USED: Root

MAGICKAL: The ancient Greeks hung it in their homes over windows to protect from invading forces that sought to do harm or cause mischief. Powdered and mixed with equal parts of Patchouli herb, Valerian makes a fine substitute for the graveyard dust called for in many spells.

GENERAL: When purchasing Valerian for use as a sedative, do not substitute Indian Valerian (*Valeriana Wallichii*). Although it is often tempting at about one-sixth the price, you will not be pleased with the results. Often, herb shops advertise "Valerian Root" at a great price—not so great when you realize that you are purchasing a far cheaper herb.

Valerian, American—Cypripedium hirsutum/ Cypripedium pubescens/Cyprepedium parviflorum—Feminine, Saturn, Water

Also known as Lady's Slipper, Nerve Root, Noah's Ark, Yellow Lady's Slipper, Yellow Moccasin Flower

ASTROLOGICAL: *Primary*: Aquarius, Capricorn; *Secondary*: Cancer, Pisces, Scorpio

GODS: Eleggua, Obatala

NOTE: American Valerian has the same medical properties as Valerian (*Valeriana officinalis*), except that American Valerian is not as powerful

Valerian, Indian—*Valeriana Wallichii*—Feminine, Venus, Water

Also known as Tagar

ASTROLOGICAL: *Primary*: Libra, Taurus; *Secondary*: Cancer, Pisces, Scorpio

MAGICKAL: Indian Valerian is used to draw men to women. In a tincture, it acts as a love-drawing perfume, even though it is not exactly the most pleasant odor. Drink it as a tea prior to meeting new people, and you just might find it lends enough to the exchange that you will find the love of your life.

Valerian, Red-Spur—*Centranthus rubra*

Also known as Bouncing Bess, Delicate Bess, Drunken Sailor, Drunken Soldier, Pretty Betsy

NOTE: I count myself fortunate for having experimented with this friendly plant while in Germany, where its leaves are sometimes served in salad and its roots used in soup. I say fortunate because I have not seen it available in the United States, and if it were, I doubt I could find it fresh enough for culinary use. Red-Spur Valerian seems to have none of the properties of other plants by similar common name, but the flesh of its root makes for good substance in vegetarian soup.

Vandal Root—*See* Valerian

Vanilla—*Vanilla aromatica/Vanilla planifolia/ Vanilla tahitensis*—Feminine, Venus, Water

Also known as Banilje, Tlilxochitl

ASTROLOGICAL: *Primary*: Libra, Taurus; *Secondary*: Cancer, Pisces, Scorpio

GODS: Shango

GODDESS: Ochun

Vanilla

MEDICAL: Anodyne. Vanilla bean is used to sooth toothaches. Grind to a powder and add water to make a paste. Apply to the painful area and visit a dentist as soon as possible.

PART USED: Bean

MAGICKAL: Vanilla is used in cooking to induce lust in both men and women. The scent of Vanilla attracts men when worn by women. Grind a single bean and carry in a sachet or simmer in water for the same effects.

Vanilla Leaf—*See* Deerstongue

Van Van—*See* Vervain

Vapor—*See* Fumitory

Vegetable Sulphur—*See* Moss, American Club

Velvetback—*See* Mullein

Velvet Dock—*See* Elecampane and Mullein

Velvet Flower—*See* Amaranth

Velvet Plant—*See* Mullein

Venus Hair—*See* Fern

Verbena—*See* Vervain

Vetiver—*See* Vetivert

Vetivert—*Andropogon zizanioides/Vetiveria zizanoides*—Feminine, Venus, Earth
Also known as Vetiver, Kush Kush, Moras
ASTROLOGICAL: *Primary*: Libra, Taurus; *Secondary*: Capricorn, Taurus, Virgo
GODS: Eleggua, Obatala, Oggun
GODDESS: Yemaya
MAGICKAL: A strong infusion of Vetivert root is added to bath water to make oneself more attractive to potential sexual partners. Powdered root is also used in sachet and incense recipes for the same purpose, as well as to attract money. Oil of Vetivert is diffused to place one in the right mind-set for spells designed to attract money. It is also diffused in retail establishments to increase customer spending.

Violet Bloom—*See* Woody Nightshade

Verge d'Or—*See* Goldenrod

Vervan—*See* Vervain

Vervain—*Verbena officinalis*—Feminine, Venus, Earth
Also known as Brittanica, Enchanter's Plant, Herba Sacra, Herb of Enchantment, Hoodoo Herb, Herb of Grace, Herb of the Cross, Holy Herb, Juno's Tears, Pigeon's Grass, Pigeonwood, Simpler's Joy, Van-Van, Verbena, Vervan, Voodoo Plant
ASTROLOGICAL: *Primary*: Libra, Taurus; *Secondary*: Capricorn, Taurus, Virgo
GODS: Shango, Eleggua, Hanuman, Hermes, Jupiter, Juno, Mars, Mercury, Obatala, Oggun, Parashurama, Tegid, Thor, Thoth, Vishnu
GODDESSES: Aradia, Isis, Cerridwen, Ochun, Venus
MEDICAL: Astringent, Antispasmodic, Diaphoretic, Febrifuge

PARTS USED: Flowers, Leaves
MAGICKAL: A strong infusion of Vervain is used to wash the floor of an altar room. Alternatively, it can be powdered and sprinkled on the carpet at night, then vacuumed in the morning. Used in the rest of the home, Vervain is calming and brings peaceful thoughts. A small besom/broom made of Vervain is a most appropriate tool for sweeping the altar surface. Romans used such tools in the care of altars dedicated to Jupiter. Vervain is associated with the Summer Solstice. Some lore states that Vervain gathered on that day will be particularly powerful in each of its magickal uses. Vervain has been cited as one of the three herbs sacred to the Druids. The other two in the same citations are Water Mint (listed here under Mint) and Meadowsweet. The problem with this citation is that there were certainly other herbs sacred to the Druids. Consumed as a tea, Vervain is said to drive out sexual desire and lessen lust. However, its scent seems to have the opposite effect, drawing both love and lust. Consuming the infusion also drives away bad dreams and nightmares. A tea made from 1 part Lavender, 1 part Vervain, and 3 parts Chamomile is an ideal blend for a restful night's sleep (do not sweeten). The very popular Van-Van oil used in New Orleans-genre Voodoo spells is typically an oil infusion of Vervain. To make this oil, simply saturate Vervain in a vegetable oil and simmer for 3 hours. Then cool, strain, and bottle for later use. Occasionally a drop of Patchouli oil is added to the finished product; other times Patchouli herb is mixed with the Vervain during the simmering process. There are a thousand more variations.

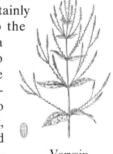

Vervain

Vervain, Blue—*Verbena hastata*
MEDICAL: Diaphoretic, Expectorant. Used as an infusion.
PART USED: Herb

Vine—*Vitis vinifera*—Feminine, Moon, Water
Also known as Grape, Grapevine
ASTROLOGICAL: *Primary*: Cancer; *Secondary*: Cancer, Pisces, Scorpio
GODS: Adonis, Asclepius, Aristaeus, Bacchus, The Buddha, Dionysus, Hymen, Krishna, Liber Pater, Oeneus, Ra, Vishnu
GODDESSES: Hathor, Sura, Yemaya
MEDICAL: Astringent (seeds), Diuretic (fruit)
PARTS USED: Fruit, Seeds
MAGICKAL: One of the 9 woods referred to in the Wiccan Rede; thick Grapevine is an ideal wood for constructing wands to call on Dionysus and Bacchus. A crown of Grapevines can be worn when calling on these gods as well as Hathor, although a woman should only do the latter. Eating Grapes increases both reproductive fertility in women and cognitive functions in both men and women.

Violet—*Viola odorata*—Feminine, Venus, Water
Also known as Blue Violet, Sweet Violet
ASTROLOGICAL: *Primary*: Libra, Taurus; *Secondary*: Cancer, Pisces, Scorpio
GODS: Shango, Eleggua, Obatala, Oggun,
MEDICAL: Laxative (mild), Nervine, Sedative (mild), Tonic. Warm water infusion of the leaves is a great source of vitamin A, improves eyesight, and calms the mind. Acts as a mild sedative and an evening tonic. A warm water infusion of the root acts as

Violet

an herbal alternative to the pink stuff you buy at the drugstore. It treats both upset stomachs and diarrhea. Fresh flowers and greens contain large amounts of vitamin A.
PARTS USED: Flowers, Leaves
MAGICKAL: Mix 1 part Violet with 1 part Lavender and 2 parts Chamomile; boil for a moment and then allow to simmer for 20 minutes.

Sweeten with Honey and share with your lover prior to gentle lovemaking followed by sleep. Your dreams will intertwine, as did your bodies.

Virginia Creeper—*See* Ivy, American

Virginian Scullcap—*See* Scullcap

Virginian Poke—*See* Pokeweed

Virginian Prune—*See* Cherry, Wild

Virginian Snakeroot—*See* Snakeroot

Virgin's Glove—*See* Foxglove

Viscid Groundsel—*See* Groundsel, Viscid

Vomitwort—*See* Lobelia

Voodoo Plant—*See* Vervain

Wad—*See* Woad

Wall Rue—*See* Fern

Wall Fern—*See* Fern

Wallwort—*See* Comfrey

Walnut—*Juglans regia*—Masculine, Sun, Fire
ASTROLOGICAL: *Primary*: Leo; *Secondary*: Aries, Leo, Sagittarius
MEDICAL: Astringent, Laxative. As topical astringent or internal laxative, 1 ounce of the bark and/or leaves is decocted in 1 quart of water. Reduce by boiling to 1 pint, strain, and serve 4 ounces at a time as laxative or use topically as astringent.
PARTS USED: Bark, Leaves
MAGICKAL: Eating Walnuts provides heightened cognitive abilities as well as a sense of well-being.

Wand Wood—*See* Ash, Mountain and Willow

Warnera—*See* Golden Seal

Water Betony—*See* Figwort

Watercress—*Nasturtium officinale*—Masculine, Mars, Fire

ASTROLOGICAL: *Primary*: Aries, Scorpio; *Secondary*: Aries, Leo, Sagittarius

Watercress

MEDICAL: Antiscorbutic, Diuretic, Tonic. Served fresh, Watercress will increase appetite. An expression of fresh Watercress makes a fine ointment for blemishes of the skin. Acts as a mild diuretic and cleanses the kidneys. Contains high amounts of vitamin C and iron, making it an excellent tonic for vegetarians and others who may need an iron boost.

MAGICKAL: Eating fresh Watercress will increase reproductive fertility in women.

Water Dock—*See* Dock, Water

Water Fern—*See* Fern

Water Figwort—*See* Figwort, Water

Water Flag—*See* Blue Flag

Water Hemlock—*See* Hemlock, Water

Water Iris—*See* Blue Flag

Water Lotus—*See* Lotus

Watermelon—*Citrullus vulgaris*—Feminine, Moon, Water

ASTROLOGICAL: *Primary*: Cancer; *Secondary*: Cancer, Pisces, Scorpio

GODS: Olocun

GODDESS: Yemaya

MEDICAL: Diuretic, Tonic. An infusion of dried seeds is a good treatment for high blood pressure. By the way, the seeds don't actually cause pregnancy, despite what your parents told you.

PARTS USED: Fruit, Seeds

MAGICKAL: When consumed, Watermelon lifts the mood and promotes spiritual healing, especially from a broken heart.

Water Mint—*See* Mint

Water Parsley—*See* Hemlock

Water Plantain—*See* Plantain, Water

Watu—*See* Fenugreek

Wax Dolls—*See* Fumitory

Wax Works—*See* American Bittersweet

Waybread—*See* Plantain, Common

Way of Bennet—*See* Avena

Weat—*See* Woad

Weazel Snout—*See* Nettle, Yellow Dead

Weiszer Germer—*See* Hellebore, White

Weisze Nieszwurzel—*See* Hellebore, White

Welcome-Home-Husband-Thou-Never-so-Drunk—*See* Houseleek

Welcome-Home-Husband-Thou-Never-so-Late—*See* Houseleek

Wendles—*See* Plantain, Ribwort

Western Gorse—*See* Gorse

Weusswurz—*See* Solomon's Seal

Weybroed—*See* Plantain, Common

Wheat—*Triticum spp.*—Feminine, Venus, Earth

ASTROLOGICAL: *Primary*: Libra, Taurus; *Secondary*: Capricorn, Taurus, Virgo

GODS: Min

GODDESSES: Ceres, Demeter, Ishtar, Onatha

MAGICKAL: Grains and whole sheaves of Wheat have been brought into the home to increase prosperity and fertility. While that practice is alive and well today, unless you live off the land or in a community where Wheat supports either fertility or prosperity it is not likely to work well for you because neither your conscious or subconscious mind will make the connection. Then again, it can't hurt.

Whig Plant—*See* Chamomile, Common

Wheat

Whin—*See* Gorse

Whinberry—*See* Huckleberry

White Archangel—*See* Nettle, White Dead

White Balsam—*See* Balsam, White

White Briony—*See* White Briony

☠**White Bryony**—*Bryonia dioica*—Masculine, Mars, Fire

Also known as Goat Root, Ladies' Seal, Mad Root, Navet du Diable, Snake Grape, Tamus, Tetterberry, Wild Hops, Wild Vine, Wood Vine, English Mandrake

ASTROLOGICAL: *Primary*: Aries, Scorpio; *Secondary*: Aries, Leo, Sagittarius

MEDICAL: Cathartic, Irritative

PART USED: Root

MAGICKAL: Its root is an excellent magickal substitute for Mandrake (*Atropa mandragora*) root, which is next to impossible to find these days. Outside of use as a substitute, I have not found a use for White Bryony. However, White Bryony root isn't much easier to acquire. Don't even think about using it, as a popular movie implies, in a love potion. Both White Bryony and Mandrake are considered poisons.

NOTE: White Bryony is sometimes spelled White Briony.

White Dead Nettle—*See* Nettle, White Dead

White Desert Sage—*See* Sage, White

White Endive—*See* Dandelion

White Hellebore—*See* Hellebore, White

White Horehound—*See* Horehound, White

White Lily—*See* Lily

White Maidenhair—*See* Fern

White Man's Foot—*See* Plantain, Common

White Mullein—*See* Mullein

White Mustard—*See* Mustard, White

White Poppy—*See* Poppy, White

White Sandalwood—*See* Sandalwood, White

White Saunders—*See* Sandalwood, White

Whitethorn—*See* Hawthorn

White Wood—*See* Cinnamon, White

Whitty—*See* Ash, Mountain

Whorled Mint—**See** Mint

Whortleberry—*See* Huckleberry

Wicken-Tree—*See* Ash, Mountain

Wiggin—*See* Ash, Mountain

Wiggy—*See* Ash, Mountain

Wiky—*See* Ash, Mountain

Wild Ash—*See* Ash, Mountain

Wild Celery—*See* Celery

Wild Chamomile—*See* Chamomile, German

Wild Cherry—*See* Cherry, Wild and Chicory

Wild Cotton—*See* Dogbane

Wild Cranesbill—*See* Geranium

Wild Curcuma—*See* Goldenseal

Wild Endive—*See* Dandelion

Wilde Yamwurel—*See* Yam, Wild

Wild Fennel—*See* Fennel

Wild Geranium—*See* Geranium

Wild Hops—*See* White Bryony

Wild Hyacinth—*See* Hyacinth, Wild

Wild Hydrangea—*See* Hydrangea

Wild Ice Leaf—*See* Mullein

Wild Ipecac—*See* Dogbane

Wild Lemon—See Mandrake and Mandrake, American

Wild Lettuce—*See* Lettuce, Wild

Wild Liquorice—*See* Sarsaparilla

Wild Mint—*See* Mint

Wild Pansy—*See* Heartsease

Wild Plum—*See* Plum, Wild

Wild Oregon Grape—*See* Barberry, Holly-leaved

Wild Sarsaparilla—*See* Sarsaparilla

Wild Snowball—*See* New Jersey Tea

Wild Succory—*See* Chicory

Wild Sunflower—*See* Elecampane

Wild Vanilla—*See* Deerstongue

Wild Vine—*See* White Bryony

Wild Cinnamon—*See* Cinnamon, White

Wild Yam—*See* Yam, Wild

Willow—*See List*—Feminine, Moon, Water
Also known as Osier, Pussy Pine, Pussy Willow, Saille, Salicyn Willow, Saugh Tree, Tree of Enchantment, Wand Wood, Witches' Aspirin, Witches' Wood, Withe, Withy
> **Crack Willow**—*Salix fragilis*
> **Goat Willow**—*Salix caprea*
> Also known as Pussy Pine
> **White Willow**—*Salix alba*

MEDICAL: Antiperiodic, Astringent, Nervine, Tonic

PART USED: Bark

ASTROLOGICAL: *Primary*: Cancer; *Secondary*: Cancer, Pisces, Scorpio

GODS: Jehovah, Mercury, Oko, Osiris, Olocun, Tegid

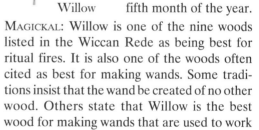

GODDESSES: Artemis, Athena, Belit-Ili, Callisto, Ceres, Cerridwen, Diana, Hecate, Hera, Luna, Persephone, Psyche, Selene

CELTIC TREE CALENDAR (Saille)—April 15th thru May 12th—The fifth month of the year.

Willow

MAGICKAL: Willow is one of the nine woods listed in the Wiccan Rede as being best for ritual fires. It is also one of the woods often cited as best for making wands. Some traditions insist that the wand be created of no other wood. Others state that Willow is the best wood for making wands that are used to work with the moon.

Willow-Wort—*See* Loosestrife, Yellow

Winter Cherry—*See* Cherry, Winter

Wintergreen—*Gaultheria procumbens*—Feminine, Moon, Water
See also Pipsissewa, as Wintergreen is also a common name for that plant.

Wintergreen

ASTROLOGICAL: *Primary*: Cancer; *Secondary*: Cancer, Pisces, Scorpio

MEDICAL: Astringent, Diuretic, Emmenagogue, Stimulant, Tonic

PART USED: Leaves

Winter Savory—*See* Savory, Winter

Winterweed—*See* Chickweed

Witchbane—*See* Ash, Mountain

Witchen—*See* Ash, Mountain

Witches' Aspirin—*See* Willow

Witches' Bells—*See* Foxglove

Witch Hazel—*Hamamelis virginiana*

MEDICAL: Astringent, Sedative, Tonic. Used as tea. A decoction is used topically, especially in conjunction with a poultice. A warm water infusion (or decoction) can be applied to clean cloth and used as a poultice on closed eyes to treat mild irritation and strain. Apply for 30 minutes while you take a catnap. Great during a break at work.

Witch Hazel

PARTS USED: Bark, Fruit, Leaves

Witch's Berry—*See* Belladonna

Witches' Hair—*See* Dodder

Witches' Herb—*See* Basil

Witches' Mannildn—*See* Mandrake

Witches' Pouches—*See* Shepherd's Purse

Witches' Thimble—*See* Thornapple and Foxglove

Witches' Thimbles—*See* Foxglove

Witches' Wood—*See* Ash, Mountain and Willow

Withe—*See* Willow

Withy—*See* Willow

White Oak—*See* Oak

Wild Marjoram—*See* Oregano

Wind Flower—*See* Anemone

Winter Rose—*See* Hellebore, Black

Wishing Thorn—*See* Sloe

Woad—*Genista tinctoria/Ivatis tinctoria*

Also known as: Guado (Italian), Guede (French), Pastel (Spanish and French), Teinching (Chinese), Wad (Anglo-Saxon), Weat (Dutch)

MEDICAL: Astringent, Diuretic, Cathartic, Emetic. Because Woad is an incredibly strong astringent, it should never be used internally. An infusion of the leaves is often used to cleanse wounds and decrease bleeding.

PARTS USED: Whole plant

MAGICKAL: Just what was that blue paint that Mel Gibson wore into battle in the movie *Braveheart*? Chances are it was just that, blue paint. But what they were going for was a historically accurate representation of a Woad-painted warrior. One of the things they didn't mention was that these blue warriors often met combat either completely or partially naked with hair spiked wilder than the punk rockers of the early 1990s. Woad is yet another example of magick that has become science. Although the exact formula that was used in the days of the real-life William Wallace has not been preserved, there is a strong belief that when it was prepared correctly it worked topically as a psychotropic, the drug entering the blood through the skin. Now here is where it gets fun. Woad is used medically to slow bleeding. It accomplishes this by causing the body to restrict blood flow to the capillaries. Thus, one can imagine blood pressure increasing in other vital areas (including the genitals). Now imagine that you are a young Roman soldier who has been warned that you have to defend your empire against the horrific barbarians who are over the next hill. You hear the thundering war cries of hundreds of these barbarians, so you look up at the crest of the hill where you see hordes of naked blue giants with spiked hair. As they get closer, you realize they are sporting both swords and erections. What would be in your mind as they ran towards you in a psychotropic haze? What would you think when you realize their wounds don't bleed nearly as much as you thought they would? If you survived and someone told you that the blue stuff was Woad, what would you think about this wonderful little plant? Now, if you were one of the blue giants, what would you say about it?

MAGICKAL: Lore states that it will strike fear into one's enemies and ensure victory in battle. Magick, science, or a little of both?

GENERAL: The French and Spanish word for this plant is Pastel. There is little doubt that the ground root of this plant led to the modern use of the word pastel.

Wohpala—*See* Nutmeg

☠**Wolf's Bane**—*Aconitum napellus/Arnica latifolia/Arnica montana*—Feminine, Saturn, Water

ASTROLOGICAL: *Primary*: Aquarius, Capricorn; *Secondary*: Cancer, Pisces, Scorpio

GODDESS: Hecate

MEDICAL: Anodyne, Diaphoretic, Diuretic. Historically, a tincture is the method of extraction. However, the use of this plant is best avoided because it is a deadly poison.

PARTS USED: Whole plant

Wolf's Claw—*See* Moss, American Club

Wolf's Milk—*See* Spurges

Womandrake—*See* Mandrake

Wonder-of-the-World Root—*See* Ginseng, American

Wood Aloes—*Cardia dichotoma, Aquilaria agaillocha*—Feminine, Venus, Water

Also known as Lignum Aloes, Lolu, Mapou

ASTROLOGICAL: *Primary*: Libra, Taurus; *Secondary*: Cancer, Pisces, Scorpio

MAGICKAL: Medieval Europe saw Wood Aloes burned during magickal evocations. In ancient Egypt it was used in incense form for the same purpose as well as to attract luck and the blessings of the gods. Wood Aloes are often powdered and added to other incenses to strengthen the mixtures intent. This is especially the case with incense and mixtures designed to promote love.

Wood Betony—*Stachys betonica, Stachys officinalis, Betonica officinalis*—Masculine, Jupiter, Fire

Also known as Bishopwort, Lousewort, Purple Betony

ASTROLOGICAL: *Primary*: Pisces, Sagittarius; *Secondary*: Aries, Leo, Sagittarius

MEDICAL: An infusion of Wood Betony is often used to calm both asthma and heartburn. An expression of the fresh plant material is used on small cuts to ease pain and speed healing. Soaking the dried leaves in water and using them in a poultice will accomplish much the same results as an expression of the fresh leaves.

PART USED: Herb

Wood Betony

MAGICKAL: Wood Betony is often sewn into pillows to prevent dreams of any type. Traditionally, Wood Betony was burned in bonfires (especially at Summer Solstice) for purification. Combined with Cedar, and you have a purification fire. Jumping over the flames and through its smoke was thought to purify mind, body, and soul. The same practice at Beltane by a couple newly initiated to each other can cleanse the relationship of concerns and jealousy over past lovers. For these reasons, Wood Betony is often added to incense recipes for purification. In the garden, Wood Betony is said to protect the yard, making it an ideal ornamental for decorating the ritual area. Cut and dried, it is sometimes scattered along the Circle for added protection. Dried and powdered, it is a substitute for Black Salt (which keeps away bad neighbors). Scatter at the point where your property line joins. Because Black Salt will kill your lawn, I like to describe this simple spell as "good Witchcraft makes for good neighbors."

Wood Boneset—*See* Boneset

Wood Vine—*See* White Bryony and Ivy, American

☠**Woody Nightshade**—*Solanum Dulcamara*—Masculine, Mercury, Air

Also known as Bitter Nightshade, Bittersweet, European Bittersweet, Violet Bloom, Felonwort, Scarlet Berry, Dulcamara.

ASTROLOGICAL: *Primary*: Gemini, Virgo; *Secondary*: Aquarius, Gemini, Libra

GODDESS: Athena

MEDICAL: Narcotic (mild)

PART USED: Twigs

MAGICKAL: Lore states that Woody Nightshade was worn by shepherds and their animals to protect from evil influences. There are much better and less dangerous herbs for that purpose.

NOTE: If you are looking for Bittersweet, this is probably it. However, it could also be American Bittersweet (*Celastrus scandens*) that you are looking for.

Woodbine—*See* Honeysuckle

Wood Pimpernel—*See* Loosestrife, Yellow

Woodruff—*Asperula odorata/Galium odoratum*—Masculine, Mars, Fire

Also known as Sweet Woodruff.

ASTROLOGICAL: *Primary*: Aries, Scorpio; *Secondary*: Aries, Leo, Sagittarius

GODS: Ochosi

MEDICAL: (*Asperula odorata*) Stomachic. A warm water infusion is calming to the mind and stomach.

MAGICKAL: Carried to bring luck, victory, and prosperity.

Woodruff

Wood Rose—*Ipomoea tuberose*

MAGICKAL: Historically, the Wood Rose seed has been consumed for vision quest.

Woollen—*See* Mullein

Woolmat—*See* Hound's-Tongue

Wormseed—*See* Mustard, Treacle Hedge

Wormwood—*See* List

GODS: Apollo, Ares, Castor, Horus the Elder, Eleggua, Mars, Montu, Ochosi, Orunla

GODDESSES: Artemis, Diana

Wormwood, Common—*Artemisia absinthium*

Also known as Absinthe, Green Ginger

MEDICAL: Anthelmintic, Febrifuge, Stomachic, Tonic. 1 ounce is infused with 1 pint of water. Simmer for 15 minutes, strain, and serve 4 ounces at a time.

PARTS USED: Herb

Wormwood, Roman—*Artemesia pontica*

MEDICAL: Stomachic

PART USED: Tops

GENERAL: Although most references include only *Artemisia absinthium*, Roman Wormwood has been used in the creation of Vermouth and, in Germany, Wormwood Wine.

Wormwood, Sea—*Artemesia maritima*

Wound Weed—*See* Goldenrod

Woundwort—*See* Goldenrod and Yarrow

Wu jia pi—*See* Acanthopanax

Wymote—*See* Mallow, Marsh

Xian he cao—See Agrimony

Yam, Wild—*Dioscorea villosa*
Also known as: Colic Root, Dioscorea, Rheumatism Root, Wilde Yamwurzel
MEDICAL: Antispasmodic. Consumption of the rhizome (rootstock) helps to ease symptoms of asthma. Because Wild Yam provides nutrients that mimic estrogen, it is useful in easing the symptoms of menopause and provides a natural alternative to postmenopausal estrogen needs. It is also said to act as a natural birth control; however, it is not nearly as effective as modern pharmaceuticals. A warm water infusion of the rhizome is said to help with colic and rheumatism.
PART USED: Rhizome

Yanisin—*See* Anise

Yarrow—*Archillea millefolium*—Feminine, Venus, Water
Also known as Achi Uea, Arrowroot, Bad Man's Plaything, Carpenter's Weed, Death Flower, Devil's Nettle, Eerie, Field Hops, Gearwe, Hundred-leaved Grass, Knight's Milfoil, Knyghten, Lady's Mantle, Milfoil, Militaris, Military Herb, Millefolium, Noble Yarrow, Nosebleed, Old Man's Mustard, Old Man's Pepper, Sanguinary, Seven Year's Love, Snake Grass, Soldier's Woundwort, Stanch Grass, Stanch Griss, Stanch Weed, Tansy, Thousand Seal, Wound Wort, Yarroway, Yerw
ASTROLOGICAL: *Primary*: Libra, Taurus; *Secondary*: Cancer, Pisces, Scorpio
GODS: Babalu Aye, Eleggua, Eros, Horus the Elder, Obatala

GODDESS: Ochun
MEDICAL: Antiperiodic, Astringent, Nervine, Tonic. Relief from mild pain, sleeplessness, and headaches can be had from a warm water infusion of Yarrow. Calms the mind. Acts similarly to Willow but tastes a great deal better (note that I did not say good). The same infusion is good to clean cuts and scratches. Yarrow is a great dietary supplement for vegetarians and vegans as it is rich in both calcium and iron.
PART USED: Herb

Yarrow

MAGICKAL: Yarrow is used in sachets and incense to bring on courage. It attracts long-lost friends and causes one to notice potential friends that one might have overlooked. As an infusion, it is a good floor wash for driving baneful energy from a home. Essential oil of Yarrow is diffused to enhance self-respect and to promote mutual respect and love between all who share the scent. As such, it is often used to enhance relationships and to assist in calmly addressing issues that, without the presence of the scent, might turn into an argument. It is also good oil to diffuse to encourage intuition.
NOTE: Many of the common names for Yarrow seem to be unique to the modern Pagan community and seem to have come specifically from Cunningham's *Encyclopedia of Magical Herbs*.

Yarroway—*See* Yarrow

Yasmin—*See* Jasmine

Yellow Archangel—*See* Nettle, Yellow Dead

Yellow Avens—*See* Avena

Yellow Bark—*See* Buckthorn, Californian

Yellow Bedstraw—*See* Cleavers (A)

Yellow Dead Nettle—*See* Nettle, Yellow Dead

Yellow Dock—*See* Dock, Yellow

Yellow Flag—*See* Iris

Yellow Gentian—*See* Gentian

Yellow Iris—*See* Iris

Yellow Lady's Slipper—*See* Valerian, American

Yellow Loosestrife—*See* Loosestrife, Yellow

Yellow Moccasin Flower—*See* Valerian, American

Yellow Mustard—See Mustard, White

Yellow Oleander—*See* Be-Still

Yellow Root—*See* Goldenseal

Yellow Puccoon—*See* Goldenseal

Yellow Sandalwood—*See* Sandalwood, White

Yellow Snowdrop—*See* Adder's-Tongue

Yellow Willow Herb—*See* Loosestrife, Yellow

Yellow Wood—*See* Ash, Prickly

Yerba Buena—*See* Spearmint

Yerba del Sapo—*See* Holly, Sea

Yerba Louisa—*See* Lemon Verbena

Yerba Santa—*Eriodictyon glutinosum/Eriodictyon Californicum*
Also known as: Bear's Weed, Consumptive's Weed, Gum Bush, Holy Herb, Mountain Balm, Sacred Herb
MEDICAL: (*Eriodictyon glutinosum*) Stimulant. Old medical texts and herbals recommend smoking the leaves for relief from asthma. Either smoked or in a warm water infusion, Yerba Santa will act as a mild stimulant, calm

hayfever, and has even been recommended for relief from hemorrhoids. The specific application of the latter was not mentioned.
PART USED: Leaves

Yerw—*See* Yarrow

☠**Yew**—*See List*—Feminine, Saturn, Earth
  Common Yew—*Taxus baccata*
  Japanese Yew—*Taxus cuspidata*

Yew

ASTROLOGICAL: *Primary*: Aquarius, Capricorn; *Secondary*: Capricorn, Taurus, Virgo
GODS: Odin, Mimir
GODDESSES: Athena, Banbha, Bestla, Hecate, Saturn
CELTIC TREE CALENDAR (Idho)—Winter solstice

Yn-leac—*See* Onion

Yohimba—*See* Yohimbe

Yohimbe—*Corynanthe yohimbe*
Also known as Johimbe, Pausinystalia, Yohimba, Yohimbehe
WARNING: Do not use in conjunction with alcohol or any other drug (including nonprescription, prescription, legal, or illegal).
MAGICKAL: It has been used to enhance the enjoyment of sex, mating rituals, and orgies for centuries. It seems to dramatically lower inhibitions, allowing today's lovemaking to be free from yesterday's issues. Consuming Yohimbe an hour prior to making love seems to allow a couple to overcome inhibitions in such a lasting way that after the issue has been addressed with the use of Yohimbe, it is not likely to return. This means that although the chemical effects of Yohimbe fade, the lesson learned while under its influence remains. Today, it is sold in pill form at virtually every health food/supplement store. Unfortunately, even with its long-documented history connecting Yohimbe

with mating customs and rituals, it is most often used simply as a recreational drug for its action as a stimulant and mild hallucinogen.

Yohimbe Wedding Tea
4 cups fresh water
1 ounce Yohimbe bark
1/2 ounce Common Chamomile

Bring water to a boil and add all ingredients; reduce heat and allow to simmer for 30 minutes. Serve warm; sweeten to taste with honey. Effects will begin in approximately an hour.

Yohimbehe—*See* Yohimbe

Ysopo—*See* Hyssop

Yssop—*See* Hyssop

Yulluc—*See* Comfrey

Zabila—*See* Aloe

Zaboca—*See* Avocado

Zaffer— *See* Saffron, Spanish

Zauberwuzel—*See* Mandrake

Ze Xie—*See* Alismatis Rhizome

Ziele—*See* Sesame

Ztworkost—*See* Comfrey

Final Words

In most of my books, I reserve a page or two for some final words. They are usually something deeply personal that I want to share with my readers. In *Wicca for Couples*, I ended the book by telling the world that I wanted to be loved. In *A Wiccan Bible*, I told the world that I had found my love and asked her mother for permission to wed that love. Guess what! At the Real Witches Ball 2003, her mother said yes. I am now a husband and the father of the brightest new star in the universe. So what else could I possibly have to say?

Our Lord and Lady do listen to our prayers and I have a wife and healthy baby to prove it.

Please stay in touch. The press might think I am the world's most infamous Witch, but I like to think of myself as the world's most interactive author. My wife Aimee and I can usually be found lurking around *www.PaganNation.com* and invite your to join us.

Blessed be and live free,

A.J. Drew

Endnotes

Chapter 1

1. This statement is found as a common concept in the teachings of many traditions of Wicca. I received it while in Frankfurt, West Germany in 1984 or 1985. It is also the title of a chant written by Starhawk and recorded in 1987.

Chapter 2

1. Aleister Crowley, *Magick in Theory and Practice*. (New York: Castle Books, n.d.), 64.
2. Ibid.

Chapter 3

1. Aleister Crowley, *Magick in Theory and Practice*. (New York: Castle Books, n.d.), Introduction, Page XXIII.

Bibliography

Baker, Margaret. *Gardener's Magic and Folklore*. New York: University Books, 1978.

Blackwell, W.H. *Poisonous and Medical Plants*. Upper Saddle River, N.J.: Prentice Hall, 1979.

Blamires, Steve. *Celtic Tree Mysteries*. St Paul, Minn: Llewellyn Worldwide, 2002.

Blunt, Wilfred. *The Illustrated Herbal*. New York: Thames and Hudson, 1979.

Chase, Pamela. *Trees for Healing*. Franklin Lakes, N.J.: New Page Books/New Castle, 1991.

Crowley, Aleister. *777*. York Beach, Maine: Red Wheel/Weiser; Weiser Books, 1973.

Cunningham, Scott. *The Complete Book of Incense, Oils, and Brews*. St Paul, Minn.: Llewellyn Worldwide, 1989.

———. *Cunningham's Encyclopedia of Magical Herbs*. St. Paul, Minn.: Llewellyn Worldwide, 1985.

———. *Magical Aromatherapy*. St. Paul, Minn.: Llewellyn Worldwide, 2002.

Ellis, Peter. *A Brief History of the Druids*. Berkeley, Calif.: Carroll & Graf, 2002.

Grieve, Maud. *A Modern Herbal*. New York: Random House, 1986.

Glare, P.E. (editor). *Oxford Latin Dictionary*. Oxford: Oxford University Press, 1983.

Hopman, Ellen Evert. *Tree Medicine, Tree Magic*. Blain, Wash.: Phoenix, 1991.

Leek, Sybil. *Cast your Own Spell*. New York: Pinnacle, 1970.

————. *Herbs: Medicine and Mysticism*. Chicago: Henry Regnery, 1975.

————. *Sybil Leek's Book of Herbs*. New York: Thomas Nelson, 1973.

Leyel, C.F. *Herbal Delights*. Boston: Houghton Mifflin Co., 1938.

————. *The Magic of Herbs*. Toronto: Coles Publishing, 1981 (originally published 1927).

Miller, Richard. *The Magical and Ritual Use of Aphrodisiacs*. Rochester, Vt.: Destiny Books, 1993.

————. *The Magical and Ritual Use of Herbs*. Rochester, Vt.: Destiny Books, 1993.

————. *The Magical and Ritual Use of Perfumes*. Rochester, Vt.: Destiny Books, 1993.

Montenegro, Carlos. *Magical Herbal Baths of Santeria*. New York: Original Publications, 1996.

Muryn, Mary. *Water Magic*. New York: Simon & Schuster/Fireside, 1995.

O'Hara, Gwydion. *The Magick of Aromatherapy*. St. Paul, Minn.: Llewellyn Worldwide, 1998.

Pliny the Elder. *Natural History*. Cambridge, Mass.: Harvard University Press, 1992.

Smith, Steven. *Wylundt's Book of Incense*. York Beach, Maine: Red Wheel/Weiser; Weiser Books, 1989.

Tarostar. *The Witch's Formulary and Spellbook*. New York: Original Publications, 1996.

Williams, Jude. *Jude's Herbal Home Remedies*. St. Paul, Minn.: Llewellyn Worldwide, 2004.

Index